Pathways of Hope and Faith
Among Hispanic Teens

Pathways and Journeys
for a New Generation

Volume 1

Pathways of Hope and Faith Among Hispanic Teens

Pastoral Reflections and Strategies Inspired by the National Study of Youth and Religion

Edited by

Ken Johnson-Mondragón

Instituto
FE Y VIDA
Institute for Faith & Life

Stockton, California

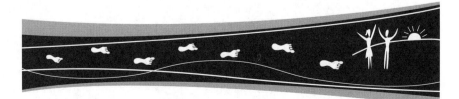

Editorial Team

General Editor:	Ken Johnson-Mondragón, D.Min. cand.
Writers:	Carlos Carrillo, M.Ed. Carmen M. Cervantes, Ed.D. Arturo Chávez, Ph.D. Elizabeth Conde-Frazier, Ph.D. Lynette DeJesús-Sáenz, M.S.W. Edwin Hernández, Ph.D. Ken Johnson-Mondragón, D.Min. cand. David Ramos, M.Div., M.S.W. Tomas V. Sanabria, M.Div.
Focus Group:	Juliet de Jesús Alejandre Kenneth G. Davis, OFM Conv. Elvira Mata, MCDP Patrick Mooney, M.A. José Montenegro Felisa Román
Copyediting:	Aurora Macías Dewhirst
Design:	Alicia María Sánchez
Illustrations:	Alicia María Sánchez Martha Elena Sánchez
Layout:	Edith Vega

OCUS
Comunicación visual

Contents

Foreword

When in the year 2000 I first began to envision the research project that would eventually become the National Study of Youth and Religion (NSYR), I was aware that the findings of such a study could be interesting not only to scholars who study religion and adolescents, but also potentially informative and practically useful to adults "on the ground" who work with youth. Reliable information about people's lives can often be helpful for knowing how better to relate to and work with people. One of the key premises of the NSYR when it began was that we lacked adequate knowledge about the religious and spiritual lives of American youth at a national level. It was only natural to think that improving our knowledge in that area could be helpful to youth pastors, clergy, church ministers, youth mentors, denominational leaders, community workers, and parents. Therefore, as program officers from Lilly Endowment Inc., which funded the NSYR, and I began working on the structure of the project, we agreed on the value of building into it resources to help disseminate our research findings to a variety of communities and constituencies that work with youth. Included in that was the intention to commission a set of thoughtful pastoral workers who minister with different kinds of American youth to reflect on the sociological findings of the NSYR and to write some theological and pastoral reflections to be published for the benefit of similar youth ministers.

This book is one of the results of that commissioning. During the collection of the first wave of NSYR data, I asked two members of the project's Public Advisory Board, Carmen Cervantes and Edwin Hernandez, if they would be willing to organize a team of highly qualified scholars and pastoral workers to develop this book. They happily agreed and quickly brought Ken Johnson-Mondragón on board the project. Those three put their minds together and proposed back to me an unusual and creative approach to writing this book. Rather than tasking only one or two major authors to write a book on ministry with Hispanic youth, they proposed to gather together small teams of experienced leaders to engage, digest, and reflect theologically and pastorally upon the sociological findings of the NSYR when it came to Hispanic youth. The idea sounded great, so I commissioned them to run with it. With additional support from a Louisville

Institute Grant, Ken, Carmen, and Edwin formed a set of impressive teams to take on different aspects of the matter at hand. The products of their work are represented now in the chapters of this book.

I am very pleased to see this collaborative work come to fruition. It is the result of diligent years of work by the able hands of Ken, Carmen, and Edwin and their collaborators. It hardly needs to be said to anyone who knows American society that the Hispanic population in the United States has been growing dramatically and is transforming the character of American religion, both Catholic and Protestant. Anyone who hopes to grasp the central issues of American religious life and culture cannot afford to ignore this important Hispanic presence. Anyone who hopes to minister effectively among American teenagers cannot afford to simply treat them as if they were all Anglos, but must understand the cultural distinctiveness of different ethnic groups. But taking seriously the Hispanic presence of youth in the life of the church by conducting informative research has been hampered by the lack of solid information.

Before the NSYR, many of the best sources of information about the religious lives of U.S. adolescents were school-based samples that systematically excluded youth who were not in school or who were absent more than a typical number of days. This introduces a non-response bias against Hispanic adolescents, particularly among older Hispanic teenagers, many of whom either have dropped out of high school or are recent immigrants that are not in school because they came to the U.S. in search of work. Furthermore, most of the good studies of American youth were conducted in English only, which of course also systematically excludes some Hispanic youth from participating, especially when a parent is also a respondent or must give permission for their minor children to participate in the study. For these and other reasons, most of our best previously existing data on U.S. adolescents have not supported reliable studies of Hispanic teens.

The NSYR was determined to do better. That meant among other things making sure we had adequate survey and interview sample sizes to be able to conduct meaningful analyses of our Hispanic adolescents. It also meant conducting our survey in both English and Spanish for both the youth and parent respondents. It meant being sensitive to how we asked our survey questions about immigration and citizenship. And it meant making sure that we asked a set of questions about religious practices specifically relevant to our Hispanic respondents. We were very pleased in the end with the representative sampling, response rate, total sample size, and Hispanic participation of our NSYR study. Our data, therefore, are unique in the world of survey scholarship in the opportunity they present for a reliable analysis of the religious and spiritual lives of Hispanic youth in the U.S. The rigorous research design we implemented and study outcomes we achieved mean that books like this one can with confidence be understood as based on solid, rigorous social scientific data representative of the population in question.

But this book does not simply report sociological research findings. Rather, the authors of the various chapters of this book bring their expertise in pastoral work with Hispanic teenagers and young adults to reflect on the theological and pastoral implications of the NSYR's research findings for effective ministry with young Hispanics in the United States. In successfully accomplishing that task, I believe this book provides many different kinds of readers with a unique and important resource. The high quality of the data on which it is based, the collaborative nature of the thinking and writing that went into this book, the rich experience of the authors who deliberated about and wrote the following chapters, the practical focus of the analyses, and the book's ecumenical scope which considers both Catholic and Protestant Hispanic youth: all of these together make this a truly exceptional and valuable publication. It is with pride that I see it published, and much gratitude to the editors and authors who brought it to completion. I commend it to readers from all backgrounds who care about the lives of American youth—particularly those who need to deepen their appreciation for the religious, spiritual, and cultural dimensions of adolescents' lives. I hope and trust that this book will find its way into the hands of many youth ministers, church leaders, seminary faculty, and parents.

Christian Smith, Ph.D.
Principle Investigator of the National Study of Youth and Religion

Introduction

You've seen the headlines in the papers. Hispanics are the largest and fastest growing "minority" group in the United States today. Their presence is changing the way America does business, education, and politics, as well as what it listens to, watches, reads, and eats. These changes can also be seen in the pews and pulpits of parishes and congregations across the country, from Miami, FL, to Anchorage, AK, and nearly everywhere in between.

In the life of the church, the most obvious change is when a Spanish-speaking congregation appears in a neighborhood, or worship services in Spanish are added in an existing faith community. Nevertheless, language is only the first of many issues that must be resolved in order to develop a comprehensive and effective outreach to Latino/a teens. Some of the questions that pastors, youth ministers, and parents may be asking themselves are:

- What is really happening in the lives of the Hispanic teens living in my community? What are the most pressing pastoral needs that I should be addressing with them?

- Why is it so hard to get some of the Latino/a teens to come to church or to participate in youth ministry programs? What knowledge and skills do I need in order to improve my outreach to them?

- What can I do to ensure that teens with different national or cultural backgrounds all feel welcome and comfortable at church, especially when there are ethnic or racial tensions in the larger communities of school, neighborhood, or town?

- How can I partner with parents and other family members in the religious formation of the Hispanic teenagers in my faith community?

- What concrete actions can I take to support and encourage leadership training for ministry with the young Hispanics in my community? And how can I support young Latino/as in their development as leaders in church and society?

- As a Latino/a parent, how can I be of greater support to my adolescent children in their religious, emotional, intellectual, moral, social, and cultural development?

The National Study of Youth and Religion

If you have asked yourself these questions, or others similar to them, this book is for you. Over the last five years, researchers for the National Study of Youth and Religion (NSYR) have been conducting a longitudinal study of the religious beliefs and practices of teens throughout the United States. Two of the goals of the NSYR are:

- To provide a nationally-representative description of the religious and spiritual practices, beliefs, experiences, histories, concerns, and involvements of American youth.
- To identify how the religious interests, concerns, and practices of American youth vary between people of different races, ages, social classes, ecological settings (rural versus urban), and between boys and girls.

Research methodology of the NSYR

The NSYR's data collection is being carried out in three waves over the course of six years, from 2002 to 2008. Each wave includes a telephone survey and personal interviews with a subset of the young people surveyed. The longitudinal telephone survey began as a nationally representative survey of 3,290 English and Spanish speaking teenagers between the ages of 13 and 17. The baseline survey was conducted, with the teen respondents and one of their parents, between July 2002 and April 2003 by researchers at the University of North Carolina at Chapel Hill. A random-digit dial (RDD) telephone method was employed to generate numbers representative of all household telephones in the 50 United States. Among the respondents, 385 teens identified themselves as Hispanic or Latino/a. In addition, researchers recorded and transcribed personal interviews with 267 teens, 38 of whom were Hispanic.

The second wave of the NSYR is a re-survey of the Wave 1 teen respondents. Like Wave 1, the Wave 2 survey was conducted by telephone using a Computer Assisted Telephone Interviewing (CATI) system. The survey was conducted from June 2005 through November 2005 when the respondents were between the ages of 16 and 21. Every effort was made to contact and survey all of the original NSYR respondents, including those out of the country and in the military. Of the original respondents, 2,604 participated in the second wave of the survey resulting in an overall retention rate of 78.6%. The predominant source of attrition in the second wave was from participants who could not be found. Of the Wave 2 respondents, 242 were Hispanic, giving a retention rate of 62.9% among Latino/as. The Wave 2 interviews were conducted with 122 of the interview participants from Wave 1, 15 of whom were Hispanic or Latino/a.

Process utilized in the preparation of this book

Taken together, the NSYR survey responses and transcribed interviews provide unprecedented insight into the spiritual concerns and personal lives of teens in the United States today. The NSYR Hispanic Theological Reflection Project, of which this book is the final product, was designed to make the insights of the NSYR regarding Latino/a adolescents available to pastors, youth ministry leaders, and parents in Catholic and Protestant faith communities throughout the country.

While the NSYR surveys and interviews provide the empirical foundation for the reflections in this book, the data is only one part of the richness contained in these pages. The pastoral insights and recommendations reflect the combined wisdom of an ecumenical team of 15 pastoral theologians, pastors, and youth ministers (8 Catholic and 7 Protestant) who have spent many years serving Latino faith communities in a variety of social and pastoral settings.

These professionals gathered in the summer of 2004 to discuss the implications of the NSYR Wave 1 data for youth ministers and parents of Hispanic adolescents. Chapters 2 through 7 of this book were prepared by forming three focus groups of four professionals; each group included two designated writers and two dialog partners who worked together to select the themes for their assigned chapters. All of the participants had access to the NSYR survey data and interview transcript materials pertinent to their chapter topics, as well as an early draft of Chapter 1 of this book.

Once the writers completed the first draft of their assigned chapters, they received feedback from each of their peers in the focus group before they submitted their manuscript for final editing. Chapter 8 was added as a brief update on the insights and recommendations of the first seven chapters once the NSYR Wave 2 data became available. Finally, Chapters 9 and 10 focus on the broad implications of the insights presented in the first eight chapters for ministry with Hispanic adolescents and their families in Protestant and Catholic faith communities, respectively.

Guide to using this book

As already mentioned, this book is intended for pastors, youth ministry leaders, and parents who have Hispanic adolescents in their care. For this reason, the presentation of data from the NSYR in each chapter is generally followed by a pastoral-theological reflection on the meaning of the data for faith communities, youth ministry leaders, and parents. In some cases, theoretical models are introduced to help the reader understand the variety of challenges faced by Latino/a teens in their daily lives. It is hoped that these features will make this an attractive volume for seminarians and sociologists of religion as well.

The presentation and discussion of the data are followed by a series of recommendations for pastors and youth ministry leaders to assist them in the development of programs that are more responsive to the needs of the Hispanic teens in their community. Each chapter ends with a series of questions that may be used for personal reflection or for discussion, either within a youth ministry team or by the parents of Hispanic adolescents. The notes and a list of additional resources for each chapter are found at the back of the book, starting on page 369.

Whenever possible, excerpts from the NSYR interview transcripts have been included to illustrate or clarify the insights from the survey data. To protect their identity, the teens interviewed are only identified by their gender, religious tradition, and the region of the country in which they live. The quotes may have been edited to remove references to particular people or places, or to remove portions of the conversation that did not relate to the topic at hand, but in every case the words are those of the teens themselves.

How to read the tables

Unless otherwise indicated, the reader should assume that all tables refer to data drawn from the NSYR teen survey. In general, the question asked of the participant is printed in boldface on the left, and the possible responses are indented underneath each question. If no question is indicated, then all of the responses relate to the topic in the title of the table (i.e. Table 2.1 on page 45). Since one of the parents of each teen was also surveyed, some tables include data from questions in the parent surveys; these results are clearly marked as such. The numbers printed to the right of each response show the percentage of the respondents in each category who gave the indicated response.

The columns of numbers on the right side of each table represent the various categories of respondents whose answers are being compared in the table. The weighted number of respondents in each category is printed in small letters at the top of each column in the format "N=xyz."[1] In some tables, the number of respondents in each category may vary from question to question within a single table; in these cases, each question is printed with its own set of Ns.

For example, the first five questions in Table 3.2 on page 89 were asked of teens who stated that they attend church "many times a year" or more. There were 190 Hispanic Catholic, 371 white Catholic, 80 Hispanic Protestant, and 1042 white Protestant teens who met that criterion. The last two questions in the table used different criteria to select the respondents in each category; the criteria are printed at the bottom of the table, and the number of respondents in each category is listed to the right of each question.

As with any survey based on a random sample, the reliability of the responses of the teens as a representation of the beliefs and behaviors of the target population in each category depends on the number of survey respondents in the category.[2] In general, sociologists like to have at least 80 respondents in each category they are comparing, but they will admit that even as few as 30 may provide results that can be generalized to the larger population.

Given the limits of the data available in the NSYR survey, it was not always possible to maintain at least 30 respondents in each of the categories being compared, especially when looking at subgroups of the Hispanic Protestant population. When there were less than 30 responses in a given category, the tables include an estimate of the sampling error based on the number of responses available. The reader should interpret these results as anecdotal evidence. In these cases, although the interpretation of the data may be strengthened by the pastoral experience of the writer, further research would be necessary to confirm or refute the differences indicated in the table. When fewer than 10 responses were available in a given category, the results were not reported.

Use of "Hispanic" or "Latino/a"

The U.S. Census Bureau identifies as "Hispanic" people whose ancestral roots and cultural heritage can be traced to places where Spanish was or continues to be the dominant language, regardless of their race. As such, the term "Hispanic" includes people of many nations. The NSYR surveys utilized the same approach to race and ethnicity as the U.S. Census Bureau, asking teens and parents separate questions about their race and whether or not they consider themselves to be "Hispanic." Thus, it is possible to be both black and Hispanic, Asian and Hispanic, etc. The racial and ethnic categories were then merged and collapsed so that comparisons between Hispanic and white teens in this book reflect the responses of Hispanic teens of any race and white teens who are not Hispanic, respectively.

It should be noted that some people object to the label "Hispanic" because their sense of ethnic identity is tied to their specific national or cultural origin. For example, some will say, "I am Cuban, not Hispanic!" They also argue that there is no "Hispanic" culture—only a collection of many national and regional cultures that happen to share language as a common element. Many of these people prefer the use of "Latino" or "Latina"

(Latino/a for short when talking about males and females together) to describe themselves because it evokes their more recent cultural ties to Latin America over and above their historic cultural roots in Spain.

On the other hand, for the descendents of Spanish-speaking peoples born in the United States, there is a growing awareness of a "pan-Hispanic" culture that is more central to their identity than the particular national origin of their ancestors. This is especially true for individuals whose parents were from different Spanish-speaking countries—for example the child of a Guatemalan mother and a Puerto Rican father. In fact, when given a chance to fill in their particular Hispanic origin in Census 2000, 12% identified themselves simply as "Hispanic," and an additional 1.3% wrote in "Latino." Together they represented more than any national group except Mexican.

Because individuals differ in their preference for "Hispanic" or "Latino/a" as the broad category to which they belong, these terms will be used interchangeably in this book. Whichever term is used, it does not mean that the many cultural and generational differences among particular groups of Hispanics have disappeared. On the contrary, youth ministers need to become sensitive to these differences so that they can avoid the types of generalizations and assumptions that will alienate or offend certain members of their youth group.

Use of "Protestant" and "Catholic" terminology

A similar tension exists surrounding the use of "Protestant" to describe mainline Christians, as well as Evangelicals and Pentecostals. Many Christians today are uncomfortable with being called Protestant because they do not consider their religious identity to be tied to protest against the Roman Catholic teachings and practices of the sixteenth century. In most cases, they prefer to call themselves simply "Christian."

The problem with this usage is that Roman Catholics are also Christians, and parts of this study describe some significant differences and particular issues that need to be addressed in ministry with young Catholic Hispanics as distinct from other Christian Hispanics, and vice-versa. For this reason, the term Protestant should be understood to include mainline, evangelical, Pentecostal, and nondenominational Christians; the term Catholic should be understood to refer to Latin Rite Catholics, also known as Roman Catholics; and the term Christian should be understood to refer to Protestants and Catholics together. Mormons (Latter Day Saints) and Jehovah's Witnesses are not included in the category of Protestants, and because they made up less than 2% of the Hispanics in the survey, there were not enough responses to draw any meaningful conclusions about them.

One of the consequences of the historical divisions between Catholics and Protestants is that we have developed different terms to describe the same or similar roles, processes, and elements of community life. In order to avoid confusion, this book follows the convention of using descriptive terms instead of favoring particular usages. The following table summarizes some of the key terms found in this book:

Protestant Term	Catholic Term	Term Used in This Book
fellowship	communion	community life
youth pastor	youth minister	youth minister
congregation or church	parish	faith community
Sunday school	catechism or CCD	religious education

By making these adjustments in terminology, it is hoped that this volume will be understandable, useful, and informative as a resource for pastors, youth ministers, parents, and anyone who is involved in preparing them for their work with Hispanic teens, irrespective of their denominational affiliation.

Acknowledgements

The National Study of Youth and Religion was generously funded by the Lilly Endowment Inc. of Indianapolis, IN, under the direction of its principal investigator, Dr. Christian Smith, the William R. Kenan, Jr. Professor of Sociology at the University of Notre Dame, and Director of the Center for the Sociology of Religion. Funding for the NSYR Hispanic Theological Reflection Project was provided by the National Study of Youth and Religion and a generous supplemental grant from The Louisville Institute of Louisville, KY.

Contributors

 Carlos Carrillo, M.Ed. has worked for the Diocese of Yakima as Director of Hispanic Youth Ministry, as a Supervisor/Therapist for the Yakima Valley Farm Workers Clinic, and currently is the Area Administrator for the Department of Social and Health Services in the State of Washington. Born in Mexico City, he started his ministry with the Hispanic community in the United States in 1985 and has been a member of Instituto Fe y Vida's editorial and pastoral teams since 1987. Carlos received a Masters in Education: Guidance and Counseling in 1992 from Heritage College in Toppenish, WA.

Carmen M. Cervantes, Ed.D. is cofounder of Instituto Fe y Vida and has been its executive director since its creation in 1994. Carmen worked as the director of the Hispanic Youth Ministry Project at Saint Mary's Press, as the director of catechesis for Hispanics in the dioceses of Oakland and Stockton, and as a researcher for the School of Education at the University of the Pacific in Stockton, California.

Carmen holds a Doctorate in Education from the University of the Pacific and a Master's degree in Socio-Cultural Anthropology from Universidad Iberoamericana and Universidad Autónoma de México in Mexico City. She is currently a professor of Hispanic youth and young adult ministry at Loyola Marymount University in Los Angeles, and she serves as adjunct professor at the Jesuit School of Theology in Berkeley, CA. Carmen received the *Distinguished Lasallian Educator Award* from the Brothers of the Christian Schools in 1998, the *Joe Fitzpatrick, S.J. Award* from the Jesuit Hispanic Ministry Conference in 2001, and the *Archbishop Patrick Flores Award* from the United States Conference of Catholic Bishops' Committee on Hispanic Affairs in 2006.

Arturo Chávez, Ph.D. is the President of the Mexican American Cultural Center in San Antonio, Texas. Arturo holds a Master's degree in Theological Studies from the Oblate School of Theology, and a Doctoral degree from the University of Denver and the Iliff School of Theology. He has worked in a variety of ministries including as a teacher, a youth minister, and a chaplain. As a community organizer and activist, he assisted grassroots communities in assessing and responding to their critical social needs. He was instrumental in developing resources to implement community development projects and innovative programs for youth and families.

Elizabeth Conde-Frazier, Ph.D. is a religious educator who integrates the discipline of religious education with theology, spirituality, and the social sciences. She has written on multicultural issues, Hispanic theological education, and the spirituality of the scholar. Elizabeth is an associate professor of religious education at the Claremont School of Theology in Claremont, CA. She also teaches at the Latin American Bible Institute in La Puente, CA, and has taught in Kazakhstan. Her scholarly passions involve her in doing participatory action research with communities working on justice issues, such as immigration and ecumenism as they relate to religious education. She is an ordained American Baptist minister with more than 10 years experience in the local church. Elizabeth received an M.Div. from Eastern Baptist Theological Seminary and a Ph.D. in Theology from Boston College.

Lynette DeJesús-Sáenz, M.S.W. has served as the Coordinator of Urban Youth Ministry for the Diocese of Rochester since 2001. Lynette was a parish youth minister for five years in Cleveland, OH, and she has over ten years of experience in social services. She also served a four-year term as a member of the National Advisory Council for the United States Conference of Catholic Bishops in Washington, DC. Lynette received a B.A. in Psychology from Baldwin-Wallace College in Berea, OH, and an M.S.W. from the Greater Rochester Collaborative Master of Work Program of Nazareth College in Rochester, NY, and the State University of New York in Brockport.

Edwin I. Hernández, Ph.D. is Director of the Center for the Study of Latino Religion at the University of Notre Dame. Edwin became program director of the Center for the Study of Latino Religion at the Institute for Latino Studies, University of Notre Dame, in January 2002. He was previously a program officer for Religion Programs at the Pew Charitable Trusts. He has also served as Vice President for Academic Affairs at Antillian Adventist University, Mayaguez, Puerto Rico, and as a faculty member at Andrews University, Berrien Springs, Michigan.

Ken Johnson-Mondragón, D.Min. cand. has worked for Instituto Fe y Vida for eight years, where he now serves as the Director of the Research and Resource Center for Hispanic Youth and Young Adult Ministry. Before that, he served as a youth minister for seven years in predominantly Hispanic parishes in Washington, DC, Arizona, and California. Ken received an M.A. in Theology from the Catholic University of America in 1995 and is nearing completion of a D.Min. in Hispanic ministry through the Oblate School of Theology in San Antonio, TX.

David Ramos, M.Div., M.S.W. is a staff minister at Faith Fellowship Ministries where he serves as the Chancellor of Faith International Training School and the Director of Covenant Ministries International. David has worked in varying vocational capacities that include the Director of Church Relations for the American Bible Society, a Policy Educator for the Beck Institute on Religion and Poverty at Fordham University and as an Assistant Professor of Social Sciences at The Kings College. David received an M.Div. from Princeton Theological Seminary and an M.S.W. from Rutgers University School of Social Work.

Pastor Tomas V. Sanabria, M.Div. is Executive Director of Ekklesia Ministry of Helps, a service ministry he founded in 1992. He has been an Associate Pastor and Senior Pastor of two storefront churches, served as the president of the Latin American Pentecostal Pastors Association, and served as chairperson of Neighborhoods With Hope, an anti-gang violence community initiative. He is currently an adjunct professor at the Hispanic Bible Seminary in Chicago and reaches out to a broader audience through preaching, teaching and writing.

Focus group members

Juliet de Jesús Alejandre is an education organizer for the Logan Square Neighborhood Association in Chicago, Illinois.

Kenneth G. Davis, OFM Conv. is an associate professor of pastoral studies at Saint Meinrad School of Theology in Indiana.

Elvira Mata, MCDP is the Coordinator of Hispanic Youth Ministry for the Diocese of Fort Worth in Texas.

Patrick Mooney, M.P.S. is the Director of Youth and Young Adult Ministry for the Diocese of Monterey in California.

José "Pepe" Montenegro is coordinator of the Outreach Advocate Program at Newport-Mesa Unified School District in California.

Felisa Román, M.Div., M.S.W. is an ordained chaplain for the Iglesia de Dios Pentecostal Church, and she is the director of the Instituto Bíblico Ebenezer in Chicago, Illinois.

Citations

During this book's preparation, all citations, facts, figures, names, addresses, telephone numbers, Internet URLs, and other pieces of information cited within were verified for accuracy. The authors and Instituto Fe y Vida staff have made every attempt to reference current and valid sources, but we cannot guarantee the content of any source, and we are not responsible for any changes that may have occurred since our verification. If you find an error in, or have a question or concern about, any of the information or sources listed within, please contact Instituto Fe y Vida.

Chapter 1:
Socioreligious Demographics of Hispanic Teenagers

Ken Johnson-Mondragón, D.Min. cand.

Dialog 1.1 – 17 year-old Hispanic Catholic female from the South:

I: *How do you see yourself fitting in at school?*
R: Normal, normal. A normal student. Just another student.
I: *How would other people at school define your group of friends?*
R: They would define me as a quiet person—a good person who does not mess around with others and studies hard.
I: *You know that in high school there are groups such as the most popular ones, those who do sports, something like that. What group are you in?*
R: The Hispanics.
I: *The Hispanics?*
R: The Latinos.
I: *Are there many whites in your school?*
R: Yes.
I: *It is the majority—whites?*
R: Yes.
I: *And are all the Latinos?*
R: We stick together...

Socioreligious Demographics
of Hispanic Teenagers

Since 2001, researchers for the National Study of Youth and Religion (NSYR) have been collecting and analyzing data from the largest nationally representative survey of U.S. teenagers' religious beliefs and practices. This portrait of American teens and their religious experiences, concerns, and beliefs is rich enough to allow for an in-depth description and analysis of particular ethnic and racial groups. In this book you will find some of the most significant findings of the NSYR with respect to Hispanic teens, as well as a discussion of their pastoral and theological implications, together with some very practical suggestions for integrating this new information into your youth programs and events, or even your relationship with your own child.

The purpose of this chapter is to describe the general social and religious context that shapes the lives of young Hispanics in the United States today. Some of this information will be taken directly from the results of the NSYR survey, while other social-scientific sources will be used to fill in the gaps left by the NSYR data. However, the numbers only tell one part of the story—it is easy to form stereotypes about Hispanic teens based on general data, thereby losing sight of the unique gifts and challenges of the Latino/a adolescents in a particular faith community. The remaining chapters in this book will make greater use of excerpts from the in-depth NSYR interviews to help overcome this tendency, filling out in human terms the portrait painted by the numbers. This chapter will conclude with a reflection on the pastoral needs of young Hispanics, as well as some reflection questions and resources for further study.

A statistical overview of Hispanic teens

Although Latino/a youth and young adults now form the largest minority group among their peers in the United States, there are significant differences among them that make it difficult to understand young Hispanics as a single group. National heritage, economic and educational resources, language, religious tradition, skin color, and immigration status are but a few of the factors that divide this young population. Youth ministers in

In those days a decree went out from Emperor Augustus that all the world should be registered. This was the first registration and was taken while Quirinius was governor of Syria. All went to their own towns to be registered. Joseph also went from the town of Nazareth in Galilee to Judea, to the city of David called Bethlehem, because he was descended from the house and family of David. He went to be registered with Mary, to whom he was engaged and who was expecting a child.
– Luke 2:1-5

faith communities that serve Hispanics must respond to all of these factors; their effectiveness will be determined by their ability to adapt to the demands of young Latino/as' diverse pastoral needs and to build upon their strengths for leadership and outreach.

A word to the wise: the next 18 pages are heavy with statistics and graphs. If you don't enjoy numbers and statistical analyses, you might want to just skim over the graphs and tables, and pick up again with the demographic summary on page 32.

Growth of the young Hispanic population in the U.S.

The news media has done a good job of communicating the growth in the Hispanic population, but most people do not realize that this growth is even more dramatic among the young. In fact, Hispanics already account for about 22.5% of the U.S. population under age 10. Chart 1.1 shows

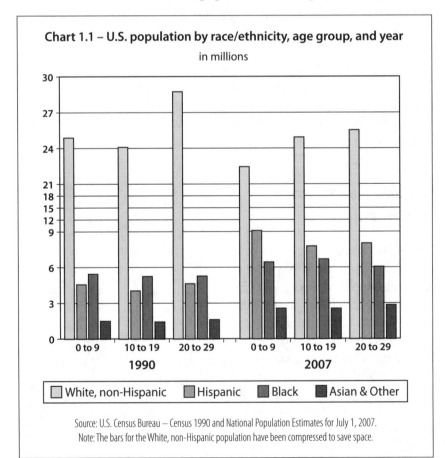

Source: U.S. Census Bureau – Census 1990 and National Population Estimates for July 1, 2007.
Note: The bars for the White, non-Hispanic population have been compressed to save space.

how the young Hispanic population has grown since 1990, as compared to other ethnic and racial groups.

At the time the NSYR survey was conducted, about 16% of U.S. residents ages 13 to 17 were Hispanic, but only 12% of the NSYR respondents were Hispanic. Although the survey was offered in both English and Spanish, Hispanic adolescents are significantly underrepresented among the respondents of the surveys and the interviews, and both the black and the white teens are slightly overrepresented. As a result, the NSYR data cannot be relied upon for certain types of ethnic and racial comparisons, such as determining the percentage of Catholic or Protestant adolescents who are Hispanic, white, etc.

Immigration and legal status

The U.S. Census Bureau's Current Population Survey (CPS) for March 2007 provides an estimate of the current Hispanic population by age and generation, as shown in Chart 1.2. It is no surprise that very few of the youngest Hispanics in the U.S. are foreign-born. Yet the proportion of young Hispanics who are the children of immigrants is remarkably high. This is due to the consistently high rate of immigration from Latin American countries, especially Mexico, since 1980. The effects of this wave of immigration can also be seen in the size of the foreign-born population among Hispanics ages 20 to 29 in the chart. Among Hispanics over age 30, nearly two-thirds were born outside the United States.

A comparison of the CPS figures and the data from the NSYR indicates that immigrant and second-generation teens are significantly underrepresented among NSYR Hispanics. In fact, only 58% of the Hispanic teens surveyed reported that they had an immigrant parent, compared to 72% of 13 to 17 year-old Hispanics in the March 2003 CPS, which was conducted at about the same time. Since the CPS sample includes more than 20 times as many households as the NSYR sample, with an oversample of Hispanic and other minority households, it should be regarded as the more reliable of the two.

Because the U.S. Census Bureau does not ask questions about the legal status of foreign-born residents, other methods for estimating the undocumented population must be employed. In January, 2002, the Census Bureau compared the number of foreign-born residents in Census 2000 to the official numbers of legal residents and naturalized citizens from around the world. Based on these numbers, it is estimated that there were 8.7 million undocumented residents living in the U.S. Of these, 3.87 million (44.5%) were from Mexico and 1.78 million (20.5%) were from the rest of Latin America. This means that as many as 50% of the Mexicans living in the U.S., and 27% of other Latin Americans, are undocumented. Chart 1.3

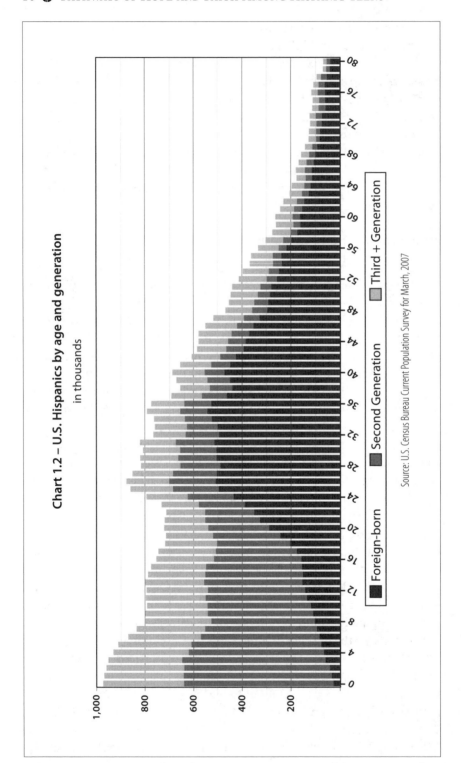

Chart 1.2 – U.S. Hispanics by age and generation

in thousands

Foreign-born   Second Generation   Third + Generation

Source: U.S. Census Bureau Current Population Survey for March, 2007

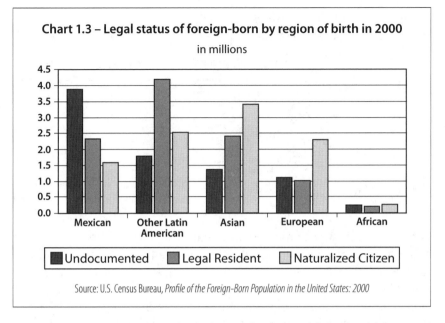

Chart 1.3 – Legal status of foreign-born by region of birth in 2000

in millions

Legend: ■ Undocumented ■ Legal Resident ☐ Naturalized Citizen

Source: U.S. Census Bureau, *Profile of the Foreign-Born Population in the United States: 2000*

includes foreign-born individuals from other parts of the world for comparison, based on Census 2000.

Although there are no data to analyze legal status by age group, the influx of at least twelve million Latin Americans who have stayed in the U.S. since 1990, together with the length of time required to obtain legal residency, suggest that the percentage of undocumented individuals among foreign-born Hispanic adolescents in the U.S. is very high—perhaps as high as 50% or more. About 20% of the Hispanic teenagers living in the U.S. were foreign-born according to the March 2007 CPS, so it is likely that about one in ten Hispanic teens in the U.S. has no legal documentation. The ratio is certainly much higher for their parents. The lack of legal documents among young Hispanics and/or their parents creates many hardships for the teens. Youth ministers should be prepared to handle such issues constructively and compassionately as they develop their outreach efforts and youth programs.

National heritage

The census does ask Hispanics to identify themselves by national heritage, but many simply identify themselves as "Hispanic," "Latino/a," or do not answer the question: 15.1% of all Hispanics described themselves this way in the 2000 census. Hispanics of Mexican heritage made up 58.5% of the total, while 9.6% were Puerto Rican, 3.5% were Cuban, and 2.2% were Dominican. These ratios correspond pretty well with the findings of the NSYR

Table 1.1 – Religious identity of U.S. adults by race / ethnicity and year (percentages)							
	1990 (NSRI & NLPS)				2001 / 2002 (ARIS & NSL)			
Religious Identity	White	Hispanic	Black	Asian / Other	White	Hispanic	Black	Asian / Other
Protestant	58	16	82	34	56	20	78	31
Catholic	27	73	9	27	23	70	7	27
Other	5	1	2	17	7	2	5	17
Not religious	10	10	7	23	15	8	11	26

survey, in which 61% of the Hispanic teens described themselves as being of Mexican heritage, 15% were Puerto Rican, and 15% were other Latin American. Of course, the national heritage of young Hispanics will vary from place to place across the country. Since national heritage is often an important dimension in a teen's identity formation process, youth ministers would do well to learn about the national and cultural backgrounds of the teens in their community.

Religious affiliation of Hispanic adults

How will the growth in the young Hispanic population affect the ethnic and racial mix in America's faith communities in the coming years? Unfortunately, the U.S. Census Bureau does not track religious affiliation, so other sources have to be consulted for this information. The best source from 1990 was the National Survey of Religious Identification (NSRI), a random telephone survey of 115,000 Americans.[1] Because the survey was done only in English, its findings for Hispanics are not as reliable as those of the Latino National Political Survey (LNPS), which surveyed nearly 3,000 Hispanics in their language of preference.[2] For comparison, we have the 2001 American Religious Identification Survey (ARIS), an English-only survey of more than 50,000 households,[3] and the 2002 National Survey of Latinos (NSL), a bilingual survey of nearly 3,000 Hispanics.[4] Although all of these surveys included only adults, their findings are summarized in Table 1.1.

Maps 1.4 and 1.5 were created by correlating the regional statistics from ARIS and NSL to the U.S. Census Bureau's population estimates by state for 2006. These maps reflect the fact that Latino/as are a young population compared to other groups, so their proportion is much higher among children than it is among adults. Given the geographic distribution of Hispanics in the United States, it is not surprising that they now form the majority among young Catholics throughout the West.

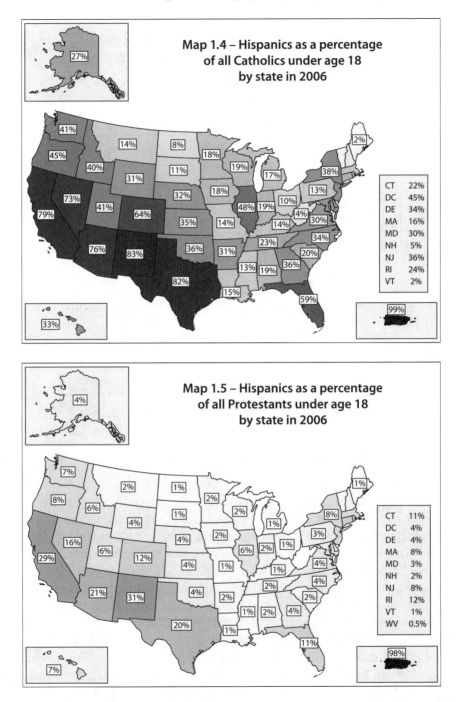

Map 1.4 – Hispanics as a percentage of all Catholics under age 18 by state in 2006

CT	22%
DC	45%
DE	34%
MA	16%
MD	30%
NH	5%
NJ	36%
RI	24%
VT	2%

Map 1.5 – Hispanics as a percentage of all Protestants under age 18 by state in 2006

CT	11%
DC	4%
DE	4%
MA	8%
MD	3%
NH	2%
NJ	8%
RI	12%
VT	1%
WV	0.5%

At the national level, assuming that the religious profiles of each racial or ethnic group will not change from their 2002 levels, Chart 1.6 clearly shows how the growth of the Hispanic population will change the ethnic

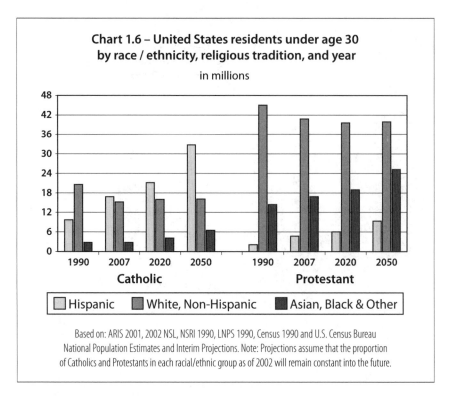

Chart 1.6 – United States residents under age 30 by race / ethnicity, religious tradition, and year

in millions

Based on: ARIS 2001, 2002 NSL, NSRI 1990, LNPS 1990, Census 1990 and U.S. Census Bureau National Population Estimates and Interim Projections. Note: Projections assume that the proportion of Catholics and Protestants in each racial/ethnic group as of 2002 will remain constant into the future.

mix of both Protestant and Catholic churches based on U.S. Census Bureau population projections.

Religious affiliation and religious switching of Hispanic teens

Since the surveys referenced in the previous section were conducted with adults only, the maps and graph are based on the assumption that young people have the same pattern of religious identity as adults. However, it is generally acknowledged that teenagers tend to be somewhat less religious than their parents, and that as Hispanics become more acculturated to life in the United States, many will leave the Catholic Church to join a Protestant church. Because the NSYR survey included questions about language usage and the religious identity of both the teens and their parents, these assertions can be checked from the data.

Many social scientists point to the dominant language as a marker for acculturation among immigrants: being English-dominant reflects a more acculturated lifestyle, while being Spanish-dominant reflects a less-acculturated lifestyle. Chart 1.7 shows the religious identities of Hispanic adolescents and their parents, broken down by the dominant language of the teen. White, non-Hispanic teenagers and their parents are also included for the sake of comparison.

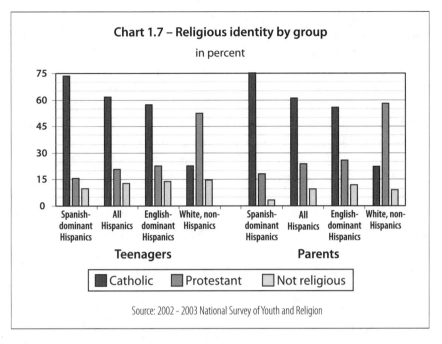

Chart 1.7 – Religious identity by group

in percent

Source: 2002 - 2003 National Survey of Youth and Religion

This graph shows that both Spanish-dominant teens and their parents are less likely to have no religion, more likely to be Catholic, and less likely to be Protestant than their English-dominant Hispanic peers. There is also evidence to support the notion that teenagers question or reject the religious beliefs of their parents: there are slightly more non-religious Hispanic teens than non-religious Hispanic parents. However, this increase is smaller than the 6 percentage point gap between white, non-Hispanic teens and their parents, suggesting that Hispanic teens are more influenced by their parents' religious identity than their non-Hispanic white peers. Even so, the number of teens who profess at least nominal adherence to a religious tradition is much higher across the board than the popular media would have us believe. To what extent this religious identity is translated into a living faith will be discussed further in Chapter 2.

On the topic of Catholic Hispanics joining Protestant churches as they become more acculturated to life in the U.S., the large gap between the 74% of Spanish-dominant teens who are Catholic and the 57% of English-dominant Hispanic teens who are Catholic indicates that more acculturated Hispanics are more likely to be Protestant and less likely to be Catholic. Indeed, 5% of the NSYR Hispanic teens report having joined their Protestant church since the age of 12. However, another 5% of them report having become Catholic since age 12. It is not clear at what age Hispanics tend to leave Catholicism to join another denomination of Christianity, but there is no evidence in the NSYR surveys of a large religious exodus among

Hispanic Catholic teens. How these teens will choose to affiliate in the long-term will depend on how well each faith community recognizes and responds to the spiritual and pastoral needs of their Hispanic families.

All of this begs the question of what is the most influential factor that leads to religious switching among Hispanic teens. Table 1.2 sheds an interesting light on the phenomenon of religious switching. The boldface number in each column represents the percentage of Catholic, Protestant, and non-religious parents whose teenage son or daughter shares their religious faith tradition. We know that as Hispanics spend more time in the United States, there appears to be a greater likelihood that they will leave the Catholic Church and join a Protestant church. However, these numbers suggest that Hispanic teens are reluctant to embrace a Protestant form of Christianity when they have a Catholic parent. By comparison, it appears

Table 1.2 – Parental religious influence on Hispanic teens by family type (percentages)	Responding Parent's Religion		
Hispanic Teen's Religion	Catholic	Protestant	Not Religious
All Hispanic families	N=275	N=107	N=29*
Catholic	**91**	13	29
Protestant	0.5	**81**	11
Not religious	7	5	**60**
Parents share the same faith	N=170	N=62	N=3***
Catholic	**96**	6	N/A
Protestant	~	**89**	N/A
Not religious	2	2	**N/A**
Parents do not share the same faith	N=20*	N=8***	N=14**
Catholic	**90**	N/A	22
Protestant	5	**N/A**	7
Not religious	5	N/A	**56**
Other religion	0	N/A	15
Single-parent families	N=84	N=38	N=13**
Catholic	**82**	21	28
Protestant	0	**73**	32
Not religious	13	5	**16**
Other religion	5	0	24

* With only 20 to 30 parent-teen pairs, these results have a sampling error of up to ±9%.

** With only 13 to 14 parent-teen pairs, these results have a sampling error of up to ±13%.

*** With 8 or less parent-teen pairs, these results are not representative, so they are not reported.

that the teenage children of Protestant Hispanic parents are significantly more likely to embrace a Catholic identity. This may be due to the influence of grandparents or other family members, or perhaps they have remained Catholic after one of their parents has become a Protestant Christian.

The influence of parents in forming the religious identity of Hispanic teens becomes even stronger when both parents share the same religious tradition. Nevertheless, even in religiously divided households, the respondents were very likely to retain the religious identity of their Catholic parent. Hispanic teens in single-parent households were the most likely to have a different religious faith from that of the parent surveyed. In addition, these teens were the most likely to respond that they are "not religious" or belong to a non-Christian religion.

Thus, while there can be no doubt that many Hispanics are switching from Catholicism to a Protestant expression of Christianity, only a small minority of the teens appear to be making the switch on their own. Rather, they are much more likely to be religious followers of their parents: if their parents make the switch, they do so as well. The following conversation with one of the Hispanic teens interviewed in the NSYR study illustrates how even older adolescents can take for granted the changes in their parents' religious beliefs:

Dialog 1.2 – 17 year-old Hispanic non-denominational Christian male from the West:

I: *And can you tell me about how you were raised religiously?*
R: For a little while—a little while, I can barely remember—I was raised Catholic, but after that it was Christian.
I: *And by Christian you mean that you go to a Protestant church?*
R: Um...
I: *Not Catholic but Christian church?*
R: Yeah.
I: *And how—when you think that change took place—like how old were you?*
R: I was about 7.
I: *So that was like your mom and dad making that change?*
R: Yeah...
I: *What have been the things that have influenced you in terms of your beliefs?*
R: Um, just I guess, just the people at church. The way my parents are. How, they, like how they like set the example.

Language

The 2002 National Survey of Latinos (NSL), a large survey of Hispanics conducted at about the same time as the NSYR, tested for the use of Spanish at home among Hispanic adults. The findings of the NSL on this point are summarized in Chart 1.8. Since the proportion of immigrants among Hispanic teens is much lower than it is in the adult Hispanic population,

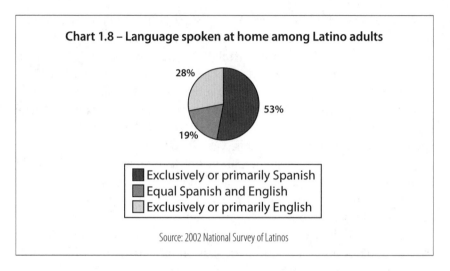

Chart 1.8 – Language spoken at home among Latino adults

28%

53%

19%

■ Exclusively or primarily Spanish
■ Equal Spanish and English
□ Exclusively or primarily English

Source: 2002 National Survey of Latinos

it is often assumed that Latino/a adolescents primarily use English. The NSYR provides detailed insight into the use of language among Hispanic teens, as shown in Chart 1.9.

Although nearly four out of every five Hispanic teens speak at least some Spanish, English is clearly the language they most use among their friends. Even among foreign-born Hispanic teens, 44% speak mostly English in conversation with their friends, compared to 12% that use mostly Spanish. In contrast, there is no clear language of choice at home. Yet when U.S.-born Hispanic adolescents are compared to their foreign-born Hispanic peers, it becomes clear that the use of English at home increases dramatically from generation to generation, as shown in Chart 1.10.

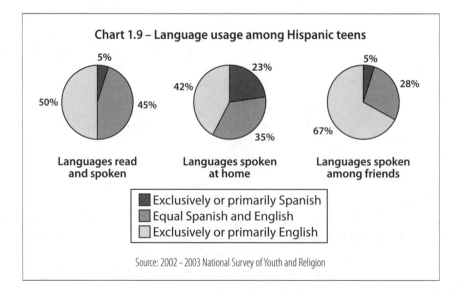

Chart 1.9 – Language usage among Hispanic teens

5%

50%

45%

Languages read
and spoken

23%

42%

35%

Languages spoken
at home

5%

28%

67%

Languages spoken
among friends

■ Exclusively or primarily Spanish
■ Equal Spanish and English
□ Exclusively or primarily English

Source: 2002 - 2003 National Survey of Youth and Religion

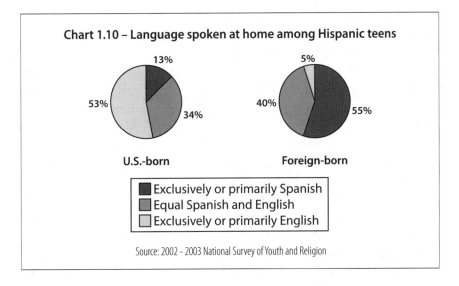

Chart 1.10 – Language spoken at home among Hispanic teens

13%
53%
34%
U.S.-born

5%
40%
55%
Foreign-born

■ Exclusively or primarily Spanish
■ Equal Spanish and English
□ Exclusively or primarily English

Source: 2002 - 2003 National Survey of Youth and Religion

Education

The *2003 Report of the President's Advisory Commission on Educational Excellence for Hispanic Americans* notes that while Hispanic educational attainment is improving, it continues to lag behind the results for other racial groups. Chart 1.11 portrays the trends over the last thirty-five years:[5]

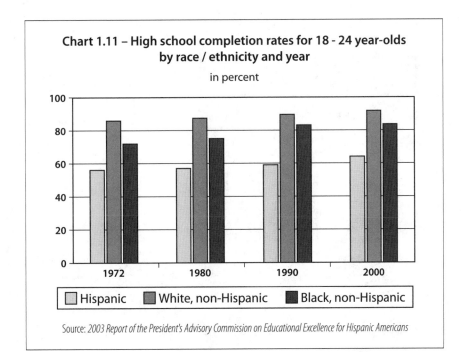

Chart 1.11 – High school completion rates for 18 - 24 year-olds by race / ethnicity and year

in percent

□ Hispanic   ■ White, non-Hispanic   ■ Black, non-Hispanic

Source: *2003 Report of the President's Advisory Commission on Educational Excellence for Hispanic Americans*

The Pew Hispanic Center reports that this underachievement is due in large part to the low educational attainment of Hispanic immigrants, with about 33% of foreign-born Hispanics ages 16 to 19 having left school without a diploma.[6] However, this low educational attainment should be understood in the light of Latin American educational and labor systems. For example, graduating from *secundaria* (roughly the equivalent of 9th grade) in Mexico at age 15 is a significant academic and practical achievement. Government offices and private businesses require a *secundaria* for a variety of careers, including commercial cashiers and drivers, sales representatives, and office clerks. Depending mainly on the family's socioeconomic status and the availability of schools, a young person at age 15 or 16 may choose to enter directly into the labor force, or enter technical or paraprofessional studies for a wide array of careers such as accounting, nursing, social work, preschool, elementary education, automotive repair, and electrical or laboratory technicians, with program lengths varying from two to four years.

Those privileged students who intend to pursue university studies need to enter into an *escuela preparatoria* or *bachillerato* (preparatory school), which may last two or three years and in some places requires paying

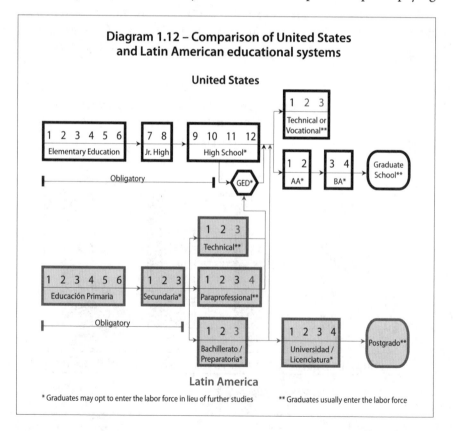

Diagram 1.12 – Comparison of United States and Latin American educational systems

tuition—if there is a preparatory school in the region at all. In the United States, Latin Americans who have not completed preparatory school are considered to be without high school, even if they have completed four years of paraprofessional studies. As a result, they add to the statistics about Hispanic high school "dropouts," and they are required to obtain a G.E.D. in order to pursue training for an equivalent certificate in the United States, as shown in Diagram 1.12.

Because many Hispanics ages 15 and higher come to the United States in search of work, the high rate of Hispanic "dropouts" in the President's Advisory Commission report should not be seen as indicative of school attendance rates for teens ages 13 to 17 (the ages interviewed in the NSYR). Although the U.S. Census Bureau does not ask whether people are currently attending school, it does ask for the highest level of education completed by individuals over age 15 in its annual Current Population Survey (CPS). From this information it is possible to approximate the percentage of teens that are not attending school. Chart 1.13 is based on data from the 2002 CPS, so it describes the dropout rate among U.S. adolescents who were roughly of the same cohort as those surveyed in the NSYR.

The disparity in dropout rates between Hispanic adolescents and teens of other racial / ethnic backgrounds is striking, and it has implications for pastoral work among young Hispanics. The reader should keep in mind that the CPS does not reach teens that are institutionalized in detention

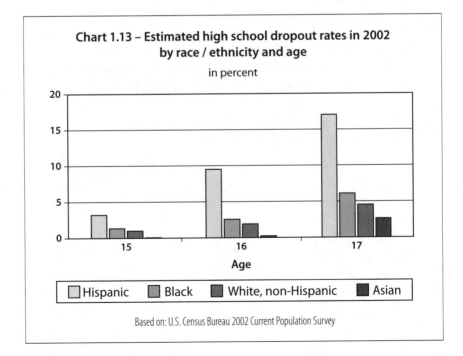

Chart 1.13 – Estimated high school dropout rates in 2002 by race / ethnicity and age

in percent

Age

Hispanic Black White, non-Hispanic Asian

Based on: U.S. Census Bureau 2002 Current Population Survey

Table 1.3 – Comparison of dropout rates among teens ages 15 to 17 in 2002 (percentages)		
Ethnic / Racial Group	NSYR Dropout Rate	2002 CPS Dropout Rate
White, Non-Hispanic	1.7	2.5
Black, Non-Hispanic	1.6	3.4
Hispanic, Any Race	3.9	9.8
Asian	0	1.0

centers, hospitals, or other types of non-traditional households. Because Hispanics are overrepresented in U.S. detention centers, and teens in detention are more likely to drop out of school, the above figures should be taken as a low estimate.

When comparing the Census Bureau's CPS figures with the findings of the NSYR, there is a significant discrepancy in the percentage of Hispanic teens that have stopped attending school. Since the CPS does not collect information about individuals under age 15, the discrepancy for teens ages 15 to 17 is summarized in Table 1.3.

While the NSYR dropout rates are consistently lower than the corresponding CPS figures, the discrepancy for non-Hispanic teens is within the margin of sampling error. The same is not true for Hispanic teens. The larger difference suggests that the NSYR may have been less effective than the CPS at reaching Hispanic households with teens that are at risk of dropping out of high school.

The same sampling bias may also have contributed to the fact that 64% of NSYR Hispanic parents had completed high school, compared to just 59% of the general population of Hispanic adults ages 30 to 59 in the March 2003 CPS. Nevertheless, the education gap between the Hispanic and white parents surveyed is considerable, as shown in Table 1.4.

Table 1.4 – Highest parental educational attainment by religion and ethnic group (percentages)				
	Catholic		Protestant	
	Hispanic	White	Hispanic	White
	N=278	N=556	N=94	N=1285
Junior high or less	16	~	6	1
Some high school	9	1	9	3
High school or GED	32	17	23	38
Some college, AA, or vocational/technical school	27	31	39	38
Bachelor's degree or some graduate school	8	30	13	24
Graduate or professional degree	7	21	10	16

The numbers in the table represent the highest educational level achieved by either parent, and the high school graduation rates range from 75% for Hispanic Catholics to 99% for white Catholics. The parental education gap is particularly large between Hispanic and white Catholic families. Because most of the Hispanic parents have not experienced what it takes to obtain a university degree, many of their children need additional support in order to get into a college and complete a degree program. Far too many high schools in low-income areas are not able to provide that support, but youth ministry programs could make a big difference for Hispanic teens by providing the direction and encouragement they need to finish high school and set their sights on a college degree.

Another significant factor in the educational portrait of young Hispanics is the type of school they attend—public or private. Whereas the national dropout rate for Hispanics in public education lies somewhere around 25%, the graduation rate among Hispanics attending Catholic high schools is over 90%, and 95% of those who graduate from Catholic school will obtain a university degree.[7] According to the NSYR, about 9% of Hispanic teens are either being home schooled or are attending a private high school, compared to about 12% of White teens. Much more work is needed to encourage Hispanic teens to complete high school and to provide them with mentorship leading to success in colleges and universities—especially for those enrolled in public high schools. These issues will be addressed in depth in Chapter 5.

Economic status

When it comes to household income, the U.S. Census Bureau's annual American Community Survey (ACS) is generally regarded as the most reliable source of information. The ACS revealed that between 2000 and 2005, Hispanic household median income increased by 8%—from $33,450 to $36,275. This compares with $30,950 for black and $50,625 for non-Hispanic white households. Thus, the median Hispanic household income was only 71.5% as much as the median white household income. However, Hispanic households are generally larger than white households, so the Hispanic per capita income is only $14,460, or roughly 50% as much as the white per capita income of $29,025.[8]

In 2005, about 22.4% of Hispanic households were living below the poverty threshold, compared to 25.6% for the black, and 9.0% for the white, non-Hispanic population. Among children ages 5 to 17, the poverty rates increase to 28.3% for Hispanics, 10.0% for whites, and 31.9% for blacks. Chart 1.14 summarizes how Hispanic household income compared with that of other racial groups in 2005.

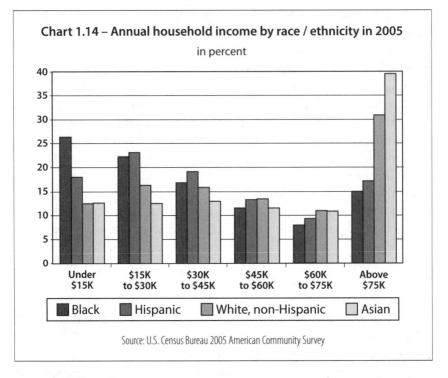

Chart 1.14 – Annual household income by race / ethnicity in 2005

in percent

Source: U.S. Census Bureau 2005 American Community Survey

While household income is certainly an important factor in describing the economic prospects of a family, there are other factors that are equally important. For example, a retired couple with no mortgage, no debt, and a $200K retirement fund living on a fixed income of $20K per year clearly has a different economic status than a family of five with $5K in credit card debt and monthly rental and car payments, living on the same income. The NSYR parents surveyed were asked about their level of indebtedness, their annual income, and whether they owned their home. Combining these measures, it is possible to segment the NSYR families into low, middle, and high economic status groups, as shown in Table 1.5.

Although white Catholic families have a higher economic profile than their Protestant counterparts, Hispanic Catholic families have the lowest economic profile. Clearly, the low economic status of many Hispanic families goes hand-in-hand with lower educational attainment and the undocumented status of so many Latino/a immigrants. For both Catholics and Protestants, the economic disparity between Hispanic and white members of the faith community should be taken into consideration when developing programs and activities that are intended for all of the teens.

For example, access to transportation, the availability of spare time apart from school and family obligations, neighborhood safety for going out at night, the ability of parents to pay a fee for programs and activities,

Table 1.5 – Economic status by religion and ethnic group (percentages)				
	Catholic		Protestant	
	Hispanic	White	Hispanic	White
	N=278	N=556	N=94	N=1285
Low*	40	7	27	13
Middle*	39	33	35	35
High*	19	59	35	50
* See the Appendix on page 361 for definitions of the economic status categories.				

Internet access at home, and in some cases even telephone service cannot be taken for granted. In addition, many Latino/a teens living in low-income areas of large cities are faced with the daily enticements of escaping their harsh reality through substance abuse, or making some easy money through criminal activity. Any of these considerations can become an obstacle to participation at church. Parents and youth ministry leaders should engage in honest and open conversation about these realities in order to find ways to overcome the obstacles that may present themselves. These issues will be taken up again in Chapter 3.

Gangs and delinquent behavior

The 2004 National Youth Gang Survey (NYGS) reports that of 760,000 active gang members in the U.S. in 2004, about 48% were Hispanic, 36% were black, and 10% were white. Also, 62% were over 18 years old, while 38% were from 15 to 17 years old.[9] Assuming that the age distribution was about the same for each racial/ethnic group, there were around 140,000 active Hispanic gang members under the age of 18 in 2004. Since law enforcement officials report that about 92% of active gang members are male, this number represents about 8% of all Hispanic boys and 1% of all Hispanic girls ages 13 to 17 in 2004.

Delinquency among minors is defined as committing an offense that would be a crime for an adult. One measure of the prevalence of delinquent behaviors among various groups is the number of residents in juvenile detention facilities. According to the U.S. Office of Juvenile Justice and Delinquency Prevention, about 0.5% of all Hispanics ages 10 to 17 were in detention in 1999 (the most recent data available at the time of writing). This compares to about 1% for blacks and 0.2% for whites in the same age group.[10] Statistics were not reported by individual years of age or by gender, except to note that detention rates were significantly higher among older

Table 1.6 – Offense profile of Hispanic juvenile offenders in 1999	
Most Serious Offense	Percent of Hispanic Offenders
Aggravated Assault	13
Probation or Court Order Violation	13
Burglary	11
Robbery	9
Drug Possession	7
Simple Assault	6
Auto Theft	6
Weapons	5
Theft	5
Sexual Assault	5
Drug Trafficking	3
Criminal Homicide	2
Status Violation (runaway, truancy, etc.)	2

Source: U.S. Department of Justice, Office of Juvenile Justice and Delinquency Prevention, 2004.

teens, and among boys. In 1999, Hispanics represented 18% of all juveniles in detention. Their offenses are categorized in Table 1.6. When compared to other racial and ethnic groups, Hispanics were most notably overrepresented in offenses for weapons, criminal homicide, aggravated assault, and auto theft. At the same time, they were underrepresented in offenses of status violation and sexual assault.

Since the NSYR did not survey any adolescents in juvenile detention facilities, its results are not representative of this small sector of the young Hispanic population. A bigger question is whether the NSYR survey reached young Hispanic gang members, who may represent as much as 8% of Hispanic boys ages 15 to 17. There is nothing in the design of the study that would exclude gang members, but it is possible that they may have been more likely than others to exclude themselves from participating in the survey. Either way, the NSYR data currently provides the most reliable picture available concerning the impact of religious faith on the moral beliefs and decisions of young Latino/as—including some teens that might be classified as habitually delinquent or gang members. Chapter 6 will address in greater detail the findings of the NSYR on the relationship between faith and moral choices among Hispanic adolescents.

Demographic summary of young Hispanics

With all of the above information about young Hispanics, what can really be said about them as a group? Without a doubt we can say that young Latino/as are rapidly increasing both in the size of their population compared to other groups, and in their social and religious influence. While the majority of young Hispanics continues to identify as Catholic, the Protestant

minority is slowly but steadily growing. Hispanic teens that are "not religious" are also growing in number, although a bit more slowly than among
their White, non-Hispanic peers.

Hispanic teens are mostly the children of immigrants, but their national and cultural heritage is very diverse. Even so, they seem to be developing an awareness of a pan-Hispanic cultural identity. The vast majority
can speak at least some Spanish, yet all but the most recent immigrants
prefer English with their friends. The challenges faced by the children of
immigrants in the United States are not new—many previous generations
have had to deal with high dropout, poverty, and delinquency rates, as well
as the allure of substance abuse and gangs. Yet this generation is still very
young, and the course it will take in response to these challenges is still
unfolding.

This means that the churches and schools, and in particular the parents, teachers, and youth ministers, have a tremendous opportunity to help
young Hispanics address the challenges they face in creative, constructive,
and prayerful ways. In many cases, the ones that persevere in school and
take an active role in their churches are doing so in the face of much greater
adversity than their non-Hispanic peers. This perseverance is undoubtedly
forming the character of the next generation of Hispanic leaders for church
and society. Catholic and Protestant churches alike must do more to call
forth the gifts of these bright and resourceful teens for the evangelization
of their peers. The following section provides a description of some of the
pastoral implications that arise from this demographic portrait.

Pastoral categories of Latino/a adolescents

From the preceding statistics, it
should be clear that young Hispanics in the U.S. today are a very diverse
group. One of the great challenges
for youth ministers is to find ways
to welcome and empower *all* young
people, developing leaders that re-

> "You are worthy to take the scroll and
> to open its seals, for you were slaugh-
> tered and by your blood you ransomed
> for God saints from every tribe and
> language and people and nation; you
> have made them to be a kingdom and
> priests serving our God."
> – **Revelation 5:9-10**

flect the ethnic, cultural, socioeconomic, and/or racial characteristics of
the community's families. Developing a youth ministry team that is competent for cross-cultural or multicultural ministry and creating programs
that are culturally appropriate and relevant to the needs of the teenagers
should be the first priorities.

Leadership development is critical when it comes to reaching adolescents who are culturally, linguistically, or socioeconomically different from the majority of the young people in a faith community. Too often these "minority" young people choose to avoid youth ministry programs because they do not feel at home in them. Unless the youth ministers intentionally include teens of diverse backgrounds in leadership and decision-making, they risk catering to a homogeneous subgroup of the adolescents in their community, leaving others without the benefit of their services.

The first step should be to identify the depth and breadth of the diversity in the community, and create strategies for ministering with and developing leadership among adolescents of every background. Faced with this challenge, it may be helpful to segment the young Hispanic population into groups that provide a higher degree of homogeneity than the young Latino/a population as a whole. What follows is a pastoral segmentation of the young Hispanic population, loosely based on the statistical portrait outlined in the first section of this chapter.

The lives of Hispanic adolescents involve complex interactions between individual experiences and cultural influences. As a result, not every young Hispanic will fit neatly into just one category, but segmenting the population offers a point of reference for evaluating how well the parish or congregation is reaching and meeting the needs of teens with different characteristics. In general, when a faith community implements pastoral strategies to care for teens in all four categories, young Hispanics of any background are likely to find a place for themselves in its youth ministry programs.

Identity seekers

The NSYR data suggest that the largest segment of young Hispanics are looking for a sense of identity and belonging in a world that is neither their parents' nor their own. Mostly the

Identity Seekers
- Mostly bilingual
- Few will go to college
- Mostly born in the U.S.
- Low self-esteem
- Children of immigrants
- Unmotivated / apathetic
- Some struggle to stay in high school and graduate
- May find hope in work or family relationships
- Some seek refuge in alcohol, drugs, or sexual promiscuity
- Mostly in lower-middle part of the economic spectrum

children or grandchildren of immigrants, they are citizens of the United States, but they and their loved ones have felt the sting of social and religious discrimination, poor education, and dehumanizing public policy. They are frequently bilingual but mostly use English among their peers.

These "identity seekers" are likely to be enrolled in public schools. The majority will finish high school, but few have the combination of desire, financial resources, and support to pursue a bachelor's degree. At school, they tend to avoid associating with their peers in both the mainstream culture and the gang subculture, because they feel neither accepted nor respected by them. For this reason, they will also avoid participating in church youth groups, unless there is a critical mass of young Hispanics like themselves among the leadership and the participants.

With the proper support, these young "identity seekers" have the potential to integrate into either the mainstream youth ministry of the U.S. or the immigrant Hispanic ministry, depending on whether they are more inclined to use their English or their Spanish. Their greatest personal struggle lies in developing and maintaining a healthy self-esteem. They need positive role models and a safe place to gather with other teens with whom they can relate and who will not judge them for the color of their skin, their neighborhood, or the music they enjoy.

Without proper support, they tend to busy themselves with immediate-gratification activities such as listening to music, dancing, driving flashy cars, gossiping, and watching television or movies. During this time, they are neglecting their studies and their preparation for the future. They may even develop a culture of resistance to the mainstream ideals of education, hard work, and individual achievement, such that they will criticize their peers for working too hard in school or being too involved in church activities. As their self-esteem deteriorates, they may become involved in self-destructive behaviors such as drug or alcohol abuse, promiscuous sexual activity, or suicidal thoughts. When their hope diminishes to the point of despair, they may turn to life in a gang, criminal activity, or even suicide as a final escape.

Mainstream movers

Another segment of the young Hispanic population might be described as "mainstream movers" because they are well educated and they know what it will take to get ahead in the

Mainstream Movers
- Mostly English-speaking
- Motivated and hopeful
- Mostly born in the U.S.
- Willing to work hard
- Will likely go to college, and some attend private schools
- Do not associate much with lower-income Hispanics
- More likely than other Hispanics to leave Catholic Church
- May look down on other categories of Hispanics
- Mostly in middle-upper part of economic spectrum

United States. Most of them are second- or third-generation Americans with parents who understand the value of education, and who can provide the benefits of a middle class, upwardly mobile lifestyle. Some are immigrants who arrived legally and have a good formal education or sufficient financial resources to make a new start here. A significant portion of these young Hispanics have also benefited from education in Catholic or other private schools.

As they witness the pitfalls and struggles of other young Hispanics, some try to lend a helping hand by seeking careers in public service work, education, or politics. Other mainstream movers view these less fortunate Hispanics as obstacles in their path to success, so they deliberately separate themselves from their cultural heritage. Many do not speak Spanish, and they may resent the assumptions that are made about their language based on the color of their skin. Those who are drawn to the church tend to integrate into mainstream youth groups or campus ministries without much difficulty.

Immigrant workers

Most of the foreign-born Hispanics who come to the U.S. after age 15 can be considered "immigrant workers." More than half are from Mexico, the rest coming from Puerto Rico, Cen-

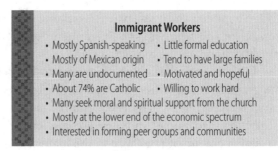

Immigrant Workers
- Mostly Spanish-speaking
- Little formal education
- Mostly of Mexican origin
- Tend to have large families
- Many are undocumented
- Motivated and hopeful
- About 74% are Catholic
- Willing to work hard
- Many seek moral and spiritual support from the church
- Mostly at the lower end of the economic spectrum
- Interested in forming peer groups and communities

tral and South America, and the Caribbean. They are highly motivated to work, and they are usually able to find jobs in the farming, manufacturing, and service sectors of the economy. The majority arrives without a high school education, and unless they have strong encouragement from others and are documented (about half are not), they likely will never complete their studies. Most continue to speak Spanish at home and at work, and they prefer to attend church services in Spanish.

Some of the adolescent children of recently-arrived immigrant parents might also be considered immigrant workers, even though they are likely to be in school. In addition to their school work, they will be expected to work to help support the family, and the pressure of family needs combined with the cost of higher education will make it very difficult for them to go to college. In addition, the lack of college-educated role models, and the struggles associated with being undocumented (for those who are), often will lead them to take a low-end job after they graduate. Even so, they carry memories of the limited economic prospects in their country of origin, as well as a strong cultural devotion to family, so they may continue to be optimistic about their life in this country despite the hardships.

Because of their hopefulness and willingness to work hard, their potential for pastoral leadership is tremendous; what is often lacking is the human and spiritual formation to provide stability and direction for the development of their gifts. In faith communities around the country, many of these immigrant workers are seeking training and offering their gifts for ministry among their peers. Creating spaces for them, especially when they are newly arrived, in more traditional youth ministry programs can be difficult—their limited English and the fact that they are working for a living instead of, or in addition to, going to school means that they have little in common with other adolescents in the U.S., although they may have the same chronological age.

Gang members and high-risk teens

In the final category, it is helpful to distinguish between gang members and other high-risk teens on the one hand, and at-risk adolescents on the other. Gang

Gang Members and High-Risk Teens
- Limited bilingual abilities
- Little formal education
- Mostly born in the U.S.
- Anger towards society
- Many live in inner cities
- Experience despair
- Most are unemployed
- Many are incarcerated
- May become habitual drug users / sellers
- Mostly at the lower end of the economic spectrum
- Will only get involved at church in specialized programs

members are individuals who join a gang for protection or a sense of belonging—usually out of despair that their future will never offer them anything better. High-risk teens are young people whose lives have been filled with experiences of violence and suffering, leading to a criminal lifestyle which in many cases is at least partially the result of substance abuse. At-risk teens are those whose lives are surrounded by gangs and role models engaging in high-risk activities, and who need extra support at home and at school to avoid falling into the traps of gangs, drugs, violence, and other criminal behavior. Strictly speaking, the at-risk teens usually fall within the segment of "identity seekers."

Pastoral experience suggests that no one is attracted to the gang lifestyle, but rather defeated young people are pushed into it when they see no other alternatives, and most of them live to regret that decision. Gang members are seldom immigrants, unless they came to this country at a very young age. They may come from many different types of families, but in almost all cases they were raised in poverty.

They are bilingual to a certain degree, yet they generally are not fully proficient in either Spanish or English. Very few finish high school, and without marketable skills, many turn to selling drugs or other criminal activity as a way to survive. Chances are good that they will be incarcerated or killed before they reach age thirty. Some will make a choice to separate themselves from their criminal lifestyle and associations as they move into young adulthood. For many of these, it is their religious faith that provides the motivation and support to their choice to turn their lives around.

Table 1.7 – Pastoral needs of Hispanic adolescents by category

	Identity Seekers	Mainstream Movers	Immigrant Workers	Gang Members and High Risk Teens
Spiritual life	Need mentoring to integrate faith and life amid cultural transition	Need guidance to overcome individualism and consumerism, and to value Hispanic spirituality	Need to form faith-based communities grounded in their culture of origin	Need faith to heal and move from anger / hatred to forgiveness
Intellectual development	Need encouragement to finish high school and set goals for higher education	Need financial aid and help understanding U.S. system of higher education	Need an accessible alternative system of education	Need an accessible alternative system of education
Affective maturity and socialization	Need assistance to develop self-esteem and faith in themselves	Need positive role models of social and cultural integration	Need a healthy environment for developing relationships	Need a peer group and a safe place to belong with positive role models
Acquisition of human virtues	Need guidance and direction in life	Need to value community service and social justice	Need help to avoid the pitfalls of vice and addictions	Need counseling to overcome bad habits and attitudes
Percent of Hispanic adolescents	40% to 50%	20% to 30%	10% to 20%	10% to 15%

Pastoral needs by category

The pastoral needs of these four categories of young Hispanics are sum-marized in Table 1.7. A comprehensive approach to ministry with young Hispanics will require different strategies to address the distinct pastoral needs of each of the four categories. Because of the uniqueness of each faith community, leadership development becomes the critical issue for reaching Hispanic young people. Once the leaders begin to reflect the diversity of the community, they must be empowered to create activities, programs, and environments that are culturally appropriate, relevant to the needs of their peers, and in harmony with the Gospel. Because they are learning to transform their own lives, they will be creative, passionate, and ultimately very effective in their efforts to bring the Good News to others.

Questions for reflection

A good starting point for youth ministry teams is to discuss the following questions:

1. Which of the four pastoral categories of young Hispanics are present within our community, and what efforts have we made to find groups that may be hidden?

2. How have we involved young Hispanics from each of these categories in developing their skills for leadership as members of our youth ministry team?

3. Are there Hispanic young adults in our community who have similar backgrounds to our Hispanic teens, and who can serve as positive role models for them in a variety of ways?

4. Gather a diverse group of Hispanic teens and their parents and ask them (or if you already have a diverse leadership team, ask them): Are our programs and activities culturally appropriate, and do they respond to the pastoral needs of all young Hispanics within the community? What more could be done?

Practical suggestions for developing and improving ministry with Hispanic teens can be found at the end of each chapter in the rest of this book.

Chapter 2:
Personal Religious Beliefs and Experiences

Pastor Tomas V. Sanabria, M.Div.

Dialog 2.1 – 15 year old non-religious Hispanic male with Catholic leanings from the South:

I: *When you think about God, what do you think of? Who or what is God to you?*

R: Just a greater force out there that makes things happen for a reason.

I: *Okay. Do you think of God as active or removed from human affairs?*

R: I think he is active in most people's lives. I mean, I think he looks down on people, has a purpose for everybody.

I: *Okay. Do you think of God as more loving and forgiving, or demanding and judging?*

R: Loving and forgiving.

I: *And how did you get these ideas about God?*

R: Ah, I guess from reading various parts of the Bible, watching all those shows on TV with the preachers and just stuff like that.

I: *Okay, so you watch the televangelists?*

R: Ah, I don't watch them, but ah, I'll flick through the channels and stop for like two minutes and just listen a little bit and then I'll move on.

I: *What religion, if any, do you consider yourself to be?*

R: Ah, Catholic, I think.

I: *Okay. You said you think? You're not really...*

R: Well, ah, I, I don't really consider myself a Catholic. I mean, not that I consider myself anything else... 'cause I'm not really religious at all. But ah, I guess if I was anything I'd be Catholic.

I: *Okay. And you definitely consider yourself Christian?*

R: Yes.

I: *Okay. Can you tell me the beliefs of your own personal faith? Or morality?*

R: Ah, I don't really have any real beliefs. I mean, just that there is a God and we all have a purpose...

Personal Religious Beliefs and Experiences

When it comes to believing in God, who can describe adequately the religious experiences of Hispanic teenagers, and who can explain their beliefs about religion, faith and God? Only they can. The 393 Hispanic responses to the National Study of Youth and Religion (NSYR) survey, and the 38 one-on-one interviews with Hispanic teens provide unique insights into the religious beliefs and practices of Hispanic adolescents—we hear them speaking about their faith (or lack thereof) in their own voices.

Since Latino/as currently make up about 17% of the high school-age population in the United States, these responses give religious leaders, youth ministers, and members of faith communities valuable insights that can help shape youth ministry and the way that we respond to the spiritual needs of young people in our congregations. As a pastor, previous youth worker and community organizer, I will share my reflections on the religious experiences of Hispanic teens and their beliefs as they are found in the NSYR.

A reflection on faith and belief

I would like to begin by marking the distinction between belief and faith. Whereas believing is a process that requires *the working out* within the mind of an impression as stimulated by feelings, persuasion, conviction or even a doctrine, a tenet, or an opinion, faith, on the other hand, *is arriving at* a secure belief in God and a trusting acceptance of God's will in one's life. It is demonstrated by the way it is lived out.

> "Let the children come to me; do not prevent them, for the kingdom of God belongs to such as these. Amen, I say to you, whoever does not accept the kingdom of God like a child will not enter it." Then he embraced them and blessed them, placing his hands on them.
> – **Mark 10:14b-16**

faith (fāth) n. 1. Confident belief in the truth, value, or trustworthiness of a person, idea, or thing. 2. Belief that does not rest on logical proof or material evidence. 3. Loyalty to a person or thing; allegiance. 4. often **Faith** *Christianity* The theological virtue defined as a secure belief in God and a trusting acceptance of God's will. 5. The body of dogma of a religion. 6. A set of principles or beliefs.[1]

As an experience with the divine, faith is not dependent on logical proof or material witness but rather on trust. The Holman Bible Dictionary states, "Paul wrote that 'faith,' both in the sense of Christian piety and of the trust and confidence one puts in God, determines action in life... Faith is the living out of religion; it is Christianity in action."[2] Faith, therefore, includes the dimension of belief, but it is much more. It includes trust, experience, action, and ultimately it is a goal to be worked toward in the concrete decisions of daily life.

The challenge for Christians in every generation is to provide their children with both the experience of the risen Lord, and the understanding of this experience as handed down through the ages, above all in the words of the Bible. In this way, it is hoped that young Christians will not only know the triune God (Father, Son, and Spirit) through personal faith experiences, but will also have the vocabulary to be able to talk about these experiences and share them with others. By examining the religious experiences, beliefs, and practices of adolescents, we can gain insights into what is being handed on in our communities and families, how it is being transmitted, and how deeply it is penetrating the lives of teens today.

In the discussion that follows on religious beliefs, experiences, and practices, our interest lies in understanding the experience of faith from the perspective of the Hispanic teens as represented in the NSYR survey and interviews. Not all of the Hispanic respondents are considered—only those who identified themselves as either Catholic or Protestant. Because the religious expressions of Catholics and Protestants are different in significant ways, in most cases we compare the responses of Catholic and Protestant Hispanic teens, and as a point of reference we also look at the responses of the dominant cultural group—the white Catholic and Protestant teens. Through these responses, now placed in the public domain as NSYR statistics, we learn that the echoes from the past and from present experiences still reverberate as yearnings in their souls for a spirituality grounded in the experience of God through faith, worship, and religious practices—a spirituality that can give direction and meaning to their lives.

Religious beliefs of Hispanic teenagers

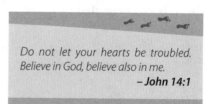

Do not let your hearts be troubled. Believe in God, believe also in me.
– John 14:1

Several questions in the NSYR survey asked the young people specifically about their religious beliefs. In answering these questions, the teens shared their ideas about religion, church, doctrine, and about other religions and spiritualities. The raw data from some of these questions are summarized in Table 2.1. The following two sections explore briefly the tabulated responses and illuminate them with direct quotes from the personal interviews with some of the Latino/a teens.

Table 2.1 – Religious beliefs (percentages)

	Catholic		Protestant	
	Hispanic	White	Hispanic	White
	N=278	N=556	N=94	N=1285
Definitely believes in God	89	84	96	92
Believes God is a personal being	78	80	90	86
Believes in a judgment day	70	66	92	82
Does not believe in psychics/fortune tellers	65	67	77	76
Definitely believes in angels	60	59	75	75
Definitely believes in divine miracles	60	53	82	72
Does not believe in astrology	54	54	67	65
Does not believe in communicating with the dead	52	51	76	65
Does not believe in reincarnation	34	44	66	63
Definitely believes in life after death	43	47	53	58
Definitely believes in evil spirits	28	30	66	53
Does not believe in evil spirits	31	26	12	17
Does not believe in a judgment day	26	28	5	15
Does not believe in life after death	13	10	20	12
Believes in an impersonal god/cosmic life force	15	16	4	9
Definitely believes in communicating with the dead	15	9	7	8
Definitely believes in reincarnation	15	14	5	8
Definitely believes in astrology	12	10	2	7
Definitely believes in psychics/fortune tellers	6	7	7	5
Does not believe in divine miracles	7	7	2	4
Does not believe in angels	7	6	6	4
Does not believe in God	1	1	1	1

Beliefs about God

With 84% of the 3,290 teenagers surveyed saying that they definitely believe in God, it can be said that most teens in the U.S. do believe in God. More specifically, of the Hispanic Catholic respondents, 89% said that they definitely believe in God, while among Hispanic Protestant respondents, the ratio was 94%. In both cases, this belief ratio is higher than that of white adolescents in their respective faith traditions. When asked again in the personal interviews whether they believed in God, the vast majority of the responses showed conviction, or at least a very matter-of-fact approach to God, even in cases when the teens did not consider themselves to be very religious, as the following example shows:

**Dialog 2.2 – 15 year-old non-religious Hispanic male
with Catholic leanings from the South:**

I: *Do you think of yourself as a religious or spiritual person?*

R: No.

I: *Okay. Do you believe in God?*

R: Yeah...

I: *Okay. So the next question is: do you consider yourself to be any particular religion, or not?*

R: Well ah, I, I don't really consider myself a Catholic. I mean, not that I consider myself anything else... I'm not really religious at all, but ah, I guess if I was anything I'd be Catholic.

I: *Okay. And you definitely consider yourself Christian?*

R: Mm-mm [yes].

I: *That's a yes?*

R: Yes...

I: *Okay, so what do you think about like Hindus and Buddhists and Muslims? Like how do they fit into the one God idea?*

R: Well they, they believe in totally different gods, like, like Buddha and stuff. I think that's, that's just wrong... I don't, I don't believe in that, really. I mean, I believe there's only one God and, and, some guy just branched off little gods, idol thingies.

Whenever Catholic and Protestant teens can articulate foundational truths of their faith it is always a reason to celebrate—particularly when they can describe the God of the Bible in terms that demonstrate who God is: a living being immersed in personal relationships with people who call themselves God's children. According to the NSYR data, belief in God as a personal being involved in the lives of people today was upheld by 78% of the Hispanic Catholic teens as well as 90% of the Hispanic Protestant teens. As Christians this is good news for us.

However, because the numbers in this research reflect how believing Christian adolescents view God, I argue that not only must we pay attention to the beliefs of the majority, but we must take into account the views of the minority. Why is this important? It is in the lower percentages that we find another side to the story—these minority replies are important because they also reflect the souls of young Latino/as and their yearnings. In this regard, we find that 10% of Hispanic Catholic teens and 3% of Hispanic Protestant teens are not sure whether they believe in God, and 1% of each group states that they do not believe in God at all. In addition, 15% of Hispanic Catholic and 4% of Hispanic Protestant teens say they see God as impersonal, a kind of cosmic life force that sets the universe in motion but does not get involved in people's lives. A good example of the uncertainties surrounding religious belief for some teens can be found in the following transcript:

Dialog 2.3 – 15 year-old Hispanic Baptist male from the South:

I: *Do you believe in God?*
R: Ah, I have questions, but mostly yes.
I: *What kind of questions?*
R: I mean, does he really exist? How do, how can you prove that he's created all this? And yeah.
I: *What other questions?*
R: Like that's pretty much it.
I: *So you're not sure that God exists?*
R: Yes. Yes, I'm not sure.
I: *Okay. If you had to put it on a scale of like zero to a hundred, how sure are you that God exists?*
R: Seventy percent.
I: *Okay. When you think about God, what do you think of?*
R: Ah, a spirit.
I: *What do you mean by spirit?*
R: Like a spirit in the sky, I don't know.
I: *Okay. Who or what is God to you?*
R: I have no idea.
I: *Do you tend to think of God as personal or impersonal?*
R: Impersonal.
I: *Active in human's lives or sort of removed?*
R: It depends on how Christian you are or whatever.
I: *What do you mean?*
R: Like if you really believe in God then yes, but.
I: *Active?*
R: Yes.

In general, the personal interviews support the survey statistics, showing that the vast majority of both Catholic and Protestant Hispanic teens believe in a God that is active and involved in the lives of people. However, it was not always clear that the young people had in mind the God of Jesus Christ, who is both loving and demanding, and who accompanies us in our suffering, but does not always remove the hardships faced by believers in this life. The following conversation is a typical example:

Dialog 2.4 – 14 year-old Hispanic non-denominational Christian female from the West:

I: *When you think about God, what do you think of?*
R: Like a father, father figure.
I: *Who or what is God to you?*
R: A person who is like a counselor. He can help you with your problems and um, he can help you with things that you want, maybe. Like if you really want something really, really bad and then it comes true, you know God helped to make that come true...
I: *Do you think of God as more loving and forgiving, or demanding and judging, or something else?*
R: Loving and forgiving.
I: *And how did you get these ideas about God?*

R: Going to church and reading the Bible and...
I: *So what are your own religious beliefs?*
R: Um, I believe in God. I believe that God makes everything that is here today and what's gonna come. And he's like your future—he plans out your future.

Although the majority of Catholic and Protestant teens reported that they believe in a judgment day, their descriptions of God's activity rarely included a discussion of God's judgment of human actions or the way God guides and challenges people to grow in faith and discipleship to Christ. The overall impression is of a God whose primary objective is to protect people from harm or any kind of suffering, and to give them the things that they want in life. Among the personal interviews, only two out of the 16 Catholic Hispanics and six out of the 14 Protestant Hispanics could describe the more balanced Christian understanding of God's activity as both loving and demanding. All eight of these young people had significant experiences of religious education—whether in Catholic school, a Confirmation program, a Bible study, or through active participation in the life of their church community.

Among the other 22 Hispanic Christian teens interviewed, only 8 were regular participants in church services or a religious youth group. The fact that so many Catholic and Protestant teens are not actively engaged in any form of ministry should be of great concern to anyone who cares for the faith life of Hispanic adolescents. Fundamental to the development of any youth ministry is reaching out to the teens where they are by meeting their spiritual needs in the present—the seeking out of the "lost sheep," as Jesus put it. As we rejoice with the many who view God from within the sheepfold, let us remember those that remain outside.

At the same time, the NSYR interviews give us cause for concern about whether even those within the sheepfold are being properly fed for their spiritual journeys. The fact that less than half of the young Hispanics who *are involved* in their church's ministry can describe God in terms that resemble traditional Christian doctrine is all the more reason why parents and youth ministers must reevaluate what is being provided in ministry to their teens.

Sources of religious beliefs among Latino/a adolescents

Beyond the core beliefs about God and a judgment day, Table 2.1 shows that there is very little consistency among Protestant and Catholic teens about other religious beliefs. Instead of giving a detailed analysis of each question in the survey, it is more helpful in this case to consider how the teens came to believe their religious ideas. The range of sources identified in the interviews includes: friends, teachers, sound bites gleaned from televangelists while flipping the channels, parents, grandparents, the Bible, church leaders, school teachers, movies, television, and even their own imagination! Perhaps the fact that they are drawing from so many different contradictory sources accounts for some of the discrepancies between traditional Christian teachings and the expressed beliefs of Hispanic teens, although in many cases it can be attributed to the fact that the teens have spent very little time thinking about their religious faith. Consider the following two examples:

Dialog 2.5 – 15 year-old Hispanic Catholic female from the South:

I: *Is religion a source of conflict or of sharing with your parents?*

R: No.

I: *And do you talk about religion in your house?*

R: Almost never...

I: *Uh-huh... And does God get mad when you do something wrong?*

R: I don't know.

I: *You don't know? And where did you get your ideas about God?*

R: From church.

I: *From church? And what are your own religious beliefs?*

R: I believe the same things as... all Catholics.

I: *Uh-huh... What have been the important influences on you when it comes to religion, faith, belief, or spirituality?*

R: Oh... My mom and my dad. Well, my dad not that much... but my mom has.

I: *How? What did she do?*

R: Well, she influenced me into saying my prayers each night.

I: *How important is religion in your life?*

R: It is, but not that important...

I: *You know, different people have different ideas about what they believe about things like angels, demons, divine miracles, life after death, and so on. Do you believe in those things?*

R: Not life after death, but I believe in angels. My little, well my older brother, I think he's an angel.

I: *Oh really, how so?*

R: Cause um, he died when he was 8 months, he would be 18 today and um, um, we knew, me and my mom always know that he's watching over us and it's just that I know that he's there.

I: *How about things like astrology?*

R: I really believe in astrology.

I: *Tell me about that.*

R: 'Cause I would read my horoscope and some things don't happen but some things really do happen. Like one of my scores, my horoscope said that you will have a relationship, a new relationship with a Scorpio. And I met this really cool guy, and we hit it off really good, and he's a Scorpio. So that like really put two and two together and it was really cool.

I: *Do you believe that there is any kind of punishment after death for bad things people have done in life?*

R: No.

Dialog 2.6 – 17 year-old Hispanic non-denominational Christian male from the West:

I: *And do you believe in God?*

R: Yes.

I: *And when you think about God, what do you think of? Who or what is God to you?*

R: That I'm in trouble.

I: *[laughs] That he's like looking out over?*

R: Yeah, I'm just like, "God, help me out."

I: *So it's like maybe a way to get out of trouble?*

R: Yeah, you know, it's like, it's just a comforting feeling when you know that there's someone there listening to you, or someone there that you can talk to...

I: *And do you think of God as active or removed from human life?*

R: My family and me, I think it's more active.

I: *Um, where do your ideas about God come from?*

R: Church.

I: *Church?*

R: Family.

I: *Church and family?*

R: Yeah.

I: *And we already mentioned this but you would consider yourself Christian now?*

R: Yeah.

I: *Let's say somebody comes up to you and asks you... what is it about being Christian, what does that mean for you?*

R: Uh, just the way you... Huh, I don't know how to explain it. Uh, just the way I live my life—the rules. Not rules, but you know, what makes you feel good, and, and knowing that you can pray to God and you have that comforting spirit. Or, or uh, or the way you worship, 'cause when I was Catholic it was really like tame and mellow, but now you like clap and sing and praise. Um, just it's the way I feel when I go to church. It's fun, and you know, you get a feeling that you're doing something right and you know that it's going to help you in life. And of course there's the Bible lessons and teachings, that still apply today from back then. And yeah.

In Dialog 2.5, one gets the impression that the girl really doesn't know what she believes, so she simply says, "the same things as all Catholics." This interpretation is reinforced when considering that her family almost never talks about religion and they no longer go to church. Without opportunities to discuss her faith with her parents or religious leaders, she continues to pray to God, but she is perfectly at ease about incorporating a belief in astrology into her religious worldview.

Dialog 2.6 has a line that reads, "my family and me think..." The interviews give strong support for the influence of parents and grandparents in shaping the religious beliefs of Latino/a teens, and in many cases their sense of religious identity is intimately tied to their sense of belonging within the family. The following examples are typical discussions about the role of parents and grandparents:

Dialog 2.7 – 17 year-old Hispanic Catholic male from the South:

I: *Okay. Can you tell me about how you were raised religiously?*

R: We go to church every Sunday, and my dad's been the number one thing there...

I: *Let's see, so how similar or different are your religious beliefs from your mother and father?*

R: Me and my father's, we're the same, we are very alike. My mother, her New Year's resolution was to go to church and be more religious and she has been and I congratulate her for that. But I just think she needs to do more than just going to church. I mean, maybe read the Bible or something. But, I don't, I really don't see myself, when I have a family... I don't know if we, if I really want them to be Catholic... And even my dad says so. He's, he's like, "I wish we could go to another church." A church, I'm not sure what you would call it, but one... We have a crucifix in our church and, and the Bible says like don't bow to any things of Jesus or something. And I mean it's the Catholic way but my dad like, ah, he goes because it's church. But, but I think I will not, not not be Catholic, but just go to like a different church and raise my kids... Or hopefully my wife will want to learn like the ways that me and my dad think...

I: *Okay, so if you went to a different church, you would still want to be Catholic, just a Catholic church that was more along what you think?*

R: If I wasn't Catholic, I'd be, I'd be okay with that. But, I, I'd probably be, just be another denomination. But, um, basically I'm just going by like the Bible. I mean what, what, anything my dad says I'll, I, I will believe unless it's like totally wrong, like, like worship the devil. Or something like, whoa, why would you want to do that? But I follow my dad, yeah... 'Cause my ad, I mean, I follow him and I, just it's basically my dad. I mean, I listen to him. He knows. I, I totally trust that he's wrong and right about what not to believe in and what to believe in and what to do and stuff like that.

Dialog 2.8 – 18 year-old Hispanic Catholic male from the West:

I: *Where do your ideas about God come from?*

R: Come from my parents. Um, that's where they all originate. Um, before my grandma passed away, she was a big influence. And she was the one that really pushed, you know the whole religion, and you know I, being Catholic is something my parents taught me through church, I always prayed, there wasn't a time when I didn't. And then I think now, a lot more of my beliefs are coming from that whole Confirmation pact. So they, you know, they come from church and...

I: *Tell me what are your own religious beliefs are… Your personal faith, tell me a little bit how, being Catholic, tell me what you believe?*

R: Um, well I am Catholic and you know I, I guess I try to follow what the Bible says and what the ten commandments and what, the basic, you know I try to, I try to follow those kinds of things.

I: *What have been the important influences on you when it comes to religion, faith, belief, or spirituality, those types of things?*

R: Like, well, like I guess, parents, church...

I: *You mentioned your grandma?*

R: My grandma.

I: *In what ways did she?*

R: She was very religious, she just, she had this, she kind of taught me how to pray, the right way to pray. She, I remember she prayed just like, "be with me." She would, she could just add something extra to it, and well like a lot of my beliefs and my influences, that, she influenced me a lot.

The boy in Dialog 2.7 has "total trust" in the religious judgments and teachings of his father, and the one in Dialog 2.8 describes how his grandmother deeply influenced his faith by her example and her spirituality. In general, the Hispanic interviews give a resounding confirmation to the notion that Latino/a teens continue to be deeply influenced by the religious beliefs—or lack thereof—of their parents and grandparents. In cases where one parent did not believe, the teen typically embraced the faith of the believing parent. In fact, the only interview with a Catholic or Protestant Hispanic teen who did not embrace the faith of at least one parent involved a teen whose parents were not religious, but who came to faith through involvement with his school's Christian club.

Both of the conversations above also mention the importance of the Bible in directing and shaping the religious beliefs of these teens. While it cannot be said that this is true for the majority of Hispanic adolescents, it is nevertheless true for a small minority of the Catholic and a large minority of the Protestant Hispanic teens in the personal interviews. The following transcript is a good example of the power the Word of God can have in the life of a young person:

Dialog 2.9 – 17 year-old Hispanic Seventh-day Adventist female from the Northeast:

I: Can you tell me about how you were raised religiously?
R: Well, since I was born I was taken to church and up to now I still am of the Adventist religion. And I was brought up right, as it should be, in the church.
I: How similar or different are your religious beliefs from those of... your mother and father, are there different beliefs?
R: No, no.
I: Like, you think something and your father doesn't think the same?
R: No, whenever there is a point that all of us don't... agree with... we sit at the table, get the Bible, and look for that point.
I: And you are all sure that's it? What it says, that's it?
R: Because it's in the Bible, right? Then whoever is not right, rectifies him/herself. Whoever is in error, rectifies him/herself. We correct ourselves...
I: And do you believe in God.
R: I believe, yes.
I: When you think about God, what do you think of?
R: Well, I consider God as a friend because I... I pray to him and I tell him all my problems.
I: Uh-huh. Who or what is God to you?
R: God is... the Lord of the Universe because he created everything... Everything we have now, all of nature, right? And man…
I: Uh-huh. Where did you get these ideas about God?
R: Ideas, because I read the Bible, right?

Summary

While the great majority of Latino/a teens believe in God, their responses to both the NSYR survey and the interviews reflect a wide variety of beliefs about God and the religious dimension of life. When they are articulate and clear about their Christian beliefs, it is usually due to the influence of parents, grandparents, church, and/or the Bible. When these influences do not guide religious development, Hispanic teens use their own creative imaginations, or things they hear from the media, friends, secular school teachers, and others to develop religious beliefs that frequently are not in continuity with the traditional tenets of the Christian faith.

The good news for parents, grandparents, and youth ministers is that they can be a powerful influence on the religious development of the teens in their family or community, despite the predominant secularism of U.S. media and culture. The question then becomes: how are parents, grandparents, and youth ministers utilizing their capacity to shape the religious lives of the teens around them? The evidence shows that the reality for the majority of Hispanic teens—for Catholics even more than for Protestants—is that families and churches are not doing an effective job of transmitting anything more than the most basic belief in the existence of God to the next generation.

Beliefs about religion

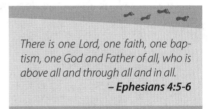

There is one Lord, one faith, one baptism, one God and Father of all, who is above all and through all and in all.
– Ephesians 4:5-6

Before delving into Latino/a teens' beliefs about religion, it is important to understand that most teens are still in the information-gathering phase of their lives, and in many cases they have not yet solidified their world-view and beliefs, especially with respect to religion. Although the Hispanic cultures have deep roots in Christianity, especially in its Catholic form, young Hispanics in the U.S. today are often exposed to a broad range of religious or "spiritual" beliefs, including Islam, fortune tellers, reincarnation, Eastern religions, and even paganism. Is it any wonder, then, that young Hispanics may be confused about what to believe? Consider the following example:

Dialog 2.10 – 17 year old non-religious Hispanic male with Catholic background from the West:

I: *Have your religious beliefs changed over time?*
R: Not yet. They did for like, last, like, a couple months ago, but not yet so far.
I: *Like how?*

> R: Like I used to be Buddhist, like I said before, you know. And then, uh, so I didn't know which religion was right, but now I'm back. I guess if you were putting me in a category, Catholicism.
>
> I: *How long were you Buddhist?*
>
> R: I was Buddhist for like a month or so. Maybe two or three months.

As religious folks, we must remember that adolescents are dealing with sexual awakenings, the physical changes of puberty, the first stages of abstract thinking, and the transition from dependence to autonomy. Along with these changes come deep personal questioning, parental testing, and social experimentation. With regard to God and religion, Latino/a teens are asking: Is it real? What's the benefit? Why should I believe in church teachings when so many adults say they believe but they do not give witness with their life? And what do I think about my friends with other belief systems?

In the plurireligious environment of the U.S., traditional Christian teachings, such as the necessity of salvation in Jesus Christ or the importance of participating in weekly fellowship, worship, and/or Eucharist, are easily questioned. In fact, Table 2.2 shows that a large majority of young Catholics and a sizable minority of young Protestants believe that many religions may be true. The difference between Catholics and Protestants on this point may be due in part to the fact that most Catholics

Table 2.2 – Beliefs about religion (percentages)

	Catholic		Protestant	
	Hispanic	White	Hispanic	White
Beliefs about religion's truth	N=278	N=556	N=94	N=1285
Only one religions is true	19	20	52	39
Many religions may be true	66	72	30	55
There is very little truth in any religion	14	7	11	4
True believers need to attend church				
Agree	31	32	60	31
Disagree	69	67	40	68
Beliefs aboth religious particularity				
It is okay to practice religions besides own	51	57	19	40
People should only practice one faith	44	35	68	50
It's okay to pick and choose religious beliefs without accepting the church's teachings as a whole				
Agree	53	55	36	40
Disagree	44	45	59	57

consider Christians of other denominations to be of a different religion, while for many Protestants, Christians of any denomination all belong to the same religion.

In any case, the surveys as well as the interviews show that many young Hispanics today live in households that are religiously divided, or that offer little or no religious guidance. In this context, it should not be surprising that so many express doubts about the truth of their own religion as compared to others. The other point that becomes clear in the interviews is that most teens will adapt their religious beliefs to embrace the examples they receive from their parents, friends, and other acquaintances. Consider the following examples:

Dialog 2.11 – 17 year-old Hispanic non-denominational Christian female from the West:

I: *If it were totally up to you, how often would you attend religious services?*
R: As much as I could, weekly.
I: *Okay, so pretty much like you do now?*
R: Yeah.
I: *Okay. Some people say that in order for a person to be truly religious and spiritual, they need to be involved in a church and not just a lone individual. What do you think about that?*
R: I agree with that because… um… I really don't see how… You could get pretty far that way but you definitely need other Christians. I'm not saying that you don't have any other Christians in your life, but being around other people and uh… listening to other teachers… Is that answering your question?
I: *Yeah, absolutely. That these folks are positive influences you're saying.*
R: Yeah, just to make sure that you're not like preaching your words, I guess.
I: *Okay, sure. Some people think that it is okay for people to pick and choose their religious beliefs however they want to without having to accept their religion's teachings as a whole. Do you agree or disagree?*
R: I disagree.
I: *So you think people should accept the religions teaching as a whole?*
R: Yeah.
I: *And why is that?*
R: Because…maybe I'm going to answer this wrong, but why would you accept something if you thought part of it was wrong?

Dialog 2.12 – 17 year-old Hispanic Catholic female from the South:

I: *Some people think that it is okay for people to pick and choose their religious beliefs however they want to without having to accept their religion's teachings as a whole. Do you agree or disagree? For example, I may say I am a Catholic but I don't believe in the virgin… Is that okay?*
R: Then you are not a Catholic. Look for a religion where they believe in God but not in the virgin.
I: *Then I can't be… I can't say that…?*
R: You are a Catholic.

I: *Yes. So... You may not choose the beliefs in the religion you want...?*
R: Uh-huh.
I: *You have to accept them all?*
R: Yes.
I: *And do you believe... does it have... does your religion have any particular teaching or morality view point when it comes to sex?*
R: That you shouldn't do it before... marriage, but... I think... I mean... if it happens before marriage, I don't think it is bad... I don't see it that way! If the person has been your boyfriend for a while and you love each other, I don't think it is wrong.
I: *But you said that you have to accept everything.*
R: That's why... That is why, I... I mean, I am a bit confused because my religion... yes, yes...

The girl in the first example is not shy about saying that people need to go to church, because this is the experience she has within her family. Her response also supports what was reported in Table 2.2—that Hispanic Protestants are much more likely than Catholics or even their white Protestant peers to consider going to church as necessary. However, many Hispanic families today have at least one parent that does not go to church on a regular basis, and the result is that the teens in these families tend to question whether this is a necessary part of being a faithful follower of Jesus—they have a hard time making a negative judgment about themselves or their parents. The second interview above is a good example from a teen who is not active in her church. She wants to embrace what the church teaches, but when it comes into conflict with what she believes or practices, she gets very confused. Even among those who have an active faith life, there are many who feel that religious belief is entirely up to the individual, and any religion is as good as any other, as in the following example:

Dialog 2.13 – 17 year-old Hispanic Catholic male from the South:

I: *Do you try to take one day a week to rest, to worship, to take a break from normal routines? Do you set any time especially aside for religious purposes?*
R: I guess Sunday morning, that's about it. Like, I have to schedule things around church, make sure church. I do go to church, that's about it.
I: *How does that affect you.*
R: I don't, I don't think it really does affect me, really. It's just something I do. I mean it's a habit. I mean, I don't think it really affects me.
I: *If it were totally up to you, how often would you attend religious services?*
R: Once a, once a, once a week. I mean, I think that's fair enough. I mean giving once a week is good...
I: *Okay. Some people say that in order for a person to be truly religious and spiritual, they need to be involved in a church and not just lone individuals. We talked a little bit about this before, I think. Do you agree or disagree and why?*
R: I believe it doesn't, it really, really doesn't matter. I mean, you, a person doesn't have to go to church, and he can pray on his own and read the Bible on his own and do his own religious beliefs on his own. He doesn't have to go to church.

I: *Okay… and why?*

R: Well, it's, it's saying like, you have to go to church to be a good person, and if you don't then you're a bad person. I mean, that's totally like wrong. I mean, people don't go to church all the time that are religious and, and they, and they're, they're just as like good as the rest of us, I mean, morally.

I: *Okay. Do you think other people who don't practice religious faith should? Why or why not?*

R: Well people believe what they want to believe and I mean… It's all how you were raised, and if you… I think people should find something to believe in, and I think they should believe in something. Yeah. Yeah, I believe all people like should try to believe in some religion.

I: *Like, why does that matter?*

R: I think it keeps them on track on what they do. I mean, any kind of religion, like it's something there for you. I mean, something you, for you to follow.

All of this suggests that Hispanic teens today are influenced in their beliefs about religion by what they see their parents, peers, and religious leaders doing—and not just by what they are being taught in Sunday school or religious education. As parents and religious leaders, it is so important to avoid selling out our integrity because teenagers need spiritual leaders and role models. With the failure of priests and ministers to maintain ministry integrity making headlines across the country, it is no wonder a good number of teens have grown disillusioned with traditional church settings. So, like their clothing or hair—it is anyone's guess what they will wear, or what color it will be—the young people of this "whatever" generation are free thinkers: mixing, matching and amalgamating ideologies to fit what they see. Is this the Christianity that will be handed on to future generations? Indeed, is it not the watered-down Christianity that many Hispanic parents today are already passing on to the current generation of teenagers when they do not provide their children regular opportunities to practice and reflect on their religious faith?

As these echoes of religious experiences and belief reverberate within the hearts of Hispanic teens, religious leaders, pastors, priests, youth ministers, and parents must genuinely face their own spirituality and their commitment to the Christian faith. Beyond the church rituals and traditions, they must become the true spiritual mentors that the young people need. They need living witnesses to provide a sense of God as they come to terms with their own experiences and beliefs. Despite past failings and future imperfections, it is the youth workers, parents, and pastors with vision that will create environments for young Latino/as to question their faith, find answers, grow, and mature, so that the Good News of Jesus Christ may take root in their lives.

Religious experiences

Regarding their daily lives, the vast majority of Catholic and Protestant teens agree that their faith is important (at least "somewhat")—but they

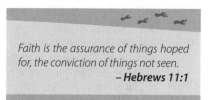

Faith is the assurance of things hoped for, the conviction of things not seen.
– Hebrews 11:1

differ on the degree of importance. The Protestant teens on average give their faith a higher priority than the Catholics, and among both Catholic and Protestant teens, the Hispanics say they are more directed by faith than their white peers. These differences are paralleled among the parents of each group, and the parents generally say they are more faith-directed than their adolescent children. With respect to major life decisions, it is interesting that the white teens responded almost exactly the same as they did regarding their daily lives, but the Hispanic Catholics said their faith was more important in big decisions, while the Hispanic Protestants said it was less important.

When it comes to sensing God's presence in their lives, 34% of the Hispanic Catholic respondents said they felt "extremely close" or "very close" to God, compared to 51% for the Hispanic Protestant teens. Adding in those who reported feeling "somewhat close" brings the total for both groups to about 5 out of every 6 that feel at least some closeness to God, with the Protestants reporting on average a higher degree of closeness than their Catholic peers. For ministers and parents, it is encouraging that so many of our young people feel close to God, but it is worth examining this feeling to see if it corresponds to any differences in behavior or attitude.

When probed to see if they had taken a step further by making a personal commitment to live for God, the Protestant teens were far more likely to answer that they had done so. Perhaps this is not surprising, considering that the question itself is very closely related to the Protestant concept of conversion as a personal decision to follow Christ, while Catholics tend to describe conversion in various ways: as a turning away from sin, a lifelong transformation to think and act as Jesus did, and a commitment to participate in the sacramental and communal life of the church. Yet when asked in the personal interview what they thought was the purpose of life, by far the most common responses for both Catholic and Protestant Hispanics were "I don't know" and "to have fun." In fact, only one out of the 16 Hispanic Catholics and six out of the 14 Hispanic Protestants interviewed gave an answer that had something to do with God or their faith—and half of those responses were very vague, as the following response shows:

Table 2.3 – Religious experiences & attitudes (percentages)

	Catholic		Protestant	
	Hispanic	White	Hispanic	White
Importance of religious faith shaping daily life	N=278	N=556	N=94	N=1285
Extremely important	11	9	23	27
Very important	35	28	50	36
Somewhat important	42	43	20	28
Not very important	8	15	4	7
Not important at all	5	4	0	3
Importance of religious faith shaping daily life (parent respondent)				
Extremely important	35	38	59	55
Very important	46	28	27	24
Fairly or somewhat important	17	27	10	17
Not very important	1	6	2	3
Not important at all	0	2	2	1
Importance of faith shaping major life decisions				
Extremely important	17	9	21	27
Very important	35	28	43	35
Somewhat important	37	44	30	29
Not very important	6	14	3	7
Not important at all	5	6	3	2
How close teen feels to God				
Extremely close	13	7	18	13
Very close	21	24	33	32
Somewhat close	48	41	32	34
Somewhat distant	15	23	16	15
Very distant	1	4	1	3
Extremely distant	3	1	0	1
Does not believe in God	1	1	1	1
Religious experiences				
Made a commitment to live life for God	38	41	81	74
Experienced very moving and powerful worship	33	38	59	69
Experienced a definite answer to prayer	41	40	73	61
Witnessed or experienced a miracle from God	38	37	63	54
Interest in learning more about their religion				
Very interested	30	16	55	39
Somewhat interested	46	50	32	41
Not very interested	15	22	5	10
Not at all interested	3	6	0	3
Don't know / refused / not asked	5	6	8	7

Dialog 2.14 – 15 year-old Hispanic evangelical male from the South:

I: *What do you think is the purpose of life?*

R: I don't know, I haven't got that far yet. [laughs]

I: *When is that far?*

R: When I start going to church more and learn more about life and God and all that.

I: *So... let me see if I got this right. You don't think much about the purpose of life, but you think it has something to do with church.*

R: Yes, and God.

I: *Like what?*

R: Like he creates all people and heaven and earth and...

I: *So the purpose of life has something to do with that.*

R: Mm-hmm [yes].

Another way to analyze a teen's commitment to live for God is to compare their commitment with how close they feel to God. For Hispanic Protestants, the vast majority has made a commitment to live for God—even among those who feel distant from God, as shown in Table 2.4. In fact, 77% of Hispanic Protestant teens who felt somewhat distant from God had made this personal commitment, compared to just 27% among similar Hispanic Catholic teens. Clearly, expressing a commitment to live for God is an important step in the faith life of nearly all Protestant teens, but judging from their closeness to God, many who have made this commitment are no longer living it in their daily lives. In contrast, more than 30% of Catholic teens who feel extremely close to God have never made such a commitment—it simply is not as important a marker of the faith life

Table 2.4 – Teens who have made a commitment to live life for God, by closeness to God, ethnicity, and faith tradition (percentages)					
	How Close Teen Feels to God				
	Extremely Close	Very Close	Somewhat Close	Somewhat Distant	Very / Extremely Distant
Made a commitment to live life for God	N=36	N=57	N=133	N=41	N=10*
Hispanic Catholic teens	69	44	32	27	20
	N=37	N=131	N=230	N=125	N=28
White Catholic teens	63	59	39	26	18
	N=17	N=31	N=30	N=15*	N=1
Hispanic Protestant teens	100	79	75	77	N/A
	N=165	N=410	N=433	N=199	N=61
White Protestant teens	95	87	72	52	41

* With only 10 to 15 responses, these results have a sampling error of ±13%.

for Catholics as it is for Protestants. In any case, the interviews with both groups of Hispanic teens suggest that the vast majority of Hispanic adolescents who have committed themselves to living for God are far from really understanding and integrating this concept into their lives and worldviews, whether they be Catholic or Protestant.

Experiences of God

We report joyfully that 33% of the Hispanic Catholic respondents and 59% of the Hispanic Protestant respondents give evidence in their responses that they have had an experience of spiritual worship that was very moving and powerful. Still, I ask: between the Catholic and Protestant Hispanic teens, which want more of a spiritual experience? They both do!

The other side of this important story begs the following question: what about the other 67% of Hispanic Catholic teens or the 41% of Hispanic Protestant teens who do not report having felt, seen, sensed or discerned God in a spiritual worship that was both moving and powerful? In short, the NSYR research gives evidence that, for the most part, Catholic adolescents between the ages of 13 and 17 are not discerning a powerful spiritual movement or moment during the Eucharist. Nevertheless, this lack of a powerful "religious experience" does not mean that they do not experience or feel close to God, as revealed in the following interview:

Dialog 2.15 – 14 year-old Hispanic Catholic male from the West:

I: *Have you personally had any significant "religious experiences?"*
R: Ah, no.
I: *Would you say that you feel close to God or not?*
R: Yes.
I: *In what ways?*
R: Well, when I pray to him I feel that he, he hears me and he believes in me and he trusts me.
I: *What does it mean to you to feel close or not close to God?*
R: It means a lot to me.
I: *Like, like what? You said a lot.*
R: Because he believes in me and all that so I should love him back.
I: *Are there any times in your life in which you felt particularly close, like you were talking about, when you prayed.*
R: Yeah, only when I pray ever, I feel very close to him.
I: *Are there any specific times that you can think of when you felt even more close?*
R: Um, Mass, Christmas, holidays, birthdays, yeah. That's about it.
I: *Have you ever experienced anything that seemed truly supernatural? Like a miracle?*
R: No, uh-uh.

Although 26% more young Hispanic Protestants report experiencing moving and powerful worship compared to their Catholic counterparts,

I must still ask: what about the 41% who do not report such an experience? If the most significant spiritual activity we as Christians can celebrate regularly in the sanctuary is worship, should we not then expect a greater stirring among the teens in worship today? As priests, pastors, and worship leaders, what can we do differently, if not additionally, within the activities of worship? Through either the Mass, youth services or church services, how else can we help our teenagers experience God?

Perhaps a partial answer can be found when we look at the topics of miracles and answered prayers. For clarity, the American Heritage Dictionary defines a miracle as "an event that appears inexplicable by the laws of nature and so is held to be supernatural in origin or an act of God."[3] When the Holy Spirit moves among us, just as Jesus Christ moved physically among his followers, God's presence is experienced. (cf. John 14:7-10; 15:26) Like the crowds that followed Jesus looking for proof of God's mercy on earth, so the Hispanic teens of today are awaiting an experience of God in their lives.

Table 2.3 shows that 63% of the Hispanic Protestant teens and 38% of the Hispanic Catholic teens reported having witnessed or experienced what they believed was a miracle from God. In addition, 73% of the Hispanic Protestants and 41% of the Hispanic Catholics had experienced a definite answer to prayer. Does this mean that young Hispanic Protestants are more attuned to the movement of the Holy Spirit in their lives than their Catholic peers?

Judging from the numbers, one would have to answer "yes." But the numbers beg the question: how are young Hispanic Protestants different from Catholics in the way they see and experience God in their lives? The NSYR survey found that 61% of Hispanic Catholic teens and 79% of Hispanic Protestant teens believed that God is "a personal being involved in the lives of people today," while 32% of the Catholics and 16% of the Protestants believed that God does not get directly involved in people's lives. This suggests that in some way, the Protestant teens are more disposed to recognizing God's activity in the world. When the Catholic teens were asked about their experiences and beliefs about God, many of their answers were unclear or even contradictory, as in the following examples:

Dialog 2.16 – 13 year-old Hispanic Catholic female from the South:

I: *Is there any time that you don't feel close to God?*

R: Um, no.

I: *No? Okay. Have you ever experienced anything that seemed truly supernatural? Like a miracle?*

R: No.

I: *An experience of angels or demons?*

R: No...

I: *How important or central do you think your religion or spirituality is in your life?*

R: It's important but not as important as people say. Like my step dad, he said it's the most important thing in your life, the only thing that matters... That it doesn't matter if you're educated, that the only thing that matters is if you're religious and you believe in God. I don't think it's that bad.

I: *Okay. In your life now, though, do you think that religion is important to you?*

R: Yeah.

I: *Okay, how so?*

R: Um, important, not very important, though.

I: *How is it important, like what do you do?*

R: Um, cause for example, they say that faith... If you have faith in God, you know, um, your problems might be cured. Um, for example, last time there was this friend of my grandma's and they, he, they detected he had cancer and that he couldn't have um... Like he was, like he was gonna die. And they, he had faith, and they said that he was cured because he had faith. And he didn't go to the doctors but he just got cured, like that.

I: *And that's important to you?*

R: Yeah.

Dialog 2.17 – 16 year-old Hispanic Catholic female from the South:

I: *Do you tend to think of God as personal or impersonal?*

R: How, personal?

I: *Like... does God help you or is he just looking after everyone? Is God personal...?*

R: After everyone.

I: *Everyone, yes? Uh-huh... And do you think he is active or removed from human life?*

R: Removed from human life. I mean he isn't with us...

I: *Yes. Uh-huh...*

R: I always believe that he is with us.

I: *Is he always with everyone?*

R: With everyone.

I: *Individually?*

R: Yes.

Not all of the Catholic responses were so unclear, and the Protestant interviews could be equally confusing in some cases, but overall more of the Protestant teens were articulate about the way they experienced God in their lives, as exemplified in the following conversation:

Dialog 2.18 – 15 year-old Hispanic non-denominational Christian female from the Northeast:

I: *And who or what is God to you?*

R: My...my creator, my savior, my friend.

I: *Do you tend to think of God as personal or impersonal?*

R: *Personal*

I: In what ways?

R: Because he cares about every…I think he cares about every detail, not only in the world but in people. He sends somebody to help you and um, you know… I think it's just like he comforts you if you need him, and stuff, if you really need him. Otherwise he's still there to help.

I: *Do you consider God active or removed from human life?*

R: I think he was active, but then we removed him.

I: *How so?*

R: Um, basically, people just started, stopped, yeah, stopped caring. Like you know along came a lot of people who came along saying God is not real and whatever, and God is whoever you make it to be. And then you grow up hearing these things and then you're like, "Oh, God doesn't care." And then you see anything that is wrong in your life and then you're like, "Yeah, God doesn't care." And so I think people have really moved away from God.

This young lady has articulated for us what the survey results show: for many teens today, the scientific worldview provides a sufficient explanation of their experiences, and they do not feel a need to explain things as a miracle from God. Yet for a person of faith, the signs of God's activity in daily life can speak powerfully of God's care and presence—such as God sending someone to help you when you need it, as our Protestant teen suggested above. It seems that Catholic teens are less accustomed to speak about such experiences as being signs of God's presence and activity in the world, and as a result they are less likely to recognize the movement of the Holy Spirit in their own lives. In their minds, an experience of God would have to be something that defies the laws of nature, and when they are asked if they have had such an experience, their most frequent answer is "no." These echoing responses challenge the overall Christian church to be more responsive to the spiritual growth of its adolescent members.

The responses to the final question in Table 2.3 bear out that the vast majority of young Hispanics attending both the Catholic and Protestant church are interested in learning more about their religion—even more so than their white counterparts. We thus return to the question posed earlier in this section, "How else can we help our teenagers experience God?" A very practical suggestion would be to help young Hispanics—especially the Catholics—to recognize and name God's activity in their own lives. We pray that someday they may be able to testify to the abiding presence and action of God in their lives before ever becoming dismayed in their faith in the long term!

Personal religious practices

In studying the individual interviews with Hispanic teens, it was evident that the answers they expressed regarding their religious practices were showing signs of what they had al-

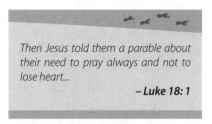

Then Jesus told them a parable about their need to pray always and not to lose heart...

– Luke 18: 1

ready learned or were still learning from parents, and other family members, church, and television. Popular religiosity has maintained itself alive in many households—even among families that do not regularly attend

Table 2.5 – Personal religious practices (percentages)

	Catholic		Protestant	
	Hispanic	White	Hispanic	White
Personal spiritual practices in last year	N=278	N=556	N=94	N=1285
Prayed rosary, novena, or to a special saint	44	45	N/A	N/A
Has sacred images or altars in home	58	43	N/A	N/A
Practiced meditation not including prayer	6	12	13	8
Burned religious candles or incense	46	30	15	16
Fasted or denied self something as spiritual discipline	17	33	25	24
Read a religious book other than Scripture	20	23	48	41
Tried to practice a weekly day of rest or Sabbath	32	30	38	37
Attended a religious music concert	17	22	43	52
Wore religious jewelry or clothing	40	42	39	49
Shared faith with someone not of faith	36	36	56	54
Listened to religious music or radio programs	30	36	71	66
Frequency of praying by self alone				
Many times a day	13	7	30	19
About once a day	27	22	24	26
A few times a week	18	15	15	16
About once a week	10	14	7	13
1-2 times a month	15	17	11	13
Less than once a month	5	12	8	6
Never	12	13	5	7
Frequency of reading Scriptures by self alone				
Never	47	54	27	26
Less than once a month	14	19	5	16
Once or twice a month	22	16	17	23
About once a week	7	5	15	11
A few times a week	6	3	15	11
About once a day	2	1	14	9
Many times a day	2	~	6	3

church. Too often the teens do not know the significance of these practices, but they hold on to them as manifestations of faith. Among Catholic teens, Hispanics are 15% more likely than their white peers to have sacred images or altars in their homes. Other popular devotions include praying rosaries, lighting of candles, and listening to religious music or radio programs. However, personal prayer was by far the most common response when the teens were asked to describe their personal religious practices in the interviews. Among Hispanic Catholics, 68% said that they pray at least once a week, and for Hispanic Protestants it was 76%. Even some who claimed not to be religious admitted that they pray:

Dialog 2.19 – 14 year-old non-religious Hispanic female from the West:

I: So how often do you say your prayer?
R: Every night.
I: And what do you think prayer is?
R: Um, usually I try to tell him like, you know, thanking him for blessing me with a wonderful family and for like the wonderful food in the house he's given us. And mostly blessing some people that need it. Like mean people to me, even though there's people I don't like, I usually, say, bless them a lot. So like, you know, all that stuff, but I really try to not say hate because my mom gets kind of upset with me when I say the word hate on people.
I: So what is prayer though, in general?
R: I don't know, I usually just pray like by thing. I think it's like thanking God for stuff he's given you.
I: And how do you feel about praying?
R: Um, I feel good sometimes, like if I miss one night, I feel…I don't know why…I don't like skipping a night of praying.
I: Do you feel guilty? Or… what?
R: No, I don't feel guilty, but I just don't… I don't know, I get a funny feeling inside of me, so, no.
I: Are your prayers answered?
R: Um, [pause] I don't know. I really don't know.

The fact that most Hispanic teens today say they have a habit of praying only begs the question: how do they pray? This question was asked in the interviews as well, so the teens had the opportunity to describe their prayer life in their own words. It is instructive to look at a couple of examples:

Dialog 2.20 – 14 year-old Hispanic Catholic female from the West:

I: What do you think prayer is?
R: Um, I think it's just talking to God. Just um, telling God about recent things, asking him for forgiveness or whatever.
I: How often do you pray? You said that you pray at meals and you pray at night. Is that every day?
R: Yeah.

I: *Are those the only times you pray or are there other times you pray?*
R: Ah, we pray at Mass. We just, we pray when people are sick. We pray when people are about to die, that, that they go to heaven, and yeah.
I: *Do you pray often alone, or with family, friends, what?*
R: I pray often with my family.
I: *What do your prayers sound like? Like what kinds of things do you pray for?*
R: Sick people, less fortunate, pray for the things that we have. I pray for better days. Yeah, that's about it.
I: *Do you think your prayers are answered?*
R: Ah, I think they're heard, but some of them aren't answered.
I: *How do you feel about praying?*
R: I feel comfortable.

Dialog 2.21 – 15 year-old Hispanic non-denominational Christian female from the South:

I: *Okay. So what kind of religious or spiritual things, if any, do you actually do? Do you pray?*
R: Yeah, I pray every night, and in the morning.
I: *So, twice a day?*
R: Well, usually. I don't know, I pray a lot, but like those are like the two main things. Like other times it's just like I pray if I feel like I need prayer.
I: *What would let you know that you needed prayer.*
R: I don't know. If I was feeling like uneasy about something, I just pray about it. Or like if my friends need prayer, like, if they're going through like a tough time, I pray about it.
I: *And what do you think prayer is?*
R: It's just talking to God, letting him know your problems and stuff.
I: *What is it like when you pray? What do your prayers sound like?*
R: I don't know, just like conversation.
I: *So, do you just speak or do you pause? Like give me an example.*
R: I don't know. I just say, I talk like if I was talking to one of my friends or like my mom or something.
I: *Do you do this out loud or in your head?*
R: Most of the time in my head, sometimes out loud.
I: *What kind of things do you prayer for? You mentioned praying for help for your friends, or when you feel uneasy. Is there any other time that you pray?*
R: Just, I don't know. I pray to say thank you just for like God blessing me or something, you know? Or, I don't know. I just pray mostly for my friends. I pray for them a lot, or just like to pray for like people that don't know him, just like to get saved. And like I don't know, just people that I know, that like I'm not really friends with. People in my school, I pray for them.
I: *Are your prayers answered?*
R: Yeah, a lot of the time. No, I don't know. Most of the time, yeah.
I: *How do you feel about praying?*
R: I don't know. I don't know. I think everybody should pray.
I: *Okay, so you think, you think everybody should?*
R: I think it's important.

When asked to describe their prayer, the most common answers were "a conversation," "asking for blessings or things," and "asking for forgiveness." This suggests that, especially for young Hispanic Catholics, the experience of prayer has become much more relational and personal, and less formulaic than it might have been in prior generations—there was very little mention of reciting formal prayers that they had been taught to memorize or repeating ritual prayers that they did not understand. Also largely absent from these descriptions were the practices of meditative prayer and praising God in prayer. All things considered, the fact that so many of today's young Hispanics are in relationship with God through prayer is good news for parents and youth ministers alike—yet as always, there is much more that could be done to enhance their spiritual lives.

With respect to reading the Bible, the survey results show that among both Catholic and Protestant teens, Hispanics are more likely than their white peers to engage in Scripture study. Nevertheless, among the 16 Hispanic Catholic teens interviewed, there was not one who reported having a habit of reading the Bible alone. In contrast, five out of the 14 Hispanic Protestants interviewed expressed that they have a regular habit of reading the Scriptures alone, as in this example:

Dialog 2.22 – 15 year-old Hispanic non-denominational Christian female from the Northeast:

I: *Okay… Do you read the Bible regularly?*
R: Yes.
I: *Why?*
R: Most the time I'm made to, but a lot of the time I'm interested in it, so.
I: *Do you like it?*
R: Yeah.
I: *How does it affect you, reading the Bible?*
R: Um…it makes me find out new things about what I believe...
I: *Are there things that you do on a regular basis that have some sort of religious or spiritual meaning for you?*
R: Church. Prayer. Reading the Bible. Stuff.
I: *And how important are your religious practices to you? Attending church, praying, all these practices…*
R: Very important. They strengthen my faith.
I: *How hard would you say that you have to work at your religious faith or being the kind of religious person you would like to be? Is it a struggle or does it come naturally?*
R: Um…I think it comes naturally. It's not like a struggle, or something that you have to do, like "Oh my God, I didn't do this! I didn't pray at a certain time, I'm dead!"
I: *Where do your own views of right and wrong come from?*
R: The Bible. [giggles]
I: *The Bible?*
R: Yeah.
I: *Like literally, you read the Bible when you're wondering?*
R: Not literally, because there's some things that are like, if you disrespect your parents you shall be stoned at the doorpost in Leviticus somewhere. So that's like, uh, no… So basically, basic laws you know. Love your

neighbor, and that would be caring about them and not wanting harm for them, and just you know, basics. Don't steal, it's not yours. Don't kill, because people deserve to live just like you deserve to live. All that stuff.

The overall impression one gets from reading the interviews is that the teens in the survey may have overstated the frequency with which they are accustomed to reading the Scriptures by themselves. Even in the interview excerpt above, the young lady says that most of the time she is made to read the Scriptures, but then she finds that she is also interested in what they have to say. It appears that her "habit" of reading the Scriptures has been instilled by a structured discipline given to her by her parents. In any case, it is clear that young Hispanic Protestants are more likely to participate in this spiritual practice than their Catholic counterparts. Since the Catholic Church considers knowledge of the Scriptures to be essential for all Christians—in the words of Saint Jerome, "ignorance of the Scriptures is ignorance of Christ"—the fact that so few of its adolescent members have developed a practice of reading and reflecting on the Scriptures should be a cause for concern among all Catholic parents, pastors, and youth ministers. Even among Hispanic Protestant teens, there is much room for improvement.

Reflections on the religious beliefs and practices of Hispanic teens

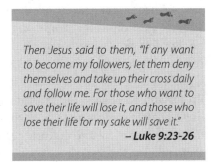

Then Jesus said to them, "If any want to become my followers, let them deny themselves and take up their cross daily and follow me. For those who want to save their life will lose it, and those who lose their life for my sake will save it."
– Luke 9:23-26

In their book *Soul Searching*, in which they describe the main findings from the National Study of Youth and Religion, Christian Smith and Melinda Lundquist Denton offer two valuable concepts to assist parents and religious leaders in assessing the spiritual lives of adolescents:

- First, they divided the teens in the survey into four religious types: the *disengaged*, the *sporadic*, the *regulars*, and the *devoted*.
- Second, they describe the religion of most teens in the U.S. as a form of "moralistic therapeutic deism" (MTD).

Religious types among U.S. adolescents

Not all the teens fit neatly into one of Smith and Denton's types, so they concentrated their analysis on those that most closely fit the "ideal types."

They found that the markers for individual well-being were consistently much higher for the religiously devoted teens than for the other groups. They also found that conservative Protestant teens were much more likely to be religiously devoted than mainline Protestants, and that Catholics were by far the least devoted of any Christian group. Because these findings were drawn from the overall population of U.S. teens and Hispanics are a small segment of that population, it is important to ask: do the religious differences between Catholics and Protestants in the general population also hold true with regard to Hispanic teens?

An initial difficulty with this question arises from the way the types are defined. For Smith and Denton, the "devoted" teens included only those who: a) believe in God; b) attend religious services weekly or more; c) say that their faith is very or extremely important in their lives; d) regularly participate in religious youth groups; e) feel very or extremely close to God; and f) pray and read the Bible regularly. This definition is a problem for Catholics for three reasons. First, among Catholic teens, participation in a religious youth group is often not a very good indication of religious devotion. Chapter 3 of this book will explore in more detail the current state of youth ministry participation among Hispanic teens, both Catholic and Protestant; for now it is sufficient to note that, in an analysis done by Ken Johnson-Mondragón on the same NSYR data being studied in this book, it was found that some of the most devout Hispanic Catholics may be choosing not to participate in their parish's youth group *because it is not religious enough for them.*[4]

Second, it has already been shown that Catholics are less likely than Protestants to engage in Scripture study. While this may not be the ideal that Catholic pastors and youth ministers would like to see in teens today, there are historical and cultural reasons that have led Catholics to express their religious devotion in other ways. The cumulative impact of these historical and cultural differences between Protestants and Catholics is still evident in the spiritual lives of today's teens in both traditions, and it is unfair to categorize a Catholic teen's religious devotion according to criteria that reflect a historically and culturally Protestant expression of religious practice.

Third, Hispanic Catholics tend to be much less individualistic about their faith than Hispanic Protestants. Because the Catholic faith has dominated the official religious landscape of most Latin American countries for centuries (although that is rapidly changing today), most Catholics were baptized and raised in their faith from infancy. For devoted Catholics, prayer and religious celebrations are family and community activities. Religious identity is formed simultaneously with family, cultural, and national identity, and there is usually very little emphasis on personal prayer, personal Scripture study, or in some cases even on a "personal" relationship with Jesus or God. The devoted Hispanic Catholic may have a rich prayer life and may read (or at least listen to) the Scriptures or other religious materials many times each week, but may not participate in either of these activities alone. In contrast, the Protestant Tradition in Latin America distinguishes itself from the historically dominant Catholic form of Christianity by heavily emphasizing personal prayer, personal Scripture study, and a personal relationship with God in and through Jesus Christ. Because Smith and Denton utilized *personal* prayer and *personal* Scripture reading as criteria for identifying the devoted teens, once again they excluded some devoted Hispanic Catholic adolescents because they do not fit the criteria for a typically Protestant expression of religious practice.

That being said, there is still significant evidence in both the survey data and the personal interviews that shows Hispanic Catholic teens are less knowledgeable and active in their faith life than their Protestant peers. A subjective analysis of the personal interviews confirms this, with six out of 16 Catholic respondents describing their faith as having a meaningful impact on their lives (only one of whom was an active participant in a youth ministry program), compared to eight out of 14 of the Protestant respondents. A further confirmation comes from the survey data.

Even after adapting the religious types defined by Smith and Denton to take into account the differences between Catholic and Protestant forms of devotion, Catholic teens are significantly less religiously engaged than their Protestant peers, as shown in Table 2.6. In this table, Smith and Denton's terminology for "regulars" and "devoted" teens has been changed to "engaged" and "committed" to reflect the fact that the numbers are based on adapted religious types—see the Appendix on page 361 for a detailed explanation of the criteria used to define these types.

Table 2.6 - Adolescent religious types (percentage)	Catholic		Protestant	
	Hispanic	White	Hispanic	White
	N=278	N=556	N=94	N=1285
Committed	4	8	28	19
Engaged	43	44	40	47
Sporadic	22	25	11	15
Disengaged	3	7	1	3
Mixed	28	16	20	16

It is interesting that Hispanic Catholic adolescents overall exhibited less religious commitment than their white peers, while Hispanic Protestants were more committed than their white counterparts. As a result, Smith and Denton's observation of greater religious laxity among Catholic adolescents is even more marked when Hispanic Catholic teens are compared to their Hispanic Protestant peers. The chapter on Catholic teens toward the end of this book will go further in exploring some possible explanations for this finding.

Moralistic therapeutic deism

The second significant conceptual contribution from Smith and Denton's book comes from their description of the religious faith of most adolescents in the U.S. today as a form of "moralistic therapeutic deism" (MTD). In their understanding, MTD is "a widely shared, largely apolitical, interreligious faith fostering subjective well-being and lubricating interpersonal relationships in the local public sphere." The central tenets of this faith are as follows:

1. A God exists who created and orders the world and watches over human life on earth.
2. God wants people to be good, nice, and fair to each other, as taught in the Bible and by most world religions.
3. The central goal of life is to be happy and to feel good about oneself.
4. God does not need to be particularly involved in one's life except when God is needed to resolve a problem.
5. Good people go to heaven when they die.[5]

While this description may not resemble the traditional Christian creed, it nevertheless appears to be the dominant flavor of "Christianity" that is being passed on to the next generation of believers in churches, homes, schools, and media outlets all across the U.S. Perhaps it would be helpful at this point to list some of the ways MTD is out of step with traditional Christian doctrine:

1. God seeks to be at the center of every human life, intimately involved in every action and decision made every day, and to lead Christian souls to take advantage of daily opportunities to bear the light of Christ in a world of darkness. Living life this way requires God's help every day. In this context, prayer is not just a way to obtain God's intervention to fix the "problems" we face in our daily lives, but it becomes a discipline for continuous transformation in Christ as we learn to let go of the agenda we have set for ourselves and accept God's plan for us.

2. God's plan is for people to embrace Christ's mission of ushering in the Reign of God on earth. This involves accepting forgiveness for past

sins, proclaiming the Good News about faith in Jesus to others, living an exemplary life through the power of the Holy Spirit, and standing up for the cause of justice—especially justice for the poor and the vulnerable—until Jesus returns to set all things right in the fulfillment of God's Reign. When doing these things, it is not always possible to be nice and fair to everyone, just as Jesus did not shy away from afflicting the comfortable and self-righteous people of his day.

3. The Scriptures affirm that every life does indeed have a purpose, but that purpose is to embrace the mission of Christ in this life and to be one with the Creator in eternity—not merely to seek personal happiness and fulfillment in this life. In fact, we are called to love others as God has loved us, despite the fact that we are all sinners and do not deserve this gift of love. The practices of unconditional love and participating in Christ's mission on earth are not a guarantee of happiness; on the contrary, they are more often a recipe for much suffering. However, in the company of Christ they can also be a path to finding peace in the midst of suffering in this life, while living in the promise of eternal happiness in the next.

4. The Christian faith affirms that "goodness" is not a quality that human beings can attain on their own—we are all sinners. Therefore, it is not the "good" who go to heaven, but rather those who are redeemed and forgiven for their sins through the atoning sacrifice of Christ.

5. MTD tends to view religion as a means that parents and ministers may use to "protect" their teens from the problems that can come with sexual activity, substance abuse, violence, and criminal behavior of every sort. Using religion in this way may be a sign of immature faith on the part of the parent or minister; one wonders whether they really believe what they are passing on to the teens, or if they just see it as something that might be "good" for them, helping them to emerge "safely" from the turbulent teenage years. In addition, it often leads to a distorted presentation of the gospel message as outlined in the description of MTD above.

Since Hispanics are still a minority among adolescents in the U.S., it is necessary to ask the question: if MTD truly describes the religious faith of most U.S. teens today, does it also describe the religious outlook of Hispanic teens in particular? This question cannot be answered from the survey data alone, but the personal interviews and the preceding sections of this chapter provide ample evidence that MTD is indeed alive and well among Hispanic adolescents. In fact, 14 out of the 16 Hispanic Catholic respondents can be broadly described as followers of MTD, including one young lady who is a catechist for younger children. Among Hispanic

Protestants, seven out of 14 can be described as moralistic therapeutic deists, including two who could be described as "devoted" according to Smith and Denton's criteria. In general it is the less devoted, less actively involved Hispanic teens who embrace more of the tenets of MTD. Judging from the NSYR personal interviews, they likely form a large majority among Hispanic Catholic teens, and perhaps as many as half of the Hispanic Protestant adolescents in the U.S. today.

Pastoral recommendations

At the beginning of this chapter, it was stated that the challenge for Christians in every generation is to provide their children with both the experience of the risen Lord, and the understanding of this experience as

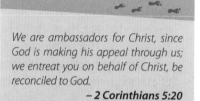

We are ambassadors for Christ, since God is making his appeal through us; we entreat you on behalf of Christ, be reconciled to God.
– 2 Corinthians 5:20

handed down through the ages, above all in the words of the Bible. The good news for parents and youth ministers is that both Protestant and Catholic Hispanic adolescents really do want to learn more about their faith—even more so than their white counterpart. They are also very adept at picking up religious cues from their parents and religious leaders. The bad news is that the cues they are currently receiving from parents, religious leaders, and many other sources are generally guiding them to a belief in moralistic therapeutic deism (MTD) rather than the traditional beliefs of the Christian faith. The following are some suggestions for ways to make youth ministry programs more effective:

1. Reach out to parents

The NSYR survey and interviews underline the important role parents have in the religious development of their teens; if parents are not involved in their church or are not actively promoting the development of faith in their children, it becomes very difficult for youth ministers to instill faith. There appears to be a great need for religious formation among Hispanic parents; without it, the pastoral care of Hispanic teens will be incomplete, and probably short-lived. This may be a greater challenge for Catholic parishes, because they tend to be much larger and more impersonal than the average Protestant congregation, and because the Catholic parents appear to be significantly less involved than their Protestant counterparts in the first place.

An additional challenge may come from differences of language, culture, and formal education; although most of the Hispanic teens speak English and are in school, many of their parents are primarily Spanish-speaking and may have a limited education. It is especially important to encourage parents and teens to worship together as a family in worship services that address the linguistic and spiritual needs of both generations.

Youth ministry must adapt to the needs and abilities of the parents, rather than forcing parents to adapt to the needs of the ministry. Although involving parents in the religious formation of their adolescent children can be very difficult, there appears to be no short-cut. Simply stated, it was the teens whose parents are actively supporting their religious development that were most confident about continuing their faith life, and most likely to describe God and religion in terms that resembled traditional Christian teachings.

2. Create worship experiences that involve the teens

When 63% of all Hispanic teens report that they have never had a spiritual experience at worship that was both moving and powerful, it is clear that much more can be done to make community and youth worship services more inviting to the adolescent participants. Besides making intentional efforts to allure them to worship, a concerted effort must be made to involve them in as many aspects of worship as possible. Some possibilities include developing rituals and church programs geared toward the young, utilizing teens in different duties within the church service (i.e. as musicians, singers, presenters, readers, ushers, altar servers, etc.), and mentoring them one on one or in small groups.

The stereotype about teens is that they get bored and disinterested at worship services. In contrast, many of the active teens in the interviews expressed how much they enjoy their community worship. Even those who are not actively involved seldom had anything negative to say about church. The problem is that so many do not go, their parents do not go, and they honestly do not feel that they are missing anything. This can only be overcome through intentional outreach to both parents and teens, offering worship services that address the spiritual hungers and the linguistic/cultural needs of both generations.

3. Provide Bible studies and retreats

The NSYR affirms that Catholic and Protestant Hispanic teens are more interested in learning about their faith than their respective white peers. Are we doing enough to satisfy their spiritual hunger? The evidence suggests that some Hispanic teens have decided to stop participating in their church youth group because it is not religious enough for them. Others have never benefited from participation in a youth group. Youth ministers must reflect on the social, economic, and religious obstacles that may be limiting the participation of Hispanic teens in their groups, and find creative ways to overcome those obstacles.

For teens who are already committed in their discipleship to Christ, in-depth Bible studies are an excellent way to provide spiritual nourishment. Retreats can also provide encouragement to continue, or they can be an opportunity to evangelize teens who have not been involved. It is a mistake to limit participation in retreats to only those teens who are already involved in the youth ministry; there should be at least one retreat each year in which the active teens can invite, and give witness to, their inactive friends and acquaintances. Such retreats should be followed by a beginning Bible study, or an invitation to youth group participation, for the newcomers.

4. Provide a clear and complete doctrinal foundation for young believers

It is evident that the vast majority of Catholic teens and substantial numbers of Protestant adolescents do not have a clear idea about even the basic teachings of their church. The task of passing the faith intact to the current generation of Hispanic teens is immense because in most cases the foundations have not yet been laid, or even worse, have been built on the false teachings of moralistic therapeutic deism. Pastors, youth ministers, and parents must dedicate themselves to this task with renewed vigor.

5. Directly challenge the false tenets of moralistic therapeutic deism

Perhaps many youth ministers and parents need to conduct an inventory of their own faith, eliminating beliefs and attitudes that reflect MTD over traditional Christian teachings. Suggestions 3 and 4 above need to be carried out with adequate explanations of the faith grounded in each faith community's theological tradition. Teens need to be taught to respect others' right to practice the religion of their choice and the importance of ecumenical and interreligious dialogue, but these principles do not equate to MTD's anything goes benign "whateverism," as Smith and Denton so eloquently described it. By becoming firmly rooted in the tenets of their own faith, Hispanic adolescents will "always be ready to make your defense to anyone who demands from you an accounting for the hope that is in you." (1 Peter 3:15)

6. Empower teens to share their faith with others

It has been said that a subject is never fully understood until it has been taught; the same can be said about religious beliefs. Until teens have had the experience of confidently sharing their faith and religious beliefs with others—especially their families and their friends and acquaintances of their own age—they may find it difficult to integrate their faith in their life. The vast majority of Hispanic teens in the interviews said that they never speak about religion with their friends, and many never spoke about it in their families.

A youth ministry structured around the evangelizing efforts of Hispanic teens will be far more effective than one structured around the efforts of adults in the community. The evidence suggests that Catholic youth groups especially may be spending too much time debating right and wrong from the point of view of utilitarian consequences, instead of helping teens to understand what God has done for them, giving them the tools and encouragement to share this Good News with others outside the youth group, and encouraging them to respond in love to God's gift by giving themselves without reservation back to God.

7. Be present—and be a role model

The NSYR survey and interviews show that Hispanic teens are very receptive to the religious modeling of parents and leaders in the church community. In fact, their responses echo with yearnings for a deeper spirituality. As they struggle with faith, adults in the community can show them love in a thousand ways (i.e. spending time with them, hugging them, playing sports with them, hanging out with them, fixing their bikes, etc.). Love can also be shared by face to face spiritual guidance through personal talks and walks, listening, sharing meals together, and going on outings. Organizing these kinds of activities for teens with adult volunteers willing to be models of committed Christian living will have a great impact in the faith of teens over time. All of these activities should include prayer and a teaching whenever possible. Modeling prayer and Christian life through our church attendance and fellowship; through presence at special, critical, and especially ordinary moments in the teens' lives; and through a willingness to speak honestly about how faith has impacted our own lives should be the cement that holds youth ministry programs and activities together.

8. Pray for the teens in the community

As youth ministry leaders, we should be praying for our teens on a daily basis—both the ones that we know in our ministry, and especially the Hispanic teens living in the community that we have not yet reached. Among Catholics, the "unreached" Hispanic teens actually account for the vast majority. In addition, we should be praying *with* the teens for their own spiritual needs, and for the success of outreach efforts to their peers outside the youth group. Finally, the whole gathered community should find ways to lift up the needs of their adolescent members in prayer. By following through with these simple prayer techniques, we unite our intentions to the movement of God's Spirit among us, and we help the teens to know that they are cherished by God and by the community. This is also a simple way to help the young people become more aware of the little miracles God is already doing in their lives, and to be able to name them and give thanks to God for them. In short, it is an effective way to promote the development and awareness of a close relationship with God among Hispanic adolescents.

Questions for reflection

In order to be a good role model for a teenager, one must first develop an ability to reflect on one's own actions and correct the subtle ways laziness or rationalization can creep into the spiritual life. The following questions may be used for personal reflection or for discussion with a spouse or partner in ministry.

On spirituality

1. As a Christian who has influence in the lives of adolescents in our community or in the lives of our own children, how active is our prayer life on a daily basis? How often do we fast? How often do we read the Bible? How often do we engage in direct service to people in need? How often do we share faith with others?

2. Do we make the mistake of trying to get teens to church merely as a means to keep them on a "safe" path in life? Is the Good News we share a reflection of traditional Christianity, or moralistic therapeutic deism? What more can we do to ensure that the next generation has faith in the God of Jesus?

On mentoring

3. When we are with adolescents, how do we provide a living example of unconditional love in our words and deeds? How do our activities with teens encourage them to raise their minds and hearts to God? How do we help them to recognize the things God is already doing in their lives?

4. What steps have we taken to motivate and empower parents, grandparents, and other family members to become evangelizers of the teens in their families?

5. What are we doing to encourage teens to bear the light of Christ for one another—seeking out the lost, proclaiming the Good News, standing up for the vulnerable, and living an exemplary life with the help of the Holy Spirit.

On availability

6. How present are we in the daily lives of the teens we serve? Do we make an effort to be there for significant moments in their lives? Are we available during the crises that may come up in their lives?

7. Do we live in the community where our church building is located? Do we make time to walk the streets, ride a bike in the neighborhood, or just hang out with the teenagers outdoors? What more could we do to reach out to a larger number of Latino/a teens?

On leadership

8. Does our youth group have a name, a focus, a shared vision? How do we invite Latino teens into leadership and foster confidence in their growing religious life?

9. Since the most significant spiritual activity we as Christians perform is in the sanctuary at worship, how have we organized religious rituals or activities under our authority to be inclusive of Hispanic adolescents?

On influence with others

10. How open is our church leadership to involving teens in the Mass or church service? What can we do to nurture their sensitivity to involving more teens in the various activities of the church?

Chapter 3:
Church and Youth Ministry Participation

Creating a Welcoming Environment
for Latino/a Teenagers

Lynette DeJesús-Sáenz, M.S.W.

**Dialog 3.1 – 15 year-old Hispanic Christian
female from the South**

I: *So you're involved in a religious youth group, right?*

R: Yeah... I go to two youth groups...

I: *What do you do there?*

R: They're... I don't know, in both of them we like praise God obviously in the beginning, and like we pray, and then just like teach you like about something, anything.

I: *They teach you about religious items or about God? What type of things?*

R: Mostly how to deal with like things in life... Just like things that like could relate to the Scriptures and everything.

I: *Do you enjoy it?*

R: Yeah, I love it.

I: *What do you get out of it?*

R: Well, I learn more about God and everything, and I don't know... I just like praising God. It makes me feel better.

I: *How important are the youth groups in your life?*

R: They're very important... one of my main priorities in life.

I: *What are the most important things about the youth group to you?*

R: I think probably learning more about God, like when they talk and stuff.

I: *So how do you think, if at all, that your life would be different if you weren't in the youth groups?*

R: I probably would have found something to get myself into on those nights. And I don't know.

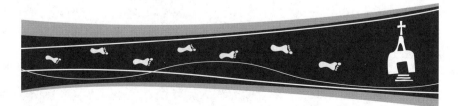

Church and Youth Ministry Participation

When ministering among adolescents in the United States, it is vital that churches take into account the reality in which young people live. Some faith communities are still neighborhood based, while others draw members from throughout the entire metropolitan area. Spirituality doesn't necessarily equate to church participation and religious devotion, individual faith communities rarely represent the diversity of society, and many churches are not able to hire a leader to pastor their teenage members. At home, parents are working longer hours, often with schedules that vary from day to day, and family structures are being questioned and redefined. Sexuality, violence, and the temptation of drug abuse are pervasive issues that cannot be ignored.[1]

As young people try to make sense of these realities on their path to adulthood, a thousand voices from parents, peers, schools, and even commercial advertisements, compete to tell them what is valuable and meaningful in their busy and confusing life. These are just a few of the challenges that young Latino/as are confronted with before ever walking through a church's doors. Some have become so overwhelmed that they would rather not have one more voice telling them what to do, so they choose to avoid the church altogether. Others accept with skepticism the motivation of their parents to participate in church activities, only to end up frustrated and discouraged when they find programs that do not touch their lives. Yet there are others who find acceptance, understanding, and compassion in the faith community, as well as the help they need to make sense out of a busy and confusing life, and guidance for successfully overcoming the many challenges they face.

Youth ministry in a competitive environment

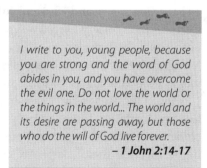

I write to you, young people, because you are strong and the word of God abides in you, and you have overcome the evil one. Do not love the world or the things in the world... The world and its desire are passing away, but those who do the will of God live forever.
– 1 John 2:14-17

Young people are constantly being bombarded with images of alternative lifestyles from TV shows, movies, music, the Internet, and other media that reach out to them. With so many choices and so many potential pitfalls, what does the church actually have to offer Latino/a teens today? Have our faith communities organized themselves to present the Good News about Jesus Christ to them in a compelling way? It is imperative that the church offer not only a safe haven for teens, but that it provide them with the knowledge and skills to navigate through society with their faith as a compass.

Faith communities need to act quickly and persuasively if they hope to make an impact on the lives of young people who are at an age of questioning who they are and who they want to become. Where financial resources are limited, as they are in many Hispanic communities, creativity, commitment, and passion for the Gospel should make up for the lack of buildings, paid staff, and abundant resource materials. The greatest asset of any faith community lies in the faith of its people; yet this living faith must be nurtured, exercised, and channeled to effectively organize the pastoral care of Latino/a teens and offer them the richness of a compassionate and liberating faith.

In 1997, the U.S. Catholic bishops issued a pastoral letter that dared to suggest that youth ministry is a reciprocal relationship between young people and the larger faith community: it is the response of the Christian community to the personal and spiritual needs of young people, and it is the sharing of the unique gifts of adolescents with the community of believers. This response has three goals:

1. To empower young people to live as disciples of Jesus Christ in our world today.
2. To draw young people to responsible participation in the life, mission, and work of the Catholic faith community.
3. To foster the total personal and spiritual growth of each young person.[2]

At the center of this approach is the ultimate goal of raising responsible members within the faith community who will live and proclaim the Good News of Jesus Christ in their families, their neighborhoods, their schools, and the workplace, and who will continue the church's mission of building God's Reign in society. Once a welcoming environment for Latino/a teens has been established, the key to achieving these goals lies in extending a warm and personal invitation to actively share their gifts in the life of the community as they willingly follow the Spirit to become disciples of Christ.

Youth ministry, as an extension of the church's mission, implicitly offers this invitation to young people of every size, shape, and color—Hispanic teens should be no exception. So how well are our churches doing in meeting these goals? Are Hispanic young people included as full and active members of their faith communities? Are they prepared to live and share the Gospel in their every day lives? This chapter will explore these questions using data from the National Study of Youth and Religion (NSYR) regarding the participation of Hispanic teens in church services and youth groups.

Latino/a teens' involvement in their faith communities

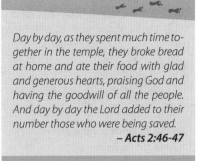

Day by day, as they spent much time together in the temple, they broke bread at home and ate their food with glad and generous hearts, praising God and having the goodwill of all the people. And day by day the Lord added to their number those who were being saved.
— Acts 2:46-47

One of the many strengths of the NSYR research is that it provides a description of both the behaviors and the attitudes of teens with respect to their faith communities and religious activities, including youth ministry programs. In addition, it is possible to compare the statistical responses of the teens surveyed to the words of individual teens in the interviews in order to gain further insight into their faith lives.

Church attendance and participation

The most striking aspect of adolescent church attendance in the U.S. as shown in Table 3.1 is the similarity of the responses between how often they currently attend church and how often they would attend church if it were totally up to them. In fact, 38% of Hispanic Catholic teens would actually prefer to go to church *more* often than they already do. Perhaps the lower number of Protestant teens who expressed a desire to go more often is at least partly due to the fact that Protestant teens—both Hispanic and white—already attend more often and report greater opportunities for participation than their Catholic counterparts. In any case, only 25% of Hispanic Catholic and 16% of Hispanic Protestant teens would prefer to go to church *less* frequently than they usually do. A reading of the NSYR interviews reveals that most Hispanic teens are happy to follow the religious direction and example set by their parents, as seen in the following example:

Dialog 3.2 – 17 year-old Hispanic Catholic male from the South:

I: *If it were totally up to you, how often would you attend religious services?*
R: Once a... once a week. I mean, I think that's fair enough. I mean giving once a week is good.
I: *And where would you attend, and why, if it was totally up to you?*
R: I'd go to church, I mean...
I: *Would you attend the same one you're attending now, or would you...*
R: Ah, I'd go to one that more of my friends are going to, really, that's where I'd go, I mean... My parents go to church because their grandparents went there and they go there, but I mean I just like, I don't know... [I'd] go to a place where my friends are, really. I mean, sometimes me and my brother go.
I: *Now your friends are also Catholics?*
R: My friends are, yeah.

Table 3.1 – Church attendance and participation (percentages)

	Catholic		Protestant	
	Hispanic	White	Hispanic	White
Teen's religious service attendance	N=278	N=556	N=94	N=1285
More than once a week	6	5	33	25
Once a week	31	36	24	27
1-3 times a month, or many times a year	31	26	28	29
A few times a year	20	23	14	13
Never	12	10	1	6
Would attend if totally up to teen				
More than once a week	9	4	38	29
Once a week	27	38	26	30
1-3 times a month, or many times a year	37	31	27	27
A few times a year	13	16	3	8
Never	12	12	7	6
Attends with:				
Both parents	50	53	53	56
Only one parent	22	18	32	22
Neither parent	8	11	7	13
Sacraments and celebrations				
Has taken First Communion (Catholics only)	73	72	N/A	N/A
In last year has been to Confession (Catholics)	36	48	N/A	N/A
Has been confirmed or baptized (not infant baptism)	34	47	55	54
In last year:				
Served as an acolyte or altar server	9	19	5	12
Taught a Sunday school or religious education class	16	15	31	27
Been part of any other Scripture study / prayer group	16	18	43	39
Played or sung in a religious music group or choir	18	18	40	36
Spoke publicly about faith in a religious gathering	22	18	52	38
Regular opportunities exist for teen to get inolved in services, such as reading or praying aloud				
Yes	48	54	76	67
No	17	12	9	13

I: Yeah, okay... So why don't you do that now?

R: Sometimes I do, me and my brother. I mean, it's just that my mother likes for the family to be together during church.

I: *Okay. Some people say that in order for a person to be truly religious and spiritual, they need to be involved in a church and not just lone individuals... Do you agree or disagree, and why?*

R: I believe it doesn't, it really, really doesn't matter. I mean, a person doesn't have to go to church, and he can pray on his own and read the Bible on his own and do his own religious beliefs on his own. He doesn't have to go to church.

I: *Okay, and why?*

R: Well, it's saying like, you have to go to church to be a good person and if you don't then you're a bad person. I mean, that's totally like wrong. I mean, people don't go to church all the time that are religious, and they're just as like good as the rest of us, I mean, morally.

The last set of answers in the quote above reveals a broadly accepted belief among most of the Hispanic students that were interviewed: namely, that going to church doesn't make a person "good," and "good" people may not choose to go to church on a regular basis. This point was discussed in greater detail in Chapter 2, since it is one of the typical attitudes of moralistic therapeutic deism (MTD—see pages 72-74), but it may also be the underlying reason why most of the teens were happy with their current level of church attendance. In practice, they consider themselves, their friends, and their parents to be good people, so if they do not happen to go to church every week, that must be okay. They do not appear to be concerned about the fact that most Christian denominations have a teaching on the importance of weekly participation in fellowship, worship, and for some the Lord's Supper. Even among adolescents who have made a commitment to going to church regularly, most do not think it is really necessary, as exemplified in the following conversation:

Dialog 3.3 – 15 year-old Hispanic Christian female from the Northeast:

I: *If it were totally up to you how often would you attend religious services?*

R: Every week.

I: *Would you attend the same church you're going to now?*

R: Yeah.

I: *Why?*

R: I get really attached. I like it. It's really nice.

I: *Some people say that in order for a person to be truly religious and spiritual, they need to be involved in a church and not just lone individuals or doing their own thing. Do you agree or disagree?*

R: I don't agree, because the church is not a building. God lives within you, so that's the way you feel, okay, as long as you're close to God. There are a lot of people in the Bible that died before going to church, getting baptized or anything and…yeah.

The number of Hispanic teens who report going to church with both of their parents is also fairly high—especially in view of the fact that 33% of the Hispanic teens in the survey only lived with one parent. Among teens living with both parents, 80% of the Protestant and 72% of the Catholic Hispanics reported attending church with both parents, and only 5% of each group attended without either parent. Among both Catholics and

Protestants, the Hispanics living with two parents were more likely to attend with both than their white counterparts.

In general the Latino/a Protestant teens are a little more involved at church than their white peers, but the rates of participation among white and Hispanic Catholic teens are generally quite similar. The areas in which Hispanic Catholic teens are clearly less active than their white peers are: going to Confession, getting confirmed, and serving at the altar.

A closer look at the Confirmation responses reveals that the Spanish-dominant Catholic teens have the same rate of Confirmation as their white peers—47%. However, only 28% of the English-dominant Hispanic Catholic teens were confirmed. Considering that 67% of them had made their First Communion (compared to 85% of Spanish-dominant and 72% of white Catholic teens), the low Confirmation rate among English-dominant Hispanic teens reveals a significant challenge for the Catholic Church: to encourage and facilitate U.S.-born Hispanic teens to complete their initiation in the faith.

Perceptions about the faith community

Perhaps my own faith journey as a young Catholic can illustrate how getting involved in church at an early age can make a big difference later in life. My family moved from Puerto Rico to Cleveland when I was 8 years old. With all the changes happening (new city, new school, new friends), it was comforting to be able to attend the Spanish Mass down the street and feel connected in some way to my previous life. It was familiar. It felt so comfortable that I would sing all the songs, which I knew by heart, at the top of my lungs during Mass. One day my father asked me if I wanted to sing in the choir. My response was "there are no kids in the choir." To him, that only meant that I would be the first. For me, it was the first step in becoming an active member, not only of my faith community, but also the larger church. Over the years, there were many more opportunities for me to learn about and share my faith—opportunities that I might not have had without that first positive experience as a child.

The surveys show that my experience of developing relationships with adults in the church community is not as common as one might hope among today's Hispanic teens, especially among the Catholics. A fifteen year-old Hispanic boy from the Northeast stated during his interview that he goes to church at least once a month. He went on, "I would go more often, I wish I went more… I just always thought, like there's no one to talk to at my church." Even so, nearly all of the active young Latino/as felt that their congregation was at least an "okay" place for talking about serious issues. The vast majority also felt that their congregation had done at least

Table 3.2 – Perceptions about the faith community (percentages)

	Catholic		Protestant	
	Hispanic	White	Hispanic	White
Church makes teen think about important things*	N=190	N=371	N=80	N=1042
Usually	52	53	71	66
Sometimes	32	33	25	26
Rarely or never	15	13	4	7
Church is boring to teen*				
Usually	16	23	7	11
Sometimes	34	42	34	36
Rarely	22	21	30	26
Never	25	14	29	27
Church is a warm and welcoming place for teen*				
Usually	66	65	74	80
Sometimes	25	28	22	15
Rarely or never	8	7	4	5
For talking about serious issues and problems, congregation is:*				
A very good place	36	34	38	51
A fairly good place	30	25	29	26
An okay place	25	29	23	17
Not a good place	5	11	9	5
Teen has adults in congregation (not family) who they enjoy talking with and who give lots of encouragement*				
Yes	59	71	78	85
No, but would like to	27	13	14	9
No, and doesn't care to	11	15	8	6
Helping me learn about my religion, congregation has done:**	N=196	N=344	N=84	N=1026
An excellent job	22	26	32	37
A fairly good job	42	41	42	40
An okay job	28	29	26	20
Not a good job or a bad job	6	3	0	3
Perceived priority of congregational ministry to teens**	N=255	N=470	N=85	N=1178
A very important priority	62	41	89	70
A fairly important priority	15	19	4	13
A somewhat important priority	15	26	4	12
A low priority or not at all a priority	4	11	1	4

* Asked of teens who stated that they attend church "many times a year" or more.

** Asked of teens attending church more than twice a year and expressing interest in learning about religion.

*** Asked of parents who stated that they attend church "a few times a year" or more.

an "okay" job in helping them to learn about their religion. Once again, the Protestant teens gave higher marks to their congregations in this regard than did the Catholic teens.

Although the teens' responses in Table 3.2 show that our Christian faith communities still have room for improvement, the overall sense one gets is that the Catholic and Protestant teens in the U.S. who go to church really enjoy doing so. After reviewing the interviews, it can be said that they generally support the positive impressions one gets from the surveys. Furthermore, the Protestant adolescents have even better things to say about their congregations than their Catholic peers. Perhaps this is a reflection of the high priority the Protestant congregations give to their teen ministries,

Table 3.3 – Youth group participation (percentages)				
	Catholic		Protestant	
	Hispanic	White	Hispanic	White
Youth group involvement	N=278	N=556	N=94	N=1285
Currently involved	20	25	44	57
Formerly involved	32	38	39	29
Never been involved	48	37	17	14
Number of years currently involved in yough group				
5 or more	5	8	11	18
2 to 4	8	12	29	30
1 or less	7	6	4	8
Type of youth group involvement				
Teen is a leader	3	6	15	19
Teen is just a participant	16	18	27	36
Both (leader and participant)	~	~	2	2
Congregation has a designated youth minister				
Full-time	16	23	26	42
Part-time	10	11	13	9
Volunteer	31	21	31	17
Has youth minister, don't know employment status	11	6	1	4
No youth minister	18	18	10	16
Evaluation of youth group*	N=55	N=139	N=42	N=730
Likes it very much	55	44	62	61
Likes it somewhat	41	45	31	29
Doesn't feel either way	2	9	7	4
Dislikes it somewhat or very much	2	2	0	6

* Asked of teens who stated that they were currently in a religious youth group.

as shown in the parents' answers to the last question in the table. What is surprising is that the Hispanic parents, both Catholic and Protestant, rated the teen ministry as having a higher priority in their faith community than their white counterparts did, despite the fact that in both traditions the Hispanic adolescents were less involved, as shown in Table 3.3.

Youth group participation

As was the case for church attendance, the Protestant teens report much more favorable experiences of their congregation's youth group than their Catholic peers: they are more likely to be currently involved, to report that they like the youth group "very much," to remain involved over a number of years, and to participate as leaders in the group. This was also reflected in the NSYR interviews: only one of the 16 Hispanic Catholic teens interviewed was involved in a high school youth group, compared to eight out of 14 of the Hispanic Protestants interviewed. The quote at the beginning of this chapter was taken from an interview with a girl who became Christian through her church's youth ministry, and it exemplifies the enthusiasm many of the Protestant Hispanic teens expressed for their church youth group. In contrast, here is the lukewarm assessment of the sole Hispanic Catholic teen interviewed who was participating in her parish's high school youth ministry:

Dialog 3.4 – 16 year-old Hispanic Catholic female from the West:

I: *You mentioned you're involved in a religious youth group. Can you tell me a little bit about that? How did you get involved, what affect has it had on you?*

R: It's once a week and it's just like when school ends and church starts, and…um…

I: *What do you all do?*

R: We start off with a prayer and it's like we go off in sections... There's senior youth which is 9th grade through, um... Well, you get confirmed when you're like in the 11th grade, but you can come back and help when you're like in the 12th grade. You're really supposed to... well you're not supposed to come back, it's your choice, but, um... And it's like nobody's coming anymore. Like as the year gets on, we start out with a whole bunch of people and like at the end of the year there's not very many. A lot of people just drop out. And um... you know, they say like something like their parents are making them come and they wouldn't come. You know there's people who've said, who've told the teachers that they wouldn't be there if their parents weren't making them. And, so, I don't know. It's just horrible. You know people aren't really caring anymore, and they say it's boring, because all we do is talk really.

I: *What do you think about that, do you share that view or not exactly?*

R: No, we do have debates you know, whether let's say, like the…the September 11th issue. We debated for like 2, 3 weeks about that.

I: *About the role of religion in that or just generally why that happened?*

R: Um, both, both. Um, about the war, we talked about that... Um, you know it's really about anything. Any problems you have you know you can go there you know, and then, yeah.

I: *Okay, that's great. Would you say your youth group has had a positive effect on you?*

R: Yeah.

I: *Do you see any differences between your religious and non-religious friends?*

R: Um… some differences, you know. The non-religious friends, no, the religious friends, they seem to care about more issues. Like they know what's, they know when something's wrong, you know. They usually, they're not usually hard partiers, they, you know, they know. They're more in school, uh, involved than... I mean I do have like a lot of non-youth attenders. They do go to church but they just don't attend youth [group].

Another key finding in Table 3.3 is that, despite the higher marks Hispanic parents gave to the priority of youth ministry in their congregations, the churches Hispanic teens attended were less likely to have a paid youth minister than those of the white teens. A closer look at the data shows that this is a significant factor in the lower youth group participation rates of Hispanic teens. Among Catholics who reported that their parish had a paid youth minister, 34% of both the Hispanic and white adolescents were involved in the youth group, although the leadership gap remained—only 3% of the Hispanics were leaders, compared to 10% for the white teens. In Protestant congregations with a paid youth minister, participation rates increased for both Hispanic and white adolescents, but the participation gap remained—54% of the Hispanics were participating, compared to 67% of the white teens.

Since a congregation's ability to hire a youth minister is at least partly determined by the economic resources available to its member families, it is helpful to compare Hispanic and white youth group participation according to family economic resources. Table 3.4 reveals that among wealthier families, the youth group participation gap between Hispanic and white teens disappears for both Catholics and Protestants. Furthermore, participation decreases steadily for both Hispanic and White teens as their economic resources decrease, although the rate of participation drops more rapidly for Hispanic families. The large participation gap in the overall figures is a result of the fact that the Hispanic teens' families have a much lower economic profile than their white peers, as shown in Table 1.5 on page 31.

In his analysis of the NSYR data, Ken Johnson-Mondragón identified two additional factors that have an impact on the interpretation of the Catholic survey responses. First, he noted that the rate of youth group participation among white Catholic adolescents in the Northeast was uncharacteristically low—only 12%, compared to 30% in the rest of the country—while the Hispanic Catholics in the Northeast participated similarly

Table 3.4 – Youth group participation by family economic status (percentages)	Low*		Middle*		High*	
	Hispanic	White	Hispanic	White	Hispanic	White
Catholic teens	N=112	N=39	N=109	N=181	N=52	N=326
Currently involved	16	18	20	23	27	27
Formerly involved	31	37	32	35	35	40
Never been involved	53	45	49	42	38	33
Protestant teens	N=25**	N=167	N=33	N=449	N=33	N=645
Currently involved	32	39	42	58	60	60
Formerly involved	56	40	27	26	31	28
Never been involved	12	21	30	15	9	12

* See the Appendix on page 361 for definitions of the economic status categories.
** With only 25 responses, these results have a sampling error of ±10%.

to their peers in other parts of the country.[3] The reasons for the significant regional drop in youth group participation among white Catholic teens are not clear in the survey data. Perhaps the fact that Catholicism is much more prevalent in the general population in the Northeast has led to complacency about the faith among their parents, only 15% of whom encouraged their teen to participate in the youth group "a lot," compared to 25% of white Catholic parents in other regions of the country.

Second, based on the NSYR survey results he concluded that 20% to 25% of the Hispanic Catholics who said they were in a religious youth group (4% to 5% of the adolescent Hispanic Catholics overall) were likely to be members of a *grupo juvenil*. Such groups usually serve adolescents together with young adults in a peer ministry conducted in Spanish, so they are both structurally and methodologically different from the mainstream approach to youth ministry. Since the NSYR survey questions did not distinguish between this type of religious youth group and the more typical adolescent-only youth groups conducted in English, it is not possible to determine with greater accuracy which style of group the Latino/a teens had in mind when they answered the question.[4]

Taking into consideration these two findings, the relatively close rates of "youth group" participation among Hispanic and white Catholic teens— 20% versus 25% respectively—mask the fact that only about 15% of the Hispanic Catholics were actually involved in a "high school" or "adolescent" youth group (not a *grupo juvenil*), compared to about 30% of the white Catholic teens in most of the country, with the exception of the Northeast.

Unfortunately, the NSYR Hispanic interviews do not provide any additional insights about this because there was only one Catholic individual who was involved in any kind of youth group—and that one was in a high school Confirmation program, not a typical "youth group" or "*grupo juvenil.*"

Participation in other youth ministry activities

The participation gap seen in the Catholic and Protestant youth groups between Hispanic and white adolescents is once again discernible with respect to other types of youth ministry activities in both faith traditions, as shown in Table 3.5. Also, there is a clear pattern of higher participation among Protestant teens, both white and Hispanic, than among their Catholic counterparts. Hispanic Catholics have particularly low levels of participation in retreats, religious summer camps, and service projects, which is not altogether surprising considering that this is the group that has the lowest economic profile (see again Table 3.4) and these types of activities

Table 3.5 – Other youth ministry activities (percentages)	Catholic		Protestant	
	Hispanic	White	Hispanic	White
Frequency of Sunday school / CCD attendance	N=278	N=556	N=94	N=1285
Once a week or more	21	20	40	34
At least once a month, but not every week	13	27	27	35
A few time a year	22	16	10	17
Never	44	37	19	14
Religious youth retreats, conferences, rallies, or congresses attended				
0	74	60	44	41
1	6	15	13	13
2 to 4	13	19	19	24
5 +	4	5	20	19
Religious summer camps attended as a camper				
0	83	75	48	44
1	8	11	18	17
2 to 4	6	10	26	24
5 +	2	4	6	14
Religious mission teams or service projects				
0	83	75	60	63
1	5	11	13	14
2 to 4	9	11	17	17
5 +	1	3	10	5

usually involve a financial contribution from the parents. Nevertheless, the teens who have experienced these other youth ministry events and activities tend to describe them in very positive terms as the interview excerpt in Dialog 3.5 shows.

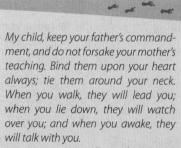

Dialog 3.5 – 18 year-old Hispanic Catholic male from the West:

I: *Have you ever been to a religious summer camp?*

R: I went to a religious retreat for Confirmation and it was… It was three days long.

I: *Uh-huh.*

R: Um, at first I didn't want to go. It was right after finals, mid-terms, and I was just… I remember I had my math final and I had to actually go home, pack, get ready, and I just wasn't in the mood to go. And it was in this bus and it was all the way in summer, you know and I… The first day I was, I wasn't just… It was a Seventh-day Adventist place, so it was just like tofu meat…

I: *Oh yeah?*

R: And at first I was just, "Oh, this sucks," you know. And then we got there and we had to go to sleep at three… But by the last day, it was different because I got to see people differently. I got to become good friends with people. I had felt closer, and I came home, I was completely stress-free.

I: *Do you think it affected your life?*

R: Yeah, it just, it still affects me, you know. I look back and I'm like wow… You know that was, that was a good time. It helped me a lot.

Parental influence on Latino/a teens' religious activities

My child, keep your father's commandment, and do not forsake your mother's teaching. Bind them upon your heart always; tie them around your neck. When you walk, they will lead you; when you lie down, they will watch over you; and when you awake, they will talk with you.
— Proverbs 6:20-22

The analyses in the previous section noted the importance of family economic resources and the presence or absence of a paid youth minister as factors that may increase or decrease the rate of Hispanic teens' participation in their congregation's youth ministry programs and activities. Nevertheless, Christian Smith, the principal investigator in the NSYR project, has argued that parents are by far the most important religious influence in the lives of their adolescent children. In fact, Smith and Denton make this claim so strongly in their book that it is worth quoting at length:

> Contrary to popular misguided cultural stereotypes and frequent parental misperceptions, we believe that the evidence clearly shows that the

single most important social influence on the religious and spiritual lives of adolescents is their parents. Grandparents and other relatives, mentors, and youth workers can be very influential as well, but normally, parents are most important in forming their children's religious and spiritual lives. Teenagers do not seem very reflective about or appreciative of this fact. But that does not change the reality that the best social predictor, although not a guarantee, of what the religious and spiritual lives of youth will look like is what the religious and spiritual lives of their parents do look like. Parents and other adults, as we have suggested, most likely "will get what they are." This recognition may be empowering to parents, or alarming, or both. But it is a fact worth taking seriously in any case.[5]

Taking Smith and Denton's point to heart, some youth ministry leaders have suggested that the lower rates of Hispanic participation in youth ministry programs and activities is primarily due to lower levels of religious commitment and involvement among their parents. Since Smith and Denton drew their conclusions based on an analysis of the NSYR data as a whole, it is important to ask the question: does the finding that parents usually "get what they are" with respect to the religious lives of their adolescent children also apply to Hispanic families in the United States?

To answer this question, Instituto Fe y Vida has devised a scale of parental religious commitment, based on the parents' responses in the NSYR survey, as a parallel to the scale of adolescent religious commitment used by Tomas Sanabria in Chapter 2. The category "mixed" refers to those individuals—teens and parents—whose responses showed a combination of

Table 3.6 – Parental religious and spiritual types (percentages)	Catholic		Protestant	
	Hispanic	White	Hispanic	White
Religious type*	N=278	N=556	N=94	N=1285
Committed	8	6	31	19
Engaged	43	38	41	40
Sporadic	7	12	5	9
Disengaged	3	10	1	4
Mixed	39	34	23	28
Spiritual type	N=271	N=519	N=89	N=1260
Charismatic	10	5	8	6
Pentecostal	6	4	28	11
Both	~	2	15	7
Neither, unfamiliar with the terms, or don't know	83	89	49	75

* See the Appendix on page 361 for definitions of the parental religious type categories.

characteristics that ranged from "disengaged" to "committed" such that they could not neatly be placed into any one of the four primary religious types. Pentecostal or charismatic identity provides another interesting comparison, since these Christians have a reputation for being more active in their faith life than other Christians, among both Catholics and Protestants.

A cursory analysis of Table 3.6 reveals that Hispanic parents are more likely than their white counterparts to be religiously "committed" or "engaged," and less likely to be religiously "sporadic" or "disengaged." Furthermore, the Protestant parents are significantly more religiously "committed" than the Catholics, as was true for the adolescents (see Table 2.6 on page 71). Also, the Hispanic parents were roughly twice as likely as the white parents to have a charismatic or Pentecostal identity. While this was true for both Catholics and Protestants, the Pentecostal identity was much more prevalent among Protestant parents, both white and Hispanic, than it was among their Catholic counterparts.

Parental religious impact in different ethnic and faith groups

Based on Smith and Denton's finding that parents generally will "get what they are," one would expect the Hispanic teens to be more "committed" and "engaged" than their white peers. This is in fact true for Hispanic Protestant teens, but not for Hispanic Catholic teens. As a further test of Smith and Denton's thesis, Table 3.7 presents the correlations between adolescent religious types and parental religious and spiritual types, broken down by faith tradition and ethnic group.

Looking only at the religious types of white adolescents, both Catholic and Protestant, one would have to conclude that Smith and Denton's assertion about parental religiosity being "the single most important social influence on the spiritual and religious lives of adolescents" is true. In fact, the boldface correlations in Table 3.7, which indicate similar levels of religious commitment between teen and parent, are strongest for white Catholic families. Significant numbers of the white children of religiously "committed" parents are merely "engaged," but there are even greater numbers among the children of religiously "sporadic" or "disengaged" parents who are *more* religiously involved than their parents. These data also appear to support the conventional wisdom regarding charismatic and Pentecostal Christians, as the white children of such parents are measurably more religiously engaged than their peers whose parents are not charismatic.

The teen-parent religious correlations among Hispanics tell quite a different story. In Hispanic Protestant families, the children of religiously "committed" parents were actually more likely to be "engaged" than "committed," but significant numbers of the children of religiously "engaged" parents were

Table 3.7 – Teen religious type by faith, ethnic group, and parental religious and spiritual types (percentages)

	Parental Religious and Spiritual Types					
	Committed	Engaged	Sporadic	Disengaged	Charismatic/ Pentecostal	Not Charismatic
Hispanic Catholic teens	N=23*	N=119	N=21*	N=7**	N=44	N=227
Committed	**15**	5	5	N/A	6	3
Engaged	39	**53**	15	N/A	33	45
Sporadic	13	13	**34**	N/A	31	20
Disengaged	0	1	10	**N/A**	3	4
Mixed	33	28	37	N/A	27	29
White Catholic teens	N=31	N=212	N=67	N=56	N=55	N=465
Committed	**69**	7	2	0	17	8
Engaged	26	**66**	33	8	34	46
Sporadic	0	12	**44**	53	21	24
Disengaged	0	1	8	**18**	6	7
Mixed	5	13	14	21	21	15
Hispanic Protestant teens	N=29*	N=38	N=5**	N=1**	N=45	N=44
Committed	**34**	30	N/A	N/A	29	30
Engaged	61	**42**	N/A	N/A	44	40
Sporadic	2	9	**N/A**	N/A	13	8
Disengaged	0	0	N/A	**N/A**	0	1
Mixed	4	18	N/A	N/A	13	20
White Protestant teens	N=249	N=507	N=119	N=57	N=307	N=953
Committed	**50**	16	6	0	24	17
Engaged	38	**64**	33	25	44	48
Sporadic	2	10	**33**	41	12	16
Disengaged	0	3	6	**6**	3	3
Mixed	11	9	22	29	17	16

* With only 20 to 30 parent-teen pairs, these results have a sampling error of up to ±10%.

** With 7 or less parent-teen pairs, these results are not representative and do not merit reporting.

more religiously involved, qualifying as religiously "committed." Regarding parental spiritual types, there was no significant difference in religious engagement between the Hispanic children of charismatic or Pentecostal Protestants and those whose parents were not charismatic or Pentecostal.

In Hispanic Catholic families, the teens' level of religious commitment drops significantly from that of their parents for all parental religious types, thus making a sharp contrast with the experience of white Catholic families. It is also interesting to see the high number of Hispanic Catholic teens with a "mixed" religiosity when compared to other groups. Furthermore, the Hispanic Catholic teens with charismatic parents appear to be somewhat ambivalent about their parents' faith practices: although they are more likely to be "committed" than their Hispanic Catholic peers with non-charismatic parents, they are also significantly more likely to be "sporadic." To better understand the religious dynamics at work in Catholic

Table 3.8 – Catholic youth involvement at church by parental religious type (percentages)

	Committed	Engaged	Sporadic	Disengaged
Hispanic Catholic teens	N=23*	N=119	N=21*	N=7**
Attends Mass once a week or more	46	52	10	N/A
Attends Mass occasionally	30	27	51	N/A
Seldom or never attends Mass	20	20	39	N/A
Has made First Communion	94	81	63	N/A
Has been to Confession in the last year	37	48	29	N/A
Has been confirmed as expression of faith	57	43	32	N/A
Currently involved in a youth group	26	24	10	N/A
Formerly involved in a youth group	24	33	51	N/A
Currently involved in a youth group as a leader	4	3	0	N/A
Has attended a religious retreat	11	38	2	N/A
Has attended a religious summer camp	9	18	12	N/A
Has served as an acolyte in last year	20	13	2	N/A
Has taught a religion class in last year	24	13	17	N/A
Attends a Catholic/Christian school	4	6	2	N/A
White Catholic teens	N=31	N=212	N=67	N=56
Attends Mass once a week or more	95	62	19	6
Attends Mass occasionally	3	26	33	18
Seldom or never attends Mass	2	12	48	77
Has made First Communion	92	92	65	48
Has been to Confession in the last year	77	61	43	23
Has been confirmed as expression of faith	66	54	42	28
Currently involved in a youth group	76	33	16	3
Formerly involved in a youth group	11	38	41	34
Currently involved in a youth group as a leader	21	9	3	0
Has attended a religious retreat	63	51	25	21
Has attended a religious summer camp	73	29	21	12
Has served as an acolyte in last year	58	26	10	0
Has taught a religion class in last year	32	16	17	4
Attends a Catholic/Christian school	16	16	9	4

* With only 20 to 25 parent-teen pairs, these results have a sampling error of up to ±10%.

** With only 7 parent-teen pairs, these results are not representative and do not merit reporting.

families, both Hispanic and white, it is helpful to consider how the children of different types of parents respond in their involvements at church.

Pastoral situation of Hispanic Catholic teens

The percentages for Hispanic Catholic teens who are children of religiously "committed" or "sporadic" parents have an asterisk in Table 3.8 because the small number of these parent-teen pairs in the NSYR sample means that the sampling error is relatively high—up to ±10%. Nevertheless, they provide a striking portrait of the differences between Hispanic and white Catholic families. For example, the Hispanic children of religiously "committed" Catholic parents in the NSYR sample are less than half as likely as their white counterparts to attend weekly Mass, about one-third as likely to participate in a church youth group, about one fourth as likely to attend a Catholic school, about one fifth as likely to be a youth group leader, and one sixth or less as likely to have attended a religious retreat or summer camp.

Because the NSYR interviews were not conducted with the parents, they cannot be used to develop additional insight into the religious dynamics between "committed" Hispanic Catholic parents and their adolescent children. However, in my own experience as a parish youth minister, I repeatedly heard stories from heart-broken Hispanic parents whose children refused to participate in the youth ministry programs, and in some cases even to come to church, because they didn't "fit in." These were very involved and dedicated Catholic parents, and they felt powerless as their children became involved in gangs or violence, got hooked on drugs, or in some cases attempted suicide. The inability of such parents to pass their faith to their children is a significant pastoral challenge that merits greater attention. In effect, the religious experience of Hispanic Catholic families forms an important counterexample to Smith and Denton's conclusion that parents most likely "will get what they are."

Pastoral situation of Hispanic Protestant teens

In contrast, the children of religiously "committed" and "engaged" Hispanic Protestant parents compare much more favorably to their white counterparts. Table 3.9 shows that the participation gap in youth ministry programs and activities between white and Hispanic Protestant teens remains, but it is much smaller than the gap between white and Hispanic Catholic teens. The Hispanic Protestant teens in the survey actually attended worship services and taught religion classes more frequently than their white counterparts. This suggests that the religious, cultural, and family dynamics that inhibit the transmission of the faith in religiously "committed" and "engaged" Hispanic Catholic families do not have the same impact in

Table 3.9 – Protestant youth involvement at church by parental religious type (percentages)

	Committed	Engaged	Sporadic	Disengaged
			Parental Religious Type	
Hispanic Protestant teens	N=29*	N=38	N=5**	N=1**
Attends worship once a week or more	86	57	N/A	N/A
Attends worship occasionally	12	34	N/A	N/A
Seldom or never attends worship	2	9	N/A	N/A
Currently involved in a youth group	67	41	N/A	N/A
Formerly involved in a youth group	21	41	N/A	N/A
Currently involved in a youth group as leader	23	15	N/A	N/A
Has attended a religious retreat	72	37	N/A	N/A
Has attended a religious summer camp	62	43	N/A	N/A
Has taught a religion class in last year	47	33	N/A	N/A
Attends a Catholic/Christian school	4	12	N/A	N/A
White Protestant teens	N=249	N=507	N=119	N=57
Attends worship once a week or more	82	62	26	9
Attends worship occasionally	17	28	36	34
Seldom or never attends worship	2	10	38	57
Currently involved in a youth group	87	62	41	11
Formerly involved in a youth group	10	28	38	42
Currently involved in a youth group as leader	41	18	15	2
Has attended a religious retreat	81	60	44	27
Has attended a religious summer camp	81	60	42	18
Has taught a religion class in last year	42	29	24	6
Attends a Catholic/Christian school	14	5	0	2

* With only 29 parent-teen pairs, these results have a sampling error of up to ±9%.

** With 5 or less parent-teen pairs, these results are not representative and do not merit reporting.

Hispanic Protestant families. Some of the reasons for this difference will be explored in Chapters 9 and 10.

Summary

At first glance, the NSYR data seem to say that Protestant congregations are much more effective at attracting and involving their adolescent members, both Hispanic and white, than Catholic parishes. A closer look reveals that the children of religiously "committed" or "engaged" white Catholic parents compare favorably to their Protestant counterparts, suggesting that Catholic parishes, and youth ministry programs in particular, depend heavily on parents to motivate and encourage the participation of their children. However, the Protestant congregations are much more effective at reaching the children of "sporadic" and even "disengaged" white parents. In order to achieve this, they must be utilizing additional strategies to reach the teens besides depending on their parents to bring them to church.

The participation gap between the Hispanic and white children of religiously "committed" Catholic parents, as well as the precipitous drop in participation among the children of less-involved Catholic parents, implies that Catholic parishes in general have not developed effective strategies to reach their marginal adolescent members. The question then becomes: who will be served? Implicit in the answer to that question is also a choice about who will not be served. By contenting ourselves with serving mostly the children of "committed" and "engaged" white parents in parishes that can afford to have a paid youth minister, we have unwittingly made a decision about who we will not serve.

Hispanic and other low-income Catholic adolescents in the U.S. have thus been victims of a kind of structural exclusion that does not sufficiently take them into account in pastoral planning for youth ministry at the parish, diocesan, and national levels. Undoubtedly, there are parishes that have made great strides to overcome this kind of exclusion, but the national picture painted by the NSYR data shows that the problem remains pervasive in the Catholic Church in the United States.

Youth ministry with gospel values

Justo González, a prominent Cuban-American theologian in the Methodist faith tradition, analyzed the Scripture passage in the box at the right as an example of reading the Bible through Hispanic eyes, and what he said is also applicable to the perspective of Hispanic teens. For González, the key to the proper understanding of the passage lies in the fact that Jesus is addressing the parable to the Pharisees who are grumbling about the fact that Jesus has been keeping

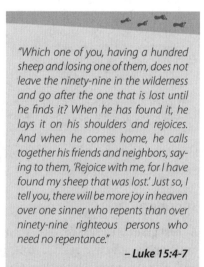

"Which one of you, having a hundred sheep and losing one of them, does not leave the ninety-nine in the wilderness and go after the one that is lost until he finds it? When he has found it, he lays it on his shoulders and rejoices. And when he comes home, he calls together his friends and neighbors, saying to them, 'Rejoice with me, for I have found my sheep that was lost.' Just so, I tell you, there will be more joy in heaven over one sinner who repents than over ninety-nine righteous persons who need no repentance."

– Luke 15:4-7

company with sinners and tax collectors. He is not speaking to the one lost sheep, but to representatives of the ninety-nine sheep that the shepherd leaves "in the wilderness" in order to go look for the one. He is not just speaking about God's love for the people on the margin, but he is telling people who believe they belong at the center that unless they too go out and seek the lost sheep, they are not true servants of God.[6]

In the spirit of this passage, Pope Paul VI wrote in *Evangelii Nuntiandi,* his encyclical on evangelization in the modern world, that "evangelizing is in fact the grace and vocation proper to the Church, her deepest identity. She exists in order to evangelize."[7] Seeking out the lost and welcoming them as they are into the sheepfold of the Christian community while teaching them to follow the path of salvation in Jesus Christ is at the heart of the church's mission in the world. A legitimate question to ask is: can our congregations and parishes really hope to engage the spiritually lost adolescents in our world if we cannot reach the marginal teens in our midst?

Bringing the Good News to teenagers at the margins

Protestant congregations have made greater inroads than Catholic parishes in reaching out to their marginal adolescent members: 51% of the white children of "disengaged" Protestant parents have at least tried a religious youth group and 11% have stayed, compared to 37% and 3% of their white Catholic counterparts. But Jesus was talking about something much more radical in the parable of the lost sheep: he literally said that we should leave the ninety-nine sheep in the wilderness to go in search of the one.

The fact that 89% of the Hispanic children of religiously "committed" Catholic parents in the NSYR survey had never been on a religious retreat suggests that even in religiously committed families there may be significant numbers of "lost sheep" who have not been reached by the church's ministry. If the best efforts of their parents are not effective at bringing them into the sheepfold, the church must do more to seek them out and bring them to a living faith in Christ.

Few ministries are as exciting as those that engage the faith of our young members; few tasks are as difficult in the pastoral setting. Congregations must be bold in their efforts to meet, greet, and gain the trust of Hispanic adolescents. Jesus modeled this discipleship when he selected fishermen to follow him. Paul modeled this kind of discipleship when he extended his ministry and trust to Timothy. We, the church, need to model this same discipleship by authentically inviting and empowering young people as respected members of the community. No community is complete until all are welcome and have a place.

The Good News for Latino/a teens

Ideally, ministry to young Hispanics is three-fold. First, it facilitates the consolidation of their religious and cultural identity in a peer community that understands and values their history, culture, and religious traditions, with adult mentors as guides. Second, it provides the knowledge, skills, and peer accountability to help them overcome the obstacles that would keep them from living the gospel message. Like other adolescents, Hispanic teens seek an open and safe place where they can form their own identity; a place where they will discover friendship, community and respect. They also seek a better understanding of the spiritual meaning of their lives.[8] These two foundations are essential for the third component: engaging Latino/a teens to live their baptismal call and embrace their evangelizing mission in their families and among their peers.

The NSYR survey tells us that Hispanic young people are open to the experience of church. The key word here is "experience." The challenge lies in the fact that their quest for fulfillment through experience can just as easily lead them to a variety of spiritual dead-ends. This philosophy makes it easy for them to pick and choose what they will or will not believe. Instant access to media with on-demand movies, 10,000 songs on their iPod, and mobile access to the Internet provide ample competition to the church's ministry of preaching the Gospel; MTV projects images and values that are much easier to come by than those of Jesus—and they are also marketed better.

Missionary outreach

If the church doesn't understand the various cultural modalities and expressions of Latino/a teenagers, how can it hope to effectively minister with them? Jesus grounded his teachings in the reality of those listening. He understood their culture and spoke to them in parables as a way to make the teachings understandable. By connecting these teachings with the life experiences of young Latino/as, church leaders can begin to make an impact on their lives. Like the ripples formed from a stone tossed into a pond, one small change will lead to many others.

The NSYR data indicate that in most Catholic youth ministry programs, and perhaps in many Protestant congregations as well, it is very rare for leaders to go searching for the "lost" adolescents in the community, unless their parents actively request the help. Much less are the ninety-nine (or in the case of Catholic youth ministry, the 25 or so youth group participants out of every 100 Catholic teens) being taught that they have a responsibility to seek out their "lost" peers. Instead, they are usually taught to guard against the dangers and bad influences of the lost sheep in the wilderness, avoiding their company at all cost and staying close to the center where they will be well loved, cared for, and protected. Such a misguided approach to youth ministry reflects a latent form of moralistic therapeutic deism (MTD) in which religion is viewed primarily as a safeguard against the moral pitfalls of adolescence (see pages 72-74 for a more detailed discussion of MTD).

To some degree, it is necessary to protect and form young people by surrounding them with positive role models and avoiding exposure to temptations that they are not equipped to handle. But this well-protected state of being should never be seen as the ultimate goal of youth ministry. Rather, young people should be built up and taught that they can serve as beacons to their peers who have lost their way—indeed, they have a mission to do so.

In the Scriptures, young people played key roles in the unfolding of God's plan throughout salvation history. We have King David, the prophet Jeremiah, and Mary of Nazareth as prominent examples, among many others. Each young person in the Bible was called for a specific task according to the gift God gave to him or her. Church leaders need to recognize that young people are full-fledged members of the faith community. As such, they have a vested interested in its future; it is only just that they be given a role to play in its fulfillment.

Clearly this requires much maturity on the part of the young people, and not all of them will be able to rise to the challenge immediately. They need to be molded and formed as disciples through intentional processes of transforming leadership. When young people encounter Jesus and accept the call to discipleship, they are transformed. Part of this transformation is accepting the responsibility to go out and transform the world. With the help of adult leaders who make outreach to the lost sheep a priority for the parish or congregation, Hispanic teens can be mentored into reaching out to their "disengaged" and "sporadic" brothers and sisters in Christ. Indeed, pastoral experience shows that it is the once-lost "sheep" who have been found by Christ that make the best evangelizers of their peers who still wander in the wilderness of gangs, drugs, sexual promiscuity, despair, or just indifference. The future, especially for young people, often seems hopeless. As they are transformed and accept their calling to be disciples, they can imagine new possibilities for themselves and the community.

Integrating teens in the faith community

When establishing outreach ministries, youth ministers should bear in mind that it may not always be possible to integrate the truly lost, or those with very different social or cultural horizons, immediately into the main youth ministry "flock"; their presence can easily disrupt or confuse the other participants. However, this does not mean that they should not be part of the faith community. Jesus came to bring a message of salvation for all people, yet his first outreach efforts were to the poor, the marginalized, and the public sinners.

What it means is that there may be a need to create a separate gang ministry, detention ministry, addiction recovery group, or even ministries for particular linguistic and sociocultural groups, in order to lower the social barriers to participation in youth ministry and overcome the conditions that cause certain teens to feel that they do not "fit in." In very large or diverse faith communities, multiple separate groups may be established on a semi-permanent basis according to the local pastoral needs, coming together as a community of communities in sacred times and places for worship and large community building.

Given the obvious challenges involved in creating youth ministry programs to seek out and engage the marginal adolescents in the community, it is imperative that pastoral leaders in our churches ask themselves: how well equipped are our current youth ministry coordinators and volunteer leaders for reaching out to welcome Hispanic, low-income, and religiously sporadic or disengaged adolescents in their parishes and congregations? The results of their current efforts at the national level as depicted in the NSYR study indicate that more training is urgently needed.

In order for communities to begin a response to the gospel call to provide pastoral care to the teens on the margins of social and congregational life, several conditions must fall into place:

- First, the pastoral agents responsible for ministry with the teenagers in the community—typically the pastor, the youth ministry coordinator, and the core team of volunteer leaders—must overcome the *pastoral nearsightedness* that only allows them to see the teens that are already participating in youth ministry and prevents them from recognizing that there are teens in the parish or congregation who are not being welcomed into their programs.

- Second, the same leaders must discern the call to reach out to these marginalized teens as a gospel imperative in their ministry.

- Third, they must equip themselves, or recruit others, with the skills necessary to carry out the pastoral action they envision.

- Fourth, they must discern how to structure and balance their ministry with the teens at the center of parish life with their outreach efforts to the marginal teens, allocating appropriate pastoral resources for each effort.

The NSYR data provides the first clear evidence of the number of Christian teens that are still being missed in Catholic and Protestant youth ministry programs, and the news is not very encouraging, especially for Latino/a teens. While it is possible that a particular faith community may be much more effective than the national average in reaching its adolescent members, the big picture certainly suggests that youth ministry teams would do well to reflect on the extent and effectiveness of their current outreach efforts. Once the above conditions are met, they will be on their way to developing a ministry that is responsive to the gospel imperative to seek out and engage the "lost" teens in the community.

Pastoral recommendations

As our young people grow in their personal and spiritual development, their level of responsibility increases and leadership skills improve. The fact that the majority of Hispanic teens stated that they anticipate attending the same congregation when 25 years old as they do now is encouraging for faith communities. Here are a few strategies to motivate them to become active in the life of the community and to be examples for the younger members.

> As Jesus passed along the Sea of Galilee, he saw Simon and his brother Andrew casting a net into the sea—for they were fishermen. And Jesus said to them, "Follow me and I will make you fish for people." And immediately they left their nets and followed him.
> – **Mark 1:16-18**

1. **Create intentional outreach efforts**
   - Learn the names of the young people in your church, and invite other members of the pastoral staff to do the same. Get to know who they are, and find out what is happening in their lives outside of the church walls. Include their concerns and struggles in the preaching and the community prayers at worship.
   - Go to the places where Hispanic young people can be found. Part of creating a welcoming community is reaching out to the young Hispanics in the area. Before you can get them into your building you need to go out to the neighborhoods, the schools, community centers—anywhere the young Latino/as gather—and get to know them and their families and friends.
   - Identify groups of Latino/as living in the area that have been difficult to reach, and strategize about how to engage them more effectively. For example:

- ° Spanish-dominant teens who have recently immigrated from other countries
- ° English-dominant children of immigrants who struggle to find their place in both the immigrant circles of their parents and the mainstream world of their non-Hispanic peers
- ° Families that have become trapped in generational cycles of violence, poverty, addiction, low educational attainment, and other self-destructive or self-defeating behaviors
- ° Teens in detention or attending alternative schools

- Invite Hispanic adults living in the different neighborhoods/barrios to serve as youth ministry leaders and mentors to young Latino/as seeking to integrate their faith and their culture in constructive ways as they prepare for their lives in the United States.

- Provide a real alternative to the allure of individualism, consumerism, and immediate gratification. Create spaces where young Latino/as can gather with their peers. If the social barriers to their participation in the existing parish youth groups or programs are too high, offer alternative groups and programs, developing leadership for each as you go.

- Plan activities and moments in which the Spanish-speaking, the English-speaking, and the various specialized youth ministries can come together to exchange ideas, share experiences, and build unity. Developing cross-cultural skills will not only create a stronger faith community but can also influence other areas of their lives.

2. **Provide vibrant worship**

- Hispanic teens want music, preaching, and rituals that engage them. They need to feel that they are a part of the body of Christ, and they need to see how what happens at church connects to their life at home, at school, or on the streets. They long for a worship experience that is passionate, that rises from the ashes of dull routine and becomes a life-giving faith event. Above all they need to be told in words and deeds that their lives and their experiences matter in the context of the whole gathered faith community.

- Invite Hispanic teens to participate in the congregation's ministries: music, lectors, ushers, Eucharistic ministers, altar servers, etc. Hispanic Catholic teens in particular have been much less likely to serve at the altar than their white peers. This reality needs to be addressed by intentionally inviting them to participate in liturgical ministries. Connect these young people with "ministry mentors" in the faith community, and prepare the mentors so that they understand the importance of the relational dimension of the ministry with the teens.

- Provide developmentally appropriate training and educational opportunities for their involvement in the worship services so they not only perform their designated functions well, but also understand the meaning behind their actions.

- Many Hispanic adolescents speak English as their primary language, yet they go to services in Spanish with their families. Provide simultaneous translations for them, or say a few words in English. This can go a long way toward creating a welcoming atmosphere and making them feel included. Another idea might be to include a Scripture reading in English or some bilingual music.

3. **Develop transforming leadership**

- Invest time and treasure in the development of young Hispanic leaders—they are your greatest asset for reaching their "sporadic" and "disengaged" peers. Give them opportunities to grow in the exercise of their leadership skills, as well as the support they need so that they will not fail. If they should make a mistake, help them to learn from the experience.

- Support the continuing education of current youth ministers and volunteers by offering accessible and inexpensive alternatives for training. If you have multiple youth ministry programs or groups, bring the leaders together for training and fellowship. In this way, you will form a common vision, share in the same spirit, increase their mutual understanding, and support each other in prayer for the diverse youth ministry efforts in the parish or congregation.

- Develop programs to empower Hispanic teens to evangelize their friends. Train, educate and send them on their mission, then support them in their continuing efforts.

- Provide special events—mission trips, retreats, conferences, and summer camps—that are adapted to the particular needs of each group, and provide financial assistance to families with few economic resources so that all may participate.

- Advocate for young Hispanics in leadership positions. Hispanic teens are significantly underrepresented in youth ministry leadership when compared to their white peers. We must call more of them to leadership and empower them to make their voice heard.

4. **Engage parents and families**

- Involve parents in ministry with Hispanic teens.

  ° Ask them about their concerns for their children's education, well-being, and spiritual growth, then develop youth ministry programs to address their needs and concerns.

  ° Engage them in planning intergenerational community celebrations of traditional Latin American devotions in which the teenagers are given a prominent role.

  ° Provide workshops in English and Spanish to help Hispanic parents in their relationships with their adolescent children, giving special attention to the ways cultural, linguistic, and generational differences can create tension and misunderstanding.

  ° Offer training and tools to assist Hispanic parents in their role as the primary educators in the faith for their children. Immigrant Catholic parents in particular may need assistance in presenting their faith in ways that are congruent with the social and religious context of Catholics in the United States, where the cultural expressions and supports for the Gospel are quite different from those in most Latin American countries.

- Build up families instead of tearing them down. When preachers and youth ministers emphasize the negative in order to "fix the problems" faced by teens and their families, many parents are made to feel inadequate. Preachers should adopt a strengths-based perspective and encourage families to build upon the positive elements in their lives.

- ¡Fiesta! Celebrate special occasions, infusing cultural expressions with gospel values, and open the celebrations to parents and other family members. For example,

  ° Celebrate Mother's Day by inviting families to participate in a blessing ritual for mothers before or after the worship service.

  ° Celebrate special events and successes specific to adolescence, i.e. *quinceañera* and high school graduation.

  ° Designate a day for the "blessing of cars," and use it as an opportunity to evangelize.

5. **Prepare the whole community**

- Include the whole congregation in ministry with young Hispanics. Use compelling media at worship and community events: music, drama, interaction, and kinesthetic worship.

- Whenever possible, send a well-prepared youth delegate to the major committees of the parish or congregation, so that the needs and perspectives of the adolescent members are adequately represented in pastoral decisions and actions.

- Advocate for teens in the community. Be visible and vocal in order to make sure their needs are being addressed at every level. The young people will see by your actions that you believe they are important.

- Provide workshops or training for all community leaders and volunteers so that they will have the skills necessary to be open and welcoming to the adolescents in the community, especially those that may be of a different culture than their own.

6. **Create ministry networks and develop congregational, diocesan, and regional pastoral plans**

- Conduct a youth ministry planning session with the youth ministry leaders in the parish, congregation, diocese, or region. Discern the most pressing pastoral needs of the teens in the community, with a gospel priority given to the "at-risk" and other marginal members, and strategize about how best to meet those needs.

- Hire a youth ministry coordinator. Communities that cannot afford a paid youth ministry coordinator are at a significant disadvantage in their pastoral efforts with adolescents, and they are often the same communities that have the most difficult pastoral challenges due to the lower economic resources of their members. Ideally, the diocese should allocate the funds necessary for these communities to hire a youth ministry coordinator with the cultural and linguistic skills to adequately serve their Hispanic adolescent members. In many places a single coordinator has been hired to serve several parishes in a cluster.

- Create a youth ministry budget that is sufficient to develop and support the programs, groups, leaders, and activities needed to address to the pastoral needs of *all* the teens in the faith community.

- Organize a diocesan or regional youth ministry council and schedule regular meetings for training, support, and pastoral planning. Outreach to at-risk and otherwise excluded or alienated teens should always be a top priority, such that the various congregations and parishes will share resources and efforts to reach the "lost" sheep in their midst.

- Collaborate with neighborhood community organizations that serve Hispanic adolescents. In order to make appropriate referrals as the needs arise, find out what service providers are available in your area to help in particular cases.

Questions for reflection

1. What was the most surprising or challenging finding of the NSYR study with regard to youth involvement at church? What are we called to do differently because of it?

2. What was the most important principle in this chapter for our ministry? How can we apply it? What will be our first step?

3. Does our faith community have a qualified youth ministry coordinator? Does the church leadership support the continuing education of our youth minister and volunteers?

4. Who are the teens in our faith community, and what are their most pressing needs? Ask this question also of the local high school principal(s), local law enforcement officers, local public health officials, and local youth-serving organizations. Do their answers match our priorities? If not, do we need to adjust them for the sake of the Gospel?

5. Are teenagers encouraged to participate in all aspects of congregational or parish life? Are they given a voice in making decisions and planning activities for the whole community?

6. Have some of the adolescent members of our parish or congregation chosen not to participate in youth ministry or to come to worship services because the social barriers to their participation are too high (i.e. they don't "fit in")? Ask this question also of a broad cross-section of the parents in the community. What should we do about it?

7. Do our current youth ministry programs and activities adequately address the pastoral needs of our Hispanic teens and the concerns their parents have for them?

8. What practical things does our faith community do to affirm, support, and celebrate the significant moments in the lives of our adolescent members?

9. What opportunities for leadership training do we provide the teens in our ministry (i.e. public speaking, planning procedures, decision-making skills, etc.)?

Chapter 4:
Faith and Culture in Hispanic Families

Carlos Carrillo, M.Ed.

Dialog 4.1 – 14 year-old Hispanic Catholic male from the West:

I: *Can you tell me about how you were raised religiously?*

R: Um, I was raised a Catholic, they taught me to believe in God and Mary and Jesus...

I: *Are you still a practicing Catholic?*

R: Mm-hmm (yes).

I: *Okay... How similar or different are your religious beliefs from your mother and father?*

R: We're all the same. My, well my mother, she's the one that's really into being Catholic. She goes to church every Sunday and all that. She's really the more religious one in our family.

I: *Is religion a source of conflict or of sharing, solidarity, with your parents?*

R: No.

I: *Um, not a source of conflict. Is it a source of sharing?*

R: Mm-mm (no).

I: *It's neither?*

R: Yeah.

I: *Okay. Do you think your family relationships are affected by religion or faith?*

R: Well, yeah. God taught us to love everybody and everything, so I guess we're just supposed to love each other... That's why we're so happy.

Faith and Culture in Hispanic Families

God chose for Jesus to be born and to grow in the Holy Family with Joseph and Mary, and since the beginnings of Christianity, the family has been at the heart of the church. Indeed, the *Dogmatic Constitution on the Church* of Vatican II repeatedly refers to the church as the "family of God".[1] In our days, we note that the social environment of Hispanic families in the United States is, in many ways, indifferent or even hostile to the faith. That is why the family today, more than ever, must become the domestic church where "the parents, by word and example, are the first heralds of the faith with regard to their children."[2]

In the United States, the presence of immigrant Hispanic families has given new life to the tradition of *familismo* (strong allegiance to family ties beyond the nuclear family) that characterizes the majority of Latin-American peoples. While relationships with the extended family tend to reinforce the faith of the younger members of Latino families, the process of acculturation often challenges this role.

This chapter will begin by describing the broad context in which the fundamental value of *familismo* in the Hispanic community is understood. That will be followed by a presentation of the family composition of the adolescents and parents in the National Study of Youth and Religion (NSYR), together with some pertinent demographic data from the survey. The chapter will also cover Latino family values and their importance, the religious practices of Hispanic families, and a description of the processes of acculturation that Latino families experience on their arrival in the United States. It will conclude with some pastoral recommendations and reflection questions for people working with Hispanic teens in the United States.

The concept of family among Hispanics

> When Jesus saw his mother and the disciple whom he loved standing beside her, he said to his mother, "Woman, here is your son." Then he said to the disciple, "Here is your mother." And from that hour the disciple took her into his own home."
> — *John 19:26-27*

In order to appreciate the results of the NSYR survey, it is necessary to understand the family context that the majority of Hispanic people share. Since the Spanish colonial period, and even dating back to pre-Hispanic indigenous origins, the value of the family group has taken precedence over the value of the individual in most areas of Latin America. The concept of family for Hispanics, as for many other minority groups, refers to the extended family, including aunts, uncles, cousins, *padrinos* (godparents), grandparents, etc. The high value placed on *familismo* means that everyone in the family has a shared sense of responsibility to care for children, to provide financial and emotional support in times of crisis, and to participate in decision-making efforts that involve other family members, even after they have reached older adolescence or young adulthood.

Studies have shown that Hispanic families tend to retain a strong sense of *familismo* even after they have assimilated in many other respects. In addition, family pride and cohesion often serve as buffers against some of the negative effects of acculturation for Latino/a adolescents. Latino/as are much more likely than non-Hispanic white people to live near other family members or maintain frequent contact with family members in their country of origin, so the teens are exposed to the values, traditions, beliefs, experiences, and customs of the family in a variety of ways. Members of the extended family consider it their duty to cooperate with parents in passing the family's values and traditions to the next generation.

It is not uncommon to find Hispanics in their country of origin, or even in the United States, who have been raised in households together with their aunts, uncles, grandparents, cousins, godparents, or other informally adopted family members. When a family or an individual moves from a small town to a distant city or another country, their ability to impart the psychosocial benefits of *familismo* to their children are drastically reduced. As a result, it is often the Hispanic teens who have greater contact with their extended families that are more secure in their identity and more self-assured.

When Hispanics who have immigrated alone begin to form their own families in the United States, they typically establish a high degree of interdependence among their few family members, and continue to share support with their loved ones wherever they may be. For example, they make great sacrifices to visit family members during vacations or for important events, and they spend a considerable portion of their income to send financial assistance to their distant family members. To summarize, the Hispanic concept of family generally includes people connected by blood or informal adoption, not just two parents and their biological children, so many young Hispanics are raised in the company of their cousins, aunts, uncles, grandparents, *padrinos,* and other family friends.

Composition of Hispanic teens' families in the United States

As a consequence of migration, poverty, and the effects of racial and sociocultural discrimination, Hispanic

> Joseph, son of David, do not be afraid to take Mary as your wife, for the child conceived in her is from the Holy Spirit. She will bear a son, and you are to name him Jesus, for he will save his people from their sins.
> – *Matthew 1:20-21*

families in the United States have undergone changes in their organization and composition. Table 4.1 provides a first glimpse into some of these changes based on results from the NSYR survey.

National origin

Almost 90% of the Hispanic teens surveyed were either born in the U.S. or have received virtually all of their schooling here, since they arrived before age seven. In contrast, more than 50% of their parents were born in other countries. That percentage is especially high among Catholic fathers, reflecting the phenomenon that single young men are often the first to leave their families in Latin America in search of a better life in the United States.

Table 4.1 – Family composition (percentages)				
	Hispanic			White, Any Faith
	Catholic	Protestant	No Religion	
National origin	N=278	N=94	N=40	N=2448
Father born in the U.S. (of teens living with father)	37	45	52	96
Mother born in the U.S. (of teens living with mother)	48	50	47	96
Both born in the U.S., or single parent born in U.S.	41	45	39	94
Both foreign-born, or single parent born outside U.S.	48	49	45	2
Teen born in the U.S.	76	80	86	99
Teen foreign-born, came to the U.S. before age 7	10	8	3	1
Number of adults (ages 18+) in household, not including parents				
0	66	69	58	76
1	24	21	31	18
2	7	9	11	5
3 or more	3	1	0	1
Number of children (under age 18) in household				
1	20	19	31	29
2	28	29	33	40
3	31	27	16	20
4 or 5	17	16	16	10
6 or more	4	9	4	2
Marital status				
Parents married and living together	62	63	55	75
Parents living with unmarried partner	7	4	3	4
Parent widowed	1	3	8	2
Parents divorced	9	19	14	14
Parents separated	6	7	10	4
Parents never married	14	4	11	2

In any case, the proportion of Hispanic teens growing up with at least one parent who was not born in the United States is very high—close to 60%.

The national origin statistics also indicate that the vast majority of Hispanic marriages are either between two people born in the U.S. or between two people born in other countries. The question was not asked whether the foreign-born spouses were from the same country, but other studies indicate that it is increasingly common to discover marital unions between Latino/as from different countries, such as one person from Puerto Rico and one from Guatemala. In addition, the 16% of Hispanic marriages that were between an immigrant Latino/a and someone born in the U.S. represent another kind of culturally mixed family, even if the U.S.-born spouse has roots in their partner's country of birth.

Household composition

As one might expect given the importance of *familismo* among Hispanics, they are more likely than white families to have adults in the household other than the parents of the teen. Nevertheless, about two-thirds of both Catholic and Protestant Hispanic families have no adults in the house other than the parents. With respect to both the number of adults and the number of children, Hispanic Catholic and Protestant families are very similar, but the non-religious Hispanic families tend to have more adults and fewer children than the religious Hispanic families. In any case, the number of Hispanic households consisting only of a nuclear family appears to be fairly high, perhaps indicating the way immigration and the types of living quarters available in U.S. cities have limited the ability of Hispanic families here to establish living arrangements together with extended family members.

Marital status

The NSYR survey shows that Hispanic teens are less likely to have parents that are married and living together than white adolescents. Protestant Hispanic teens are more likely to have divorced parents than Catholic Hispanic teens, but the Catholic teens are more likely to have parents that are living together outside of marriage, or who never married and are no longer together. This difference reflects the tendency among many low-income Latino Catholic couples to wait until their relationship stabilizes before making the commitment of marriage, even if they already have children, since the Catholic Church does not approve of divorce and remarriage. Even some couples that are in stable relationships choose not to marry until they can afford to have a church wedding in the presence of their whole extended family on both sides. Others consider that there is no advantage in getting married, so they may live together their whole lives without ever celebrating a wedding.

Among the teens selected for interviews, 11 out of the 16 Catholics and five out of the 14 Protestants were living with both of their biological parents. In addition, three of the Catholic families and two of the Protestant families included extended family members in the household, and 10 out of the 38 Hispanic teens interviewed were living in blended households with step-parents and step-siblings or half-siblings. Several of the teens spoke about their step-father as their "dad," which suggests that some of the teens surveyed whose parents were "married and living together" may have actually been talking about a step-parent. Eleven of the Hispanic teens indicated that they never had a significant relationship with their biological fathers, and others reported that their parents had been divorced because of domestic violence, use of alcohol or drugs, or infidelity. The following examples drawn from the interviews are not intended to sensationalize the negative experiences of Hispanic teens—many others are in fact living in very healthy families—but rather to raise awareness of the difficult experiences that some Hispanic teens may have had, so that pastoral workers can be sensitive to their needs while avoiding inappropriate assumptions.

Dialog 4.2 – 14 year-old Hispanic Catholic female from the Northeast:

I: *Are your parents divorced?*

R: [pause] My dad... cheated on my mom.

I: *Uh-huh...*

R: And he bought, like it's the second time he's done it already... He went to Ecuador 'cause I'm half Puerto Rican, half Ecuadorian. He went to Ecuador, and he bought an extra plane ticket for somebody, and that somebody was that girl. So he brought her from over there and then he would go and he would see her and blah, blah, blah...

I: *Were your parents still living together at this time?*

R: Uh-huh. And then um, my mom didn't know whatever, and then my mother found out, my mother found out. She was like, "Oh, we need to do something about you." And then my dad decides to leave, so he grabbed his stuff and he left. And he comes, well right now, right now, they're together, I don't really know what's going on, but I don't want them to get back together.

I: *Why not?*

R: 'Cause, I mean my mother gave him one chance first time he did it. This is the second chance, and my mother is gonna give him another chance. What's gonna happen the 4th and the 5th time, 'cause I know he's gonna do it again? And then I know my mother's gonna end up crying and... he's gonna end up doing it again, breaking my mother's heart. And then again, and then she's gonna be in the same position. So what's the point of going back, going to all that struggle for nothing?

I: *And when your dad moved out, did he move in with this other woman?*

R: No, he moved in his own apartment with a guy that lives in the same apartment. Roommates.

I: *Uh-huh. He brought this woman from Ecuador to live in the States?*

R: Yeah, to the United States.... I think she'd already been here, but she had people living, she had her mother living here so she moved in with her.

Dialog 4.3 – 13 year-old Hispanic Jehovah's Witness female from the Northeast:

I: *First, can you tell me who lives with you in your household?*

R: Um, my uncle, my grandmother, my mother and my sister. Um, my other grandmother is staying with me, um, she's visiting, but that's basically because my father's in prison and my brother is staying with his father and my older sister moved out a couple years ago, so...

I: *Okay, and which of your brothers and sisters are... Do you have some half sisters?*

R: Yeah, um, all of my other brothers and sisters have different fathers except for my second oldest and younger brother, they have the same father...

I: *Okay, and is it your same dad or a different dad.*

R: Um, no, I'm my dad's only child.

I: *Okay, and are your parents married now?*

R: No.

I: *Okay. And how long has he been in prison for?*

R: Um, roughly two years so, yeah, just about like 2 years and 6 months.

I: *Okay, so when he was out was he living with you guys?*

R: Yeah.

Divorce rates are much higher in the United States than in Latin America, and a significant number of Hispanic families have simply been abandoned by the fathers. When divorced parents remarry, they create blended families with step-parents, step-brothers and sisters, and half-brothers and sisters. In other cases, men who have come to the U.S. to provide better support for their families in Latin America end up forming new families in this country. All of these situations can be stressful for adolescents, demanding psychological, social, and economic adjustments that can be overwhelming for many.

Divorce and remarriage poses a particular challenge to Catholic families because the parents are excluded from full participation in the Eucharist. In many Latino Catholic communities, even divorce without remarriage can lead to a sense of isolation or rejection from the community. Adolescents may internalize these feelings of rejection, to the point that they prefer to stay away from church. In some cases, such families may be drawn to other Christian denominations that offer divorced, separated, and unmarried families equal opportunities to participate in the community.

Forgiveness and family unity are values that are shared among Catholic and Protestant communities alike. However, they differ pastorally in the way they reach out to families in difficult situations. Many Protestant communities offer a specialized ministry for divorced or unmarried parents, inviting them to conversion and healing in their relationships, both old and new. Catholic communities are challenged to offer alternative ways to include parents and couples that do not represent "the ideal family," so that their children can benefit from the catechetical and sacramental services of the parish without feeling stigmatized or rejected because of their parents' life circumstances.

Among Hispanic teens surveyed who were living in single-parent households, 90% were living with their mother. The many obligations that single mothers have toward their families often make it impossible for them to bring their children regularly to church. Thus, divorce or separation often means that adolescent children will stop going to church, even if they or their parents do not feel rejected or alienated in any way. The NSYR interviews indicate that when such changes of family routine occur, the teens generally do not question the direction set by their parent(s)—they are quite content to do as their parents do. Faith communities must find ways to reach the adolescents living in these circumstances or they will risk losing a significant segment of this generation of Latino/a teenagers.

Demographic characteristics of Hispanic families

Chapter 1 has already presented a general demographic portrait of the teens and parents surveyed in the National Study of Youth and Religion. Nevertheless, it is worthwhile to revisit some of that data here in order to consider how certain realities in Hispanic families may impact

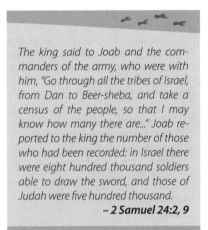

The king said to Joab and the commanders of the army, who were with him, "Go through all the tribes of Israel, from Dan to Beer-sheba, and take a census of the people, so that I may know how many there are..." Joab reported to the king the number of those who had been recorded: in Israel there were eight hundred thousand soldiers able to draw the sword, and those of Judah were five hundred thousand.
– 2 Samuel 24:2, 9

their quality of life, as well as the ability of parents to transmit their faith to their children. Table 4.2 highlights some of the more important factors for Latino families.

Language usage at home

The survey results show that Spanish continues to be a common language used in the home among Hispanic parents. In fact, it is nearly the majority language for Hispanic Catholic parents, reflecting the fact that recent immigrants tend to be more Catholic than generations born in the United States. Among Hispanic adolescents, Spanish is significantly less dominant, yet Spanish continues to be used at home at least as much as English for about two-thirds of Hispanic Catholic teens and half of Hispanic Protestant and non-religious teens.

Table 4.2 – Demographic characteristics (percentages)

	Hispanic			White, Any Faith
	Catholic	Protestant	No Religion	
Primary language spoken at home by parent(s)	N=278	N=94	N=40	N=2448
English	51	60	69	99
Spanish or other	48	40	31	1
Language(s) spoken at home by teen				
Only or mostly English	35	49	53	N/A
Only or mostly Spanish	25	20	25	N/A
Both Spanish and English equally	39	31	22	N/A
Highest level of education completed by either parent				
Junior high or less	16	6	11	~
Some high school	9	9	13	3
High school or GED	32	23	39	16
Some college, AA, or vocational/technical school	27	39	25	35
Bachelor's degree or some graduate school	8	13	3	26
Graduate or professional degree	7	10	10	19
Parental employment status				
Both parents working	40	39	40	52
Father working, mother not working	21	25	13	19
Mother working, father not working	4	3	0	4
Single mother, working	15	24	24	13
Single mother, not working	13	7	14	4
Single father, working	2	2	5	3
Household economic status*				
Low	40	27	36	12
Middle	39	35	39	34
High	19	35	25	52
Safety of neighborhood				
Very safe	35	40	43	64
Mostly safe	32	28	24	28
Somewhat or not very safe	33	31	34	8

* See the Appendix on page 361 for definitions of the economic status categories.

Language affects adolescents in two different ways: through its content (what it signifies) and through its process (how is used). This reality merits greater attention, since youth workers continue to ask what role language plays in the transmission of the faith among adolescents. Joan D. Koss-Chioino, an anthropologist in Arizona, and Luis A. Vargas, a child psychologist in New Mexico, emphasize that for teens who have learned English as a second language, the emotional and cognitive associations with an event that occurred in early childhood are expressed much more powerfully in the language in which they were experienced, and they lose their flavor and their emotional impact when translated or declared in another language.[3]

Similar to emotions and feelings, the language of faith has greater impact when it is expressed in the language of first exposure to religious concepts in early childhood. Research recently conducted by Instituto Fe y Vida has found that there is a high level of correlation between the language of the home and the language of personal prayer among Hispanic young adults.[4] Because the NSYR survey shows that most Hispanic teens are bilingual and Spanish continues to be an important language at home, youth ministry leaders should consult with Latino/a teens and their parents to find out what linguistic setting will be most comfortable for each adolescent. Unfortunately, this dimension of youth ministry is generally ignored by pastoral workers serving Latino/a teens in their faith communities.

For immigrant teens with clear memories of participating in the religious celebrations of their family and community in their country of origin, it can be especially difficult to adjust to the different language and cultural expressions of the faith in the United States. In many ways, they are like the Israelites in exile in Babylon who said:

> By the rivers of Babylon—there we sat down and there we wept when we remembered Zion... For there our captors asked us for songs, and our tormentors asked for mirth, saying, "Sing us one of the songs of Zion!" How could we sing the Lord's song in a foreign land? – *Psalm 137:1, 3-4*

Similarly, many young immigrant Latino/as have become completely fluent in English, but they continue to long for the spiritual nourishment of the symbolic and cultural religious expressions of their childhood. When placed in a group that does not respond to their language of faith, Hispanic teens tend to become confused and frustrated. Although they may not be able to understand or express the reasons for their frustrations, they generally will choose not to go. In other cases, it may be their parents who cannot make the religious transition. One immigrant girl expressed her experience in this way:

Dialog 4.4 – 13 year-old Hispanic Catholic female from the South:

I: *Can you tell me about how you were raised religiously?*

R: Well, when in Honduras, I used to have to go to church every weekend. Um, like I used to have to wear dresses...

I: *Did you wear dresses like every day or just to church on the weekends?*

R: No, just to church—and tights, and these sweaters and long dresses. You couldn't show none of like your body parts—you couldn't show, not even your arms. Um, and when it was on Sunday you had to like

> cover your face or something like that and then you had to say prayers
> in front of the crowd. You have to go up and say prayers and you have
> to make offerings like bring fruit or something and make them offerings
> and stuff like that.
>
> I: And when did you come here from Honduras? How old were you?
> R: Seven or eight, I think.
> I: Okay so what happened, religiously, when you came to the U.S.
> R: When I came, um, I didn't go to church anymore. Um, I only used to like
> say um, like one prayer and I, um, I didn't worry that much about that. It
> wasn't much of a problem...

Most of the immigrant teens interviewed for the NSYR were like this girl—not very expressive about the religious changes that occurred when they arrived in this country. However, I vividly recall a conversation I had with a 16 year-old girl of Mexican origin who had come to the United States at age 13. She shared with me that once she went to live with her aunt, who had been born in the U.S. and spoke more English than Spanish, she started going to church services in English. She felt like something was missing because she no longer went on pilgrimages, Christmas was celebrated differently, the songs and prayers used at church did not touch her, and the religious practices felt empty. She deeply missed preparing the tamales with all the women of their town, as well as the novenas, the rosaries, and the parish fiestas. Then she told me that "praying in English doesn't make me feel the same way as when I pray in Spanish."

In effect, reciting the "Our Father" in Spanish brought to mind a rich collection of memories and relationships from special moments in her life. Praying it in English related it to nothing. At the beginning of this chapter, it was noted that parents are called to be the first heralds of the faith to their children. For most Hispanic teens, this initial proclamation was made in Spanish. Faith communities need to prepare themselves to offer adolescent faith formation that builds upon what the teens have learned at home and in their earlier religious experiences, whether in the United States or in Latin America. The use of familiar language, music, and ritual experiences are indispensable tools, but ultimately the youth ministry team must engage in a continuous dialog with the Hispanic parents in order to better understand the religious hopes and aspirations they have for their adolescent children.

Parental education and employment status

Table 4.2 indicates that the Hispanic parents have a much lower educational profile than their white peers, and among Hispanics, the Catholic parents were less likely than the Protestant parents to have completed high school or to have a college degree. This may be partly due to the fact that the Catholic parents are more likely to be immigrants, so they were less likely to have the benefit of growing up with a free public education through high school.

One of the religious challenges of having parents with limited education is that the parents likely received their religious instruction in a very experiential way. This is especially true for Catholics in Latin America, where the faith has been transmitted for generations by means of family and community rituals and celebrations that have a religious meaning or message. This creates a double challenge for immigrant families: 1) the traditions and rituals of Catholicism in the United States are different, so parents cannot depend on the community to provide the same teachable moments that they had received in their childhood; and 2) religious education here has adapted to the needs of a highly literate and secular culture, so it tends to be presented in a conceptual manner, rather than based on lived experiences.

Because the parents do not have the academic or doctrinal training to reinforce what is being taught at church, they are not able to respond adequately to their children's questions, leaving many Hispanic adolescents without help when their friends of other religions challenge them about their beliefs or practices. Take for example the following conversation from one of the NSYR interviews:

Dialog 4.5 – 17 year-old Hispanic male without any religion from the West:

I: *Can you tell me about how you were raised religiously?*

R: Uh, well I was raised as a Catholic. You know I went to Catholic school for 7 years and got baptized, had my First Communion as a Catholic... Then like earlier this year, like from like December to like February or March or something I was like looking into Buddhism... Then uh, one of my uh, friends you know gave me this book you know about conversations with God, and I started reading that 'cause I didn't know which religion to believe in... 'Cause you know every religion says their religion is right and everyone else is wrong or something like that. So I looked into that and the guy asked him you know, how do you know what religion to believe in? And God said "I sent all those teachers out to different groups of people." And so you know I just believe in you know my God and you know, what my heaven is like, 'cause, that's basically all it is...

I: *So... would you consider yourself a particular religion at this point?*

R: Uh…not really. I just, I just believe in there's a God. You know, I do believe in Jesus and Mary and them, but you know I don't consider myself a certain type of religion.

The lower educational levels of Latino parents also have an impact on the type of employment they are able to secure. The parental employment figures in Table 4.2 show that Hispanic families are actually less likely than white families to have both parents working. This is an indication of the value Hispanic families place on having the mother in the family at home with her children—even if she is a single parent. What the statistics do not tell is the sacrifices that Latino families make in order to survive with limited employment prospects. The following conversation illustrates the difficulties encountered by one immigrant family:

Dialog 4.6 – 17 year-old Hispanic Seventh-day Adventist female from the Northeast:

I: *First, tell me, who lives with you in your household?*

R: I live with my dad during the week and with mom only when she comes on weekends.

I: *So, your mom is there only on weekends?*

R: Yes, she works.

I: *She works. But they are not divorced or anything.*

R: No, no, no.

I: *Tell me about your relationship with your mother. How well do you get along with your mother?*

R: Well, I consider my mother as a friend because she gives me advice. I tell her everything, everything that goes on with my feelings, that goes on at school and then she gives me good advice... I've lived with her for 15 years; I came here only seven months ago and only now do I live with my father—like that, together.

I: *Uh-huh.*

R: We never lived like that before. With my father we've lived like for one month a year and that's all, because he went to work in different countries. Then with my mother I've lived more time.

I: *And how long… how long have you lived with your father?*

R: Practically, like... in a year we've lived together for 3 weeks, 4 weeks; because he went on trips. Only now am I living with him for 8 months. We don't talk too much but... I'm trying to get along with my father because he has a very strong personality...

Working two jobs, on weekends, or at odd hours is common for parents with a limited education. As a result, it is not always possible for them to go to church every week, or to provide extracurricular activities for their children, including youth ministry programs. Faith communities should be sensitive to the living circumstances of their lower-income members, especially single parents, and develop ways to support them in the religious education of their children at home, or to facilitate their teenagers' participation in youth ministry programs.

Economic situation of the Hispanic families

Given the lower educational levels of Hispanic parents, it is not surprising to see that they also have a much lower economic status, based on household income, indebtedness, and home ownership. A further consequence is that they are forced to living in neighborhoods where they do not feel very safe, especially at night. Youth ministry programs frequently do not fully take into consideration the economic situation of the families, so teens in low-income families are excluded simply because of a variety of expectations that cannot be met by the family.

For example, it is often the older girls in a family that are expected to take care of their younger siblings, starting at a very early age; they may be asked to prepare dinner, pick up their siblings at school, watch the little ones, or work to provide additional income for the family. Occasionally the oldest son will step in for an absent father by abandoning any hopes for a higher education in order to go to work to help support the family.

Psychologically, low-income Latino/a teens also express a certain frustration when they compare themselves to their wealthier companions. I had the opportunity to work with a Latino teen who was accepted on his school's football team; he soon stopped going to practice because one of the players made a comment about his parents and the house where he lived. His matter-of-fact explanation for his decision to leave the team was: "I am so tired of being poor." When Hispanic teens are asked to participate in youth ministry programs with teens of a much different socioeconomic status because there is no other alternative offered, they will most often refuse or quit after a few visits. They will then either internalize their frustration and anger in the form of low self-esteem, or project it against the faith community that is not sensitive to their reality.

Latino family values

As a counselor, therapist, social worker, and youth minister for more than 20 years, I am convinced that families are called to be small communities of faith and life, comprising people with common interests and shared responsibilities, united by love. The social environment is built on the values that are lived in the heart of the family. For this reason, parents are called to guide every educational

> As God's chosen ones, holy and beloved, clothe yourselves with compassion, kindness, humility, meekness, and patience. Bear with one another and, if anyone has a complaint against another, forgive each other; just as the Lord has forgiven you, so you also must forgive. Above all, clothe yourselves with love, which binds everything together in perfect harmony.
> *– Colossians 3:12-14*

activity in the home. Their responsibility is to educate with kindness, generosity, detachment, and a willing spirit of self-sacrifice. The home is where children learn the values that they will carry all their lives—values like love, justice, honesty, courage, fairness, work, respect, love of God, communication, trust, forgiveness, and many more. Table 4.3 demonstrates how some

Table 4.3 – Hispanic family relationships by religion and religious type (percentages)

	Teen Religion			Teen Religious Type*			
	Catholic	Protestant	No Religion	Committed	Engaged	Sporadic	Disengaged
How close do you feel to your parents? (mother/father)	N=278	N=94	N=40	N=47	N=172	N=82	N=32
Extremely close	32/18	30/18	34/14	30/28	35/18	27/13	25/19
Very close	38/23	38/24	41/26	42/29	35/29	46/18	37/11
Fairly close	13/15	23/18	13/9	18/4	18/16	10/15	19/16
Somewhat close	8/9	4/6	8/4	0/2	6/11	11/13	11/5
Not very or not at all close	5/7	1/3	0/10	2/1	2/7	1/7	5/10
How often do you talk with your parents about personal subjects? (mother/father)							
Very often	30/14	23/5	8/4	30/15	28/10	23/10	16/3
Fairly often	19/5	21/11	36/18	20/7	22/11	17/5	27/10
Sometimes	32/24	39/27	30/13	31/26	36/29	35/23	16/14
Rarely	10/16	7/15	16/14	6/10	0/19	17/15	22/14
Never	5/13	8/11	5/15	6/5	2/12	7/15	16/19
How often do your parents praise and encourage you? (mother/father)							
Very often	63/30	48/38	55/29	55/32	64/41	58/19	43/16
Fairly often	16/16	24/10	18/16	25/19	20/16	16/17	27/17
Sometimes	15/17	23/15	13/3	11/11	12/18	18/23	10/10
Rarely	3/7	2/3	5/8	2/2	2/6	7/4	10/5
Never	~/2	0/2	5/8	0/0	0/1	0/4	8/3
How much do you feel your parents understand you?							
A lot	39	35	36	40	34	37	32
Some	41	47	30	36	50	41	25
A little	17	15	15	16	14	13	24
None	3	3	19	8	2	8	19
How much do you feel your parents love and accept you?							
A lot	82	87	71	83	83	77	62
Some	15	11	11	17	13	17	14
A little	2	2	18	0	2	4	24
How well do you get along with your siblings?							
Extremely well	18	8	0	11	16	13	6
Very well	31	31	36	46	32	29	40
Fairly well	26	34	23	29	29	36	24
Not so well, poorly, or badly	3	9	10	4	4	7	3
No siblings	20	19	31	11	20	16	27

* See the Appendix on page 361 for definitions of the adolescent religious types.

of these values are at work in Hispanic families, and how they are enhanced when the teens are religiously involved.

The value of trust

God demonstrated complete trust in us when we were endowed with a free will. Similarly, parents can create an environment of trust if they demonstrate an open attitude toward the interests and aspirations of each of their children. When there is love and trust in a family, each member reflects an interest in the wellbeing of the others with minimal competition or jealousy about whose needs are met when there is conflict. This happens because each person trusts, consciously or unconsciously, that the greatest need of any member will always be served, and everyone will have their needs met, within the realm of what is possible for the family as a whole.

One measure of the level of trust in a family can be found in the Hispanic teens' responses to the questions: How close do you feel to your mother and father? The survey results show that most Hispanic teens have a closer relationship with their mother than with their father, and there was very little difference between Catholics, Protestants, and non-religious Hispanic teens on this point. However, the Catholic and Protestant teens that were most religiously "committed" (see Chapter 2, pages 69-72, and the Appendix on page 361 for an explanation of the religious types) had significantly closer relationships with their fathers, and they were less likely to have a poor relationship with either parent than their less religiously involved peers.

The foundation of trust in a family is transmitted by parents to their children mostly between 0 and 2 years of age, but it continues to develop and change as children grow, including in the adolescent years. An atmosphere of trust and security is created when parents respect their children, when children respect their parents, and when parents help their children to respect one another's personal possessions. Adolescents have a lot to say and to share with their families. When they receive appropriate attention and discover that they can share their ideas without being judged, their self-esteem grows, allowing them to develop their gifts responsibly without emotional trauma or insecurity.

The NSYR interviews provide many examples of the obstacles that tend to inhibit the development of trust in Hispanic families. Most of the Latino/a teens clearly expressed a great deal of love and admiration for their parents, but the living situations of many families and the resources they have sometimes make it difficult for them to create an open and trusting environment in the home. Domestic violence and substance abuse play a role in breaking down trust in some of these families, while the lack of commitment in marriage or an irresponsible attitude toward parenthood contributes toward the same process in others. It is difficult to trust parents or children who do not keep their word, are not present, or are not committed to helping the family. In these situations, religion appears to help cultivate the value of family trust. Although the young man in the following conversation does not say that religion is responsible for the positive changes in his family, it is easy to see that his going back to church made a difference for everyone:

Dialog 4.7 – 18 year-old Hispanic Catholic male from the West:

I: *Have there ever been any turning points in how well you have gotten along with [your parents] in recent years?*

R: Um, I didn't used to get along with my dad at all. 'Cause he did used to drink and there was problems... Then he stopped [and] it went a lot better now. So that was like the biggest turning point...

I: *So you think the turning point in... how you got along with him was him making the decision to stop drinking?*

R: Yeah.

I: *Okay. Can you tell me about how you were raised religiously?*

R: Well, I went to a Catholic school when I was a little kid, for kindergarten, first grade. And then somehow, I went to public school and I kind of separated... You know I didn't go to the church that often. Then uh, this past year, I actually got suckered into it, to like going to church and going to get my Communion and stuff... At first, I was just I don't want to do this, this is stupid. But then after a year and after getting to really understand it, I, you know I did it for my own things. So I had like Communion, Confirmation. I think I'm pretty religious now, much more than I was...

I: *Are [your parents] going to church more now than you are, or...?*

R: Yeah. When I started going to church, it's like they sent me, but they didn't really participate.

I: *Okay.*

R: And when I started going to church, I know they hadn't gone to Confession. And when I was going to Confession, they decided to go, so it was kind of like they decided to go with me...

I: *Uh-huh. And do you think that there's anything else about religious faith or spiritual outlook that affects the quality of relationships in your family?*

R: I think it does, because I think a lot of religions have, they set sort of like rules and... Like that you should be kind to your family members. And I think if you have that in the back of your head, you know, you won't do certain things. You'll take things... You'll be more considerate...

I: *Okay. Who, if anybody, are the people that you most admire?*

R: I admire my mom. I do admire my parents, you know, because they've gone through so much and they, they've gone past you.

I: *And what is it about them that you find admirable?*

R: With my mom, I think... She knows how to get through things. She knows how to survive through, you know, the worst of things. And my dad, I think he knows now how to recognize when he's wrong. And I think that's a really admirable quality...

The value of communication

Communication is a vital tool that is needed to maintain the cohesion and unity of all families. Communication makes it possible for two or more people to come together; it is the starting point for every interpersonal relationship. Through communication we also come to know and understand ourselves, from the most superficial characteristics to the very deepest parts of our inner being.

The NSYR survey offers important insights into the frequency and quality of communication between Hispanic teens and their parents when it asks the questions: How often do you talk to your parents about personal subjects? And how often do your parents praise and encourage you? Table 4.3 shows that the channels of communication are much more open and encouraging between the Latino/a teens and their mothers than they are with their fathers. Furthermore, the Catholic teens appear to communicate with their parents a little more frequently than their Protestant peers, but both groups communicate with their parents about personal subjects much more regularly than the non-religious Latino/a teenagers. It is comforting to see that the vast majority of Latino/a teens receive praise and encouragement from at least one of their parents fairly often. In this regard, mothers again easily outshine the fathers, and Hispanic Catholic mothers are especially inclined to motivate their children.

When compared by levels of religious involvement, it is clear that the more religious teens tend to have more frequent personal communication with their parents. Nevertheless, even among the religiously "committed" teens there is a significant minority of 12% to 15% who say that they rarely or never talk to their parents about personal matters. Furthermore, the religiously "engaged" Latino/a teens appear to receive more parental praise and encouragement than their more active "committed" peers.

These statistics combined with a close reading of the personal interviews reveal that some religiously committed teens have difficultly relating with their parents, and they may be spending extra time at church as a way to avoid the negativity they feel at home. In other cases, parents may have a tendency to provide less praise and encouragement to their religiously committed children because they feel it is not needed since the teens are already on the right path. In any case, it should not be assumed that the most involved adolescent leaders in the faith community always have healthy relationships at home; there is room in all families to improve the communication between parents and teens.

Open channels of communication help teens to understand other members of the family, and to consider their experiences, attitudes, beliefs, thoughts, feelings, etc. On the other hand, when adolescents are not able to communicate well with their parents, they may accumulate grudges or even desires for revenge. As a result, there is no better gift parents can give to their adolescent children than to speak with them often from the heart. In contrast, masks, lies, and superficiality can destroy the spirit of a family and prevent teens from maturing in their ability to develop and maintain healthy relationships with others.

Hispanic teens consistently report that they wish they had better communication with their parents. It is not that they never talk, but rather that they need better techniques to increase mutual understanding. Communication between Hispanic teens and their parents can be especially difficult in the United States due to the circumstances of their lives here:

- Sometimes they are not fully proficient in speaking each other's primary language.
- Immigrant parents have not experienced what it is like to be a teen in the U.S.
- Cultural and ideological differences create a chasm between parents and teens.
- The time parents have available to give their children is very limited due to work commitments, the extra activities of the teens, homework, chores, and the time spent watching television.

The community of faith can be an ideal place to encourage and teach families to deepen the communication between parents and children by providing helpful ways to open the dialog and reflect together on daily life and the topics found in the Scripture readings each week. It will be especially challenging, but much needed, to increase the communication between Latino/a teens and their father figures—if they have one. The place of the father in the family is much more demanding today, going way beyond the traditional role of making a living. When fathers are more involved in the lives of their children, it makes a big difference in their growth and development through adolescence and into adulthood. Youth ministry has the responsibility to work not only with the adolescents, but with their parents and the entire family. It is not enough just to offer programs and activities for the teens; youth ministry leaders must become familiar with the needs of the parents and respond to them.

The value of forgiveness

In every family there are times when the feelings of one member are hurt by the actions of another. That is why families need to develop a commitment to seeking reconciliation among their members, based on mutual love and respect. Families that strive to live a religious life based on

Christian principles realize that the value of forgiveness is very important to maintain household unity. Harmony in the family is achieved when each member understands the others, when they feel loved and accepted, when they get along well, when they communicate. In every human relationship, there are moments in which this harmony is broken.

The results of the NSYR survey shown in Table 4.3 are very hopeful because they show that the vast majority of Hispanic adolescents feel understood, loved, and accepted by their parents, and they get along at least "fairly well" with their siblings. Nevertheless, there are significant numbers of non-religious or religiously "disengaged" Latino/a teens who only feel "a little" love and acceptance from their parents, and do not feel at all understood by them. Because they do not usually come to church, it is challenging for faith communities to connect with these families, but there is a clear need for outreach efforts to provide guidance to Latino parents in establishing healthy and supportive relationships with their adolescent children.

Furthermore, there is a minority of religiously "committed" Hispanic teens who do not feel at all understood by their parents. Youth ministry leaders should be aware of the need to look for signs of troubled home life in order to provide appropriate pastoral care, even with some of their most involved teens.

Another concern raised by the NSYR surveys is the fact that there is a significant gap between Latino/a boys and girls with respect to how much they feel understood, loved, and accepted by their parents. Table 4.4 provides the pertinent response rates. It is not possible to know from the survey data whether Hispanic parents actually love and understand their sons more than their daughters, but it is clear that the girls do not feel as appreciated as their brothers. Parents should take the time to reflect on their relationships with their children to see if there is a need for reconciliation and better understanding with any of them, especially the girls. In addition, youth ministers could provide a needed service by raising the awareness among parents that there is a perception of preference for the boys, and offer suggestions for ways to deepen and improve their relationships with their daughters.

Often the emotional pain of adolescents is brought about unconsciously by their parents and siblings. At times there may be an attitude of indifference toward the hurt feelings of others because the reasons for their reaction are not understood. There are many obstacles that can prevent seeking forgiveness: fear, pride, a perception of weakness, ridicule, thinking that the other person deserves what they got, expecting the other person to take the initiative, etc. There are also obstacles that may make it difficult to forgive: sexist attitudes, resentment, anger, hatred, fear of being taken advantage of, superiority complexes, etc.

Table 4.4 – Hispanic parent-teen relationships by gender (percentages)		
	Male	**Female**
How much do you feel your parents understand you?	N=215	N=236
A lot	44	30
Some	37	43
A little	13	21
None	6	5
How much do you feel your parents love and accept you?		
A lot	84	76
Some	10	19
A little	4	4

Adolescents need to grow in an environment of forgiveness and understanding in order to discover that God is rich in mercy. Living in an environment where children, parents, and siblings forgive one another, helps them to feel the presence of God, who is love, in their home. Here are some tips to consider for putting Christian values into practice at home:

- Listening is put into practice when family members pay attention to each other and open their hearts when they are asked to do something, without feeling disregarded.

- Mutual respect means making a point not to make fun of other members of the family.

- Humility implies acknowledging mistakes, not trying to defend them.

- Responsibility is shown when people are on time for family commitments and follow through with what is required of them as a parent or child in the family.

- Loving service is a choice to help with the chores around the house and to pay attention to the needs of the others.

The value of freedom

Teenagers long for freedom. However, they need guidance to understand the difference between the Christian value of freedom and the vice of licentiousness or permissiveness. Christian freedom develops when a person becomes aware of the responsibility to make good decisions in accordance with the values, norms, and laws established in the family, in the community, at school, at work, or in the church. Freedom is the capacity and the right to express ideas, feelings, goals, and opinions, and the choice to act responsibly. Freedom is to do or not to do; to speak or not to speak; to protest or to remain quiet; to act or not to act at any given moment in time.

It is the role of parents and educators to form responsible young people who can act freely by exercising appropriately their capacity to choose. True freedom involves a shared responsibility, as St. Paul wrote in his letter to the Galatians: "For you were called to freedom, brothers and sisters; only do not use your freedom as an opportunity for self-indulgence, but through love become slaves to one another." (Galatians 5:13) In other

Table 4.5 – Parental supervision of Hispanic teens by religion and religious type (percentages)

	Teen Religion			Teen Religious Type*			
	Catholic	Protestant	No Religion	Committed	Engaged	Sporadic	Disengaged
How much do your parents monitor the television and movies you watch?	N=278	N=94	N=40	N=47	N=172	N=82	N=32
Always	16	25	11	24	18	18	8
Usually	32	25	19	34	34	30	24
Sometimes	25	22	36	31	24	23	21
Rarely	12	17	21	7	8	18	25
Never	15	11	13	3	16	11	22
How much do your parents monitor who you hang out with?							
Always	40	50	41	65	40	35	24
Usually	21	17	18	15	22	22	17
Sometimes	22	18	21	16	21	16	30
Rarely	9	6	18	0	9	15	24
Never	9	9	3	4	8	13	5
How often do your parents know what you're doing away from home?							
Always	41	41	36	60	40	37	16
Usually	32	35	38	16	32	38	59
Sometimes	21	18	14	17	23	13	14
Rarely	4	6	8	5	5	6	8
Never	1	1	3	2	~	4	0
How much freedom do your parents give you to express your own views?							
Too little freedom	16	20	15	14	17	20	16
The right amount	79	70	78	77	78	67	78
Too much freedom	5	9	8	9	5	13	6
When your parents find out you did something wrong, how often do they punish you?							
Always	36	39	24	34	45	21	19
Usually	25	27	21	25	24	34	29
Sometimes	22	15	36	15	16	22	29
Rarely	12	14	15	19	10	18	19
Never	6	5	3	6	5	5	3

* See the Appendix on page 361 for definitions of the adolescent religious types.

words, adolescents need to learn that they are not free when they violate civil, family, or spiritual laws, or the rights of others. They are not free when they act with violence or aggression because in such actions they are dominated by their feelings instead of taking control of them. In freedom there is no room for deceit or manipulation because they affect the dignity and freedom of others. Teens are not free when they give in to vices or bad habits, because in doing so their personal dignity is abandoned.

In this context, parents are called to create in their home a "school for human enrichment."[5] This means limiting children's freedom to do whatever they want, whenever they would like, until they have demonstrated the responsibility and maturity to be able to make healthy and loving choices for themselves and others. Table 4.5 reflects the limitations Hispanic parents have placed on their teenage children in order to prepare them for the responsible exercise of their freedom as they grow into adulthood, as found in the NSYR.

Comparing the supervisory practices of Hispanic parents by religious tradition, it appears that the Protestant parents tend to provide more supervision than the Catholic parents, and both religious groups watch their teenage children more closely than non-religious parents. What is most striking in the numbers is the high degree of correlation between adolescent religiosity and parental supervision—the most religiously involved teens tend to be the ones that have the most supervision at home, and the most consistent consequences when they do something wrong. Chapter 6 will look more closely at the moral choices made by Hispanic adolescents, but undoubtedly the degree of parental supervision in more religious households is an important factor in shaping the behavioral outcomes of the adolescents in those families.

Religious practices in the family

The family is called to be a privileged place where children experience religious practices as a natural part of their lives and adolescents begin to integrate them into their lives with a personal conscious commitment. The Christian faith is cultivated through the celebration of religious devotions at home and in the faith community,

> A certain woman named Lydia, a worshiper of God, was listening to us; she was from the city of Thyatira and a dealer in purple cloth. The Lord opened her heart to listen eagerly to what was said by Paul. When she and her household were baptized, she urged us, saying, "If you have judged me to be faithful to the Lord, come and stay at my home." And she prevailed upon us.
> *– Acts 16:14-15*

including going to church on a regular basis. In the following example, it is clear that a religious commitment has taken root in the teen's life:

Dialog 4.8 – 14 year-old Hispanic Latter Day Saints male from the West:

I: *Different kinds of religious and spiritual people "do" different kinds of things to express their faith. Are there any kinds of religious or spiritual things that you "do," any practices or habits or regular things that are part of your religious faith or beliefs?*

R: Um… I just pray and read the Scriptures and attend church.

I: *Okay, so… you said you read the Scriptures, what Scriptures do you mean?*

R: The Scriptures is the pearl of great price, the doctrine and covenant, is the Book of Mormon and the Bible.

I: *Okay, what do you read?*

R: All of them.

I: *How does that affect you?*

R: It gives kind of examples in the past of how they did things and… what I should do to be like them.

I: *Okay, is there any other religious stuff that you read?*

R: Um, yeah… I read church magazines 'cause they have stories of how you can look at examples from life for direction and counsel.

I: *Are there any things you do because you are LDS or are different from your friends that are [of] different religions? For instance the way you use music, take care of yourself, use your talent and money, express yourself to others… fasting, giving money or service?*

R: Yeah, I do fast and we also give money to people who are less fortunate and we do not necessarily take drugs or anything because we know it's bad for us… We do not have sex before marriage or anything like that, and we keep our standards high.

I: *How often do you fast?*

R: Um, once a month, or if it happens or if I just need to enhance the meaning of my prayers.

I: *Okay, how often do you end up doing it would you say?*

R: Um…I do it once a month regularly and I do it in case of any family conflict or I need some guidance.

I: *How do you feel about going to church? You go to church every week you said, right?*

R: Uh-huh.

I: *Okay, what does attending church do for your faith?*

R: It helps it by understanding that there is someone to care for you… There is like people that love the Gospel as well.

Traditionally, Hispanic families have shared an essential spirituality that reflects their ultimate dependence on God. This spirituality sees the divine as very close at hand, a constant companion in daily life. Daily prayers and devotions contribute to the way children are socialized into their families, informing the way they relate to God, nature, and other people. Today, Hispanic families demonstrate a greater diversity of expressions in their spirituality. Table 4.6 presents some of those expressions as found in the responses to the NSYR survey.

Table 4.6 – Religious practices in Hispanic families (percentages)

	Teen Religion			Teen Religious Type*			
	Catholic	Protestant	No Religion	Committed	Engaged	Sporadic	Disengaged
Regular religious practices at home	N=278	N=94	N=40	N=47	N=172	N=82	N=32
Give thanks before or after mealtimes	40	69	43	90	49	29	19
Pray together with parents, other than at meals	42	70	20	86	54	29	8
Talk about God, prayer, the Scriptures at least weekly	43	76	40	100	47	29	17
Parent prays for teen daily	72	84	51	86	77	60	44
Frequency of religious service attendance							
Once a week or more	37	57	0	100	70	0	0
One to three times a month	20	18	3	0	30	20	0
Many times a year	11	10	0	0	0	17	0
A few times a year	20	14	11	0	0	62	16
Never	12	1	86	0	0	0	84
Attends church with:							
Both parents	50	53	0	48	64	32	5
Only one parent	22	32	2	39	25	32	0
Neither parent	8	7	0	13	10	7	0
Never attends	20	8	98	0	0	28	95
Religious practices in the last year (Catholics only)				N=10**	N=120	N=61	N=10**
Religious pilgrimage, procession, or way of the cross	19	N/A	N/A	60	23	8	16
Prayed a rosary, novena, or to a special saint	44	N/A	N/A	60	54	26	21
Celebrated the Virgin Mary (i.e. Guadalupe)	57	N/A	N/A	75	63	43	21
Has a sacred image or altar at home	58	N/A	N/A	90	61	47	21
Extended family members at teen's church (attenders only)	N=235	N=83	N=12**	N=41	N=158	N=58	N=12**
0	43	45	75	35	45	59	78
1 to 3	15	21	8	31	18	12	9
4 to 9	20	22	17	21	16	11	9
10 or more	23	12	0	13	21	17	4

* See the Appendix on page 361 for definitions of the adolescent religious types.

** With only 10 to 12 respondents, these results have a sampling error of ±15%.

Religious practices at home

The NSYR survey asked the teens and their parents about some typical activities for Christian families: giving thanks to God before or after meals, family prayer at other times, talking about spiritual subjects as a family, and how often the parents pray for their adolescent children. On all of these measures, the Hispanic Protestant families showed significantly higher activity rates than their Catholic counterparts. In fact, on two of the measures, the families of the Catholic teens were not significantly than those of the non-religious teens.

Several of these practices were used as criteria to help sort the teens into the four religious types (see the Appendix on page 361 for a full explanation of the differences between the religious types), so it is not surprising that the religiously involved teens engage in them at home, while the religiously "sporadic" and "disengaged" teens do not. In any case, it is interesting that many Latino parents make it a point to pray for their children every day, even if there is very little other evidence of a living faith in the home or the family routines. In their book on Hispanic Seventh-day Adventists in North America, Johny Ramírez and Edwin Hernández mention that "praying for one's children is important, but praying with them is crucial."[6] Teens have a greater opportunity to mature in their faith when parents engage with them in open dialog about spiritual experiences, doubts of faith, and Jesus' life, mission, and teachings, rather than telling them what to do and what to believe in a dogmatic fashion.

Family and cultural impact on religious service attendance

Chapter 1, pages 20-23 and Chapter 3, pages 85-88 explored in detail the religious service attendance of Hispanic adolescents, as well as the impact of parental religious affiliation on the religious identity of their teenage children; that information will not be repeated here. As with the religious practices at home, attendance at worship services was far more frequent among Latino/a Protestants than it was among Latino/a Catholics. In fact, 32% of the Hispanic Catholic teens said they went to church a few times a year or never, compared to just 15% for their Protestant peers.

Does this mean that Catholic families are less serious about their faith than Protestant families? The answer to this question is: yes and no. With nearly three times as many Hispanic Catholics as Hispanic Protestants in the survey, there were far more religiously "engaged" and "committed" Catholics than Protestants among the Hispanic teens surveyed. Because Catholicism has been the dominant form of Christianity in Latin America for 500 years, there are many Hispanic families that identify themselves as

Catholic out of a sense of cultural or family identity that only manifests itself minimally in their lives. With no cultural inertia reinforcing a Protestant identity, Latino/a teens who were raised in non-practicing Protestant families tend to say that they are simply not religious. As an example, two of the five non-religious Hispanic teens interviewed in the NSYR were raised in Protestant churches.

On the other hand, Catholicism is integral to the identity of many Latino families that are very active in their faith communities. Chapter 3 showed that cultural and religious dissonance with the non-Hispanic teens in their parish may sometimes discourage the adolescents in these families from participating in their parish youth ministry programs. In fact, a significant proportion of the most active Latino Catholic parents in the U.S. are really struggling to pass their faith to the next generation. Their efforts are manifested in the fact that 67% of religiously "engaged" and "committed" Hispanic Catholic teens in the survey attended religious services with both parents, compared to 62% for their Protestant counterparts.

Practices of popular Catholicism

The phrase "popular Catholicism" is used to describe a variety of devotional practices that are common among Catholics of Latin American heritage, but which are not part of the official liturgy of the Catholic Church. These practices include novenas (nine-day prayer rituals), rosaries, pilgrimages, lighting candles, wearing scapulars or religious medals, the use of holy water, the blessing of homes and cars, and many others. The NSYR survey included questions about four such practices, but they were only asked of the adolescents who identified themselves as Catholic.

Since these devotional practices are generally conducted as a family or in small groups, the results of the survey indicate that Latino families in the U.S. continue cultivating practices of popular Catholicism. Among religiously "committed" Hispanic teens, the devotions are especially popular, and the level of participation decreases progressively with decreased religious involvement. Nevertheless, the practices are still alive in the homes of even the religiously "sporadic" and "disengaged" teens, most of whom do not go to church. The NSYR personal interviews suggest that many Latino/a adolescents do not really know the meaning of these practices; only four of the 16 Catholic Hispanics interviewed actually spoke about rosaries, holy water, or other devotional practices when they were asked in general about their religious practices, and one of them only mentioned the rosary to say she does not use it:

Dialog 4.9 – 18 year-old Hispanic Catholic female from the West:

I: *What religion, if any, do you consider yourself to be now?*

R: I would have to consider myself Catholic, because my mom would consider me to be Catholic. I was baptized, you know, in a Catholic church, and things like that. But I don't, you know like practice it you know.

I: *What are your own religious beliefs?*

R: I don't really have religious beliefs. Like when I pray, I pray to God, because you know, I was brought up to pray to God. And like, usually when I just pray to him, it's just like, oh, you know, like just like a certain, help me, you know, take care of my family and things like that... Not like, oh I need this and that, you know. I never had that, and I don't light candles, I don't do things like that. I don't pray to the rosary and stuff.

I: *How involved or active would you say you are in religion or spirituality?*

R: All I do is pray. I don't like, I don't go to church or anything like that.

I: *How important do you think your religion is in your life?*

R: I think it's important, because it kind of gives you a sense of what you're working for, you know. Like kind of like, oh, I have to be good. It's like, why be good if you don't have a reason for it, and stuff like that. But it's like if you kind of like have a belief, it's kind of like you know, I believe in that. It makes me a person, it kind of like makes you who you are. That's my belief.

The religious role of extended families

Table 4.6 shows that the percentage of Hispanic teens with extended family members at their church goes higher as religious involvement increases, based on the teens' religious type. This correlation suggests that having extended family members nearby serves to enrich and deepen the religious commitment of Latino/a children and adolescents. The interviews reveal that Hispanic grandmothers in particular have an important role in the religious formation of their adolescent grandchildren. In fact, ten out of the 38 Hispanic teens interviewed specifically mentioned their grandmothers as religious influences in their lives. The following conversation offers an example of how the grandmothers make sacrifices on behalf of their grandchildren.

**Dialog 4.10 – 16 year-old Hispanic Baptist
female from the Northeast:**

I: *So... you didn't live with your mom when you were younger?*

R: Uh-uh. I moved in with my mother when I was twelve.

I: *And you're fifteen now?*

R: Uh-uh. Sixteen.

I: *Sixteen... So four years ago. And where were you living before?*

R: I was living with my grandmother...

I: *And how did it affect you when you weren't able to live with [your mother]?*

R: It didn't bother me much 'cause I went right straight out to the house with my grandmother. And I used to call her mom. I used to think that's my mother until I was like 9 or 10 years old... 'Cause I used to think my mother was my sister. So, then I found out that was my mother...

I: *And how was your relationship with your grandma when you were living with her?*

R: Oh, I love my grandmother. I love her more than my mother.

I: *Really?*

R: Yeah…

I: *Can you tell me about how you were raised religiously?*

R: Oh, my, I was raised Pentecostal. 'Cause my great-grandmother, she helped raise me with my grandmother, which is her daughter. So, it was like she was Pentecostal and I would have to go to church with her. I still do once in a while. But it was just like I felt, I'm not… Like I am religious, but I just don't like that you have to wear skirts all the time, and can't wear pants. And it's just like you gotta be plain, like you can't wear no kind of jewelry, nothing. No earrings, just skirts and dresses. And I tell my great grandmother that I'm uncomfortable with that, and she was like, "I respect that."

I: *But you were raised Pentecostal?*

R: Uh-huh [yes].

I: *And um, what is your mom?*

R: She's Pentecostal. All of them's Pentecostal. That's what I grew up with.

Family dynamics in the process of acculturation

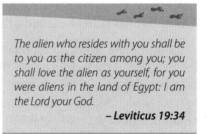

The alien who resides with you shall be to you as the citizen among you; you shall love the alien as yourself, for you were aliens in the land of Egypt: I am the Lord your God.
– Leviticus 19:34

In order to develop an effective ministry with Hispanic teens, it is necessary to reflect on the dynamics of generational diversity among Hispanics in the United States. Chapter 1 indicated that 72% of Hispanics ages 13 to 17 living in the United States in 2003 (the year of the NSYR survey) had at least one foreign-born parent, and 26% of the teens themselves were born in another country. Given this reality, many youth ministers are asking: What can I do for the Hispanic adolescents in my community to help them integrate into our youth ministry programs?

Before this question can be answered, it is necessary to understand the process of acculturation and how it relates to the religious and social development of Latino families. The analysis that follows demonstrates the need for youth ministry teams and programs that help Hispanic and mainstream teens to understand and overcome the naturally conflictive situations in which they find themselves. It also sheds light on the difficulties that immigrant and second-generation adolescents may have when participating in youth groups where the majority of the members are of the mainstream culture.

Culture, enculturation, and acculturation: some definitions

The Blackwell Dictionary of Sociology defines *culture* as "the accumulated store of symbols, ideas, and material products associated with a social system, whether it be an entire society or a family."[7] At a practical level, culture creates a shared identity and establishes the boundaries of a human group by defining patterns of behavior that allow individuals to feel confident in their interactions with other members of the group. Culture is both learned and in a constant process of being created as it is passed from generation to generation.

The elements of a culture can be described as forming five distinct layers; access to the deeper layers is generally dependent on familiarity and competence with the cultural elements in the more superficial layers, as shown in Diagram 4.1.

- The *visible aspects* of a culture form the first layer, which includes styles of dress, music, technology, housing, tools, and foods.

- *Traditions and customs* are the parameters for conducting daily life and family relations. Social norms in personal and business interactions, the meaning of gestures and body language, and the way special events in life are celebrated are all part of the second layer.

- The third layer of culture consists of the attitudes, habits, and assumptions about time, work, and family life that are integrated into a coherent *system of values* to organize and prioritize the activities of daily life.

- Social *institutions* that direct the activities of daily life and organize stages in the life cycle form the fourth layer. Schools, churches, governmental institutions and systems, sports, and the economy are all examples of cultural institutions.

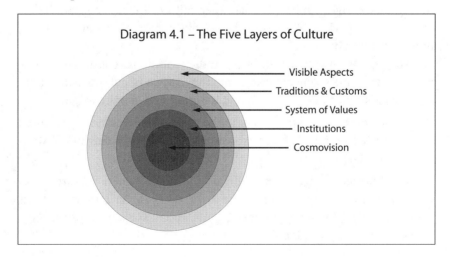

Diagram 4.1 – The Five Layers of Culture

Visible Aspects
Traditions & Customs
System of Values
Institutions
Cosmovision

- The *cosmovision* or worldview makes up the deepest layer of culture. It is the underlying framework by which a person interprets the meaning of life and the significance of particular events.

The use of language cuts across all five layers of culture. At its most superficial level, language is used to discuss or explain objects and events that can be directly experienced between two or more people. At the deeper levels, spoken and written communications are often used to express and reinforce the traditions and customs of a culture; they are grounded in the assumption of shared values so that meaning can be implied without explicitly stating what is intended; and social institutions play an important role in defining and contextualizing the meaning of words and establishing patterns of communication. At the receiving end of the communication process, language is interpreted from the context of the cultural cosmovision, which is presumed to be held in common.

While most people can readily talk about the visible aspects of their culture, each succeeding layer becomes more and more difficult to express in words. Interactions between people of different cultures are often awkward and subject to misunderstanding because the deeper layers of culture are not shared—even though they may be speaking the same language. As a result, the communication is interpreted based on assumptions that do not apply, so the intended meaning gets lost even though there may be openness and sensitivity toward the acceptance of cultural differences.

Cultural competence refers to the ability to interact comfortably and confidently with others in a particular cultural framework by appropriately utilizing or referencing the assumptions, customs, values, and symbols of the culture. When people communicate with others of their own culture, this is usually done intuitively and without any self-conscious effort. However, when dealing with people of another culture, it takes conscious effort and years of experience to master the use of the symbols, values, customs, and touchstones of the culture.

No one is born with a culture, but rather culture is acquired over time by exposure to the social environment. The process of cultural acquisition from birth is called *enculturation,* and it occurs in two basic ways:

- *Endoculturation* occurs mainly in the home, where culture is acquired primarily through repeated exposure to the values, behaviors, and actions of the parents.

- *Socialization* occurs mainly outside the home, where culture is acquired through repeated exposure to the values, behaviors, and actions presented in the media, in peer groups, and in social institutions such as schools and churches.[8]

In traditional monocultural societies, endoculturation and socialization support and reinforce one another to transmit cultural values, norms, traditions, and religious faith from one generation to the next. In the United States today, the pace of cultural change has accelerated due to the influence of the mass media and the progress of science and technology. In addition, the separation of age groups in many of our social institutions (including schools and churches) tends to accentuate the cultural influence of peer groups among the young. Consequently, the endoculturation teens receive from their parents is sometimes at odds with the socialization they are receiving from their peers, the media, etc.. This cultural divergence has been called a *generation gap,* and it often causes adolescents to question the values they are receiving from their parents—including their religious beliefs and practices.

When people find themselves in a new cultural setting, some of the daily life behaviors and assumptions about the world that they developed from childhood no longer apply. The process of developing cultural competence in this new setting is called *acculturation.*[9] Initially, it is common to experience frustration from dealing with people who do not behave "as they should" because they are operating from different customs, assumptions, or values. This frustration is called *cultural dissonance,* also known as culture shock, and it can easily be generalized into ethnocentric judgments about the people of the other culture. When people of two or more cultures live in close proximity to one another, these experiences may develop into attitudes or patterns of ethnic distrust, prejudice, and discrimination.

On the other hand, when two distinct cultures are brought into regular contact with one another, both the people and the cultures themselves may be transformed over time by integrating or rejecting elements of the other culture. The degree of reciprocity in this exchange is largely dependent on the number of people from each culture involved and their relative power or prestige in the social environment. *Mestizaje* is the transformation and integration of two or more cultures over an extended period of time, especially through intermarriage, so that a new culture and a new people are formed.

For Latino/a adolescents in the U.S.—especially among the 72% that has a foreign-born parent—the generation gap between parents and children tends to be compounded by the confusing and often contradictory cultural cues the adolescents receive from the Latino cultures of their parents and the dominant culture of the social environment. As a result, it often takes Hispanic teens longer than their peers of the dominant culture to develop confidence in dealing with adults of either culture. As they struggle to make sense of their culturally ambiguous world, frequent experiences of mistaken assumptions and the frustration of trying to reconcile the sometimes incompatible values systems of their families, their schools, their friends, and their churches tend to weaken and confuse their personal identity and contribute to a lack of self-confidence and to low self-esteem.

A model of acculturation

The reasons for immigration and the life circumstances of each immigrant group affect the process of acculturation at a personal and social level. For example, the acculturation of African-Americans in a context of racism and slavery was very different from that of European immigrants, who experienced milder sociocultural contrasts because the initial discrimination against them was not based on racism. By the middle of the 20th century, the many immigrant European cultures had undergone a process of *mestizaje* with the Anglo-American culture to form the mainstream culture of the United States.

In contrast, the Latino cultures that had been in North America since the 1500s did not participate in the process of *mestizaje* to the same degree as the European cultures did. Furthermore, Latino immigration has continued constantly throughout the history of the United States, and we are presently in the midst of a new wave of immigration from all parts of Latin America. The processes of enculturation and acculturation among young Latino/as in the U.S. today are different for each person based on their particular history, culture of origin, and new social environment. Nonetheless, they will invariably have a major impact on the development of their personality, how they live their faith, and their experience of the church.

It is beyond the scope of this book to describe the historical, cultural, and social characteristics of the many Latino groups in the United States. Even so, youth ministry leaders should take the time to learn about the national origins of the Latino/as in their community, as well as the historical and social forces that have brought them to this country. There are some excellent resources listed at the end of this chapter for further study. In any case, the pattern of acculturation followed by each person depends on the frequency with which they interact with people from the mainstream culture and their culture of origin, and how motivated they are to improve their relationships with each group.

The four modes of acculturation among immigrants—as shown in Diagram 4.2—express the combined level of cultural competence in both the ethnic culture of origin and the new host culture:[10]

- *Biculturalism* occurs when adults who were raised in one culture migrate to a place with a new host culture, where they slowly become culturally competent through frequent or intentional interactions with the people of that culture. They also interact with people of their own

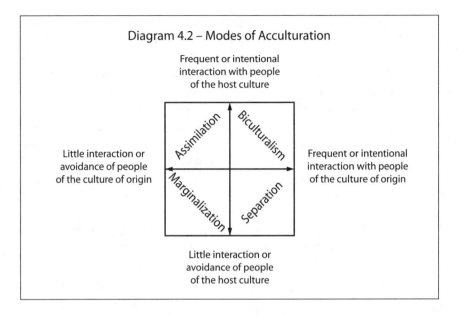

Diagram 4.2 – Modes of Acculturation

Frequent or intentional interaction with people of the host culture

Little interaction or avoidance of people of the culture of origin

Frequent or intentional interaction with people of the culture of origin

Assimilation

Biculturalism

Marginalization

Separation

Little interaction or avoidance of people of the host culture

culture, either in their new location or by maintaining ties with people in their homeland, so that they do not lose their competence in their native culture. Biculturalism may also occur when a child is raised in an environment in which they have regular interactions with people of both cultures.

- *Assimilation* takes place among immigrants when they have an intensive participation in the host culture and little or no interaction with anyone from their culture of origin for an extended period of time. Little by little, the cosmovision and values of the ethnic culture are replaced by those of the host culture, and the person adapts to the new institutions, traditions, and customs. At the end of this process, the person may be so changed that they would experience cultural dissonance, or reverse culture shock, on return to their culture of origin.

- *Separation* only occurs when a significant number of people of a particular immigrant culture are living in close proximity to one another, within a broader social context of the host culture. Immigrants in the separation mode adapt to their new location by avoiding interactions with people of the host culture and forming a tight community with others of their own culture. As a result of this separation, they do not develop cultural competence for the host culture. Children raised in such communities may experience cultural dissonance in ways similar to an immigrant when they start to venture beyond the ethnic enclave.

- *Marginalization* means that a person does not feel comfortable interacting with people of either culture. This situation may develop when a family moves to an area where there are few people of their own ethnic culture, and due to experiences of discrimination, xenophobia, or their own inability to adapt to the linguistic and cultural differences, they do not feel confident when interacting with people of the host culture. In order to avoid uncomfortable social encounters, they become isolated or take on an oppositional stance toward both cultures, thereby making it harder for them to develop competence in either one.

  Among marginalized adolescents, substance abuse sometimes provides momentary relief of the psychological pain of isolation. If they find a peer group of other marginalized individuals, they may choose to associate primarily with them in gangs and engage in risky antisocial behaviors as a protest against the society they blame for their feelings of alienation. In a sense, they take control of their social environment by creating an alternative subculture in opposition to the cultures around them.

Acculturation in the second generation

The process of acculturation is more complex for the children of immigrants and for children who migrated with their families to a new host culture at a young age. Recent studies have shown that acculturation in the second generation usually falls into one of four distinct patterns, depending on the respective modes of acculturation of the parents and their children. These four patterns are summarized in Diagram 4.3.[11]

- *Consonant assimilation processes* occur when both the parents and the children favor the development of cultural competence in the host culture over the ethnic culture. When the ethnic community has little social capital, the parents may not see an advantage in fostering the ethnic culture in their children. In other cases, there may not be opportunities for parents to connect their children with other families of their culture of origin, so they focus on preparing their children to integrate into the mainstream society, even as they themselves are in the process of becoming culturally competent. In these situations, the children experience parental, peer, and social affirmation of the host culture, and they may see negative stereotyping of their culture of origin.

  While the parents may become bicultural, the outcome in the second generation is usually the loss of the parents' language, unawareness of their ethnic history and cultural heritage, and feelings of discomfort in interactions with the ethnic community. If the children feel acceptance and belonging in the host culture, they will generally

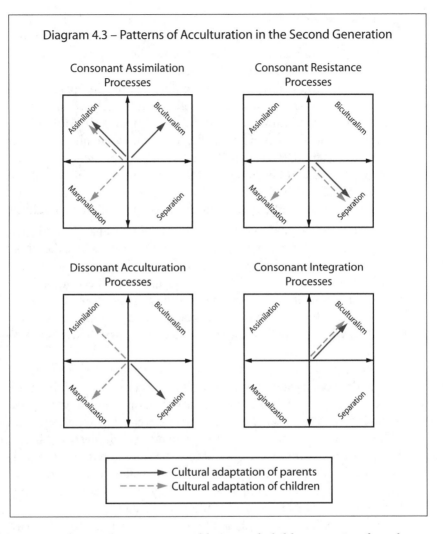

Diagram 4.3 – Patterns of Acculturation in the Second Generation

assimilate without major problems, and children coming from lower socioeconomic classes may experience upward mobility. However, if experiences of discrimination and prejudice predominate, the children may be pushed into a marginalization mode.

- *Consonant resistance processes* occur when both parents and children engage primarily in social relationships with people of their own culture. In some areas, such as large parts of Texas and California, this occurs simply because the vast majority of the local population is Latino/a. In other areas, experiences of discrimination based on race, ethnicity, or socioeconomic class may contribute to the tendency to avoid interactions with people of the host culture. Either way, socialization is provided mainly within the ethnic community, and the children experience parental and peer affirmation of the ethnic culture over the host culture. Some socialization through schools and other institutions of the host culture is unavoidable, but even that may be met with an attitude of resistance on the part of the children.

Although the parents may be comfortable relating primarily to people of their own culture, this pattern often leads their children to low educational attainment, low social mobility or downward mobility, and continued discomfort in interactions with people of the host culture. These children are generally bilingual, yet they tend to develop a limited historical understanding of both cultures, and they are at risk of being marginalized because their disjointed socialization may not provide the opportunities to become fully competent in either culture.

- *Dissonant acculturation processes* are similar to consonant assimilation processes in social location: they usually occur in places where the ethnic community is weak or has low social capital. Consequently, the primary socialization of the children is accomplished through peer and institutional affirmation of the host culture over the ethnic culture. At the same time, the parents either find it impossible to develop competence in the host culture because of their life circumstances, or they choose not to do so for their own reasons.

  The disparity of linguistic and cultural competence between parents and children often leads to role reversals in the family when children are asked to translate for their monolingual parents at school or in business transactions. In addition, the children may develop low self-esteem and feelings of embarrassment about their parents or their lifestyle at home. Many eventually choose to fully embrace the worldview of the host culture and abandon their ethnic community and language. Others retain a degree of competence in their parents' language and culture, but they feel most comfortable in the host culture and language.

  For the children's assimilation to be successful and lead to upward mobility, they generally need healthy adult role models and personal support during the cultural transition. Without these benefits, they are at a higher risk of becoming marginalized, which may lead them to engage in self-defeating behaviors such as substance abuse, violence, sexual promiscuity, and attempted suicide.

- *Consonant integration processes* occur when parents and children are regularly exposed to both the ethnic culture and the host culture, and they develop competence in both. For this to happen, the ethnic community generally needs to have a high level of social capital so that it can make strategic accommodations to the host culture from a position of strength. The ethnic community is then able to be the primary agent of socialization for the children, even in social institutions such as church and school, and there are parental, peer, and institutional affirmations of both the ethnic culture and the host culture.

The outcome produced by this pattern is often called *integration without assimilation*. In this case, the traits of the second generation are: bilingualism, high self-esteem, preservation of cultural values, upward mobility, awareness of ethnic history and cultural heritage, and a selective embracing of elements from both cultural worldviews. In other words, the children effectively become bicultural. Of the four acculturation patterns, this is the only one in which marginalization is not likely to occur.

While the acculturation patterns described above help to illuminate the experiences of Latino/a adolescents being raised between two cultures, they should not be taken as absolute predictors of life outcomes for these teens. Exceptions to these patterns may occur based on the gifts, limitations, personality traits, and life circumstances of a given person. In addition, many people who did not develop a particular cultural competence when they were younger find the motivation as young adults to become competent in either the host culture or their parents' culture of origin.

Implications for youth ministry with Latino/a adolescents

Because the vast majority of Latino/a teens in the U.S. today are either immigrants themselves or the children of immigrants, their acculturation pattern plays a prominent role in their religious formation. In most cases, the language and cultural expressions of the faith in Latin America are quite distinct from those in the United States, even though the religious tradition may nominally be the same. Part of the challenge of cultural transition for Latino/a adolescents is to negotiate the differences within their religious tradition and faith community.

For Hispanic adolescents following the patterns of consonant assimilation or consonant integration, this is generally not a problem: they can simply integrate into the mainstream youth ministry programming, as long as they feel comfortable with their mainstream peers. However, providing pastoral accompaniment and faith formation to Latino/a adolescents following the consonant resistance and dissonant acculturation patterns tends to be much more challenging. In both cases, the cultural dissonance they experience may go to the very heart of their religious identity.

For example, some Hispanic teens will find it difficult to relate to the religious expressions of the local faith community at worship, whether the services are conducted in English or in Spanish. The rejection of their parents' culture in dissonant acculturation may also extend to a rejection of their parents' religious faith, such that the teens do not want to have anything to do with church—or at least not their parents' church. In the consonant resistance pattern, the teens may be content to participate in worship services in Spanish, but they are likely to find participating in youth ministry programs with teens of the host culture to be uncomfortable because of the cultural dissonance they experience with them—even though they speak English.

For the Hispanic Catholic children whose parents are charismatic or very traditional in their religious devotions, especially those who are accustomed to attending prayer meetings with their parents, there is the additional risk that they will find the parish youth group to be too secular. Unless the youth ministry team is very aware of the cultural differences in religious expression, spirituality, values, and worldview, the youth ministry programs likely will not support or connect with the religious formation the teens have received from their parents. Socioeconomic differences and ethnocentric attitudes on both sides can create additional barriers to participation for these *culturally squeezed* Latino/a teens, and they will generally choose not to participate in the youth ministry programs. Even in areas that are predominantly Hispanic, the linguistic and cultural differences between recent immigrants and U.S.-born Latino/as can be problematic.

For these reasons, youth ministry leaders who are not bicultural should adopt a missionary approach to ministry with the Hispanic adolescents in their community. This means that they must depend heavily on adult and adolescent Hispanic leaders in the team to design and carry out the pastoral efforts intended to reach the Latino/a teens that are not comfortable in settings grounded in the host culture. They should then follow the lead of the team in deciding whether to create separate programs for the marginalized and Spanish-dominant Hispanic adolescents, or simply adapt the content and style of the existing programs, and engage all of the teens in a process of cultural awareness and appreciation, to make the Latino/as feel more welcome.

Pastoral recommendations

Working with Hispanic teenagers can be very challenging, because the youth ministry leaders need to have a thorough knowledge of the Latino/a teens' diverse family structures and

These are the things you must insist on and teach. Let no one despise your youth, but set the believers an example in speech and conduct, in love, in faith, in purity. Until I arrive, give attention to the public reading of scripture, to exhorting, to teaching. Do not neglect the gift that is in you.
– 1 Timothy 4:11-14

the constant tensions these adolescents face in their daily lives. Add to that the social, cultural, and religious dimensions of their still-emerging identity, and it becomes clear that ministry with Latino/a teens provides endless opportunities to exercise innovation and creativity. The following recommendations offer some starting points to help youth ministry teams improve the quality of their pastoral care of Hispanic adolescents and their families.

1. Get to know the Hispanic families and their living situations

Working with Latino/a adolescents in the United States requires home visitations, building relationships with their parents, seeing the teens in their neighborhood, and understanding the hopes, fears, and needs of their parents. Do the teens have to take care of younger siblings at home? Do they have transportation to youth ministry gatherings? Are registration fees an obstacle to their participation in retreats, workshops, conferences, excursions, etc.? Who are the main promoters of faith in their homes? What religious goals and ideals do the parents have for their children? How do they practice their faith at home? The answers to these and many other questions are not usually found in registration forms.

For Hispanic teens, belonging to a family is an important part of human development and contributes to growth in Christian maturity. Youth ministers should make it a top priority to provide religious and pastoral support to the families. This means asking for the parents and other relatives of the teens to become involved in the ministry through consultation, as volunteers, or simply by giving them tips on how they can follow up on a youth ministry event at home. It also means constant communication with the parents to discover their needs, and providing pastoral care and workshops to help parents in their role as the religious leaders of the family. More and better materials for Hispanic parents to use with their adolescent children at home are urgently needed. These family resources will improve the religious formation of the whole family, while also improving the bonds of family unity and love.

2. Involve Latino/a adults who can serve as role models

As Hispanic teens work through the process of acculturation, they need to have contact with adults from the faith community who have successfully integrated their faith and their culture in a way that makes sense in the religious and cultural context of the United States. Such adults can talk to the Hispanic adolescents about the struggles they are experiencing, thus diminishing their sense of isolation and providing hope for a way forward. These role models can also help other youth ministry leaders to be more aware of cultural differences, seeing them as a source of enrichment for everyone and not a weakness or a defect.

3. Develop Hispanic leadership

The leadership team for youth ministry should reflect the diversity of the families in the faith community—among the youth leaders and the adult leaders alike. Because Latino/as are currently underrepresented in youth ministry leadership in both Catholic and Protestant churches, there needs to be an intentional effort to invite them into leadership. Youth ministry coordinators should be careful to invite individuals that are at different stages of acculturation and who come from a variety of Latino cultures and generations, if such diversity exists in the faith community. While it may not always be appropriate to have parents serving as leaders in the youth ministry programs, the channels of communication with parents need to be open so that their concerns for the religious formation of their children can be heard and addressed.

4. Invest in the cultural competence of the youth ministry team

Youth ministry leaders should be able to recognize the pattern of acculturation in each Hispanic family and understand how it affects the religious and social development of their adolescent members. In most communities, there are counselors or educators who can provide workshops on intercultural sensitivity, cultural competence, and the sociocultural contours of the local Hispanic community. If not, it is always possible to conduct listening sessions with adults and teens in the community that are dealing with cultural transitions.

The youth ministry team should be prepared to offer programming alternatives if cultural or religious dissonance becomes an obstacle to Hispanic teens' participation in groups that are intended to be for all of the teens in the faith community. However, the first requirement is to be able to recognize the signs of cultural dissonance so that appropriate responses can be developed. An adequate assessment of the cultural and religious diversity in the community, together with an awareness of the potential pitfalls that may arise out of the sometimes conflictual acculturation processes within immigrant families, will help the youth ministry team to develop programs that are culturally appropriate for all the teens in their care.

5. Value the religious and cultural heritage of the Hispanic teens

Many Hispanic teens have learned traditional religious devotions at home from their mothers, grandmothers, or other family members. For them, culture and religion are not two separate entities, but a single reality that informs the way they experience both the sacred and the secular in their lives. Through the process of acculturation, these teenagers will incorporate many elements of the mainstream culture into their lives, but preserving the value of their religious and cultural heritage is an integral part of their development into mature young Christians. Youth ministry should help young people to develop a critical consciousness of their own culture and that of others, as well as to discover and appreciate the personal, religious, and cultural dimensions of their own identity.

6. Recognize the importance of the language

In many faith communities, there is an assumption that if an adolescent can speak English, he or she ought to participate in youth ministry programs offered in that language. The reasons for this vary from place to place, but some of the frequently mentioned concerns include: the Latino/a teens need to learn English anyway, so providing youth ministry in English will help them in other areas of life; most of them prefer to speak English with their peers; there are not enough resources in the community to provide duplicate programs; and separating the language groups creates a system of segregation that helps to perpetuate racial and ethnic stereotypes, prejudice, and discrimination.

Although it is true that the vast majority of Hispanic teens can speak English, it is also true that millions of young Latino/as received their early religious education at home in Spanish—and in many cases at church as well. When these children are suddenly asked to participate in youth ministry programs in English as adolescents, they often find that it does not relate to the spiritual and psychocultural ethos of their religious upbringing. Furthermore, their parents may have difficulty understanding and supporting what is happening in the program. In some communities, the teens are even asked to attend particular worship services in English every week, thereby dividing the families or forcing parents to attend services they do not understand. On the other hand, when youth ministry programs provide worship and religious formation experiences that connect linguistically and culturally with Latino/a teens, they will feel the validation of their religious upbringing at home and a sense of spiritual nurturing in the faith community.

Depending on the demographic makeup of the adolescents in the community and the experience of the youth ministry team, it may not always be necessary to provide youth ministry programs in Spanish. In some cases, it is enough to incorporate a bilingual approach in which teens are able to form small discussion groups in English and Spanish, especially if the leaders are prepared to incorporate the religious traditions, prayers, and music of the local Latino community into the program.

Unfortunately, bilingual or bicultural programs often run the risk of creating uncomfortable cultural dissonance for everyone, not just the

Hispanics—especially if the leaders are not fully competent in both cultures. When this risk results in large numbers of teens choosing not to participate, it would be better to offer several alternative small groups or programs grounded in the language, spirituality, and culture of the participants. In this way it becomes possible to reach many more of the adolescents in the community.

In some parts of the country, it may be necessary to offer programs in Spanish for no other reason than the fact that the pool of available Latino/a adults who can serve as leaders do not speak English. Before deciding whether to offer programs in Spanish or bilingually, each faith community should assess the linguistic and cultural needs of the teens, as well as the abilities of the leaders and the concerns of the parents, in order to develop the best possible solution.

7. Work with the parents of the family

For many Hispanic families, the search for work has led to a separation from the support of the extended family, and parents often do not have the skills they need to establish a healthy home environment for their children without the extra support. This is especially true for single-parent families, which are quite common in Latino communities. Immigrant parents also need to be informed about the U.S. norms regarding child abuse, and instructed in the use of positive discipline as an alternative to the generally accepted disciplinary measures in their culture of origin.

Churches provide a valuable service when they offer parenting classes or workshops in both English and Spanish, making sure that they are accessible for people who work nights or weekends. It might be beneficial to bring in culturally competent professionals to discuss issues such as discipline, oppositional behavior, communication, conflict, self-esteem, and healthy adolescent development. Immigrant parents could also benefit from discussions about how to be more effective advocates for their children's education, and how to manage the dynamics of acculturation within the family. Many community organizations already offer parenting classes in low-income neighborhoods; it may be possible to establish an alliance that is mutually beneficial by offering the use of church facilities for these classes.

8. Encourage the young people to fulfill their family obligations

Some of the most religiously committed Hispanic teens appear to be using their participation at church as a refuge from the problems they experience at home. Adult youth ministry leaders should watch for the signs of this phenomenon among their adolescent leaders, and be prepared to offer the family pastoral accompaniment or a referral for counseling so that they can deal with their conflicts at home in an appropriate way.

In addition, while it is important to inform adolescents about their legal rights when their parents are abusive, it is also important from a Christian point of view to provide information about the obligations of children toward their parents and other family members. For example, in many Latino families, all of the children are expected to make a contribution to the welfare of the family as they are able, even if it means sacrificing certain personal goals or activities. Before making a judgment that Hispanic parents are placing unreasonable burdens on their teenage children, youth ministers should be prepared to assess the reality of the family within its cultural context.

9. Accompany Hispanic teens in their search for hope

As a result of the socioeconomic environment in many inner cities where large numbers of young Latino/as live, and the low social and economic capital of their families, many Latino/a teens are exposed to violence, discrimination, and seemingly insurmountable obstacles on a daily basis. In their struggle for a sense of identity and purpose in life, they need people who can help them deal constructively with their solitude, anxiety, fear, frustration, anger, sadness, and confusion. Youth ministry is called to give hope to those who have lost it, and to open new horizons of opportunity so that they may discover the strength and comfort of God's loving presence. These things will only happen when the teens really trust their youth ministers, and that trust is won by staying with them when the going gets tough.

10. Attend to the recent immigrants and their families

In virtually every state in the country, families from Latin America continue to arrive in search of work and a better life. These families represent a pastoral challenge because their adolescent members speak little English, and they may not be enrolled in school. Instead, they work to help support their families in whatever job they can find; some move from place to place as migrant agricultural workers. The challenge for the faith community is to offer short-term missionary programs that serve this segment of the Hispanic adolescent population in Spanish, so that their relationship with God is not adversely affected by their living conditions. More stable residents should also be provided opportunities to develop their gifts as leaders. Far too often, these families are forgotten in the pastoral planning of parishes, congregations, and dioceses, yet the steadfast faith that sustains them amid the most difficult of circumstances in a foreign country is a powerful testimony for the whole church.

Summary

The NSYR survey and interviews reveal that Hispanic families are blessed with a deep sense of family commitment, although many have suffered through separations due to economic circumstances, struggles with vice or addiction, or the failure of a marriage. Living in the United States poses many challenges to Latino families as they work through processes of linguistic and cultural transition with limited economic and academic resources. Because of cultural and linguistic differences, youth ministry leaders require intense preparation in order to help Hispanic adolescents and their families face these challenges. Nevertheless, faith communities are ideally positioned to offer real help to Latino families in ways that other social service organizations and institutions cannot. The mission is clear, but many youth ministry leaders still do not have the skills and knowledge they need to build on the religious traditions and expressions the Hispanic teens received as young children in their families. It is hoped that this chapter will provide the motivation and direction needed to reverse that situation.

Questions for reflection

For youth ministers

1. Does the general demographic portrait of Hispanic families in the United States match what we see in our community? What is different?

2. How can we build on traditional Latin American values to strengthen the Hispanic families in our community?

3. Are there public or non-profit organizations serving Hispanic families in our area? What can we do to leverage or complement their efforts in our ministry?

4. Name ten Latino/a adults in the faith community who could serve as role models for our adolescent members. If needed, ask one or two Hispanic members of the community to help make the list. How can we get them involved in youth ministry?

5. Do the descriptions of culture and the processes of acculturation make sense? If not, ask an immigrant member of the faith community to read them and share his or her opinion.

6. What aspect of this chapter was most motivating or hopeful? What was most challenging or discouraging? What are we called to do about it?

7. How might we assess our church's current ministry with Hispanic adolescents and their families? List three priorities for improvement based on the insights from this chapter.

For parents of teenagers

1. Which findings help to illuminate my relationship with my son or daughter? What can I do to improve that relationship, or to help my child integrate culture and faith more deeply into his or her life.

2. What do I do to help my children mature in the use of their freedom? What might I do differently?

3. Do my children know that I love and accept them as they are, and that I have high hopes for what they can achieve? Do they know how important my faith is in my life?

Chapter 5:
The Moral Imperative of Latino/a Educational Investment

The Future is Now!

David Ramos, M.Div., M.S.W.

Dialog 5.1 – 17 year-old Hispanic Catholic male from the West:

I: *How much do you think about your future?*

R: A lot.

I: *What do you think about?*

R: How am I going to survive, you know, what kind of job am I going to get.

I: *What do you imagine you will do with your life when you are an adult?*

R: Um…you know go to a two-year community college and then a two-year university, and you know just get a good job. Get an apartment or house or something.

I: *How do you think your life is going to turn out?*

R: Good.

I: *Do you look to the future with hope or fear or?*

R: Both.

I: *Like in what ways, in what ways for hope and in what ways for fear?*

R: Hope like, you know, I hope I do good and I, you know, I graduate school and everything. And fear it's just like, you know, I don't know what might happen. I might get in trouble or I might not do as good as I think I'm going to do.

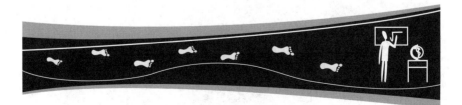

The Moral Imperative of Latino/a Educational Investment

One of the most important issues facing the Latino/a community is the issue of education, since education serves as the portal of opportunity for economic upward mobility and family stability. Concerns about education are even greater for young Hispanics, many of whom must overcome enormous challenges in order to continue their studies. Poverty, language barriers, racism, immigration status, family needs, urban violence, substance abuse, and the allure of gangs conspire to derail the educational aspirations of far too many young Hispanics today.

The prevailing educational statistics for Latino/as are daunting. In 2004, there was a 23.8% dropout rate among Hispanics between the ages of 16 and 24, compared to 6.8% for white and 11.8% for black individuals of the same age range.[1] Hispanic males fared significantly worse than Hispanic females, with a dropout rate of 28.5% compared to 18.5% for the young women. The high dropout rate for Hispanics is partly due to the higher dropout rates among Hispanic immigrants, many of whom come to the U.S. seeking work as young adults who have not completed the equivalent of a high school education. Nevertheless, Latino/a teens born in the United States are still more likely to drop out than their counterparts of any other race/ethnicity with the exception of Native Americans.[2]

What is needed is nothing short of a national campaign to promote education and academic excellence among Hispanic teenagers throughout our country. In this context, the National Study of Youth and Religion (NSYR) raises some interesting questions about the relationship between Hispanic teens' socioreligious backgrounds and their educational prospects. How do young Latino/as' faith traditions relate to their educational goals and accomplishments? How important is their parents' educational level for student achievement in the next generation? How does their economic status affect their educational prospects? How do Latino/a students' academic aspirations compare to those of other adolescents today? What role do mentors and authority figures play? What role does the church play in mentoring Latino/a teens toward academic achievement and excellence? The following reflections will attempt to address some of these issues.

NSYR findings

Parental educational attainment

The NSYR study shows that among white, black, and Hispanic adolescents, Hispanics had the largest number of parents with less than a high

> And now, my children, listen to me: happy are those who keep my ways. Hear instruction and be wise, and do not neglect it. Happy is the one who listens to me, watching daily at my gates, waiting beside my doors.
> **– Proverbs 8:32-34**

school education. Among Hispanics, 22% of the fathers had less than a high school education, compared to 4% of black and 5% of white fathers. Similarly, 28% of Hispanic mothers had less than a high school education, compared to 11% of black and 5% of white mothers. Among Hispanic parents, the Protestants reported significantly higher levels of education than the Catholics, while most of the parents of teens with no religion had education levels in the middle, having completed high school or some college. Especially notable is the relatively low number of fathers without a high school diploma among teens with no religion, nearly matching the high school graduation rate of the white parents. Furthermore, the average Hispanic mother's education surpassed that of the average Hispanic father, irrespective of their religious faith. In contrast, the white fathers generally had more education than the white mothers.

The impact of limited parental education on young Latino/as cannot be underestimated, especially in inner-city environments where many parents' work commitments prevent them from being able to supervise their children after school, and their education levels prevent them from being effective tutors even when they are at home. Low income levels associated

Table 5.1 – Parental educational attainment (percentages)

	Hispanic			White, Any Faith
	Catholic	Protestant	No Religion	
Education of resident father figure	N=278	N=94	N=40	N=2448
No resident father	28	31	36	17
Elementary or less	18	11	3	1
Some high school	10	9	3	4
High school graduate or GED	21	17	22	18
Vocational, AA, or some college	14	19	20	26
College graduate (BA or BS)	5	9	3	17
Master's degree (MA, MS, MDiv, etc.)	1	2	3	12
PhD or professional degree	2	4	0	4
Education of resident mother figure				
No resident mother	3	2	9	4
Elementary or less	17	7	9	1
Some high school	15	9	21	4
High school graduate or GED	27	28	29	23
Vocational, AA, or some college	26	39	27	35
College graduate (BA or BS)	6	7	0	22
Master's degree (MA, MS, MDiv, etc.)	5	7	3	8
PhD or professional degree	1	1	2	2

with limited parental education often leave Latino/a parents with few options other than living in the barrios where violence, drugs, and inferior schools are the norm. Latino/a young people are keenly aware of these challenges, even if they have found ways to overcome them, as the following conversation with a young man living in an inner-city area shows:

Dialog 5.2 – 19 year-old Hispanic Baptist male from the West:

I: *Where do your own views of right and wrong come from?*

R: From my upbringing.

I: *From the way your mom raised you?*

R: Yeah, the way she raised me. So it depends on how you were raised. If you were raised, I mean you ain't got to live in no suburban area to know what's right or wrong—to know what to do in life, to be successful in life, or whatever. If you were raised right, then you were just raised right...

I: *Could you just tell me a little bit what you mean by raised right?*

R: Uh, basically, um, like my mom, "Get home from school, get off your school clothes, get that books out, get ready for dinner." I mean, that type of stuff, don't let them hang out, run the streets, do what they want to do, that type of stuff. I mean you have to have like um, rules and regulations. Every parent should have their rules and regulations, and if you don't live by those rules and regulations, it will just lead you to the wrong way.

I: *Do you think that everybody should have the same sort of rules and regulations? Like your mom should have the same as somebody else?*

R: I don't think that 'cause everybody has different beliefs, and they're all... Like I said, everybody has different beliefs. Some parents don't believe in what my mom believes in. Like the hanging out... that's one of my mom's main beliefs. Get home, get out your school clothes, get ready to do your chores, do your homework, get ready for dinner, watch some TV, ready to start the day all over. Everybody's parents don't do that. Some people's parents would rather just... I mean there's two hard working parents out there and they don't have time to do that stuff, but somewhere in your life you have to find that time to be able to do that. If not, your child will end up like the trench coat mafia kid, or a rapist or a killer or in prison. And I mean it's all about you upbringing, if you're raised right then.

Chapter 1 reported that 72% of Hispanics ages 13 to 17 living in the United States in 2003 (the year of the NSYR survey) had at least one foreign-born parent. As young Hispanics become acculturated in English-dominant schools and neighborhoods, many do not become proficient Spanish speakers, which can exacerbate communication difficulties between foreign-born parents and their children. In other cases, young kids and teenagers serve as interpreters for their parents at school, at the bank, or in other environments. This imbalance of knowledge and cultural skills compounds the difficulties immigrant parents may experience in supervising their children's education, thereby contributing to the lower academic achievement of immigrant and second-generation Latino/a teens.

Table 5.2 – Type of school and educational goals (percentages)

	Hispanic			White, Any Faith	Hispanic Religious Type*			
	Catholic	Protestant	No Religion		Committed	Engaged	Sporadic	Disengaged
Currently attending	N=278	N=94	N=40	N=2448	N=47	N=172	N=82	N=32
Public school	89	84	96	86	88	89	98	87
Catholic/Christian private school	6	8	2	8	12	6	2	6
Home schooled or other	2	8	1	5	1	4	0	3
Not going to school	3	1	2	1	0	1	1	3
Importance of doing well in shcool (teen survey)								
Extremely important	51	54	52	46	66	54	46	44
Very important	35	35	43	38	31	33	37	43
Somewhat important	10	9	3	12	3	12	15	8
Importance of teen graduation from college (parent survey)								
Extremely important	66	66	55	57	65	64	69	78
Very important	32	29	41	30	26	32	26	22
Somewhat important	2	3	2	10	6	2	2	0
Not very or not at all important	~	2	2	2	2	2	3	0
Ideally how far would you like to go in school?								
High school or less	7	4	14	5	13	5	8	10
Vocational, AA or some college	10	9	10	6	10	11	6	10
College graduate (BA or BS)	66	62	53	62	57	65	75	44
Post-graduate (MA or higher)	15	18	21	22	15	15	9	30
Realistically, how far do you think you will go in school?								
High school or less	21	7	19	9	6	18	18	17
Vocational, AA or some college	11	14	5	9	14	12	9	10
College graduate (BA or BS)	53	49	28	59	46	54	60	29
Post-graduate (MA or higher)	11	13	26	17	19	11	6	38
Actual educational attainment at ages 25 to 29**	Hispanic, Any Faith							
Less than high school	38			6	---	---	---	---
High school graduate	31			28	---	---	---	---
Vocational, AA or some college	21			31	---	---	---	---
College graduate (BA or BS)	9			28	---	---	---	---
Post-graduate (MA or higher)	1			7	---	---	---	---

* See the Appendix on page 361 for definitions of the adolescent religious types.
** Taken from the U.S. Census Bureau's March 2003 Current Population Survey.

Academic aspirations

Among Hispanic teens, those with a religious connection (either Catholic or Protestant) were more likely to express a desire for a college degree than those who had no religion. In fact, 81% of Catholic and 80% of Protestant Hispanic teens aspired to acquire a bachelor's degree or higher, compared to 74% of non-religious Hispanic teens. Among both Protestants and Catholics, Hispanic females expressed greater ambitions for post-secondary degrees (84%) than their male counterparts (77%). Nevertheless, when asked in personal interviews what they wanted to do with their lives, only about one in four could name a specific career, and the majority could not clearly articulate a connection between educational goals and future career plans. The following conversation is a typical example:

Dialog 5.3 – 17 year-old Hispanic Catholic male from the South:

I: *How much do you think about the future?*

R: Oh, I think a lot, you know? Because it's already my last year and I have to see what I'm going to do after this.

I: *And what do you think about when you consider the future?*

R: Well, mainly in having an education and afterwards working.

I: *What do you think you will do with your life when you are an adult?*

R: Well... continue studying, going to a university and... getting a good job.

I: *How far in school do you want to go? Like, graduate, medical school... how far?*

R: Well, I like different things, I would like to do a little bit of each. And have the opportunity to... experience each one of the things I want to do.

I: *But do you want to get a bachelor, master...?*

R: Oh yes, I would like each one...

I: *Or doctorate...*

R: No, not doctorate. Too much time studying...

When asked how far they "realistically" thought they would get in school, there was a significant drop in expectations for all Hispanics, while the corresponding drop for white adolescents was much more modest. Among the boys, only 53% said they actually expected to obtain a college degree, compared to 71% for Hispanic females. Even so, these expectations contrast sharply with the fact that only 10% of 25 to 29 year-old Latino/as in the U.S. had actually obtained a bachelor's degree or higher in 2003, and 38% had not completed high school, compared to 35% and 6% respectively of their white peers. One young Latina expressed her concerns about future educational attainment as follows:

Dialog 5.4 – 13 year-old Hispanic Catholic female from the South:

I: *How much do you think about your future?*

R: I don't really think of it that much, um, but I, I know what I want.

I: *And what do you want?*

R: Um, I want to go to University of Miami, and like I want to study art, like singing or acting. Or if not I want to like, um, be a lawyer.

I: *How do you think your life is going to turn out?*

R: I think if hopefully I keep on studying that I'll reach my goal.

> I: Do you look to the future with hope or fear?
> R: Hope and fear at the same time.
> I: What are you hopeful about?
> R: That I get to be um, I get a good career. But I fear that I won't or that I, I don't finish college or studying. Or I just don't make it.
> I: What would stop you from making it?
> R: Um, money, um, or maybe um, family problems, family issues.
> I: Like what kind of family issues.
> R: Um, like for example, if something happens to one of my, to my mom or something like that and I can't finish paying for college. Or I have to work and I just can't finish paying it or stuff like that.

There are also some interesting educational differences between the Hispanic teens based on their respective levels of religious commitment. In *Soul Searching*, Christian Smith and Melinda Lundquist Denton describe four levels of religious devotion evident among the teen respondents to the NSYR survey: the devoted, the regulars, the sporadic, and the disengaged. As discussed in Chapter 2 of this book (see pages 69-71), Smith and Denton's definitions do not work well for Catholic teens, so an alternative set of criteria was developed to describe the religious commitment of the Hispanic teens. A detailed explanation of the criteria used to categorize the teens into four religious types is found in the Appendix on page 361. In any case, Tables 5.2 and 5.3 provide comparisons of the academic aspirations and experiences of Hispanic teens based on their religious commitment; teens with mixed religiosity characteristics are not reflected in the tables.

It is not a surprise that the religiously "committed" teens are by far the most likely to be attending a Catholic or Christian school. There is a double causality for this finding: teens from religiously devoted families are more likely to be sent to these schools, and teens attending religious schools are more likely to become deeply involved in their faith because of the additional exposure they receive at school. There also is a clear correlation between religious commitment and the Hispanic teens' perceived importance of education.

However, it is somewhat surprising that there is an *inverse* correlation between the Latino/a teens' religious commitment and the importance of education as perceived by their parents. Also, the "sporadic" teens were the most likely to aspire to a college degree, and the "disengaged" teens were by far the most likely to hope for a post-graduate degree, despite the fact that as a group they said education was less important than did their more religious peers. It is possible that the greater concern about education expressed by the less religious teens' parents is a reaction to the fact that their children are actually doing less well at school, as shown in Table 5.3. If this is the case, the fact that the less religious teens indicated a greater desire for higher education may be a reflection of the messages they are receiving

Table 5.3 - School life (percentages)

	Hispanic			White, Any Faith	Hispanic Religious Type*			
	Catholic	Protestant	No Religion		Committed	Engaged	Sporadic	Disengaged
What kind of grades do you get in school?	N=278	N=94	N=40	N=2448	N=47	N=172	N=82	N=32
As and Bs or better	48	48	32	56	51	52	43	40
Mostly Bs and Cs	32	21	45	25	31	31	27	37
Mostly Cs and Ds	7	7	3	8	3	6	14	3
Mostly Ds and Fs	3	1	5	1	0	2	4	11
Mixed	5	12	7	5	8	5	12	2
How much are you part of the popular group at school?								
A lot	36	30	40	29	46	32	34	27
Some	40	41	33	43	44	42	46	40
A little	11	13	14	14	11	9	13	17
None	9	8	12	9	0	12	4	10
In the last year, how many times have you cut class?								
Never	52	44	44	67	56	54	59	27
1 or 2 times	30	35	28	18	41	27	25	33
3 or more times	14	12	26	10	3	14	15	33
In the last 2 years, how many explusions / suspensions?								
None	77	70	69	81	80	74	80	57
1 or 2 times	16	16	22	11	15	18	15	21
3 or more times	4	6	3	4	4	3	5	5

* See the Appendix on page 361 for definitions of the adolescent religious types.

from their parents, rather than an accurate representation of their personal goals in life. Further research is required to confirm this interpretation.

Academic environment and performance

The NSYR survey included four measures of school involvement and performance, as shown in Table 5.3. The data show that among Latino/a teens, Catholics had slightly better grades and attendance records than their Protestant peers, and both religious groups did significantly better than their non-religious peers. However, none of the Hispanic groups reported grades or attendance measures approaching those of the white adolescents. Despite these facts, it was the non-religious Hispanic teens that most felt like part of the "popular group" at school, while the white teens and Protestant Hispanics on average felt the least popular. One may wonder what leads to such disparities in the way teens perform and fit in at school.

Religious participation can play a significant role in the development of young Hispanics. What is not shown in the tables is that among Hispanic teens, the Catholics score significantly lower on the tested measures of religious involvement than their Protestant peers. A contributing factor may be that there appear to be more opportunities for youth leadership within Protestant congregations than in Catholic parishes. According to the NSYR survey, 52% of Hispanic Protestant teens have spoken publicly about their faith in a religious meeting, compared to 22% of Hispanic Catholic teens. Similarly, 43% of the Hispanic Protestants in the survey reported participation in a Scripture study or prayer group, compared to 16% of the Hispanic Catholics. Finally, 17% of the Hispanic Protestants were leaders in their church youth group, compared to only 3% of the Hispanic Catholics.

The denominational difference may be partly due to the fact that young Hispanic Protestants are far more likely to have adults they can turn to for help within their congregation: 71% have this benefit, compared to only 45% of Hispanic Catholic teens. Involvement in church can thus provide role models and help young people to develop self-esteem and reinforce positive behavior while acting as a deterrent to negative behavior and/or negative influences from acquaintances. The educational and leadership opportunities, positive safe environment, skill development, and support provided by local churches can easily be transferred into improved academic performance. By becoming deliberate about helping young Hispanics transfer these skills and opportunities into their studies, congregations can go a long way toward addressing the need for academic support among Hispanic adolescents.

Given these advantages, it is not surprising that the religiously committed Hispanic teens reported significantly better grades in school than their sporadic or disengaged fellow-believers. In addition, they were more likely to feel that they were part of the popular group at school, and less likely to cut class or be suspended, especially when compared to their religiously disengaged peers. Nevertheless, the general impression one gets from the interview transcripts is that the committed teens made very little connection in their minds between the values and benefits they receive at church and the work they do in the classroom. The following example is typical of both the Protestant and Catholic teens who are committed to their faith:

Dialog 5.5 – 17 year-old Hispanic Seventh-day Adventist female from the Northeast:

I: *How do you see yourself fitting in at school?*

R: Well, I'm just beginning to fit little by little, right? It hasn't been easy, but I'm trying hard.

I: *How would other people define... other people at school define your group of friends?*

R: Well, my friends are healthy, they are correct... in my opinion.

I: *How does your group of friends relate to other groups at school?*

R: Well, they don't have many friends, either.

I: *Uh-huh. Do you personally identify much with your school—with the school spirit?*

R: No.

I: *Uh-huh. What kind of grades are you getting?*

R: Eh... eighty and above.

I: *How much do you care or not about doing well at school?*

R: I care, because I want to win a scholarship, then I need to exert myself.

I: *Do you think your religion has anything to do with your feeling about grades and achievement?*

R: No. No, no, no.

I: *What do you think it means to be a good Adventist at school?*

R: It's like an example given. Because we don't... attack, we don't fight all the time. No. We are correct, disciplined and we respect, right?

I: *Uh-huh. Do you need to do anything in particular to be a good Adventist at school?*

R: No, normal... Be a normal person. Not to attack, not to say bad words, normal...

I: *Uh-huh. Are there things you do at school because you are Adventist?*

R: No.

While religious participation clearly plays an important supporting role in the academic development of young Hispanics, a number of other factors contribute to the educational opportunities available to Latino/a teens—and their ability to take advantage of them. Table 5.4 highlights the impact of generational differences, economic status, and gender stereotypes on the academic performance of young Hispanics today.

Differences between immigrant generations

First generation

The girl quoted above in Dialog 5.5 is a good example of the impact of immigration on educational outcomes. She was born in Peru, and she makes mention of the fact that she is trying to fit in but finds it difficult. The experience of immigration can be highly stressful, even traumatic, for many young people. In addition to having to learn new cultural expectations and a new language, they experience the loss of significant relationships and the social roles that provided them with a sense of how they fit into the world. As many as 85% of immigrant teenagers experience a separation from one or both of their parents for periods of six months to ten years. Even reunification with parents can be a difficult transition, because children lose contact with their caregivers and must adjust to new family constellations that may include stepparents, stepsiblings, and siblings they have never met.[3] Furthermore, the low educational attainment and low wages earned by many immigrant parents mean that many immigrant

Table 5.4 – School life correlations for Hispanic teens (percentages)

	Generation*			Economic Status*			Gender	
	First	Second	Third +	High	Middle	Low	Male	Female
What kind of grades do you get in school?	N=95	N=165	N=191	N=111	N=167	N=164	N=215	N=236
As and Bs or better	55	50	39	57	47	38	43	49
Mostly Bs and Cs	33	30	33	25	36	34	32	32
Mostly Cs and Ds	3	7	8	6	3	10	9	4
Mostly Ds and Fs	1	3	4	~	4	4	3	3
Mixed	6	7	7	8	5	8	8	6
How much are you part of the popular group at school?								
A lot	37	28	40	39	35	34	42	29
Some	35	51	31	39	38	40	41	38
A little	15	9	12	12	12	12	10	13
None	10	9	9	6	11	10	4	13
In the last year, how many times have you cut class?								
Never	38	60	45	50	54	44	49	49
1 or 2 times	40	28	30	30	26	38	29	33
3 or more times	18	11	17	16	17	13	19	12
In the last 2 years, how many explusions / suspensions?								
None	75	79	70	83	74	72	69	79
1 or 2 times	19	16	14	9	17	18	20	12
3 or more times	4	3	7	5	5	6	6	3

* See the Appendix on page 361 for definitions of the generation and economic status categories.

children live in the poor and often violent inner cities, and their parents are forced to work two or more jobs, so the young people are left without much parental supervision, and in many cases are responsible for the care of their younger siblings.

While immigrant teens and their parents recognize the importance of an education and value the opportunity for a free education in the U.S., their life circumstances often necessitate sacrificing certain academic opportunities for the sake of family survival. This fact is reflected in the high levels of "cutting class" among first-generation (immigrant) Latino/as in the NSYR survey as shown in Table 5.4. It is likely that some of these missed classes involved caring for sick younger siblings, helping parents with bureaucratic processes at banks or other service agencies, or even embarrassment about not having the proper clothing or equipment needed for school. Nevertheless, immigrant teens report higher grades on average than their U.S.-born Latino/a counterparts. Having experienced life in another country with less economic opportunity, they are motivated to learn and improve the living situation for themselves and their families.

Second generation

Life and education in the U.S. can be equally challenging for the U.S.-born children of immigrants (the second generation). These children must learn to make sense of a world in which the cultural markers and expectations of their parents do not always mesh with those of the world around them. The questions in the NSYR interviews did not focus on experiences of cultural differences and how they impact the self-image of cultural "minority" adolescents. As a result, it is difficult to find in either the survey data or the interviews any reference to the sort of academic and social challenges young immigrants experience, and how those challenges can deepen in subsequent generations. Nevertheless, these challenges are well established in other studies, and it is worthwhile to include here the following quote from a Mexican-American girl who grew up in Indiana, as reported by sociologist Ken Crane:

> "[The Mexicans think] I'm just a white girl, you know... I'm not with Mexicanos, I'm just a white girl and that's still hard right now. Right now it's just like oh, well, Mexicanos, they don't treat me as a Mexican because I'm not Mexican but then white people are like, well, I'm not a white, you know. I'm not American. So I'm right in the middle. So I'm not there and I'm not here, you know, so it's very hard for me... You know, you don't speak any Spanish so you're white. You're an Americana and that's what they call me, like Gringa or that kind of stuff. Oh, that gets me so mad... I'm Mexican-American and I'm not Mexican and I'm not American. I just, right there in the middle, you know, and it gets me so mad because like they're, they think that I'm white and I'm not and they think I'm Mexican and I'm not and, oh, that gets me mad. That gets me really, really, really mad..."[4]

When compared to their immigrant peers, second-generation Hispanic adolescents are less likely to cut class or be expelled. This reflects the greater levels of family stability typically found in the families of second-generation Latino/as by the time they reach adolescence. As immigrants themselves, the parents are still highly motivated to see their children succeed in school, and they are able to provide more support than most recent immigrant parents can offer.

Nevertheless, the teens do not have the experience of living in their parents' country, so instead of seeing the comparative life improvement that their parents have experienced, they judge their standard of living from the perspective of consumer media messages and comparisons with the lifestyles of their classmates. As a result, they often become discouraged about their living situation and lose motivation for doing well at school. This is reflected in the lower grades reported by second-generation Hispanics in the NSYR survey. In addition, because they do not fit in with either the teens of the mainstream culture or with the more recent Latino/a immigrants, they may have difficulty developing self esteem and a positive sense of identity. This is reflected in the low number of second-generation teens who say they feel they are a part of the popular group at school.

It is interesting to note the use of language among Latino/a teens: 39% of the Hispanic adolescents surveyed reported that they can read and speak English and Spanish equally well. However, this number drops from 58% in the second generation to only 16% in the third generation. It appears that having U.S.-born parents makes a significant difference in the development of language in young Latino/as. The way schools handle English instruction can make a significant difference in their long-term academic success for first- and second-generation Latino/as whose first language was Spanish. If schools are not deliberate about offering math and science instruction in Spanish simultaneously with English language classes, by the time teens become proficient enough in English to join the mainstream classrooms, they will be so far behind their peers that they will more than likely need remedial classes. Once they are placed on the remedial track, they may never receive the help they need to catch up with their peers in college preparatory classes, thus making college virtually inaccessible to them.

Third generation

By the third generation, the academic experiences of Hispanic teens tend to become polarized. Many second-generation parents who had difficulty adjusting to life and school with limited resources and support in culturally conflicted environments never developed the maturity or the skills to provide the nurturing environment that their children need to thrive, so the generational cycle of violence and poverty begins. On the other hand, the second-generation parents who were able to overcome the challenges of developing self-esteem, integrating their ethnic and American identities in a constructive way, and attaining higher education are able to pass the benefits of stability and high expectations to their children in the third generation.

Some of these third-generation Hispanic teens have fully assimilated to the mainstream U.S. culture (many have only one Hispanic parent), while others maintain cultural and linguistic ties to their ethnic heritage. This polarization of outcomes in the third generation is reflected in the NSYR survey results in that the third-generation Hispanic teens are the most likely to say they feel like they are part of the popular group at school, yet on average they have lower grades and are more likely to cut class or be expelled than either generation before them. Clearly, there are far too many third-generation teens that have become trapped in the cycles of poverty and violence, and not enough that have achieved an integrated sense of identity and self-esteem.

Economic status

As already mentioned, the lower economic and educational resources of immigrant parents create challenges for the academic achievement of their children. Once the cycle of poverty and violence begins in the lives of young Latino/as, it may be difficult to break the cycle in subsequent generations. Not surprisingly, the NSYR survey shows that grades diminish and cutting class, suspensions, and expulsions increase as the family income levels go down. Indeed, the academic performance of high-income Hispanic teens on these measures as reported in Table 5.4 is very close to that of white adolescents, and on the measure of popularity at school, the high-income Hispanics do significantly better than their white peers. The challenge for Hispanic communities is to find ways to prevent the low income levels of immigrant families from limiting the academic achievement of the children, and to break down the factors that contribute to a cycle of poverty and violence in the second and later generations.

Twenty percent of the Hispanic families surveyed had annual household incomes of less than $20,000, compared to only 7% of the white families. Hispanic Catholics fared even worse, with 23% reporting income under $20K, versus 14% among Hispanic Protestant families. Similarly, 46% of the Hispanic families rented rather than owned their own homes, compared to only 15% among the white families. Furthermore, 73% of the Hispanic families said they were in debt or just breaking even, and only 25% claimed to have savings and other assets, the lowest ranking among those surveyed.

Such economic hardships reverberate throughout the lives of children and can adversely affect their education. Religious private schools could significantly impact the educational prospects of Hispanic teens in low-income environments, but the cost of tuition and scarcity of scholarships has made this a reality for only 2% of low-income Hispanic teens. Many Hispanic parents work two or even three jobs in order to make ends meet. The resultant lack of parental involvement and supervision leads some children to adopt negative behaviors, such as substance abuse for solace and getting involved with street gangs for a sense of belonging. Poverty, inadequate support services, and poor educational opportunities create a vicious cycle that frequently condemns yet another generation of young Hispanics to the same fate.

Gender

It has already been noted that Hispanic teens generally trail their white peers with respect to grades and school attendance. Among Hispanics, the boys also trail the girls on these measures by significant amounts, yet the girls were less likely to say they were part of the popular group at school. The lower academic performance and higher social performance of Hispanic boys may be partly explained by resistance theory. According to this theory, *not learning* what schools teach can be interpreted as a form of political resistance to the dominant culture. What may begin as a series of cultural misunderstandings on the part of teachers and administrators of the dominant culture, over time often becomes interpreted by teens as a hostile attitude toward people who are not like the majority.

Limited job opportunities and experiences of discrimination teach young Hispanics that studying hard will not benefit them as much as it would a white person, so they develop an aggressive or passive-aggressive attitude toward the classroom. Failure to do homework, inattention in class, misbehavior, cutting class, and criticizing peers for "selling out" by studying too much are manifestations of this resistance. Ironically, the students most dedicated to these counterproductive behaviors are made to feel more popular as they gain the respect of their peers for not selling out to the system. Taken to the extreme, a student will drop out of school as a final act of resistance; many other capable students are intellectually "on strike" even though they may be present in school.[5]

Recent studies have shown that immigrant girls typically get better grades, have higher academic aspirations, spend more time on homework, and consider school to be more important than their male counterparts. One such study accounts for these differences as follows:

> Immigrant girls may be protected from risk factors like harsh school environment by the supportive networks of teachers, peers, and parents they meet in their pursuit of education. Girls had better relations with teachers and more support in school than did boys. Girls had friends who were more serious about schoolwork and more supportive of academics, while boys were more likely to be negatively influenced by their peers. In addition, girls perceived higher expectations in schooling from parents than did boys, and parents also monitored girls more closely than they did the boys.
>
> The immigrant boys, however, had fewer sources of social capital either within or outside the family... At home, parents gave them more freedom to date, be with friends, and be on the street. As a result, it may

have been easier for them to be distracted from school, because unlike the girls, they had more alternatives. Lack of parental supervision increased the opportunities for their exposure to negative influences on the street, such as gangs and drugs. Furthermore, for many minority boys attending urban schools, their construction of a masculine identity was likely to be in conflict with the school agenda.[6]

Qin-Hilliard goes on to point out that maintaining their native culture and language may also play a protective role, for girls even more so than for boys. For this reason, schools should encourage immigrant students to retain their culture and language while learning English. Churches and community organizations can play an important role by providing space after school for Hispanic teens—girls and boys alike—to study and interact with peers in a healthy and cognitively stimulating environment.

Theological points of departure

As noted at the beginning of this chapter, the educational challenges now facing adolescent Latino/as are indeed daunting. The preceding section noted how religious faith and devotion, cultural values, economic status, and gender can influence His-

> In the presence of God and of Christ Jesus... I solemnly urge you: proclaim the message; be persistent whether the time is favorable or unfavorable; convince, rebuke, and encourage, with the utmost patience in teaching.
> – *2 Timothy 4:1-2*

panic teens' ability to handle these challenges. Parents and youth ministers need to work together to leverage the family and community resources for the educational success of Latino/a adolescents. How does the Bible inform these educational and community issues? What theological concepts might be used to better understand this situation? How can churches respond to these needs and be faithful to their mission? This section explores a variety of ways that faith communities can assist young Latino/as further their education and build a greater sense of hope for their future.

Theology of presence: the incarnation and authentic pastoral care

Jesus is the grand example of incarnational ministry. In what is known as the divine *kenosis,* God emptied himself of all divine power and majesty (Philippians 2:5-7), becoming human in order to fulfill his salvific mission. Jesus slept, ate, laughed, cried, and died in the midst of the people he was serving. If we want to have an impact in the lives of young Hispanics at risk of repeating the vicious cycle of poverty, violence, and low educational attainment, we can do no less. We must go where the young people are, walk the streets they walk, feel the fear they feel, and share their ironic laughter as they deal with the paradoxes that filter through their daily lives. We cannot reach urban Hispanic adolescents if we can only stand in judgment of their music, reject their expressions of fashion, dismiss their questions, and demean their culture. Jesus earned the right to speak to the lives and experiences of those he served—so must we.

In the NSYR interviews, many Hispanic teens described the loneliness they felt and expressed feelings of not belonging or frustration about not having the support they needed. Others expressed the appreciation that they felt for having adult role models and other caring individuals in their lives. As any experienced minister will tell you, a theology of presence implies "being there" with parishioners through the peaks and valleys that color the landscape of their life journeys. Ministers often describe how their lives are woven together with those they serve. They speak of the joys mutually experienced at weddings, graduation ceremonies, and baptisms, as well as the grief shared at funerals, hospitals, and other critical events. To gain the trust of Latino/a young people, we must be present when they fly, founder, flourish, and fail. We can only speak to their experience when we become a part of their lives.

Theology of place: the call to social location

For many ministers, the calling of God did not come as a vague invitation to serve "the church" at large, but as a clear burden about the needs of a specific people, or a specific cause, at a specific place. They were called to work within various particular communities or neighborhoods, and their passion and commitment to the people resulted in successful ministries. Moses was called to Egypt, Jesus was determined to go to Jerusalem, and Paul knew he had to end up in Rome. In a similar way, David Wilkerson, the founder of the renowned Teen Challenge ministry, was burdened to travel to New York to work with the street gangs there. Many thought he was crazy, but he obeyed, and the result has been an international ministry whose successful impact on substance abusing young people has been the subject of many research studies.

In Luke 10:1-12, Jesus sent his disciples ahead to every town and place he intended to go. It is significant that he did not send out the seventy disciples with flyers to post at the entrance to each town, inviting everyone to come and hear Jesus when he makes the rounds. Instead, he sent them out as sheep in the midst of wolves, utterly dependent on God's grace. What would happen if youth ministry teams in parishes and congregations went into the Hispanic barrios, sharing a meal and bringing the Word of God?

If the statistics regarding young Hispanic educational realities do not move us, perhaps witnessing the existential realities of their lives will. When we take the time to taste the foods they eat, take daily walks in the streets of their neighborhoods, listen to the music they dance to, and share their laughter and tears amid the joys and tribulations of life—only then can we begin to appreciate the call and the task before us.

If parishes and congregations are really called to serve the people of a particular place, the youth ministry leaders must make every effort to enter into the neighborhoods and build relationships with the young people *where they are.* This is the most effective way to overcome the pastoral nearsightedness that obscures the vision of too many youth ministry leaders so that it never occurs to them that they should be serving anyone other than those young people who have responded to a general invitation to participate in the youth group. As youth ministry leaders, if we hope to impact the educational outcomes of today's young Latino/as, we must first find ways to be in relationship with them on an ongoing basis. This will only happen if we grow in our understanding of how God calls us to serve the young people—*all* the young people—of *this* place, at *this* time.

Theology of culture: the imperative of contextualization

Theological reflection provides a means to understand sacred truths more deeply by interpreting them from the perspective of the lived experience of the local community. The NSYR survey offers a glimpse into the lives of Latino/a adolescents in the U.S., so it is a rich source for contextualizing our theological reflection at the national level. Pastoral responses to the reality seen in the data will be most relevant if they are constructed around a profound understanding and appreciation for Latino cultures—their histories, literature, art forms, contributions, challenges, and aspirations—and their local manifestations in the present. Far too many youth ministry teams have committed the error of believing that Hispanic culture is the same for all Hispanics. In doing so, they ignore the myriad differences in sociopolitical, economic, linguistic, historical and even religious manifestations found between Hispanics of different national origins, regions of residence, and generations since their family's arrival in the U.S..

To be effective in ministry with young Latino/as, we must conduct a cultural exegesis of the population—or populations—we are attempting to serve. In his introductory chapter to this book, Ken Johnson-Mondragón provides a helpful schema for understanding some of the pastoral differences found in various segments of the young Latino population (see pages 33ff). In addition, H. Richard Niebuhr's classic, *Christ and Culture*[7] still provides an excellent rubric to understand culture from a theological/Biblical

perspective. Niebuhr helps us to understand that it is not necessary to reject youth culture completely—or the various expressions of culture among
young Latino/as—in favor of some idealized universal "Christian culture"
that somehow is supposed to work for people of every place and every
time. Pope Paul VI provides a very helpful construction of the relationship
between Gospel and culture in his encyclical on evangelization:

> The Gospel, and therefore evangelization, are certainly not identical with
> culture, and they are independent in regard to all cultures. Nevertheless,
> the kingdom which the Gospel proclaims is lived by men who are pro-
> foundly linked to a culture, and the building up of the kingdom cannot
> avoid borrowing the elements of human culture or cultures. Though in-
> dependent of cultures, the Gospel and evangelization are not necessarily
> incompatible with them; rather they are capable of permeating them all
> without becoming subject to any one of them... Therefore every effort
> must be made to ensure a full evangelization of culture, or more correctly
> of cultures. They have to be regenerated by an encounter with the Gospel.
> But this encounter will not take place if the Gospel is not proclaimed.[8]

Orlando Crespo refers to the mutual realities of being Hispanic and
Christian as a "parallel journey," not one that one ends as the other begins,
but that these realities operate simultaneously.[9] There is a need for both
Latino/as and non-Latino/as to understand this as they negotiate these realities and embark upon ministry in our communities. Being a Christian
does not negate one's ethnic identity.

While many may agree that ethnicity is a core component in the con-
stellation of elements that form an individual's identity, some would like to
limit the understanding of ethnicity to the practices that are found in the
cultures of origin. In this way, they would deny extending the same stature
to the dynamic expressions of Latino youth culture as it takes shape and
adapts to new environments in the U.S. It cannot be denied that Latino
youth culture often incorporates aspects of other cultures as new generations seek to create an image and identity for themselves in the multicultural marketplace of contemporary cities. For instance, the fusion of hip-hop
with reggae, salsa, and merengue into reggaetón is but one artistic manifestation of this phenomenon. While some will view this as diluting authentic
"Latino culture," the pastoral task of evangelizing culture means that these
expressions cannot be rejected; rather they must be understood and transformed from within by the values and content of the gospel message.

Will we seek to understand Latino/a teens and their perennial creative work of forming an image and a space to call their own within the
landscape of the status quo (or in the virtual landscape of the Internet on
popular websites like MySpace.com)? Or will we merely reject their creativity, their authentic voices, and the locus of their endeavors within our

communities? When we give them the room to appropriate their own symbols and negotiate the world on their own terms, we have an opportunity to struggle with them as they frame and ask the questions of their generation. On the other hand, if we judge them, their culture and their contributions with our ready-made answers, custom-designed to address the aspirations and concerns of another cultural group or another generation, we risk alienating these young Latino/as not only from ourselves and our churches, but even from the gospel message we so enthusiastically proclaim.

Social justice: the challenge of systemic evil

As we endeavor to work with Hispanic adolescents and the challenges they face, it is imperative that we revisit our notion of sin and evil. For example, in Esther 3:8-10, through a unique interplay of political favors, financial kick-backs, and racism, Hamon advocates for genocidal laws to actualize a personal vendetta. This is a graphic example of the way sinful attitudes can become institutionalized within the laws and policies of a country or state. Similarly, the institutional and environmental racism that condemns children to under-funded, failing schools is also a pernicious evil.

If we are to stem the tide of poor educational performance among young Hispanics, it is imperative that the church revisit its notion of sin and justice, and involve itself in public policy advocacy addressing the political, economic and systemic challenges of public school education. Even in our own Catholic and Christian schools, more energy and resources are often dedicated to funding the construction of new buildings or recruiting athletic superstars than on finding creative ways to open spaces for the poor and the migrants in our communities to obtain a better education. Esther intervened on behalf of her people to save them from sure death; Christians must also intervene on behalf of the poor and marginalized who face a cycle of poverty, if not provided with a good education.

Ecclesiology: the creation of communities of meaning

How do we conduct church life? Is it youth-friendly? Does it offer room for dialogue with young people, or do they see it as a monologue directed by the active leader(s) to a passive church? What are the entrance points through which individuals and/or groups of Latino/a adolescents can contribute to the life of the church? In order to become communities of meaning for young Latino/as, our churches must give them opportunities to participate meaningfully and contribute positively to the life and well-being of the community. Without authentic mutuality, young people quickly get bored or begin to feel used as tokens in contexts where their input does not really matter. The way we conduct our services and programs will either be life-giving and life-transforming for them, or ritualistic and staid.

Do we dare to allow Latino/a young people, with all the baggage they bring, to inform and transform our liturgy, our worship, and our communion with one another? Do we trust them as leaders in the evangelization of their peers, empowering them to give shape and direction to our youth ministry programs? Or are our communities of faith more interested in method and practice than in life and its often organic shifts and surprises? Have we become the enforcers of a regime or are we pilgrim companions exploring new possibilities in the Spirit of love and fellowship? The answers to these questions define who we are as a church community and show whether or not we truly believe that Latino/a teens are members of the body of Christ.

Eschatology: the future is now!

As we struggle to improve the educational opportunities for young Hispanics, it would be helpful to review our notions of eschatology, our doctrine of the end times. What does eschatology have to do with the struggling Hispanics? In the past, many Christian leaders have used the promise of the after-life to mitigate the importance of this life. The result can be a certain indifference to the plight of the poor because life in this world is seen as less important. It is easy to negate the importance of this world from the comforts of a well-furnished home, and from the view of finely manicured lawns. However, it is a quite different reality for many young people afraid to go to school because of the rampant violence they have witnessed there.

For Christians, the Reign of God is both "now" and "not yet." Yes, we have a promissory note for a New Jerusalem, a new heaven, and a new Earth in the future, but there are also promises for this life. Eschatology should bring hope for salvation in this life as well. Do we make room in our eschatological views for "God's Reign" to break in with a spirit of renewal and a hope for restored communities? Salvation is both now and not yet; so must our hope be for the communities and the educational opportunities of young Hispanics. The Reign of God is now, therefore the future must be now!

Pastoral theology: the witness of the theological virtues

Pastors, priests, and lay ministers alike are called to be purveyors of faith, hope, and love within their communities. Latino/a young people must develop faith in God, faith in themselves, faith in their churches, and faith in their communities, if they are going to overcome the many obstacles that make education a challenge for them. Ministers must model faith in times of hardship, faith when things go wrong, and faith in spite of opposition. By witnessing a faithful life, young people can believe that alternative futures crafted by hard work, a commitment to excellence, and right living are possible. While faith is not an amulet to ward off misfortune, it nevertheless provides foundational principles for success in life.

Ministers must also project a vision of hope for their communities. Leaders with such a vision create communities of transformation. It is a vision of hope that sees an empty lot as a garden, an abandoned building as a new home, and a young gang member as a leader in the church, or a struggling student as a Harvard graduate. These seeds of hope sowed in the lives of young people grow to be the transforming vision of possibility and aspirations for a community.

Love is both a noun and a verb—the message and the method of the Gospel. Love is necessary to see at-risk young people as both the preferential recipient and potential leader of the church's ministry, and not just as a dangerous presence in the community from which the "good" teenagers must be protected. Gospel love will sustain young people through disappointing times, disheartening setbacks, and catastrophic loss and/or failure. We can love young people to life, we can love churches to life, we can love communities to life—and we must!

By now the astute reader may have noticed that most of this theological reflection has focused on the practice of ministry with Latino/a teens, instead of the challenges they experience in school. The challenges are very real, and there is no simple solution to bridge the educational gap between Latino/a students and their peers of the mainstream culture. The point of this reflection is that youth ministers cannot help young Latino/as overcome their educational challenges if they are not in relationship with them through the ministry of the church.

In the Gospels, Jesus went first to the sick, the suffering, the public sinners, and the outcasts, bringing them a message of hope and salvation. If youth ministers today will do the same, they will find Latino/a adolescents who are alienated from their schools, their teachers, their peers who are doing well academically, and in many cases from their churches as well. Finding ways to overcome their alienation from church, and the peer community they encounter there, is the first step in becoming an effective advocate for the educational success of Latino/a teens.

Pastoral recommendations

Beyond the challenge of reaching out in ministry to Latino/a adolescents, the NSYR research underscores many needs within the Latino community that require intervention. Once Latino/a young people become involved in the life of the church community, there are a variety of strategies that might be employed to improve their academic performance and encourage them to set goals for higher education. Below are some examples of interventions that can be helpful.

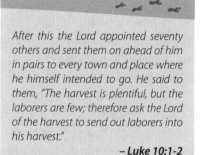

After this the Lord appointed seventy others and sent them on ahead of him in pairs to every town and place where he himself intended to go. He said to them, "The harvest is plentiful, but the laborers are few; therefore ask the Lord of the harvest to send out laborers into his harvest."

– Luke 10:1-2

1. Training and education

A. ESL training. The church can help by providing English as a Second Language (ESL) classes to its immigrant members, both parents and teens alike. Through ESL, the church empowers parents with the tools to make themselves more marketable for improved employment opportunities. This service also enables parents to communicate better with their children, who typically become proficient in English at school. Moreover, when parents know English they do not need their children to be language brokers for them in the adult world of teachers, doctors, etc.—a position that creates an awkward role reversal.

For older children and adolescents who are recent arrivals to the United States, every day that is spent learning English represents another day they can fall behind their peers in other subjects, such as math, science, history, literature, and social studies. As a result, schools are under intense pressure to mainstream their English-language learners as quickly as possible. Many immigrant Latino/as are placed in remedial math and science classes because they do not have sufficient English skills to understand the subtleties of what their teachers and books are saying. Once they have been placed in remedial classes, it is very difficult for them to transition to college preparatory classes as they get older. Through church-based ESL classes, Spanish-dominant young people can continue studying English after their school's ESL classes have ended. Because the students all have similar backgrounds, they can ask questions about the meaning of words without feeling embarrassed. The improved English skills they acquire will generally lead to better academic performance in school. There are even ESL curricula that use the Bible as a point of departure for learning English.[10]

B. Religious private schools and scholarships. Very few parishes or congregations are able to establish private high schools on their own, but there are thousands of religious high schools across the country. The challenge lies in the fact that the cost of tuition places private education out of the reach of most Hispanic families. To address this fact, some schools have been set up on the Jesuit "Cristo Rey" (Christ the King) model, in which local businesses pay the tuition for five students who rotate working for the company one day each week. In other communities, childless couples have taken it upon themselves to give a child from a low-income Christian family an education in Christian schools from kindergarten through high school and beyond. Religious schools need to demonstrate greater creativity and initiative in collaboration with the faith communities in their area to make the education of teens from low-income families a gospel priority in their ministry.

2. Tutoring and mentoring

A needed service for many Latino/a young people is tutoring. By providing tutoring, churches can play an important role of investing in the academic and professional development of their young people while connecting them with an older mentor in the community. Latino/a adolescents can also serve as volunteer tutors for younger children in church-based after school programs that: a) provide a safe environment after school for children of all ages whose parents work; b) improve adolescents' self-esteem by giving them an outlet to use their gifts to positively impact the lives of children in their community; c) reinforce the importance of valuing education; and d) give Latino/a children educational role models from within their own community before negative stereotypes about being "too studious" can take root. Tutoring also renders a strategic service to the emerging generation that can have a future impact on the life of the church.

For the college-bound, mentoring can be extremely helpful. Many Latino/as are the first in their family to attend university and need help with applications, financial aid, etc. When churches invest in the academic preparation of their adolescent members, they are more likely to remain loyal and involved in their church as they become upwardly mobile, investing in turn in the community that invested in them—through their time, talent and treasure. This mutuality helps build the local church as it fulfills its mandate within the community it serves.

3. Job fairs

Job fairs are excellent methods for helping young people crystallize their vocational goals—especially in urban inner-city environments where career opportunities often appear to be very limited. By meeting with professionals in various fields and being able to ask them questions, young people begin to visualize themselves in those very roles. Job fairs conducted by colleges tend to emphasize career paths related to the degree programs they offer, but when conducted by the church they can also underscore other legitimate vocational paths such as ministry, and professional or blue-collar roles often not found in college fairs.

4. Career counseling

Career counseling should begin as early as young people start to explore their interests in particular fields. This involves the tandem tasks of gathering information about occupations and identifying the strengths, interests, and giftedness of each individual. Far too often, the counseling services offered by schools in Latino communities are insufficient to meet the needs of their students, and many teens go without service. If no one in the church is qualified to conduct such counseling, professionals should be hired to conduct workshops during designated times of the year. Some are willing to provide these services pro-bono, if identified and scheduled well in advance. Role models within the community can also be helpful as they explain how they overcame obstacles to reach their goals.

5. Conduct listening sessions and intergenerational panels

Many adults in our churches are accustomed to lecturing, orienting, preaching, counseling or reprimanding young people. When was the last time adults deliberately created a formal session to *listen* to young people's cares, critiques, and concerns? Adults ought to attend a meeting where teens control the agenda, in a setting of their choice. Every effort should be made to include a broad representation of the young people in the community, so that no one's voice is excluded. Similarly, an intergenerational discussion or panel addressing the concerns of each generation can assist communication and create mutual understanding. This insight can be generalized so that in all church events and activities, someone takes responsibility to ensure that generational interests are represented and addressed.

6. Field trips and partnerships with local colleges

Exposing Latino/a adolescents to the beauty of campus life, and the wonderful opportunities to be found in college can motivate high school sophomores and juniors towards academic excellence and concretize their educational aspirations. When they witness students like themselves who already attend, they can more easily visualize themselves attending as well. Youth ministers might consider establishing partnerships with local colleges that are recruiting in the area to conduct special visits and career orientation courses at the local church. As affirmative action programs are dismantled, many institutions of higher education are looking for new ways to attract a diversity of students and would welcome an overture by a nearby church.

7. **Collaboration with local businesses**

Churches can collaborate with local businesses to create internship programs in which students are hired to work for a weekly stipend. Upon successful completion of the internship, students would receive a scholarship to help them towards their academic studies. Even the church itself might offer such an internship with funding provided by members of the community. By developing internship programs with a variety of businesses, churches can provide their teens with the added benefit of exposure to diverse occupational fields to help form their vocational goals.

8. **Academic projects or research within a community**

Some academic institutions provide opportunities for professors to create partnerships with community-based organizations and/or faith-based organizations on joint community and research projects. For example, researchers could conduct studies on the impact of community service learning projects, after school programs, or urban mission endeavors. By collaborating with professors, churches and their members may benefit from the creation of new approaches to community intervention and renewal. Providing ways for teens to participate in such research is a tremendous added benefit as they become involved in meaningful work with a visible impact in their communities. Outcome-based research is incredibly valuable for community-based and faith-based initiatives, as it can provide the basis for grant applications to philanthropic organizations and/or government sponsored *requests for proposals* (RFP's).

9. **Educational summit or expo**

Conducting an educational summit where Latino/a role models can share their lives, struggles, doubts, and journey is inspirational for teens who often feel that adults do not feel the same raw emotions that they experience. As successful professionals share about their doubts and failures with young people and de-mythologize academic and occupational processes, adolescents begin to form their own strategies towards successful academic and career tracks. Another variation of this would be to have an expo in a certain field, thus allowing young people to develop a clearer picture of the multiple careers available in that area. Priority should be given to the service professions (health care, education, counseling, ministry, legal services, politics/public service, etc.) where there are never enough professionals to serve the growing Latino population in Spanish and/or in culturally appropriate ways.

10. **Youth acknowledgment ceremony**

At least once a year, churches should acknowledge the accomplishments, contributions, and valor of their teenagers. Parents, small businesses, and even the local press could be invited to an awards ceremony recognizing the efforts and ability of adolescents to overcome adversity in their community. Volunteer service, good deeds, noble conduct, and excellence in other arenas such as sports and the arts also need to be celebrated. As young people experience the rewards of their labor early in life, they will be inspired to construct a life of nobility and excellence.

Questions for reflection

1. Is the atmosphere in our church welcoming, supportive and hopeful for young Hispanics? Why or Why not? What can be done to improve it? What efforts are we making to reach additional young Hispanics in the area?

2. Do we provide young people with the opportunity to express themselves authentically and meaningfully without fear of rejection, judgment or reprisal? What mechanisms can be established to create authentic dialogue?

3. What tangible support is given to the young people of our congregation to assist their development of academic excellence? Are there tutoring services, career counseling, computer training courses and/or scholarships provided by your congregation? What needs to be done to provide such services?

4. How are we involving parents in discussing, developing, and supporting programs for young people? What tangible services can we provide parents to assist them in becoming better advocates for their children's education? Do we offer a support group for parents where they can share their struggles in a non-judgmental environment?

5. What leadership, mentoring, and/or discipling structures exist in our church to assist Hispanic teens in their journey as Christians, Latino/as, and professionals? What more could we provide?

Chapter 6:
Insights into the Moral Life
of Hispanic Youth

Elizabeth Conde-Frazier, Ph.D.

Dialog 6.1 – 17 year-old Hispanic Catholic male from the West

I: *Would you say that, in general, people these days have lost a sense of right and wrong, or do you think what is right and wrong is still pretty clear today?*

R: I'm, I think it's more, not as clear.

I: *How do you think? In what ways?*

R: In the ways that society has bent right and wrong. Too many wrongs are right and more wrongs are seen as right, whereas it doesn't really matter.

I: *So people think that it doesn't matter what they really do?*

R: Yeah, and it's their lives so they can do what they want...

I: *How do you know what's right and what's wrong?*

R: For me, just my conscience and my parents.

I: *Your conscience. Is there any sort of thing that makes something, besides your parents might be disappointed or whatever, but that makes something right or wrong or?*

R: Yes. If they found out, what they would think about it—what, I guess, society would think about it.

I: *Where do your own views of right and wrong come from?*

R: My parents.

I: *Your parents?*

R: School.

I: *School? And one more time, what do you think it is that makes something right or wrong?*

R: It's what I usually think about it.

I: *How do you decide or know what is good and bad, right and wrong in life? What your parents think or what other people think?*

R: My parents or my conscience.

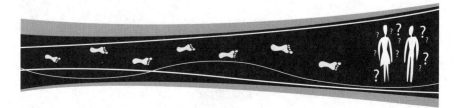

Insights into the Moral Life of Hispanic Youth

The popular media in the United States tends to portray young Hispanics as drug users, illegal immigrants, gang members, and prostitutes—if they are shown at all. Exceptions to this tendency have become more common in recent years, yet the traditional stereotypes about Latino/a adolescents are still easy to find on television and movie screens. The National Study of Youth and Religion (NSYR) provides a much-needed objective point of reference to determine whether the media depictions are an accurate reflection of the religious and moral lives of Hispanic adolescents.

With that in mind, this chapter begins with a look at several contemporary theories regarding moral development, which provide a theoretical framework for the analysis to follow. It goes on to describe the current state of moral development among Hispanic adolescents using data from the NSYR study, followed by reflections on the connection between moral behavior and participation in a community of faith. Finally, it offers six strategies and a series of reflection questions for youth ministers and parents to help them foster the ability to make decisions that reflect the values of the Gospel among Latino/a teenagers.

Contemporary theories of moral development

In the broadest terms, the field of research on moral development considers how morality develops through childhood, adolescence, and into adulthood. Moral development involves forming standards and making decisions about what is right and wrong, and the way those standards and decisions are actualized in human behavior and feelings. Contemporary research on moral development has expanded to include studies in terms of affect, cognition, emotions, behavior, and neuroscience.[1] It is not possible in the space of this chapter to provide a complete introduction to moral development, but some key concepts are needed in order to appreciate the implications of the NSYR's findings for the pastoral care of Hispanic adolescents.

> At Gibeon the Lord appeared to Solomon in a dream by night; and God said, "Ask what I should give you." And Solomon said, "O Lord my God, you have made your servant king in place of my father David, although I am only a little child; I do not know how to go out or come in. Give your servant therefore an understanding mind to govern your people, able to discern between good and evil; for who can govern this your great people?"
>
> – 1 Kings 3:5, 7, 9

In common usage, moral character usually refers to an individual's ability to put into practice the commonly held moral norms of a society or group, so the focus is on behavior. The question posed by theorists of moral development is: what motivates behaviors that are in conformity with (or against) moral norms? The field generally recognizes that reason and feelings/impulses influence the formation of moral choices. The experiences that follow on a particular action can also influence the way a person thinks and feels about their options the next time they are faced with a similar decision. Thus, moral character develops out of the interaction between thoughts, feelings, and behaviors regarding standards of right and wrong.[2] The three theoretical models that follow have been very influential among psychologists and sociologists, and although they each have their limitations with respect to explaining the behavior of adolescents in general, and Hispanic teenagers in particular, they nevertheless provide a useful vocabulary for discussing the findings in the remainder of the chapter.

Stages of moral reasoning – Lawrence Kohlberg

Early attempts to articulate a developmental model of moral character focused on the cognitive dimension of morality—how a person reasons about what is right or wrong. In the 1960s and 70s, Lawrence Kohlberg conducted empirical research to see how individuals of different cultures and stages in life actually reason about what is the right or wrong thing to do in a given situation. Based on his research, he described moral reasoning as occurring at three distinct levels and developing through six progressive stages, based on whether the reasoning was based on external or internal factors. Kohlberg's theory can be summarized as follows:[3]

Preconventional level. A person can identify family, cultural, or societal rules of right and wrong, but interprets them in terms of the reward or punishment for the behavior given by the authority figure that makes the rules (parents, teachers, police, etc.).

- Stage 1 is the *punishment and obedience orientation.* The physical consequences of action determine whether it is right or wrong, so avoidance of punishment and deference to power are valued in their own right. At this stage, "conscience" can be described as the irrational fear of punishment.

- Stage 2 is the *instrumental relativist orientation.* Right action is whatever satisfies one's needs. Elements of fairness and sharing may be present, but only in so far as they lead to personal gain; there is no concept of loyalty, gratitude, or justice. Reactions of guilt are ignored, and the potential punishment is weighed against the likelihood of getting caught and the personal benefit expected from a particular action.

Conventional level. Meeting the expectations of one's family, group, or society is perceived as a strong value in its own right, regardless of the immediate consequences. Conformity is a matter of loyalty to support and maintain the social order, which is needed for everyone's benefit.

- Stage 3 is the *interpersonal concordance orientation*. Good behavior pleases and helps others, and one earns approval by being "nice." At this stage, intentions are considered in addition to consequences, and action is motivated by the anticipated approval or disapproval of others.

- Stage 4 is the *law and order orientation*. Right behavior consists of showing respect for authority as a matter of duty, and maintaining the social order for its own sake. Avoidance of "immoral" behavior is motivated by the anticipation of dishonor (institutionalized blame) and guilt over specific harm done to others.

Postconventional, autonomous, or principled level. Moral values and principles are seen as having validity and application apart from the authority figures that put forward the norms in a particular family, group, or society.

- Stage 5 is the *social-contract legalistic orientation*. This is the "official" morality of government and constitution. Right action is defined in terms of what the whole society has agreed to be acceptable; beyond that, individuals are entitled to their own moral opinions and values, but these are relative and are not binding on others. Action is motivated by a desire to maintain self-respect ("I am a law-abiding citizen") and the respect of others / society.

- Stage 6 is the *universal ethical-principal orientation*. Right is determined by a decision of conscience in accord with ethical principles that are logical, comprehensive, consistent, and universally applicable. These are not concrete rules like the Ten Commandments, but abstract principles of justice, reciprocity, human dignity, and personal rights and obligations. Maintaining self-respect and integrity is the primary motivation for doing what is right.

The moral personality – Augusto Blasi

In the 1980s and 90s, Augusto Blasi challenged Kohlberg's primarily cognitive approach to moral development. He acknowledged that moral understanding—knowing the difference between right and wrong—plays an important role in moral behavior, but he said it is not always the determining motivator. His research centered on the behavioral gap between what a person knows is the right thing to do, and what the person does when presented with a moral dilemma in real life.

Blasi contends that this gap exists because moral values must compete with a variety of other values as motivators to action in people's lives. He acknowledges that people cannot always explain the reasons for their actions, either being completely unaware of why they did something, or offering reasons that seem more like rationalizations—after-the-fact self-justifications and attempts to manage how they see themselves and what others may think about them. Nevertheless, most people can accurately identify the "morally praiseworthy" alternatives that they are faced with in daily life when asked about them in the abstract.

In Blasi's view, people generally reflect on the various values that serve as motivators in their lives, and over time these values are organized and internalized so that the deepest values shape a person's behavior as the primary motivators to action. He calls this process the development of a *moral personality*. Reflection on moral norms and moral understanding play an important role in this process for most people, and Blasi believes that everyone engages at some level in a process of constructing the "self" by making free choices, exerting self-control, and taking ownership for the values that direct their actions in life. For some people, moral ideals become the strongest motivating values because they are intimately tied to their sense of self: "I am a moral person, therefore I will act rightly."

When such individuals do not choose a morally praiseworthy course of action, it triggers a guilt response within them because the self-image that was projected by their action does not match their internal self-image. This experience of internal dissonance motivates them to act differently in the future with greater resolve. On the other hand, people who have not tied their self-identity so closely to a sense of moral integrity can often identify what will be regarded by others as a morally praiseworthy course of action, yet they will choose not to take that action because their primary motivating values, and consequently their deepest self-identity, is not tied to the moral ideal. As a result, they may have no sense of guilt about their "moral failure."[4]

Blasi does not go into detail about the development of moral personality in adolescence, beyond stating that it is a developmental process. Although he considers the moral self to be most highly developed when the ideals of justice, altruism, compassion, etc., are self-consciously appropriated in the person's self-identity, he admits that not everyone reaches that point even in adulthood. Presumably most adolescents are somewhere in the process of constructing their self-identity, of which their moral personality is one component, but he does not speculate about where most teenagers are in that process, or how their religious faith might impact their moral development.

Plausibility structures – Peter Berger

In 1967, Peter Berger described the normative teachings of religious communities as being grounded in socially constructed and maintained *plausibility structures*. These structures consist of the network of social relationships, roles, beliefs, and practices that designate certain ideas and behaviors as good, while others are bad and ought to be resisted. People who are deeply immersed in religious plausibility structures generally accept that the moral teachings of their faith tradition are normative for themselves and everyone else in the community. Berger does not address the question of moral development *per se,* but he says that every worldview, whether religious or not, requires plausibility structures in order to effectively direct beliefs and behaviors from one generation to the next.[5]

Berger's assertion provides a sociological counterpoint to the predominantly psychological and individualistic approaches to moral development described above. In this approach, the moral choices of an individual are usually motivated by social expectations toward them based on the various roles they perform in life (parent, child, sibling, student, friend, lover, etc.). Organized religion provides a myriad of social relationships and roles that serve as plausibility structures for directing believers to act according to the moral norms of the religious faith. However, in contemporary U.S. society, these structures must compete with plausibility structures for a variety of other worldviews—especially those promoted by the public schools, the legal system, the popular media, and their peers.

In generations past, the moral standards of most religious communities and those of the broader society had a great deal in common. That is not the case today. As the NSYR data will show later in this chapter, many Christian parents do not consistently uphold the moral teachings of their faith as ideals for their children to strive toward. With a range of behavioral scripts to choose from, teenagers do not always conduct themselves according to the norms they are taught in church, or even what they say they believe. Nevertheless, the positive or negative social consequences of a particular choice with respect to significant relationships in their lives provide powerful motivation for them to behave as they are expected according to their role in the relationship—whether it be as a friend, a child, a gang member, or a romantic partner.

Christian morality – life in Christ

The various theories of moral development described above demonstrate the difficulty of accounting for human behavior, even with the helpful insights of contemporary psychology and sociology. Nevertheless, each Christian faith tradition has developed its own theological, philosophical, and anthropological understandings of human behavior, setting the boundaries of moral norms and motivating believers to conduct themselves "uprightly" in the eyes of God. This chapter is not the place to give a detailed explanation of Christian moral theology and its denominational variations. References for a deeper study can be found among the "Additional resources" for this chapter listed at the end of this book.

Whether Catholic or Protestant, most Christians would agree that living in accordance with God's law as revealed in the Scriptures is an important part of the moral life. We may disagree about whether certain concrete actions are sinful, but we mostly agree that the Ten Commandments provide a basic understanding of sins to avoid, and Jesus' teaching and example provide guidance for how we should live our lives. We would also agree that we need God's help to make good moral choices. Even so, the moral life consists of much more than simply avoiding a list of sinful behaviors, and the moral formation we provide our adolescent members should reflect the full range and depth of the Christian moral tradition.

Without a doubt, religious educators and parents must not avoid their duty to inform the consciences of their teenagers with adequate explanations of God's laws about right and wrong. However, Christian discipleship also involves the practice of loving service to others, inspired by a deep love of God. It involves proclaiming the Good News of Jesus Christ and giving witness to it in a holy life grounded in the practice of the virtues. It involves a growing awareness of personal sin, a habit of sincere repentance, and the transforming experience of God's mercy and forgiveness. It involves a commitment to prayer and worship, and for Catholics the sacramental life, both alone and in community. And it involves personal dedication to the spiritual and physical well-being of others by forgiving their offenses, rejoicing with them in their blessings, and working to transform sinful social structures that still cause suffering for many people. In the Gospels, Jesus situates all of these dimensions as moral imperatives. A comprehensive youth ministry will provide young people with experience, understanding, and mentoring in all of these dimensions of the Christian life.

Faith and the moral choices of young Latino/a Christians

If these are the hallmarks of Christian moral teachings, then it is important for faith communities to ask themselves periodically: how well are

> I say to you that listen, Love your enemies, do good to those who hate you, bless those who curse you, pray for those who abuse you... Do to others as you would have them do to you.
> – Luke 6:27-28, 31

Table 6.1 – Beliefs about right and wrong (percentages)

	Hispanic			White, Any Faith	Hispanic Teen Religious Type*			
	Catholic	Protestant	No Religion		Committed	Engaged	Sporadic	Disengaged
Have people lost a sense of right and wrong?	N=278	N=94	N=40	N=2448	N=47	N=172	N=82	N=32
Yes, lost sense of right and wrong	38	47	46	51	43	38	32	51
Somewhere in the middle	2	4	3	3	4	2	5	6
It is still pretty clear	57	40	38	45	44	59	54	32
People never had a sense of right and wrong	1	0	3	~	0	0	0	3
Don't know	2	9	11	1	8	1	9	8
Do you feel confused about right and wrong?								
Feel confused	23	26	19	18	16	24	22	21
Something in the middle	5	2	3	2	6	4	1	0
Have a good idea	72	72	79	80	78	72	74	79
"Morals are relative, there are no definite rights or wrongs."								
Agree	52	40	55	47	43	50	51	51
Disagree	44	51	36	50	50	43	43	38
Don't know	5	9	9	3	6	6	6	11
"Right and wrong should be based on a fixed standard."								
Agree	56	45	36	48	62	52	49	35
Disagree	35	43	51	47	29	38	38	60
Don't know	8	9	11	4	4	10	12	3
If unsure of what was right or wrong, how would you decide what to do?								
Do what would make you feel happy	26	21	24	28	16	22	34	27
Do what would help you to get ahead	17	12	24	10	6	18	11	21
Follow the advice of a parent, teacher, or other adult	49	32	45	41	25	53	41	49
Do what God or the Scriptures tell you is right	5	31	5	20	44	6	12	3
Other / don't know	2	4	3	2	8	2	2	0

* See the Appendix on page 361 for definitions of the adolescent religious types.

we handing on our moral tradition to our adolescent members, and have we done enough to help them integrate these teachings into their religious self-identity? In the context of this book, the questions to ask are whether Latino/a teens exhibit any particular challenges in their moral development, whether they have distinctive values that can be utilized as assets in their moral formation, and whether our faith communities are offering them moral guidance in socially and culturally appropriate contexts. Because there are tremendous regional and local variations in the moral landscape, this chapter cannot answer these questions for every community, but it does provide pointers and insights into areas that may be of concern for faith communities all across the country.

Beliefs about right and wrong

A foundational question in moral development is the idea of what constitutes right and wrong. Table 6.1 shows that when asked if people in general have lost their sense of right and wrong, young Hispanics were almost evenly split in their answers. The Catholics and the religiously "engaged" were the most likely to say that the difference between right and wrong is still pretty clear, while the Protestants and the religiously "disengaged" were more likely to feel that people are confused about it.

Nevertheless when asked whether they themselves felt confused, the Catholic and Protestant Hispanic teens were equally confident, with the vast majority saying they have a good idea about right and wrong. What is really striking is the high number of young people who say they have a good idea about right and wrong, with very little variation across religious traditions or religious types. In reading the interviews, one gets the impression that the young Hispanics actually vary a great deal in how much they have thought about what is right or wrong, and the religiously involved young people tend to be much more articulate about it. Nevertheless, nearly everyone is comfortable with their own standards, whether they have given it much thought or not. Here is an example of how one religiously "disengaged" young Latina thinks about right and wrong:

Dialog 6.2 – 17 year-old Hispanic Christian female from the West

I: *Has there ever been a time in your life when you were unsure of what was right and wrong in a particular situation?*

R: Not that I can think of at the moment...

I: *So suppose I said, "Okay, let's go steal something," and you were just like, "I don't know." How would you decide what to do?*

R: I really don't know. I would, basically, like if they would convince me, you know.

I: *How would somebody convince you?*

R: I don't know. They just keep bugging the hell out of me. I just get tired of them.

I: *Would you say that, in general, people today have lost a sense of right and wrong, or do people still know what's right and wrong today?*

R: Yes, they lost the sense, 'cause they know that they can get away with it... They can think it's not wrong. They know it's wrong, but they'll do it anyway.

I: *And why do you think that is?*

R: For the excitement...

I: Some people say that there really are no final rights and wrongs in life—that everything is relative, that morality is nothing but what people make it. So I mean, maybe you think stealing is wrong. But hey, maybe it's wrong for you, but it's right for me or something like that. Do you think there are some things that are just wrong for everybody, or everything just depends on the person?

R: I don't know, 'cause some things do just actually depend on the person.

I: Like what?

R: I really can't think of anything right now, but I know there are certain things that really do just depend. You know about a certain person. But in general, I think it should be like the same for almost everybody.

I: Okay, so where do you think that your views of right and wrong, where do they come from?

R: My morals and how I was raised up...

I: So your parents?

R: Yeah...

I: So how do you decide or know what's good and bad, right and wrong in life?

R: Just if I feel like I shouldn't do it or feel like it's that bad, just don't do it. Just you have that feeling, you know.

I: Uh-huh, so it's just a feeling you get?

R: Yep.

This conversation is actually a good example of how some young people agreed with both propositions that "morals are relative" and "right and wrong should be based on fixed standards." In fact, majorities of Hispanic Catholic teens agreed with both statements, despite the fact that they imply different moral standards. Perhaps the key word in the second proposition is "should." Like the girl above, many young Hispanics believe that there *should* be a fixed moral standard, but in practice it does not always work that way. Overall, the Latino/a Catholics were more likely to agree with both statements than their Protestant peers, and there was a strong correlation between religious engagement and the belief that right and wrong should be a fixed standard.

The last question in Table 6.1 offers insight into the importance of various sources of moral authority in the decisions of U.S. adolescents. The second through fourth responses in the list roughly correspond to stages 2 through 4 of Kohlberg's scale of moral development. The first response, "do what would make you feel happy," could fit any of the six stages, depending on how strongly the teen feels the connection between personal happiness and both internal and external sources of moral authority. In any case, there is not enough data in the NSYR survey to clearly identify the moral development stage of any of the respondents—this question only provides a very general approximation.

Latino/a Catholic teens and non-religious teens are very comparable on this question, with nearly half following the advice of an adult. In contrast, the Protestants are six times more likely to say that they turn to God or the Scriptures to know what is right and significantly less likely to seek their own advantage or follow the advice of an adult. Among the various religious types, the "committed" Hispanic teens were the least likely to seek their own advantage, and by far the most likely to say that they try to do what God or the Scriptures tell them to do.

Personal integrity and guilty feelings

Table 6.2 presents the teens' responses to questions regarding cheating, lying, and feeling guilty. Perhaps the most striking result is the relatively low incidences of lying to parents and cheating at school among Hispanic teens with no religious affiliation. For example, none of these young people reported cheating very or fairly often, compared to about 10% of both Catholic and Protestant Latino/a teens. Furthermore, 76% said they rarely or never cheat, compared to 67% of their Catholic and 52% of their Protestant peers. As a further contrast, 11% of the religiously committed Hispanic teens admitted that they cheat very often—the most of any group—and they were the least likely of all the religious types to say they rarely or never cheat.

Does this mean that being religious is related to a loss of personal integrity among adolescents? Possibly, but another potential explanation is that religious teens are more likely to respond honestly to questions that might not be very flattering to themselves. A reading of the interview transcripts suggests that the latter is the more likely explanation: of the four non-religious Hispanic teens who were asked whether they have cheated at school, three admitted that they had. Here is a typical conversation:

Dialog 6.3 – 18 year-old non-religious Hispanic female from the West

I: *Do you think it is wrong to cheat on assignments or tests at school?*
R: Oh, yeah.
I: *Why?*
R: Because it's not showing what you know.
I: *Well, I've interviewed some teenagers that say, "Who cares, I mean it's stupid stuff I'll never have to know the rest of my life. They're forcing me to learn stuff that's irrelevant, so, why not take the easy way?"*
R: I agree with that, sometimes.
I: *You agree with that?*
R: I mean sometimes they teach things that yeah you're not gonna learn.
I: *So does that justify cheating on it?*
R: No. It doesn't justify it, but...
I: *So you would say it's still wrong, you should still go with what you're expected, even if you got a worse grade.*
R: Yeah.
I: *Were you ever tempted to cheat, or did you ever cheat?*
R: Yeah.

Table 6.2 – Personal integrity and guilty feelings (percentages)

	Hispanic			White, Any Faith	Hispanic Teen Religious Type*			
	Catholic	Protestant	No Religion		Committed	Engaged	Sporadic	Disengaged
How often have you lied to your parent(s)?	N=278	N=94	N=40	N=2448	N=47	N=172	N=82	N=32
Very often	6	2	0	4	2	7	4	3
Fairly often	5	6	1	5	6	4	3	2
Sometimes	22	27	18	17	15	23	27	13
Occasionally	12	15	23	15	12	14	8	33
Rarely	36	35	35	43	49	32	43	41
Never	20	15	23	16	16	20	15	6
How often do you do things you hope your parent(s) won't find out about?								
Very often	10	5	5	6	11	7	5	5
Fairly often	8	5	10	9	5	6	10	8
Sometimes	21	28	18	16	21	19	23	25
Occasionally	10	20	8	17	12	15	10	10
Rarely	32	25	33	36	39	29	42	38
Never	20	17	28	16	12	23	10	14
How often have you cheated on a test, homework, etc?								
Very often	4	3	0	2	11	1	4	5
Fairly often	6	6	0	4	0	9	5	0
Sometimes	12	20	14	10	13	14	12	11
Occasionally	11	19	8	11	13	9	12	10
Rarely	29	26	21	34	25	32	33	19
Never	38	26	55	38	39	34	34	56
In the last year, how often have you felt guilty?								
Very often	8	6	10	4	0	5	9	13
Fairly often	14	3	8	9	6	12	6	11
Sometimes	19	32	25	17	39	16	24	21
Occasionally	10	14	14	19	14	14	12	19
Rarely	31	29	29	38	27	33	41	21
Never	18	15	15	13	14	20	9	16
How much of your guilty feelings were caused by religious influences?								
A lot	6	9	3	7	26	6	7	3
Some	19	13	3	13	6	19	14	3
A little	14	22	5	14	21	18	10	5
None	43	41	75	52	32	37	60	73
How much has religion helped to relieve your guilty feelings?								
A lot	20	45	5	27	57	25	7	6
Some	36	18	18	25	16	34	33	11
A little	13	11	11	15	6	15	26	13
None	12	6	51	19	1	6	23	54

* See the Appendix on page 361 for definitions of the adolescent religious types.

I: Were the circumstances like you didn't have enough time to study, or what?

R: I just like, you're reading and—or a question—saying I don't know. And then your, your purse is right there, so it's just kind of...

I: And did that bother you when that happened?

R: No.

I: You just said, "What the heck."

R: Oh well.

This interpretation is indirectly supported by the fact that the general trend among *white* teens is for higher levels of religious commitment to be associated with greater honesty with parents and at school (data not shown). Experts in Hispanic marketing generally agree that Latino/a adults are more reluctant than white adults to report behaviors that they think the interviewer might look down upon, unless the interviewer puts the respondent at ease and lets them know that it is okay to be honest.[6] The lack of trust between the respondent and the survey taker seems to have been a factor in the responses of some of the Hispanic teens as well, especially those without any religious affiliation. In contrast, the NSYR interviewers seem to have done a pretty good job of establishing a rapport with the teens, so it will be important in the remainder of this section to confirm survey results with patterns found in the interviews.

Another clear finding in Table 6.2 is the association between religious commitment and guilt feelings. First, greater religious commitment decreases the frequency of feeling guilty, most likely due to the fact that religiously committed teens receive frequent messages to avoid sin, so they actually avoid behaviors that would cause them to feel guilty. At the same time, their faith calls them to reflect on and question their behavior and attitudes, which can lead to heightened guilty feelings when they do something wrong. Finally, the forgiveness they experience from God releases them of their guilty feelings. All three of these dynamics are evident in the relative responses of Hispanic teens of each religious type in the last three questions: the religiously committed Latino/a teens were by far the most likely to cite religion as both causing and relieving their guilty feelings "a lot," and they reported feeling guilty less often than other groups.

As a final comparison, the Protestant Latino/a teens were much more likely than their Catholic counterparts to say that religion helps them to relieve their guilty feelings, although religion caused guilty feelings at about the same rate for both. This may be a result of the greater emphasis in Protestant doctrine on God's forgiveness of sin through a free gift in Jesus Christ. The Hispanic Catholic teens who had been to Confession in the last year were slightly more likely than their peers who had not confessed to attribute both their guilty feelings and their relief from guilt to religious causes (data not shown), but they were still less likely to report such religious relief than their Protestant peers.

Use of illicit substances

Beyond questions about guilt and personal integrity, the NSYR survey only asked a limited range of questions concerning the teens' behavior with respect to common moral norms. For example, there were no questions about violence, cursing, stealing, or gang-related activities. Nevertheless, the survey did address the use of illicit substances and sexual behaviors. Table 6.3 reports the teenagers' usage of tobacco, alcohol, and marijuana according to their religious tradition and level of commitment.

Comparing by religious tradition, there is a clear pattern of the non-religious Hispanic teens being the most likely to use illicit substances, followed by Catholics, with the Protestants being the least likely overall. With respect to religious commitment, the differences between "committed," "engaged," and "sporadic" Latino/a teens are not large, and they do

Table 6.3 – Use of illicit substances (percentages)

	Hispanic			White, Any Faith	Hispanic Teen Religious Type*			
	Catholic	Protestant	No Religion		Committed	Engaged	Sporadic	Disengaged
Smokes at least one cigarette a day	N=278	N=94	N=40	N=2448	N=47	N=172	N=82	N=32
	5	5	8	9	1	6	4	8
Frequency of drinking alcohol								
Never	59	71	53	60	68	63	56	29
A few times a year	22	15	25	21	21	18	20	46
About once a month	3	5	8	6	2	5	9	11
A few times a month	9	6	10	7	8	9	11	6
About once a week	5	2	4	4	0	4	4	0
A few times a week or more	2	1	1	2	0	1	1	8
In the last year, how often have you been drunk?								
Never / not asked	79	85	70	73	85	78	83	56
Once or twice	12	8	19	12	5	14	7	25
A few times	3	5	8	8	3	5	4	13
Every couple of weeks	4	1	0	3	0	3	0	3
Once a week	1	0	3	1	0	1	4	0
More than once a week	1	1	0	1	6	~	1	2
How often have you used marijuana?								
Never	74	82	64	75	70	83	70	48
Tried it once or twice	18	10	28	13	21	7	21	38
Use it occasionally	4	4	8	8	8	6	5	10
Use it regularly	4	4	0	3	0	4	5	3

* See the Appendix on page 361 for definitions of the adolescent religious types.

not always follow the pattern of increasing use with decreasing religious commitment. For example, the religiously "engaged" Hispanic teens were significantly less likely to have smoked pot than their "committed" counterparts. Nevertheless, the "disengaged" were much more active users of all three substances than their more religious peers.

The other significant finding in Table 6.3 is the fact that the white teens actually reported greater use of all three illicit substances than their Hispanic counterparts. However, given the already noted disproportionate tendency among Hispanic survey takers to underreport behaviors that might be perceived negatively by the survey taker, it is possible that their actual usage of these substances is more common than reported. Nevertheless, it seems unlikely that Latino/a teens deserve the widely held stereotype that they are much more likely to abuse drugs and alcohol than other young people their age.

Although it can clearly be said that religious involvement is associated with lower usage of illicit substances among Hispanic teens, there are other variables that also demonstrate clear associations. Table 6.4 reports the usage of tobacco, alcohol, and marijuana by Latino/a adolescents based on their responses to questions about parental monitoring, sources of moral authority, and generational status. Since all three of these variables also

Table 6.4 – Significant correlations to the use of illicit substances among Hispanic teens (percentages)		Smokes Daily	Has Had Alcohol in the Last Year	Has Been Drunk in the Last Year	Has Tried Marijuana Once or Twice	Uses Marijuana Occasionally or Regularly
How often do your parents know what you're doing away from home?						
Always	N=186	5	26	13	13	7
Usually	N=147	4	45	23	19	8
Sometimes to never	N=114	9	57	37	20	21
If unsure of what was right or wrong, how would you decide what to do?						
Do what would make you feel happy	N=116	3	56	34	19	22
Do what would help you to get ahead	N=73	10	53	34	21	13
Follow the advice of a parent or adult	N=195	6	32	14	16	3
Do what God or the Scriptures tell you	N=56	5	21	11	5	14
Generation since family's arrival in the United States						
First	N=95	11	29	12	10	2
Second	N=165	2	40	13	15	8
Third or higher	N=191	7	46	36	21	17

show strong associations to religious commitment (see Table 4.5 on page 135, Table 6.1 above, and Chart 1.7 on page 21), it should not be surprising that illicit substance usage is generally lowest among Hispanic teenagers whose parents closely monitor their activities; who follow the advice of parents, adults, God, or the Scriptures when they are not sure what to do; and who are immigrants—with the exception of tobacco products, where immigrants report the highest usage. It is also interesting that the differences in usage patterns between young Latinos and Latinas, and between Hispanic teens at various economic levels, were not significant (data not shown).

Attitudes about sex and marriage

On questions about sexual behavior, Protestant Hispanic teens are more conservative than their Catholic and non-religious peers. Comparing the first and last questions in Table 6.5 reveals that Latino/a adolescents in each religious tradition proportionally agree with their parents about whether they should wait until marriage to have sex. From a religious education standpoint, it is significant that so many Christian adults—especially among Catholics—disagree with the traditional teaching that people should only have sex within marriage, and presumably are providing a more secular teaching about sex to their children.

Still, there is a clear association between adolescent religious type and beliefs about waiting for sex: 84% of the "committed" Hispanic teens believe people should wait, compared to about 40% of their "sporadic" and "disengaged" peers. It should be noted that the opinions expressed on this question vary considerably with age and sexual experience. By age 17, only 51% of Hispanic teens said people should wait, compared to 69% at age 13. Similarly, only 22% of those who reported having had sexual intercourse said people should wait, compared to 67% of those who had not. Similar numbers were found among the white teens as well (data not shown).

The idea that sex is okay for teens if they are "emotionally ready" was twice as popular among Catholic and non-religious Latino/a teens as it was among their Protestant counterparts. It was also more than twice as prevalent among those who were religiously "sporadic" and "disengaged" as it was among the "engaged" and "committed." Mark Regnerus, a research associate with the NSYR, takes up this topic in his highly recommended sociological analysis of adolescent sexuality, *Forbidden Fruit: Sex and Religion in the Lives of American Teenagers.* He writes:

> So far as I can tell, emotional readiness means that it's fine for you to have sex if (a) you're ready, (b) that's what you want to do, (c) you're not being pressured, and to a lesser extent, (d) as long as you're being "safe" (practicing contraception and protection from STDs)... Furthermore, you shouldn't have intercourse with just anyone; it should be a special thing.

Table 6.5 – Attitudes about sex and marriage (percentages)

	Hispanic			White, Any Faith	Hispanic Teen Religious Type*			
	Catholic	Protestant	No Religion		Committed	Engaged	Sporadic	Disengaged
Should people wait until marriage to have sex?	N=278	N=94	N=40	N=2448	N=47	N=172	N=82	N=32
Yes, they should wait	54	73	48	56	84	69	37	41
Not necessarily, but teens are too young to be having sex	17	11	21	13	2	14	21	22
No, it's ok for teens to have sex if they are emotionally ready	29	15	31	29	14	16	38	37
Do you ever feel pressured to have sex?								
Pressured by friends	4	9	3	4	5	6	2	0
Pressured by dates	5	2	10	3	4	3	5	10
Pressured by both	2	2	4	4	11	1	1	3
No pressure from either	88	87	81	88	80	90	92	84
What is the ideal age to get married?								
15 to 19.5 years	2	5	0	4	4	2	2	3
20 to 22.5 years	22	29	28	22	18	21	20	24
23 to 25 years	44	33	34	42	46	44	46	38
25.5 to 29.5 years	22	21	18	23	21	24	24	10
30 to 34.5 years	9	4	18	6	5	8	5	21
35 or more years	1	7	4	3	6	2	4	5
Should a couple without children end an unhappy marriage?								
End it	66	63	65	61	42	70	62	76
Stick with it	30	37	19	35	58	27	33	13
Would you consider living with a romantic partner before marriage?								
Yes	57	40	60	54	33	47	59	63
No	41	59	33	44	64	51	39	30
Should people wait until marriage to have sex? (parent survey)								
Yes, they should wait	56	73	53	60	71	68	50	44
Not necessarily, but teens are too young to be having sex	27	22	28	26	14	23	36	32
No, it's ok for teens to have sex if they are emotionally ready	15	5	16	12	13	8	12	19

* See the Appendix on page 361 for definitions of the adolescent religious types.

For many girls in particular, love—however they define it—increasingly justifies the pursuit of a sexual relationship. Ironically, 'being emotionally ready' is a familiar and comfortable phrase to many adolescents, but as a norm it largely lacks standardized content and it risks being a platitude. Many definitions of it are hopelessly confusing.[7]

The vast majority of Hispanic respondents reported that they had never been pressured to have sex, either by their friends or their dates. This was surprising given that much of the literature has led us to believe that peer pressure is a very strong influence on the lives of adolescents—especially when it comes to sexual behavior. However, pastoral leaders have clarified the reason for this apparent discrepancy. Young people understand peer pressure to be some type of coercive persuasion, whereas their experience is that they are "invited," not coerced, by their significant peers to join in the different activities. Such an invitation is not perceived as pressure by most adolescents; the prevailing ethos is that "everyone is doing it," so they just fall in line and become sexually active.

Another surprise was the fact that the religiously "committed" Latino/a teens were the most likely to say that they were pressured by both friends and dates to have sex. This may be due to the fact that they are more sensitive to the subtle pressures around them than other people, as the following conversation shows:

Dialog 6.4 – 18 year-old Hispanic Southern Baptist male from the South

I: *So, do you think young people should wait to have sex until they're married?*

R: I think they should... Or if like the worst case scenario, they're like 48 and they've never been married and whatever, and they like fall in love deeply with somebody and stuff... I don't know, I don't think they should do it even then. But I mean that's a pretty, I don't know, that's pretty drastic or something like that. And they end up becoming married to the person eventually or something, I'm not sure... Personally, I think it should be in marriage all the time.

I: *Okay. Why?*

R: Because that also goes back to the moral, and that was the way that I was taught—that it's supposed to be something for marriage. It's not supposed to be something for, you know, just for fun, you know...

I: *Might it be okay for teenagers to have sex if they are "emotionally ready for it"?*

R: I don't, again, I don't think it's your emotions and stuff. I think, um, that you pretty much need to be married for that.

I: *Are friends of yours having sex?*

R: No, actually not my friends, my personal... And how do I know, I know you're gonna ask. How do I know, um, [laughs] 'cause I just know they're not like that. The girls that are my friends, or they're the friends of my friends that are guys, they're not like that. You can just tell certain girls are not gonna stand for stuff like that, and that they wouldn't do that...

I: *Have you yourself ever been physically involved with another person, more than just holding hands or light kissing?*

R: Uh, heavy kissing, but that's it.

I: *Do you ever feel pressure now to have sex?*

R: Oh yeah, you always feel pressure to have sex. Well like not from your friends, necessarily, cause my friends aren't like that. But when you open like men's health or watch TV and everybody's just screwing whatever and

> you're just... It's just to me, that's a lot of pressure. I can understand how kids succumb to that constantly, especially if they're really media oriented, because that's what they're telling you, "just do it, do it, do it," so...
>
> I: *What do you do with that pressure?*
>
> R: Um, I usually try to channel it into doing something else, you know with what I'm doing.

When asked about the ideal age for getting married, most teens replied between 23 and 25 years old, irrespective of their religious tradition or religious type. Nevertheless, a substantial minority of religiously "disengaged" and non-religious Hispanic adolescents preferred to wait until after age 30, while their Protestant counterparts were more likely to see themselves getting married before age 23. The Protestants also expressed more conservative opinions about living with a romantic partner before marriage, but they were just as likely as other teens to say that a couple without children should end an unhappy marriage. On the latter point, the religiously "committed" Hispanic teens distinguished themselves by recommending that the couple should "stick with it" more than twice as often as the other religious types.

Dating and sexual experiences

Up to this point, it is fairly clear that Hispanic teens who are more engaged in their faith life tend to hold more conservative attitudes toward sex and marriage than their peers who are less engaged. However, the question remains: do these attitudes translate into measurably different behavior with respect to sex and dating? Judging from the data presented in Table 6.6, the general answer is that they do make a difference, but the difference is not as large as one might expect.

In the first place, there is virtually no difference among the religious traditions, and only slight differences among the religious types, with respect to whether the Hispanic teens have ever been in a romantic relationship. The Protestants were slightly less likely to have been in a romantic relationship at the time of the survey, but they were just as likely as any other group to have "done more than holding hands or light kissing," with the exception of the religiously "disengaged," who surpassed all other Latino groups on this question by at least 16%.

A similar pattern emerges with respect to watching X-rated movies: there were only small differences between religious traditions, but in this case there was a linear relationship between the religious type and the frequency of viewing these movies, with the religiously "committed" being the least likely to report having done so. However, 7% of the "committed" Latino/a teens refused to answer the question or said they didn't know, so it is possible that the actual differences are smaller than they appear in the table.

Table 6.6 – Dating and sexual experiences (percentages)

	Hispanic			White, Any Faith	Hispanic Teen Religious Type*			
	Catholic	Protestant	No Religion		Committed	Engaged	Sporadic	Disengaged
Dating experiences	N=278	N=94	N=40	N=2448	N=47	N=172	N=82	N=32
Has ever dated or been in a romantic relationship	72	70	71	78	69	67	76	62
Currently dating or in a romantic relationship	36	27	40	33	20	35	24	38
X-rated movies watched in the last year								
0	70	69	66	72	79	73	71	54
1 or 2	14	19	15	13	8	14	15	25
3 to 5	5	5	9	8	4	4	10	11
6 to 10	3	1	3	3	2	2	1	3
11 to 300	5	2	5	3	0	3	3	3
Physical intimacy and pregnancy								
Has done more than holding hands or light kissing	40	39	40	43	32	35	41	57
Has had oral sex	17	16	20	24	18	18	24	32
Has had sexual intercourse	20	17	34	20	16	16	24	51
Had first sex under the influence of alcohol or drugs	2	3	0	3	13	1	1	3
Has been or has gotten someone pregnant	4	0	0	1	0	1	3	5
Is responsible for raising a baby	2	0	0	0.5	0	0	2	3
Frequency of having oral sex								
Once	3	0	0	3	0	2	5	6
A few times	8	7	8	10	9	9	12	11
Several times	3	3	8	5	3	2	4	3
Many times	3	5	5	5	6	5	3	11
Frequency of having sexual intercourse								
Once	2	1	3	2	11	1	2	6
A few times	7	5	13	6	0	5	9	19
Several times	1	3	8	4	3	1	4	10
Many times	10	7	10	6	0	8	10	14
When you have had sexual intercourse, did you and your partner use contraception?								
Every time	12	8	20	13	12	6	20	29
Almost every time	3	2	3	3	0	2	1	6
Some of the time	4	1	5	2	2	2	3	8
Never	2	5	5	1	0	5	1	6

* See the Appendix on page 361 for definitions of the adolescent religious types.

Hispanic teens report a lower incidence of oral sex than their white peers, and the two groups are comparable with respect to sexual intercourse. Interestingly, more white teens reported that they had engaged in oral sex than sexual intercourse, but the opposite was true for Latino/a teens. Mark Regnerus reports that in general, oral sex is a more common introduction to sexual activity than is intercourse, mostly because it is seen as a safer form of sexual activity, and secondarily because some believe it is a way to maintain their "technical virginity."[8] This pattern is evident among some Hispanic teens, but not to the same extent as it is with their white counterparts. In any case, the religiously "sporadic" and "disengaged" Hispanics were more likely than their more religious peers to partake in both forms of sexual activity, and the "disengaged" and non-religious teenagers were especially active with respect to sexual intercourse.

It should be noted that among sexually active teens, only about 10% reported having either oral sex or sexual intercourse just once. For most of them, their first sexual experience is not an isolated incident, but it marks a transition in life from being sexually inactive to being sexually active. On the other hand, 13% of the religiously "committed" Hispanics had their first sex under the influence of alcohol or drugs, and 11% reported only one sexual encounter. Thus, it appears that a significant minority of religiously involved teens may have become sexually active against their better judgment and are making a serious effort not to do it again—at least not until they are much older.

Despite the Catholic Church's teaching that contraception is a violation of God's plan for human sexuality, Latino/a Catholic teens are actually more consistent about using contraception when they have sexual intercourse than their Protestant peers. In fact, many of the Catholic teens are not even aware that their church has a teaching against contraception, as found in the following interview:

Dialog 6.5 – 17 year-old Hispanic Catholic female from the South

I: *What do you think have been the most important influences on how you think about sex?*

R: Influences? Well, the stories I have heard. My mother talks to me a lot. But truly, my own experience, no... I can't talk because I haven't had any.

I: *And do you believe... does your religion have any particular teaching or morality view point when it comes to sex?*

R: My own religion, yes.

I: *What does it say?*

R: That you shouldn't do it before marriage. But I think, I mean, if it happens before marriage I don't think it is bad. I don't see it that way. If the person has been your boyfriend for a while and you love each other, I don't think it is wrong... I am a bit confused because in my religion, yes, yes...

I: *And without protection... it says...*

R: Ah no. Not in my religion. Not in my religion... Yes, you may protect yourself.

I: *You may?*
R: Uh-huh.
I: *In some Catholic countries they say you may not.*
R: No, in my country you may.
I: *Uh-huh.*
R: Yes, you may. It is the Mormons who may not. The other religions may protect themselves.

Even so, none of the Protestant teens reported a pregnancy, but 4% of the Catholic teens had either been or gotten someone pregnant. Given the fact that the two groups responded with similar frequencies of sexual intercourse and contraceptive use, this is probably a statistical anomaly. On the other hand, Hispanic adolescent girls have historically had higher fertility rates than their white peers. Since both groups had similar rates of sexual intercourse and contraceptive use, it is difficult to account for the difference in fertility, which also appears in the NSYR survey. The reasons for this discrepancy merit further study.

Correlations to sexual experiences among Hispanic teens

If religious tradition and religious type are not as influential on sexual be-havior as they are on attitudes about sex and marriage, then the question must be asked: what factors play a bigger role in shaping the sexual be-havior of Latino/a adolescents? Mark Regnerus provides a helpful clue by showing that adolescent sexual activity falls into five behavioral patterns:

- *Delayers* are teens who have not yet had their first sexual experience, and for a variety of reasons they are not planning on making their sexual debut anytime soon. They make up 38% of the teen population in the United States.

- *Anticipators* likewise have not had any sexual encounters, but only be-cause they have not had the opportunity. In fact, they are anxiously awaiting the moment when the "time is right," and they are about 25% of the youth population.

- *One-timers* are those who regret or feel guilty about their first sexual activity, so they have decided not to engage in sex again, at least for the foreseeable future. Only about 4% of the teens in the U.S. fall in this category.

- *Steadies* are in a monogamous long-term relationship in which they have had sex multiple times, and they make up about 11% of adoles-cents in the U.S.

- *Multiples* have had sex with several people in different relationships, and about 23% of the NSYR teenagers are in this category.[9]

Table 6.7 – Significant correlations to sexual experiences among Hispanic teens (percentages)

		Has Seen X-Rated Movies in Last Year	Has Had Oral Sex	Has Had Sexual Intercourse	Has Been or Gotten Someone Pregnant	Used Contraception Every or Almost Every Time	Used Contraception Some of the Time or Never
Age in years							
13	N=91	16	2	4	0	4	0
14	N=91	25	9	3	0	3	0
15	N=87	26	20	16	0	13	3
16	N=92	33	33	37	4	25	12
17	N=90	35	29	45	8	30	15
X-rated movies watched in the last year							
0	N=317	0	12	14	0	9	5
1 or 2	N=67	100	26	35	4	27	8
3 or more	N=55	100	48	49	7	37	12
Should people wait until marriage to have sex? (teen survey / parent survey)							
Yes, they should wait	N=259 / N=275	19 / 25	9 / 18	8 / 19	2 / 3	4 / 12	4 / 7
Not necessarily, but teens are too young to have sex	N=68 / N=112	22 / 33	13 / 19	24 / 19	1 / ~	15 / 14	9 / 5
No, it's ok for teens to have sex if they are ready	N=121 / N=58	48 / 25	42 / 21	47 / 34	3 / 4	38 / 28	9 / 6
If unsure of what was right or wrong, how would you decide what to do?							
Do what would make you feel happy	N=116	30	29	31	2	25	6
Do what would help you to get ahead	N=73	36	25	34	5	20	14
Follow the advice of a parent or adult	N=195	24	12	15	1	11	4
Do what God or the Scriptures tell you	N=56	24	11	7	2	4	4
How often do your parents know what you're doing away from home?							
Always	N=186	15	10	14	5	8	6
Usually	N=147	33	23	24	2	19	5
Sometimes to never	N=114	38	28	30	0	21	9
Generation since family's arrival in the United States							
First	N=95	24	7	15	0	11	4
Second	N=165	19	18	16	1	14	2
Third or higher	N=191	36	25	29	5	18	11
Gender							
Male	N=215	38	24	21	2	18	3
Female	N=236	15	14	21	3	13	8

While this classification helps to explain the various attitudes about sex among adolescents today, it does not answer the question about the factors that shape these attitudes. To that end, Table 6.7 presents eight variables from the NSYR survey that are associated with diverse sexual behaviors and experiences.

The first variable in the table is also the most obvious: age. For the majority of young people, the sexual drive increases with the onset of puberty, so it is not surprising that only about 4% of Hispanic 13- and 14-year-olds have had sexual intercourse. However, this number increases steadily to 45% at age 17. For comparison, 44% of the white 17-year-olds in the NSYR survey had also engaged in sexual intercourse.

The correlation between sexual experiences and seeing X-rated movies is not as intuitive as the association with age, but it is actually even more significant. No group in the table is more sexually active than those who have seen three or more pornographic movies in the last year. This may be due partly to selection effects; in other words, the teens who were already anticipators may be more likely to view this type of video. It is also possible that sexual experience leads to an increase in watching X-rated movies. However, we cannot rule out the possibility that viewing pornographic material in itself desensitizes teens to sexual activity and leads them to see their peers as objects of sexual gratification. Most likely all three of these effects contribute to the results, but it is impossible from the data to determine which is the most significant factor.

Of particular note is the high rate of oral sex among pornographic movie watchers, which is out of step with the general tendency among Hispanic adolescents to favor sexual intercourse over oral sex. This adds to the notion that young people who see X-rated material may be taking their sexual scripts from what they see in the movies. The following conversation with a Latino who had gone to Catholic school and had not yet experienced sexual intercourse exemplifies that approach:

Dialog 6.6 – 14 year-old Hispanic Catholic male from the West

I: *What do you think have been the most important influences, people or experiences, on how you think about sex?*

R: Ah, about how it feels, about the pleasures... Um, that's about it.

I: *Who has influenced you?*

R: My friends. I mean, they haven't like pressured me or anything. They just like tell me like what they did and all that.

I: *Does your religion have any particular teaching or morality when it comes to sex?*

R: Yes, my religion says that you should just have it when you're married...

I: *Do you agree with that?*

R: Ah, yes.

I: *Why?*

R: Because it's my religion. I was taught to believe in it.

I: Okay, but earlier you said if you had the opportunity, you might do it anyway.

R: Yeah.

I: So, what do you believe versus... I mean, would you follow with your religion, or would you follow with the moment?

R: The moment...

I: Is there anything in the media that you don't like or that bothers you?

R: No.

I: Some teenagers watch or view X-rated, pornographic videos, programs, or internet sites. How do you yourself feel about pornography?

R: I feel it's natural, I guess.

I: Like can you talk a little bit more about that? Natural, how, like what do you mean?

R: Like, 'cause everybody does it. I mean, I'm not saying just 'cause everybody does it I do it, but I do it to learn—to learn or either just to watch it. Most of the time to learn.

I: To learn what?

R: Like if I get in that situation, I'll know what to do.

I: Do you or have you ever viewed pornographic websites or movies?

R: Ah, yeah.

I: What was your experience, and where, with whom was it?

R: It was at my house, no one there.

I: How do you think viewing pornography affects you, or affected you, if at all?

R: Well, it taught me a lot of stuff like, you know, what to do and all that.

I: Do you think you will continue to watch or view X-rated websites or videos?

R: Yes.

What is especially interesting about the above example is that in other parts of the interview this teen was very articulate about his faith. He clearly was paying attention in his religion classes. Nevertheless, when it comes to sexual ethics, he simply didn't believe that the Church's teachings applied to him. This example illustrates the gap Augusto Blasi described between cognitive understanding of what is right and the ability to consistently act on that knowledge. It also points to the importance of providing moral examples and creating an atmosphere of peer accountability in addition to teaching doctrine about moral behavior. Despite the fact that he knew that both his parents and his religion disapproved of sex before marriage, his peers and his choices in media were telling him otherwise. He says that they have not pressured him, but he was clearly influenced by their example.

That said, the next two questions in Table 6.7 show that cognitive understanding does play an important role in moral behavior. In fact, the least sexually active teens were those who said they believed that people should wait until marriage to have sex, and those who said that they try to do what God or the Scriptures tell them when they are not sure what to do. This may be partly due to selection effects; as noted in the previous section, teens tend to change their mind on the question about waiting for sex until marriage as they get older or become sexually active. Still, there were many examples in the interviews of Latino/a teens who believed on religious grounds that sex was only for marriage, and they were sure they would not change their opinion about it, as in the following example:

Dialog 6.7 – 17 year-old Hispanic non-denominational Christian female from the West

I: *Okay. What do you think are some of the biggest problems or pressures fac-ing teenagers these days?*

R: Uh…definitely like, drinking and sex and drugs and stuff.

I: *Have you faced any of those pressures?*

R: Yeah.

I: *And how do you deal with those?*

R: I just, I just try and stay away from it I guess. I mean I know where I stand with it and I'm not going to get into any of that stuff...

I: *Okay. So I was going to ask do you think people should wait to have sex until they are married or not, and you would respond affirmative to that?*

R: Yes, yes...

I: *Okay… Might it be okay for teenagers to have sex if they are "emotionally ready for it," or not?*

R: No, I don't think it's okay.

I: *Okay. And how much have these questions about sex been issues in your own personal life? Have you had to deal with these at all?*

R: Yeah I have but…shoot, it hasn't been for awhile. A lot of people know where I stand and they're not going to push me past that. So…

I: *Okay. Are your friends having sex or are they physically involved in any way?*

R: Uh…oh…(pause) there are people I know, but they're not, like my really close friends, people I'm always with, no.

I: *Okay, okay. And have you yourself ever been physically involved with another person, more than just holding hands or light kissing?*

R: No.

I: *Okay… Let's see… I was going to ask if you ever feel pressure now to have sex, by friends, dates, other influences?*

R: No.

I: *No? Okay. And how much is pregnancy or sexually transmitted diseases a concern for teens who are thinking about sexual activity?*

R: Uh… for my really close friends it's a huge concern. Most of them are Christians and they wouldn't even consider it.

I: *Oh, okay.*

R: But my non-Christian friends… uh… I mean if they're doing it they obvi-ously don't care too much about it, 'cause if they did I think that—I would hope that they would turn from what they're doing.

For this young woman, the fact that most of her friends understand her position on sex before marriage and support her in that choice makes a big difference—she says that she has not even had to deal with the issue for a long time. Some faith communities have recognized the importance of giv-ing teens support from their peers in their efforts to maintain sexual absti-nence. Of all the Christian Hispanic teens interviewed, only one spoke about the experience of taking an "abstinence pledge" in one of these programs:

Dialog 6.8 – 18 year-old Hispanic Baptist male from the South

I: *Thinking about your own life and your friends, do you think that people's religious faith affects their dating in any way?*

R: Yes, I think it does.

I: *How?*

R: Um... girls that are very religious and boys that are very religious are usually a lot less likely to go out and be all over each other, be inappropriate in public—things like that... There's been some girls I went out with that weren't Christian—that I could figure out pretty fast—but they were very, they were very good girls... They were still virgins, they were like very good girls and they weren't um...

I: *How did you know they were still virgins?*

R: Oh, because um, they had their True Love Waits. Of course I didn't know for sure, but I mean I could pretty much tell just by the way that they acted and stuff.

I: *What did, what about, "true love what?"*

R: True, they had their True Love Waits rings. Like some kids will get True Love Waits rings... Those rings are like, it was a big Southern Baptist push like way, about four years ago, and they still do it now. Like you get a ring when you turn like 15 or something like that, and you pledge to save yourself for your marriage and stuff.

I: *Did you do that?*

R: Did I do that? Yeah. I did it. Um, I lost my ring, though. I had to get another one... My parents were like...

I: *Why did you lose your ring? [laughs]*

R: Yeah, my parents were like, 'cause I didn't want it to give it back to my parents—that's what you're supposed to do if you lose it or something like that. You're supposed to get it back to the parents, although I'm sure kids don't constantly do that.

I: *A lot of students have taken this pledge or no?*

R: A lot, yeah, of, well, of the...

I: *Like what percent?*

R: I don't know what percent it is. But I know a lot, every single person that I've met, a bunch of people, not every single person I've met but like a lot of...

I: *And you know this how?*

R: A lot of people that I met, my, my friends, my personal friends, and stuff like that. Just because we talk about it and stuff like that, and you can actually see in somebody's life... I mean it can, you can pretty much tell if they have a good relationship with Christ and they're constantly going—you can tell the people that are going just for the social and then you know did whatever the night before, so...

Abstinence pledge programs have been controversial because their critics contend that most young people will have sex before marriage anyway, and the pledge makes it less likely that they will plan ahead when they do, therefore more likely that they will have "unprotected" sex—sex without a condom and/or another form of contraception. In fact, Table 6.7 shows that sexually active teens who believe people should wait until marriage for sex, or who try to do what God or the Scriptures tell them to do, are just as likely as not to have used contraception when they had sex. In comparison, other groups are as much as six or seven times more likely to use contraception than not. On the other hand, only 4% of these teens are having unprotected sex—less than half as many as the teens who believe it is okay for people to have sex before marriage.

Does this mean that abstinence programs such as True Love Waits are as risky as their detractors contend? There is some evidence to support both sides of the argument. Once again, Mark Regnerus summarizes the pertinent facts:

- Among the married young adults in Wave III of the National Longitudinal Study of Adolescent Health (Add Health), 88% of those who had made an abstinence pledge had engaged in sexual intercourse before marriage, as had 99% of those who had not pledged.
- Seven in ten of the pledge breakers reported having had more than one sexual partner, yet they had *far fewer* sexual partners on average than nonpledgers.
- Among the Wave III young adults who were not yet married, 44% of those who had pledged abstinence were still virgins, compared to just 12% of nonpledgers.
- The popularity of abstinence pledging within a school actually diminishes the pledge's effectiveness. A critical mass of pledgers is needed—not too few, nor too many—for the pledge to be most effective.
- Abstinence pledgers are considerably less likely than nonpledgers to use birth control at first sex.[10]

Table 6.7 also shows the clear effects of parental attitudes and strategies on the sexual behaviors of their children. The parental belief that people should wait until marriage for sex was not as powerful a predictor of diminished sexual activity as the teen's own belief in that regard, but there was still a significant correlation. Latino/a teens whose parents believe it is okay for adolescents to have sex if they are "emotionally ready" were especially likely to have engaged in sexual intercourse, yet with a ratio of nearly five to one between contraceptive users and non-users, they were among the most likely groups to consistently use contraception when having sex. Close parental monitoring also led to diminished sexual activity, and the teens whose parents always monitored what they do away from home were the least likely to have seen an X-rated movie in the last year.

Generational differences in sexual activities are also evident. One of the most significant differences is with respect to oral sex: third-generation Hispanics are more than 3.5 times as likely to do it than their immigrant peers. Even with respect to sexual intercourse, the difference is two to one. It is quite likely that these differences are related to the tendency of immigrant parents to monitor their children's activities more closely than U.S.-born parents. Even so, the preference for sexual intercourse over oral sex among immigrant Latino/as may also be a vestige of negative cultural attitudes toward sexual activities other than vaginal intercourse.

With regard to gender, the most significant difference in sexual experiences between Latino and Latina adolescents was how frequently they view X-rated movies: the boys were 2.5 times as likely as the girls to have done so in the last year. One young Latina, age fifteen, commented in her interview that "engaging in that kind of thing would be disrespectful to myself." This response shows much maturity in her reflection about this area of her life. Other interviewees responded that such viewing was "nasty" or that they simply weren't interested. The girls were also less likely to report having oral sex and less likely to have used contraception on a consistent basis.

Initial pastoral implications for Hispanic youth ministry

The young woman who gave the above response was actively involved in her faith community and focused her energies on healthy extra-curricular activities, some of which involved working toward justice. She also expressed that she felt "connected to others through prayer." She conveyed that she had adult and peer support in times of loneliness and depression. These are important connections. Community youth development programs focus on the need to create a positive environment for youth.[11]

The constructs for positive youth development include bonding, resilience, promoting social, cognitive, emotional, behavioral and moral competence, fostering self determination and providing opportunity for pro-social involvement. Ways of doing these include the very things that are a part of the young interviewee's life: involvement in the faith and/or local community; positive relationships with significant adults and peers; and a sense of connection to the family, the faith community, the school, and other community institutions. These connections cultivate becoming a contributing member of society. The NSYR study shows how young people are influenced by the example of their parents, as well as by what they are explicitly taught by them about morals.

Do faith issues play any role in this aspect of young people's lives? The study showed that many young Christians, both Catholic and Protestant, who may or may not be active in the church, claim that they turn to the Bible for moral direction. The findings of a Seventh-day Adventist study show that spirituality provides a personal sense of meaning and purpose in life while also serves as "a frame of reference by which Adventists make moral and ethical decisions."[12]

This shows how the faith community's guidance needs to work in tandem with parental advice and monitoring to help youth reflect on issues of morality. When asked how right and wrong are determined, one youth revealed that those are determined by common sense. "Common sense is what your parents taught you." So if parents specifically teach or reflect with youth about a hypothetical moral choice, the reasons for what makes it right or wrong can be owned by the young person as well as the parents. These reasons then become the parameters of moral "common sense" about the topic at hand. Without these parameters and reflections for guidance, young people fill the gap with their curiosity and the "invitations" of their peers. This predisposes them to make choices based on what "feels good," or "in the moment," with only one rule to guide them: "Be sure not to hurt others or yourself." In effect, they become stuck in the early stages of cognitive moral development (see the section on Kohlberg at the beginning of the chapter).

However, reflective discussion is not enough to ensure moral behavior, especially during the formative years of adolescence. A sense of accountability is needed. The accountability immigrant Latino/as feel toward their parents and extended family members probably plays a significant role in the fact that they engage in far less sexual activities and use of illicit substances (other than smoking cigarettes) than other Hispanics. In fact, they also fared much better than the white adolescents—despite the fact that their lower household incomes mean that they are likely surrounded by opportunities and pressures to take such risks. It was not until the third generation that Hispanic teens began to report significantly more of these risky behaviors than their white peers. In general, the young people who showed a greater capacity to reflect on mature reasons for their actions and on the consequences of such actions were those who claimed that their parents regularly monitored their activities. This parental monitoring gave them the feedback needed to internalize the parameters that guide their moral decision-making.

In this effort, parents should be careful to distinguish between monitoring and policing. Monitoring involves being aware of a teen's activities in order to direct them, whereas policing is to regulate with the purpose of controlling. The first includes non-judgmental dialogue, mutually agreed upon responsibilities, and clear consequences. The second usually does not include the adolescent in the decision-making process and assumes that unwanted behavior will take place, so controls must be put into place. Monitoring leads young people to self-awareness, as well as awareness of their environment. It creates a path of connections that young people think about in relationship to their choices and behaviors. This was exemplified by a 15 year-old young woman who stated: "Thinking about the consequences of my actions helps me decide on the right path to take."

Lastly, it is important to point out the connection between morality and community resources. Many Latino families live in areas that suffer from a critical lack of resources such as activities after school, jobs with a living wage for parents, and affordable, secure housing. Parents without these assets need to spend additional hours working, which makes it difficult for them to monitor their children or spend quality time with them. They also often lack community supports that engage young people in positive activities with adult mentors. Despite these deficits, Hispanic teens from low-income families actually reported the *lowest* incidence of drinking alcohol, getting drunk, smoking pot, and engaging in sexual activity, although the differences between economic categories in each case were small (data not shown). In these situations, the "plausibility structures" (using Peter Berger's term) established by the faith community can go a long way toward building the social support needed to help young Latino/as integrate their moral beliefs and practices into their developing moral character, filling the gap between cognitive knowledge and motivation for action.

Theological and pastoral reflection

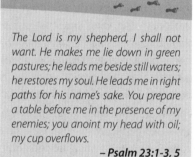

> The Lord is my shepherd, I shall not want. He makes me lie down in green pastures; he leads me beside still waters; he restores my soul. He leads me in right paths for his name's sake. You prepare a table before me in the presence of my enemies; you anoint my head with oil; my cup overflows.
> – **Psalm 23:1-3, 5**

When it comes to moral development, meaningful relationships are at the center of our work with adolescents. It is not entertainment—they have plenty of that, and they know where to find it. The insights of Augusto Blasi and Peter Berger suggest that teens do not usually develop their moral personality through personal reflection alone—they need guidance and feedback from significant relationships with adults in the community to be able to integrate a consistent moral character into their sense of who they are and who they are becoming. Healthy relationships with adults allow them to make confident choices about how they will act in the world. The quality of these relationships becomes the foundation from which they draw out a moral understanding that honors themselves and others.

A guiding image: the Good Shepherd

A pastoral approach therefore requires that our response be relational. In this regard, the Good Shepherd is a valuable relational image for our work. The shepherd image of John 10 presents us as youth ministers with a very fruitful image of our relationship with the young Christians in our communities. It begins with the understanding that the shepherd enters through the gate. (John 10:1-3) The gate is the proper place of entrance. Only when we have earned their trust will we be invited to enter into the lives of the young people.

In contrast, the thief—the one who comes to extract or to exploit for self benefit—does not use the gate. This implies manipulation, trickery, swindling, abuse, deception or imposition. Latino/a teens who do not feel comfortable in the group, or who feel forced to participate in any way, may be wary of our role in their lives. In order to overcome this, honesty, authenticity, and reciprocity in our relationship with young people are of the essence. Let us recognize that as youth workers we are often fed and taught by the young people we meet and encourage.

Following this analogy, the shepherd calls the sheep by name to lead them out to pasture, and they respond to that calling. This gives purpose to our relationship with them: we are to call and lead them out to be fed. To call is to help them discover, own, and develop who they are created to be. To lead out is "educare," the Latin root of the word to educate. This involves cognitive, affective (emotional) and volitional (of the will, behavioral) dimensions.

The process of listening and responding brings salvation (John 10:8-9), well-being, and wholeness to the young people. The thief comes only to steal, kill, and destroy, but Jesus the Good Shepherd comes to bring abundant life. (John 10:10) The abundant life comes from the strength and quality of our intentional relationships with the teens. The relationship itself is a form of nurturing ("feed my sheep" – John 21:15-17). It is the means through which young people begin to reflect upon their moral choices and to see an example of how to integrate them into their lives. The relationship also becomes the means for accountability, setting an example for how they are also called to hold their peers and families accountable to the teachings of the Gospel.

Psalm 23 deepens this image for us. The shepherd in the psalm provides for the wellbeing of the sheep: safety, a sense of belonging, protection from insects (anointing the head of the ewe served as an insect repellant), and good places to feed and drink. Teaching adolescents the skills of moral discernment is the anointing. Friendship that enhances who they are and that helps them grow is the water of our ministry with youth.

Establishing friendship entails the hard work of respecting, listening, reflecting together, facilitating growth through worship, teaching, and discovering oneself in relationship. Friendship becomes solidarity, and youth ministers become advocates for the rights of young people. Providing food and drink also involves pointing out and making accessible resources for young people, while teaching them to discern between clear streams of water and the embellished mud holes or polluted ponds that the larger society often invites them to drink.

The image of the shepherd in Psalm 23 does not only focus on the personal relationship between the shepherd and the sheep, but it calls our attention to the communal dimension of the relationship. The shepherd calls us to a trusting relationship where we can feel like children at home. We are called to be part of the family, to share community around the table (Psalm 23:5). Our daily realities are not heavenly rewards; instead, they are reminders to live under the rules of the shepherd's household and in solidarity with all of God's children.

The invitation to the table in verse five of the text implies reconciliation with enemies and offers life that overflows with goodness. The passage of Mark 6:30-44 resonates with this as Jesus feeds the crowd, first asking them to sit on the green grass (6:39). Notice how this is reminiscent of Psalm 23:2, "He makes me to lie down on green pastures." We are invited to feel safe and at home, and this allows us to rest. These are essential for the restless and vulnerable lives of youth. Do the places of ministry that we create offer safety, a sense of belonging, and rest for the young Hispanics in our communities?

The safety our young people seek is both physical and emotional. Not all neighborhoods are physically safe, and not all families are safe for the emotional nurturing of adolescents. Our ministry should provide a place of rest. This fosters reflection and self-awareness—important elements for pondering actions and consequences, as well as for internalizing the parameters that guide one's moral life. Safety also means creating a structure for behavior that affirms healthy development and life. The discussion of moral boundaries within a community of people encouraging each other to live within such boundaries invites relationship between adults and youth.

For instance, issues of sexual morality are not only related to teenagers' lives, but to the lives of adults living faithfully within the bonds of marriage or as single people. Adults must also face the challenge of respecting each other as men and women, critiquing and rejecting images, jokes, or songs that distort a healthy understanding and practice of our sexuality. Creating an environment where teens and adults can speak honestly about the struggles of learning to integrate their sexuality is a communal model that does away with the present hypocrisy of making this a moral issue that affects only adolescents, but it requires much maturity on the part of parents and adult leaders.

The communal model also creates opportunities for repentance and a journey of healing. The NSYR survey did not ask questions about domestic violence or abuse, but in the AVANCE study Ramirez-Johnson and Hernández reported that 65% of the respondents reported they had experienced some form of abuse in the family. Although what constitutes abuse was not defined in the survey, 18.8% reported that they had experienced sexual abuse and 1.5% reported that sexual abuse took place all the time in their family.[13] Such abuse leads to confusion about sexuality and sexual morality. A faith community cannot do ministry in this area without uncovering the sin of abuse in the midst of its families and seeking the resources necessary to begin and follow through on a journey of healing.

Making a commitment to foster healing affirms a sense of belonging to a community that struggles to live in faithful covenant with God and with each other. It also provides living parameters for emotional and physical safety related to sexuality, and it results in a spiritual home where young people can find rest. The Johannine text assures us that Jesus leads the sheep, provides food, and offers protection (John 10:9-13) for the purpose of sustaining life. Later in this chapter, the shepherd image with its complexity of tasks will guide my discussion of specific strategies for pastoral ministry with Latino/a adolescents. In the following sections I will look at how to provide them with the food, drink, protection, sense of belonging, and rest they need for their moral development as young Christians.

Latino/a moral values

Mexican parents define morality as the good or "correct path," grounded in moral codes that favor "filial piety, intergenerational reciprocity, gender specific ideals of social and spiritual values and the acquisition of manners and work skills that do not include competitive evaluation."[14] Thus, morality consists of values and virtues with social implications such as respect, honor, responsibility, loyalty and family unity. Because this definition includes a dimension of social implications, it cannot be narrowly defined as an individual choice. Instead, morality has to do with the web of connections or relationships in which we are engaged both at personal and institutional levels. For example, if I choose to do drugs it is a personal choice that not only affects my personal future but also the life of my family and my community.

For this reason, Latino/a moral development has to do with how a young person comes to a mature understanding of: a) the reasons for their choices, b) the practices that help them make decisions, and c) the actions that affect their priorities and commitments. The moral choices of Hispanic teens are deeply influenced by their perceptions of justice and injustice in their social environment. For example, education is a community provision that enriches the lives of adolescents and their families both in the present and the future. However, the quality of education in poorer communities is limited by budgets based on the value of real estate. In like manner, opportunities for higher education are withheld from young people who may not be citizens. These limitations affect the moral fabric of the community at both structural and personal levels.

Two things are signaled for us by this. The first is that developing the moral values of young people is connected to whether the web of life they are connected to is life-nurturing or life-oppressing. In other words, the well-being of a community contributes to its ability to foster ethical values in its young people. Conversely, when adolescents are blamed, punished, or demonized for the already toxic environment in which they live, it creates moral confusion and disorder in their lives. The second is that developing the gifts of young people nurtures the beauty of their lives and therefore fosters a virtuous life.

Values as a framework for pastoral ministry

Values provide our lives with meaning and sustenance and are an integral part of the moral life. They come from our deep personal beliefs and commitments, often in ways that we are not fully aware, and they supply the motivation that guides our behavior. When values are positive and prosocial, they enrich not only the person who lives by them but the community around them as well; they provide the framework for the expression of aspirations regarding one's educational, occupational, and relational future.

One of the places where values are embedded is in the religious beliefs and practices of the community, where they play a powerful role. Among other things, religious rituals and values serve as a protective cocoon and as a bonding process that provide community members with a sense of security and identity. When a family leaves the culture that has birthed it, everyone experiences disorientation from the loss of community values that provided boundaries and moral direction. Parents often struggle to understand how to utilize the values of the host culture as a guide for their children—if they are even aware of what those values are. The result is a diminished ability to pass on values that make sense in the context of the new culture, which can be disempowering to the new generation.

In such circumstances, the faith community can build on shared religious beliefs to promote practices that will cultivate the values of the young people. It would also be helpful to facilitate a community discussion about the two sets of values that encounter each other (those from the country of origin and those of the host country). These conversations must be carried out intergenerationally and if possible cross-culturally, so that immigrant parents, their children born and/or raised in the U.S., and people whose families have been in the culture for generations can come to a place of mutual respect, support, and understanding.

Adolescents learn self-discipline, responsibility, and respect for others by being in relationships where they are treated with respect, expected to carry out responsibilities, and exercise self-discipline in age-appropriate ways. Parent/child relationships are not enough—every teenager needs at least four significant adults in their lives. This makes us more keenly aware of the significant role that a teacher, a coach, a mentor, a youth leader, a pastor, an older sibling, or an employer may play in the life of a young person. The culture of the United States tends to separate adolescents from adults so that whereas we used to teach, listen to, and support them in informal ways, we are now spending less time with them. Meanwhile, society—especially the entertainment industry—targets them as consumers, promoting values that are in conflict with both Christianity and the traditional values of Latino cultures.

Adults must learn to overcome the social barriers that separate them from teenagers in order to help them find their place in the community. Young people wish to have adults in their lives who are caring and who listen, but they find it difficult to form relationships with adults who they see as judgmental and authoritarian figures. Many Latino families provide such constructive relationships by turning to their extended family members. In other cases, small communities of faith that embrace the whole family offer opportunities for young Hispanics to be in relationship with supportive adults who can accompany them from childhood into adolescence.

In the context of the larger faith community, when adults interact with teenagers with a tone of listening and caring, the parameters for respect, responsibility, and self-discipline can be discussed. Intentionally including young people in the life of the community is one way to help them express their emerging vocations and passions, as well as to explore their faith and form a religious commitment. This takes place when youth participate with adults and with each other in the mission and life of the church—in loving service, at prayer, and by sharing their faith with others. This relational fabric nurtures the formation, appropriation, and living out of the young person's religious values, and it is most effective when it begins in early childhood and continues throughout adolescence.

An ecology of support systems

Values do not belong to an individual alone, nor are they transmitted simply by reading about morality. To paraphrase Peter Berger, they are formed, practiced, and transmitted by a living community. Our approach to adolescent moral development therefore needs to look at the wider social structures that form and support adolescents. This is taking an ecological approach to the spiritual formation of youth.

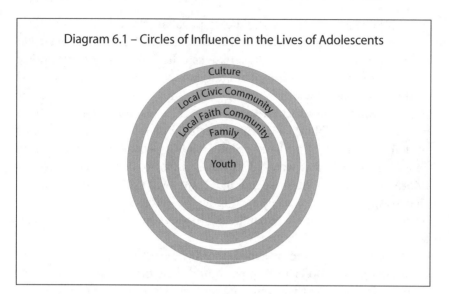

Diagram 6.1 – Circles of Influence in the Lives of Adolescents

Culture
Local Civic Community
Local Faith Community
Family
Youth

Educators Strommen and Hardel speak of various concentric circles that contribute to expanding horizons in the life of an adolescent. In the center is the young person. The next circle around it is the family, followed by the local faith community, and then the local civic community. Finally, the culture forms the last circle. Each circle contributes to the life of the adolescent in a different way.[15] Furthermore, the faith community is most effective in ministry with teenagers when it directly engages each of the other circles that have an impact on adolescent life.

Engaging the inner circle could include youth ministry programs, youth choirs, and efforts to invite adolescents into other programs and activities of the faith community. Addressing the second circle involves providing family enrichment programs and services such as parenting classes, single mother support groups, fellowships of parents, family pastoral counseling, and family-based small communities of faith. Dealing with the fourth circle entails a partnership or presence in various community supports for adolescents such as after school programs, speakers bureaus, mentoring programs, music and the arts programs, academic enrichment programs, organized sports, and community organizing or service activities. Responding to the fifth circle involves mentoring teens in the critical analysis of the culture around them and making available alternative media resources (i.e. music, movies, radio programs, etc.) with a Christian message. These are just some examples.

In many cases, one faith community alone is unable to do all of these, but several youth ministries in the same geographic area could work together. An example of this is JOLIBANI, a Latino youth partnership serving American Baptists from approximately seven faith communities. The various youth ministries collaborate on spiritual retreats, vocational discernment, and development of youth leaders for different areas of ministry with their peers, such as counseling, worship, and teaching. Another possibility is for different youth organizations to come together to intentionally channel their resources in complementary ministries and programs that will enhance the lives of the adolescents in their community.

When such a framework of assets is provided, it fosters a consistent system of values that emphasizes restraint from risk, healthy life choices, and prosocial behavior that serves to counteract the conflicting messages about risky behavior that the teens may be getting from the media and some of their peers. Within this ecological or systemic approach, religious influences can have a greater effect as part of a network of supportive relationships and common values in the different spheres of influence. When the spheres are linked to provide social development for teens, they increase the state of well-being in their lives and decrease opportunities for at-risk activities.

Pastoral recommendations

This section presents guidelines for pastoral strategies that will address the moral maturity of adolescents. The specific areas of ministry addressed will be rites of passage, the connections between identity development and moral development, a model of discernment for doing social justice and intergenerational problem solving, and ways to include both youth and adults in program planning and implementation.

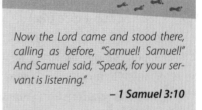

Now the Lord came and stood there, calling as before, "Samuel! Samuel!" And Samuel said, "Speak, for your servant is listening."
– 1 Samuel 3:10

1. Celebrate rites of passage

One way to bring together values, community, and commitment in a powerful way is through rites of passage. These rituals connect young people with the values of the community and provide common ground with the adults who have already been through the process, as well as with their peers who are going through similar experiences of growth. They honor the things that make the community of faith a family, reminding not only the teens, but all the community members where they come from and to whom they belong. This is one way to affirm self esteem. The rites also designate the responsibilities of the community with respect to the growth of the young people going through the rite, assigning particular mentors to accompany them in their journey of faith.

Some of the rites of passage in Hispanic communities and churches are Baptism, First Communion, Confirmation, and the *quinceañera*. A few resources for celebrating a *quinceañera* are listed among the additional resources for this chapter at the end of the book. Although most *quinceañera* materials are written with young women in mind, there is no reason why a similar rite of passage adapted for a young man cannot be offered. The following are some of the elements that make for a ritual that will generate intergenerational dialogue around values:

- Stimulate the five senses
- Provide a retreat for the young person to help them find their calling, their connection with God, their place in the community, and their purpose in the world
- After the retreat, offer a time of reflection and sharing with others who are coming through the same experience
- Ask elders in the community to teach about the values and the vision for growth embodied in the experience; the vision for growth must recognize all of the aspects of the young person's life:
  - Health and body (sexuality, diet, exercise, rest, personal hygiene, being substance free)
  - Psychological growth and development (becoming self-aware, experiencing emotions, dealing with hurt and forgiveness, recognizing when counseling may be helpful)
  - Social relationships (interacting with friends, family, intimate others, elders, employers)
  - Contributing to the life of the community (community service, involvement in the mission of the church)
  - Spiritual life (connecting with God, allowing God to direct or shape other relationships, learning the disciplines of relationship with God)
- Prepare the young people with conversations about cultural and moral habits, leading to a ritual recognition of death to the old self (child) and rebirth of the new self (adult)
- Invite the young people to embrace a code of life that honors the values of the community, perhaps by choosing a personal motto to live by
- Acknowledge the pain and grief of dying in a symbolic way as a call to growth (the transition from one state to another)

- Include the person, the family, the community, and the Holy Spirit in the ritual
- Assign elders or mentors to guide the young people in their journeys, connecting them to the work of the Spirit within them and to the values of the community
- Recognize that in any growth process, there are moments of failure; returning to our true selves and the community through confession and repentance are rituals to be continued with mentors

2. **Connect moral development with identity formation**

Identity
By Allan Johnson-Taylor

They say that I am not Latin-American
Because my given names are Anglican
They reject that I am Hispanic
Because my skin was bequeathed to me by an African
Blacks reject me because I am Hispanic
Hispanics deny me because I am African
And the Indian, reducing me to nothing, gives his back instead of his hand
Because to look me in the eye is to remember a profane time
Looking at me is to remember the rape of his fertile Indian woman
Who gave birth from her womb
Sons of the conqueror or his black slave

The question is not "to be or not to be"
For me it is to be and not belong
But Almighty God bent down to earth
And calmed the rage within me caused by three converging worlds
That were crying out for war
And then I saw John's multitude
I saw within me all of humanity enclosed

With dagger in hand, open my chest and you will see that within me flows
The blood of Nefertiti, Cuauhtémoc, and Cervantes—the blood of La Malinche
Through my veins flows the blood of three continents
Within me flows the cosmic blood
And today I know that from eternity
God declared my humanity
God declared it yesterday as well as today
That is why, even if they reject me, deny me, or ignore me
I know that I am Black, wonderfully made, and one hundred percent Latino

Erik Erikson spoke of identity formation as the central developmental task of adolescence. Contemporary psychologists generally agree that this task begins early in life and extends well beyond adolescence, but there is no doubt that it influences many areas of development in a teenager's life. Identity formation involves the integration of the different parts of the self, such as: religion, race, culture, sexuality, personality, intimate relationships, career, politics, tastes and interests, body image, etc. Decisions that may seem trivial at a given moment will begin to form the core of what an individual is about as they are repeated and reinforced over the years.[16]

Identity formation is not done in isolation; our social environment is filled with mutually exclusive identity categories, and people are constantly asked to identify with one of them (i.e. Democrat/Republican/independent, heterosexual/homosexual/bisexual, black/white/Asian/Hispanic, Christian/Jewish/Muslim/atheist, Catholic/Protestant, Pro-Life/Pro-Choice, Coke/Pepsi, etc.), or they may be categorized and stigmatized without ever being asked. Reconciling what at times are conflicting perspectives and values is no easy task. For bilingual/bicultural teens, this becomes more challenging and agonizing because they get caught between two realities or two cultures, neither of which fully embraces their experiences. When the pressures to assimilate are strong, feelings of isolation and negative outcomes including at-risk behaviors are likely to increase.[17]

For this reason, it is vital for young people to experience relationships with older peers and adults with whom they have certain core identity elements in common. Religious mentors and role models of their own cultural background play a key role, presenting models of what is possible in life and providing guidance as they move toward independence. The children of immigrants especially need such role models because their social environment sometimes makes it difficult for them to fully embrace the cultural and religious identity of their parents (see pages 148ff). Listening to the faith-stories of others with whom they can identify helps Latino/a teens to develop their own life-shaping narratives (a testimony may be a part of this) that provide a cohesive center for the whole person.

Moral development builds on the reflections and integrations that come from both identity formation and spiritual maturity. Relationships are a grounding factor in each of these. Developing a vibrant faith that can later become a central factor in moral decisions entails: sensing the love of others, feeling secure enough to trust and love in return, recognizing God's care, trusting God's promises, and learning to express love for God. This heart knowledge (relationships, emotions, and self-awareness) is paired with head knowledge (understanding of beliefs), and it results in actions that include faithful personal commitments, good citizenship, moral decisions, and reaching out to those treated unjustly or suffering hardship.

3. Utilize discernment as a Christian practice in doing social justice

Fostering a mature religious commitment among young people faith entails drawing them into responsible participation in the life, mission, and work of the faith community. For moral development it is important to integrate belief, practice, and individual piety with social action. Youth minister and religious educator David White designed an approach to youth ministry that attends to the cultural, ethnic, social, economic, and political world of teenagers. His approach elicits the gifts of the young, bringing them together with adult mentors to discern a path toward vocation which White sees as a trajectory toward the Reign of God.

The approach has four movements of discernment: listening, understanding, dreaming, and acting.[18]

i. **Listening** entails helping young people to pay attention to their inner experiences regarding how they see the world and their place within it. What bothers them? What evokes frustration and anger? What brings joy and fosters life? They can explore these feelings through the practice of prayer, walking through their neighborhood, and making observations. They may then reflect on these observations and write down questions to be researched further. As this line of questioning continues, the young people begin to get at the roots of their daily life experiences as well as the passions that lie within. They are then called to express their feelings through drama, art, music or writing. Listening is ortho-pathos or right feeling; it is loving God with all our heart. (Luke 10:27)

ii. **Understanding** engages the critical and analytical skills of the teens— their questioning and doubting energy. They explore the social, cultural, psychological, economic and political forces that impact their context, community, and the world. For example, they may ask about poverty or immigration laws. Group research is a means of delving into these questions to gain a greater understanding of the causes. This understanding is ortho-optomai or right seeing; it is loving God with all our mind.

iii. **Remembering and dreaming** is where we bring the resources of the Christian tradition to bear on the questions at hand. When Jesus sees the world in all its brokenness, what does he feel, see, think, say, and do? How do the Scriptures and the foundations of our faith ask us to imagine the possibilities for the world? Bible study, theological reflection, *lectio divina* (meditation with the Scriptures), and biblio-drama allow young people to utilize their imagination and insight for understanding the situation in the light of the Gospel. This movement gives consideration to orthodoxy or the right thinking; it is loving God with all our soul.

iv. **Acting** begins to take shape as a way to respond faithfully in the world after exploring the issue and its biblical foundations. This involves brainstorming, consensus building, and strategizing. At times it also involves creating partnerships or coalitions with others. However, it cannot end at the planning stage; it must move from ideas to actually doing something in the world. It may take the form of social protest, creating art, some form of advocacy, or acts of compassion. This is ortho-praxis or right action; it is loving God with all our strength.

Each movement has its limitations. Listening tends to define reality by what is felt, which can distort that reality and close off life-giving possibilities. Understanding can lead to a rationalism that excludes both suffering and joy. Dreaming sometimes gets stuck in the spiritual dimension, and acting can lose its center by becoming activism that eventually leads to burn out. This is why the process requires all four movements to balance each other.

Throughout this process, it is important to keep in mind that young people are idealistic and the reality of the world can be brutal. Confronting such a stubborn reality entails helping them to see themselves as only one of many parts that must fall into place in order to bring about social change. The parables regarding the reign of God remind us that it begins small (a mustard seed) and practically invisible (leaven). The vision we help to fashion must be long-range—we are cultivating not only final actions, but a Christian practice of participating with the Spirit to usher in God's Reign among us (Luke 17:21). Mentors and youth ministers are challenged to see their work with adolescents as a spiritual practice that binds them together in a way that opens them all to God and life in new ways.

4. Conduct intergenerational community problem solving

In their article on how to facilitate positive development among immigrant youth, Roffman, Suárez-Orozco, and Rhodes feature several programs that use intergenerational mentoring to address issues of identity and values between adolescents and first-generation adults.[19] One program initiated conversations about discrimination, racism, and AIDS using the arts as a medium for education and relationship building. Artists, teens, and adult educators and activists came together to have group discussions and to produce skits, plays, music, and videos as means for education and fomenting dialogue about the issues mentioned. The groups then became advocates for the prevention of HIV/AIDS while also becoming involved in expressions of compassion to individuals affected by the disease.

In this type of program, parents and teens are educated together and work together on a common cause that affects everyone in the community. It allows the young people and adults to discover, examine, and articulate their shared values while actively living them out in the larger community. They support and encourage each other as they strive to act on their values with integrity, channeling their energies into healthy relationships with each other and with the local civic community. This promotes moral and social development and creates a spirit of mutual accountability between the adults and the teenagers as both seek to live in congruence with their religious beliefs and values.

5. **Cultivate an inner voice of authority**

The formation of values requires open communication. For all that has been said in this chapter about the gap between knowing the right thing to do and actually doing it, there is no getting around the fact that knowledge of what is right is usually a prerequisite to doing the right thing. Although they cannot guarantee moral behavior among adolescents, reason and logic are nevertheless effective means of communicating values and behaviors to the next generation.[20] They also create a pattern of thought that cultivates an inner voice of authority in the young person rather than an external one. This is what Lawrence Kohlberg described as moral autonomy, the highest of his three levels of moral reasoning.

When parents set rules unilaterally without consulting their teenaged children, they inadvertently neglect to cultivate the young person's own ability to do moral reasoning. The young person therefore develops an external voice of authority which can easily be transferred to their peers, making them more susceptible to peer pressure. However, the inner voice is nurtured when teens are given opportunities to examine the human and Christian reasons for their choices, and the consequences of their actions.

Parents may model this process by opening up and talking about their own moral decisions. Family meetings should put into practice problem solving and consensual discernment whenever possible. When watching movies or the news together, discussions about the themes and moral choices they depict creates a habit of critical reflection on the information received. In addition to recognizing and understanding the consequences of actions, encouraging adolescents to take the perspective of others contributes to inward reasoning as opposed to outward compliance.

The faith community should take responsibility to help both adolescents and adults develop these skills and habits. Moral discernment should be encouraged in the community's educational programs, as well as in the way it structures its life together. Who is involved in making decisions? How does the community resolve conflict? How are ambiguities examined? When community members learn to make decisions through a process of shared reflection, their relational and analytical skills can be transferred to other aspects of their lives. Here are three strategies that can be employed to develop moral values in harmony with spirituality:

- **Teaching by example.** Parents and significant adults in the lives of teenagers must themselves be committed to the values they seek to impart to the adolescents. This does not mean that we hide or deny our inevitable shortcomings. Instead, we should openly acknowledge failures and discuss them with the teens along with theirs. Open discussion and analysis of these cases affirms the underlying values rather than creating unrealistic expectations.[21]

- **Perspective taking.** When there is conflict in daily life, it can be helpful to ask each person to take the side of the other and then discuss the issue again. Such perspective taking helps people to develop empathy, and many times it allows both people to see the other point of view so that the disagreement does not lead to an impasse that does harm to the relationship.[22]

- **Theological reflection.** Reading a biblical passage on an issue of justice and then applying it to current events while asking "Where is God while this event is taking place?" is another way to promote analysis and discussion in which we seek to align our daily actions with our faith.

Cultivating the inner voice of moral authority usually occurs in tandem with the emergence of a mature faith, both of which strengthen the behavioral dimension of moral development. It takes strength of character to develop moral habits. Mature faith takes shape when individuals examine themselves and their religious beliefs in light of their daily lives. When their discover that their faith gives meaning to their lived experience, they become motivated to live out the behavioral habits or virtues promoted by their religious tradition. The AVANCE study found that 91% of the youth with high levels of faith maturity had never engaged in at-risk behavior.[23] This leads us to our next point.

6. Foster habits that lead to good choices

Every culture recognizes the gift of human life, and as part of life, the gift of our sexuality. Sexuality is about more than just organs that make us look different or hormones that affect how our bodies function. This gift is an energy that flows in our lives, giving expression to who we are in the totality of our personhood. This energy expresses itself through our emotions, our thoughts, our creativity, attractions, and interactions with others; it is a special grace from God. For adolescents, learning to make choices that honor this grace and that prepare them to share it in life-enhancing ways is an important part of their emotional, spiritual, and moral development.

Choices entail habits. Youth ministers are called to help young people prepare to make good choices by cultivating habits oriented toward the grace of God in Jesus Christ. The Protestant Tradition focuses on grace as the gift that is mediated through Christ's sacrificial love expressed on the cross. That act mediates forgiveness and continued fellowship between God and humanity. Each time we say "yes" to that love, we also implicitly say "yes" to abiding in the love of Christ by keeping his commandments. (John 15:9-10)

Catholic Tradition focuses on the sacraments as effective mediators of grace in our lives. Baptism initiates us into the divine life of Jesus Christ by the power of the Holy Spirit. Life in Christ is a constant call to conversion from sin and participation in building the Reign of God. The sacrament of the Eucharist is our daily bread for this journey, the source and summit of the Christian life, and repentance through the sacrament of Penance and Reconciliation restores the divine life that has been weakened or lost by sin after Baptism.

Every sport and every art requires dedication to the discipline of practice in order to achieve a measure of excellence. The oboist cannot breathe life into the notes on the page without first mastering the scales in the associated key, and the players on a basketball team need to practice a variety of personal and team skills if they hope to perform well on game days. For us as Christians, the practices of obedience and the sacraments create habits that bring us into right relationship with God, others, ourselves, and the earth. These habits provide us with the grace needed to make good choices in the routine of our daily lives, as well as in times of crisis.

As an example, the NSYR surveys and interviews demonstrated that most Latino/a Christians could identify what their church teaches about the relationship between sex and marriage. A significant number even stated that they believe their church's teaching is correct, yet many of them admitted that either they had not lived up to it, or they did not expect to. What is needed is for parents and youth ministers to work with them to create habits that connect what they claim to believe with what they do on a daily basis or when faced with a moral dilemma.

One way to do this with respect to moral behavior is to guide the adolescents in a reflection on their faith commitment in order to develop a set of mutually agreed upon parameters or moral boundaries. This process presupposes that the teens already have faith, and that they understand the teachings of the Bible and their church on the subject at hand. In contrast to the behavioral scripts promoted by the secular media and many of their peers, such parameters can serve as alternative scripts for making choices that bring health and wholeness. They provide the teens with clear prescriptions for appropriate relationships, as well as much-needed guidance when they are faced with opportunities to cross the boundary of what they know is the right thing to do. It is not enough to do this exercise once at the beginning of adolescence; teens need to be regularly reminded about whose they are and at what price they were ransomed (1 Peter 1:18-19), and invited to reconsider and recommit to the parameters they have set for themselves.

Conclusion

Overall, the factors that nurture the life of the faith community are: a hospitable climate, inspirational worship, a caring environment, a thinking climate, families helping families, emphasis on prayer, a sense of mission, and intergenerational service efforts.[24] These characteristics help make the faith community a place where teens feel comfortable talking about issues important to their lives. Within each factor, the youth ministry team should provide opportunities for teens to participate in the larger faith community. Involvement may also take place at all the levels of congregational leadership.

Creating a community where teens can relate to each other in significant ways increases the opportunities for them to form relationships with adults who can serve as mentors and role models. Fun or informal opportunities for teens to gather with adults from the community allow them both to teach and learn from each other, as well as to express appreciation and respect for one another. In this way, generational barriers and tensions can be overcome.

Positive youth development entails recognizing and utilizing the gifts of teenagers. This can be done by creating opportunities for adolescents to play meaningful roles in the life of the faith community. The very programs and activities designed for them are a great place to start inviting them to offer their insights and opinions. Have we created youth ministry committees and planning boards where the teens have an equal voice with the adults and are given the chance to make a real difference?

These opportunities foster respect and bonding between generations while making for more successful implementation strategies. Adolescent participation increases as the youth ministry programs begin to respond more directly to their needs. Mutual trust, responsibility, and support between the teens and adults become the foundations for fostering conversations about moral issues, as well as for cultivating the young person's inner voice to make their own moral choices and persevere in them.

Adults also benefit as they learn about community issues from the perspective of the young and apply those insights to explore alternative courses of action for the well-being of the entire community. If adults and teens are going to form an equal partnership, each must become aware of the contributions they are making to the greater whole, including:[25]

Youth contributions

- First-hand knowledge about the interests and concerns of the young
- Forthright and creative ways of bringing attention to their needs
- Help build relationships within the organization
- Provide critical connections to larger social circles of teens
- Freedom to question current norms and suggest a more effective way

Adult contributions

- Organizational and administrative experience and expertise
- Programming skills and experience for organizational structure
- Guide and support teens as allies and equal partners
- Institutional power not accessible to adolescents
- Connections to community and financial resources

This understanding provides a framework for mutual respect and appreciation. It is important to note that equal partnership requires that the number of young people on a board or committee be significant. This marks the difference between token participation and full participation. For this to happen, it may at times be necessary to amend by-laws that have implicit barriers to adolescent participation.

Finally, it should be noted that most of the pastoral recommendations for moral development in this chapter can be implemented by parents and youth ministers with teens of any cultural background. Nonetheless, youth ministers should pay attention to the social and structural barriers that may make it difficult for certain groups, such as the Hispanic teens, to participate. The best pastoral strategies in the world are of no use if they do not reach the young people in the community. Chapters 3 and 4 describe some of the more common barriers to the participation of Latino/a adolescents in youth ministry programs and provide a variety of suggestions to overcome them.

Questions for reflection

1. How do we fare in the area of developing an ecology of support for youth? Who could be our partners for developing this?

2. What moral influences do we have upon our Hispanic adolescents? Are we helping them make connections between faith and their daily lives?

3. How can we create spaces for teens and adults to practice congruence with their beliefs and values?

4. What are the habits we want to cultivate in adolescents for healthy moral development?

5. How is the faith community incorporating teenagers in its various programs and boards? What would it take to get more teens involved?

6. How can we prepare adults for the active participation of youth in community meetings?

7. How do we do theological reflection in our community?

8. How well do we know our young people? Do we know their stories? How well do we listen?

9. What are the challenges that as adults we face in our own moral development?

Chapter 7:
The Social and Political Involvement of Latino/a Youth

Arturo Chávez, Ph.D.

Dialog 7.1 – 17 year-old Hispanic Christian female from the West

I: *Are you involved in any volunteer work or community service?*

R: No.

I: *Do you think teenagers should have to do volunteer work or community service?*

R: No.

I: *Why not?*

R: Why should they? If they want to do it then they should do it. If they don't, they shouldn't. My sister wanted to volunteer at the hospital. She did. I don't. So I didn't.

I: *Do you think you have an obligation to just—you know if you saw somebody who needed help on the street—do you think you should help them?*

R: Yeah.

I: *Why?*

R: Why not? That one person you help could be an angel. It could be God, you know.

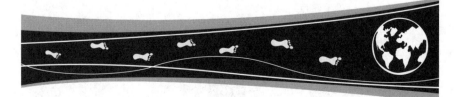

The Social and Political Involvement
of Latino/a Youth

What if God was one of us? This provocative query was famously posed by Joan Osborne in her hit song "One of Us" from 1996, but she was by no means the first to ask the question. The heart of the Christian story is the wonderful, good news that God *is* one of us. St. Paul puts it this way, "Though he was in the form of God... he emptied himself, taking the form of a slave, being born in human likeness." (Philippians 2:6-7) Even though we continually complicate the simple message of the gospel, we are at our best as a Christian community when we recognize the many faces of God in each other and especially in the brother or the sister who looks nothing like us: the stranger, the other, the one people try to avoid. These are the neighbors Jesus urged us to love. These are the angels we unknowingly help and who help us in so many unknown ways. This is what this chapter is about.

In the multidisciplinary team that worked together to develop this chapter (see the description of the process on page 3), we decided to utilize the Pastoral Circle as our methodology: we started by taking time "to see" the data collected by the NSYR research project that deals with Latino/a teens' attitudes *toward* and participation *in* volunteer services and political/social action. As Christians of various denominations and Latinos of different cultures and geographical places, we "judged" or evaluated these findings in the light of our lived faith and ministerial experiences. Finally, as a team we took "action" by helping in various ways to write this chapter on the social and political participation of young Hispanics. As the product of our efforts, we hope this chapter will provide new insights about how ministry with Latino/a adolescents must be a respectful "inculturation" of Jesus' central message to "love the Lord your God with all your heart, and with all your soul, and with all your strength, and with all your mind" and like the Good Samaritan, to love "your neighbor as yourself." (Luke 10:27)

Social and political action among Hispanic adolescents

Attitudes about others

The findings of the NSYR study regarding the social and political participation of Latino/a adolescents begin with some very good news! As Table 7.1 shows, the overwhelming majority of the Hispanic teens

> After [Jesus] had washed their feet, had put on his robe, and had returned to the table, he said to them, "Do you know what I have done to you? You call me Teacher and Lord—and you are right, for that is what I am. So if I, your Lord and Teacher, have washed your feet, you also ought to wash one another's feet. For I have set you an example, that you also should do as I have done to you."
> – **John 13:12-15**

Table 7.1 – Attitudes about others by ethnicity, religious tradition, religious type, generation, and economic status (percentages)

	Hispanic			White, Any Faith	Hispanic Teen Religious Type*				Hispanic Teen Generation*			Hispanic Teen Economic Status*		
	Catholic	Protestant	No Religion		Committed	Engaged	Sporadic	Disengaged	First	Second	Third +	High	Middle	Low
	N=278	N=94	N=40	N=2448	N=47	N=172	N=82	N=32	N=95	N=165	N=191	N=116	N=73	N=195
How much do you care about racial equality?														
Very much	41	50	41	48	47	43	35	46	44	38	50	61	43	35
Somewhat	24	19	33	26	20	26	25	33	24	24	21	11	26	27
A little	10	16	3	6	21	12	9	0	8	17	5	7	14	8
I do not really care	26	15	24	17	13	20	30	21	24	21	24	21	17	31
How much do you care about the needs of the elderly?														
Very much	46	54	43	49	57	48	44	33	49	39	56	48	47	50
Somewhat	42	36	40	39	32	41	41	44	43	44	34	39	38	40
A little	8	4	3	8	5	7	10	10	4	9	6	10	7	5
I do not really care	3	6	15	3	6	5	4	13	3	8	3	2	8	4
How much do you care about the needs of the poor?														
Very much	57	61	44	49	66	59	51	37	59	51	59	56	58	55
Somewhat	29	32	40	37	16	30	35	41	32	33	30	36	27	32
A little	10	6	16	10	12	9	9	22	8	12	7	8	10	9
I do not really care	4	1	0	3	6	2	5	0	1	4	4	1	5	3

* See the Appendix on page 361 for definitions of the adolescent religious type, generation, and economic status categories.

surveyed said they care "very much" or "somewhat" about the needs of people who are elderly or poor. Concern about racial equality was slightly lower but still significant, with two out of three Latino/a teens saying that they care at least "somewhat" in this area. The Hispanic Protestant teens expressed more concern in all three areas than their Catholic counterparts, and they were especially remarkable for the low number who expressed little or no concern for the poor. Still, the religiously "committed" Latino/a teens of any denomination easily demonstrated the highest level of concern overall. In fact, concern in all three areas tended to decrease proportionally to religious commitment. This suggests that there is a strong correlation between religious involvement and the evolving sense of justice and critical thinking skills among Latino/a young people.

There are a few additional interesting correlations to Hispanic teens' concern for other people shown in Table 7.1. For example, with respect to racial equality it was the Latino/a teens whose families had the most economic resources that expressed the greatest concern, while their peers from low-income families were nearly as likely to say they do not really care about racial equality as to say they care "very much." In contrast, when it comes to concern for the elderly or the poor, the higher-income Hispanic respondents did not distinguish themselves from their less wealthy peers. In these cases, it was the third-generation teens who were more concerned than their immigrant and second-generation peers. The table does not show a comparison between the Latinas and their male counterparts, but the girls distinguished themselves by being significantly more likely to report being "very much" concerned about the needs of the poor: 62% did so, versus only 50% for the boys.

The effect of religion on volunteering and community service

Opportunities for young people to participate in service and social action within their communities are an essential way to develop social skills and to direct youthful idealism into the real and often difficult task of bringing faith to life through action. As shown in Table 7.2, the Catholic and Protestant Latino/a teens were very similar to one another, as well as to their white peers, in terms of giving direct help to people in need. On the other hand, the non-religious and religiously disengaged Hispanics were significantly less likely to help others than any other group. Indeed, there was a direct correlation between religious commitment and the Latino/a teens' frequency of helping others in need. This pattern shows that religious families and communities have been fostering the value of service among their adolescent members.

Table 7.2 – Helping others, volunteering, and community service (percentages)

How much have you directly helped homeless people, needy neighbors, family friends, or others in need?	Hispanic			White, Any Faith	Hispanic Teen Religious Type*			
	Catholic	Protestant	No Religion		Committed	Engaged	Sporadic	Disengaged
	N=278	N=94	N=40	N=2448	N=47	N=172	N=82	N=32
A lot	8	10	4	10	17	6	5	2
Some	41	36	25	32	43	39	37	24
A little	26	32	26	32	23	30	29	25
None	24	22	45	26	17	25	27	49
In the last year, how often have you done volunteer work / community service?								
Regularly	13	9	9	13	23	15	5	14
Occasionally	14	23	16	22	23	12	15	21
A few times	30	35	19	35	29	36	33	16
Never	42	33	56	31	25	38	47	49
How much of your service was organized by a religious group?**	N=161	N=63	N=18***	N=1703	N=36	N=107	N=44	N=16***
All or most	15	33	0	23	39	23	9	6
About half	15	13	9	11	18	17	16	0
Some or a little	32	22	17	27	28	28	28	13
None	38	32	74	39	14	32	47	81
How much of your service was required by school, juvenile justice, or a parent?**								
All or most	23	21	20	20	17	20	26	34
Some	37	37	17	28	30	38	45	9
None	39	42	63	52	54	40	29	56
How much did your service expose you to people of a different race, religion, or class?**								
A lot	34	35	31	33	48	35	34	41
Some or a little	53	47	31	55	47	54	51	31
None	13	17	34	11	6	12	15	25

* See the Appendix on page 361 for definitions of the adolescent religious types.
** Among teens who had engaged in volunteer work or community service.
*** With only 16 to 18 responses, these results have a sampling error of ±10%.

The research findings also affirm that volunteer service and social action often enable adolescents to meet people of a different race, religion, and/or economic class. These encounters can help the young volunteers to see and experience life from a completely different vantage point. In addition, service can inspire teenagers to envision a future full of hope and new possibilities because it helps them to see their gifts and skills as valuable assets that can bring about positive change in other people's lives, as well as their own. Finally, community service and social action give them a sense of belonging and meaning that helps to ease the often difficult and confusing journey through adolescence.

Given all the reasons why community service and social action are so important to youth development and faith formation, our team found the following findings of the NSYR survey both troubling and challenging. The data indicate that while the majority of the Latino/a youth strongly believe in the importance of social justice and service, only an average of 12% regularly participated in volunteer work and community service. Far more had only served occasionally or a few times in the previous year, and the largest number had not volunteered or participated in any community service projects at all.

Nevertheless, the table shows a strong correlation between religious commitment and service to others, both in terms of direct service to individuals in need and with regard to the more organized forms of volunteer work and community service. Slightly less than one out of every four religiously "committed" Hispanic teens said that they regularly participate in volunteer work or community service, so even in that segment it is not as common as one might hope. Still, they were over four times more likely to regularly engage in service work than their religiously "sporadic" peers. Since a majority of the religiously committed respondents admitted that most of their service work was organized by a religious group, it is clear that being involved in a faith community is an important factor in exposing young people to this type of experience.

Although the Latino/a Catholic and Protestant teens only demonstrated slight differences in volunteer work and service to others as shown in the table, an interesting difference in their attitudes about volunteering can be found in the interview transcripts. When asked whether they thought teens should participate in community service or volunteer work, 13 of the 16 Hispanic Catholics said that teens should volunteer, though two of them clarified that it should not be forced. Six of the 14 Hispanic Protestants were not asked this question, but of the eight who were, only one said that teens "should" serve. Four others said they believe teens should serve if they want to, but otherwise they should not have to. The following conversations are good examples of the two different approaches:

Dialog 7.2 – 15 year-old Hispanic Catholic male from the Northeast

I: *What do you think about... the idea of doing community service?*
R: It's good. Like, I don't know, it makes you a good person and stuff. And if you had nothing to do there's something to do there.
I: *And do you think people have an obligation to help others or not?*

R: Should they be forced to?

I: *Or should they in any way? Do you think they should help other people or do you think it doesn't matter?*

R: People that need help and they can't... help it, people should help them.

I: *Why do you think people should help other people?*

R: 'Cause it makes both of them better—morally and stuff, spiritually and stuff. It would make them both, you know, make them both better.

I: *Okay, and do you think teenagers should be involved in volunteer work or community service?*

R: Everyone should help a little bit. That would make everything a lot better.

Dialog 7.3 – 17 year-old Hispanic Christian male from the West

I: *Do you think people have an obligation to help others or not?*

R: No, not an obligation, but I think if you can, then you should. I think that it would make you feel better if you do help other people.

I: *Yeah, so why do you think there's no obligation? It's just sort of something...*

R: If you don't want to, then why should you have to?

I: *And so if you do, what is it about helping other people that...*

R: Like if you were in that situation, you would want somebody there for you.

I: *Do you think teenagers should be involved in volunteer work or community service?*

R: I think they should, but in my... I'm in the business and finance academy where it is required that you have a certain amount of hours. But I think... if you want to, but I don't think you should have to.

I: *So... you have to put in a certain amount of hours?*

R: I have, but that church kids camp thing...

I: *Oh, so that kind of stuff counts for it?*

R: Yeah, 'cause I was... basically, I was volunteering.

I: *And so that's mostly where your volunteer stuff is at—in the church related things?*

R: Yeah.

I: *What effect on your life do you think that sort of volunteering has had on you?*

R: It just makes me feel good.

I: *Do you think that your moral beliefs or faith have anything to do with how you think or act when it comes to volunteering? Yours is mostly in your church...*

R: Yeah.

I: *Do you think that your faith has sort of motivated you to do it that way?*

R: Yeah.

I: *Why is that, do you think?*

R: Just 'cause I know it's right.

What is striking here is that the Protestant and Catholic teens are so unified in their responses to this question within their respective faith traditions. Admittedly, this contrast is mostly a difference of emphasis rather than a fundamental disagreement about the importance of helping others. Furthermore, the small sample size of the interviews means that further research would be required before making generalizations about this difference. It is also difficult to tell from the interviews if this apparent difference of opinion about whether teens "are obligated" to participate in volunteer work or community service is grounded in an awareness of the Catholic and Protestant approaches to social engagement. Nevertheless, it actually does reflect a significant theological difference between their respective traditions.

For Catholics, service to people in need is an indispensable form of witness to the Gospel—an eschatological sign that the Reign of God is already among us (Luke 17:21). The community therefore has an obligation to feed the hungry, clothe the naked, visit the sick and imprisoned, etc., and all are expected to contribute to those activities according to their ability. Without denying the fundamental importance of Christ's sacrifice for salvation, Catholics believe that they will receive a reward in heaven for such acts of Christian love (see Matthew 25).[1] Although none of the Hispanic Catholic teens interviewed were able to articulate this teaching, they seemed to convey a basic understanding of it in the way they expressed their opinions about volunteer work.

In contrast, the Protestant understanding emphasizes the gratuitous gift of Christ's atoning sacrifice on the cross and human beings' inability to do anything on their own to deserve or "merit" salvation (Ephesians 2:8-10).[2] In this context, love of neighbor and service to people in need are seen as evidence of life in the Spirit[3]—a consequence of being personally saved by accepting Christ's sacrificial gift as payment for one's sins. Therefore, neither the community nor the individual has an obligation to serve others; rather, they joyfully choose to serve others as a response to God's love.

Although many evangelical Protestant communities tend to make announcing the Gospel of salvation in Christ their first priority, the NSYR data show that they have not lost sight of the call to help people in need. Indeed, the relatively high proportion of Latino/a Protestant teens who reported that all or most of their service work was organized by a religious group indicates that these congregations are making it a priority to engage their adolescent members in service opportunities. Like their Catholic peers, the Hispanic Protestants interviewed spoke very positively about their experiences of community service. However, they generally felt that such activity was not so much an obligation as the personal choice of each individual.

Other influences on volunteering and community service

While the impact of religious involvement on Hispanic teens' community service activities is clear, it would be a mistake to conclude that it is the only stimulus in that regard. At least two other influences significantly contribute to their participation in volunteer and service activities: schools and parents. In the last fifteen years, many high schools—both public and private—have incorporated service learning experiences into their curriculum as part of the requirements for graduation. A wide body of literature has demonstrated the social benefits of engaging adolescents in the service of others: the teens become better citizens and learn important life lessons, independent of their cultural background.[4] Another approach emphasizes service activities as an opportunity for the socialization of moral behaviors that build on the empathic responses of even the youngest of children.[5] With such clear benefits, it is no wonder that many schools are requiring service-learning, as the following interview demonstrates:

Dialog 7.4 – 18 year-old Hispanic Catholic female from the Northeast

I: *Do you do a lot of volunteering?*

R: I mean, yeah. And like a lot of people think it's weird that I'll just work for no money, but like I already have... Like I have money, and like I have a lot of the things I want and so... I was also volunteering at the Housing Opportunities Commission that had these kids who needed tutors, but like when they got home: a) like their parents weren't home, and like b) their parents didn't speak English or like, not helping them with their homework. It was too hard, so like they were hiring like a bunch of little American kids to come help them with their homework. So like I would, I would help them—it was fun. I didn't get paid for it, but like it looks really good on my résumé.

I: *So you did it for your résumé?*

R: I didn't do it for my résumé, but like I did it because I wanted to do it. But now that I've done it, I'm like, I can look at my résumé and like it looks good.

I: *Would you recommend that teenagers be involved in community service?*

R: I would because they—both the Housing Opportunities Commission and Whitman Walker were my community service hours—and if they would have never asked me, cause there's the service requirement now [at school], and if they had never asked me to do that, I would have never done it. And if I would have never done it, I think I would have [been] like really culturally, like missing out. 'Cause I would have never known like how to treat individuals or like, even like kids. Like I'll see them like walking down in the mall and, they're like, "How are you doing?" I'm like, "I'm not doing your homework," and like they'll just come up to me...

I: *These are the kids you tutored?*

R: Yeah, and like they'll just come up to me and they'll be like really happy and like... 'Cause I was always like one of the youngest tutors, and like they always thought I was like cool. And I'm like okay... And like they'll come up to me and they'll be all excited.

I: *Do you think your religious beliefs or your moral beliefs have anything to do with your openness to this volunteering?*

R: I mean, I think like as far as my moral beliefs go, like they're—everybody's the same, even though they're [in] low-income housing. Like they're still kids that have a chance to do good in school, but I think like programs that help them with their homework [are] pretty good.

Unfortunately, when the teens were asked about non-religious influences on their community service activities, the survey question simply combined school and parental requirements together (see Table 7.2 on page 244). Nevertheless, the inclusion of interviews with parents demonstrates that parental attitudes, words, and example are important influences on the service activities of their adolescent children. Indeed, Table 7.3 shows that the 71% of Latino/a teens whose parents considered volunteer work to be very or extremely important for them were slightly more likely to engage regularly in service work, and much less likely to say that they never did service work. The parental influence was most evident when the parents actively encouraged their children to volunteer, and providing an example by doing volunteer work themselves also made a significant difference. Even so, the proportion of Hispanic teens who regularly participated in service work did not surpass 25% in any group.

It is noteworthy that the attitudes and behaviors of Hispanic parents regarding the volunteer activities of their children appear to have very little

Table 7.3 – Parental correlations to helping others, volunteering, and community service among Hispanic teens (percentages)		Has Given More Than "A Little" Direct Help to People in Need	Regularly Does Service Work	Never Does Service Work
How important is it to you that your teen does volunteer work? (parent survey)				
Extremely important	N=73	45	14	34
Very important	N=245	47	13	41
Somewhat / not very	N=129	45	10	47
How often have you encouraged your teen to do volunteer work? (parent survey)				
Very often	N=91	52	23	29
Fairly often	N=106	44	14	40
Sometimes	N=167	45	9	42
Not often / not at all	N=82	46	5	52
In the last six months, have you or your spouse volunteered? (parent survey)				
Yes	N=194	45	16	34
No	N=257	48	10	46
In the last year, how much have you directly helped homeless people, needy neighbors, or other people in need? (parent survey)				
A lot	N=88	56	11	50
Some	N=167	47	12	36
A little	N=108	43	17	37
None	N=89	40	7	49

Table 7.4 – Political participation (percentages)

	Hispanic			White, Any Faith	Hispanic Teen/Parent Religious Type*				Hispanic Teen Generation*			Hispanic Teen Economic Status*		
	Catholic	Protestant	No Religion	White, Any Faith	Committed	Engaged	Sporadic	Disengaged	First	Second	Third +	High	Middle	Low
	N=278	N=94	N=40	N=2448	N=47	N=172	N=82	N=32	N=95	N=165	N=191	N=111	N=167	N=164
Teen has given $20 to an organization or cause	38	47	16	37	58	37	32	17	49	30	37	38	37	36
Teen has signed a petition, attended a political meeting, or contacted an elected official	4	9	5	12	14	4	3	5	5	4	6	5	5	5
Teen has planned an event, led a meeting, or given a presentation or speech in the last year	26	31	14	32	53	31	21	19	16	34	27	38	30	19
In the last 12 months, parent has: (parent survey)					N=60	N=172	N=32	N=16**						
Contacted an elected political official	16	17	10	32	14	19	19	13	6	13	23	26	11	13
Attended a political meeting or rally	15	9	13	18	9	16	16	6	7	10	18	18	9	12
Participated in a protest, march, or demonstration	4	1	5	3	1	3	3	0	0	2	5	4	1	5
Participated in a community project	20	21	16	33	11	25	17	19	11	18	24	22	18	19
Given $500+ to an organization or cause	14	35	20	36	31	23	13	13	9	25	20	36	24	5
In national political elections, how often do you vote? (parent survey)														
Always	33	40	25	65	43	33	21	26	14	30	47	53	33	21
Sometimes or occasionally	26	30	20	25	24	24	32	23	17	23	35	28	28	24
Never	41	30	55	10	33	42	48	52	68	48	18	19	39	55

* See the Appendix on page 361 for definitions of the religious type, generation, and economic status categories. ** With only 16 responses, these results have a sampling error of ±11%.

effect on their children's tendency to directly help others in need. The reverse is also true—a strong parental example of directly helping others did not translate into more regular service work among their children. Nevertheless, there was a linear relationship between the Hispanic parents' frequency of helping others in need and that of their children. Perhaps the most important finding in Table 7.3 is the fact that the Hispanic teens were far more likely to provide direct help to people in need than to regularly participate in organized service work, irrespective of anything their parents might say or do.

Political involvement

Up to this point, the NSYR data have shown that the Latino/a teens surveyed were generally concerned about social issues such as racism and poverty, but they were not very involved in volunteer work or community service. Their lack of involvement was even more pronounced when it came to political or social action. Table 7.4 shows that only about 5% had ever signed a petition to support an important cause, attended a political meeting, or contacted an elected official, compared to about 12% of their white peers. The Protestant Hispanics were slightly more engaged than other Latino/as, with 9% reporting that they had taken such steps toward political involvement. Many more Hispanic teens said they had given their own money to an organization or cause, or had engaged in a variety of leadership activities, but these actions are not necessarily political in and of themselves. As usual, there was a strong correlation between political participation and the level of religious commitment on all three questions.

The NSYR personal interviews did not ask the teens any questions about their political activities, but the parent survey provides some additional context for understanding the pattern of political participation among Latino/a adolescents. Table 7.4 shows that like their children, the Hispanic parents surveyed were considerably less politically active on a variety of measures than their white counterparts. However, a majority of the Hispanic parents were not born in the United States, and many of them are not citizens even after living in the U.S. for years. It is therefore not a surprise that the parents of first-generation Latino/a teens reported the lowest levels of political involvement on all six questions. On the other hand, U.S.-born Hispanic parents (those whose children are of the third or higher generation) are still less politically active than their white peers, but the gap is greatly diminished.

Economic status also plays an important role—the wealthier Latino parents are nearly as politically active as the white parents, while the low-income parents are significantly less active on all measures except participation in a protest, march, or demonstration. Taken together, the generational and economic differences also help to explain the fact that the Latino Catholic parents are less likely than their Protestant peers to vote in a national election or give money to an organization, since immigrant and low-income Hispanics are more concentrated among Catholics than among Protestants (see Chart 1.7 on page 21 and Table 1.5 on page 31). Nevertheless, the Hispanic Catholic parents were significantly more likely to attend a political meeting, protest, march, or demonstration than their Protestant counterparts.

Faith and politics in historical context

One way to interpret these findings is to simplistically say that Hispanic adolescents may "talk the talk," but they obviously don't "walk the walk." Is it possible however that these statistics describe a larger social phenomenon shaping the lives of today's young people? Are they not a mirror of the

> *"Woe to you, scribes and Pharisees, hypocrites! For you tithe mint, dill, and cummin, and have neglected the weightier matters of the law: justice and mercy and faith. It is these you ought to have practiced without neglecting the others. You blind guides! You strain out a gnat but swallow a camel!"*
> *– Matthew 23:23-24*

lack of social and political involvement among adults in our communities? Even in our faith communities, is it possible that Latino/a adolescents are not being invited to be active members and recognized leaders?

Social and historical context

While it might be easy to blame the parents for their teens' lack of involvement in social action, politics, and service, it is important to critically look at the larger patterns that undoubtedly influence the attitudes, mindsets, and ultimately the actions of adolescents and their parents. For example, there is a pervasive—and often not recognized—mindset in this country as well as in much of Latin America that religion and politics must be kept separate, which tends to create a false dichotomy between faith and civic participation. Many Christians are suspicious of political and social involvement, as reflected in the low levels of direct political action among the religiously committed Hispanic parents in Table 7.4. Consequently they tend to place more importance on alleviating the suffering of those who are poor and oppressed. The words of the late Dom Hélder Câmara, former archbishop of Recife in Brazil, poignantly articulate this tension between direct service and systemic change: "When I fed the hungry, people called me a saint. When I asked why they were hungry, they called me a communist."

There are also systemic barriers that affect the opportunity for social and political participation, especially among Latino/as who are the largest and fastest growing minority group in the country, as well as the most likely to be poor, undereducated, and trapped in low-paying and often dangerous jobs in sweat shops, poultry plants, farms, hotels, and restaurants. Hispanics have historically been subjected to conquest, colonialism, exile, racism, and many other forms of social injustice. While for some this history is only a faded memory of what happened to past generations, many still experience the effects of this history as their present reality. This is especially true of newly arrived immigrants and the children of immigrants who have not been able to break out of impoverished and unsafe living situations.

On one hand, Latino/as are the oldest immigrant group in the United States; some can trace their ancestry back to the first Spanish and Mestizo explorers of the 16th century and the indigenous peoples of the Americas, long before Plymouth Rock. On the other hand, Hispanics are among the most recent immigrants who daily arrive—with or without immigration documents—in cities and rural communities across the country. Most come to escape violence, poverty, and/or injustice in their homelands. Unfortunately, many have found that even in this land of opportunity, they have been unable to escape the oppression of crime, poverty, racism and injustice. These realities keep many Latino families in a survival mode with little time to become involved in volunteer activities or political movements. Additionally, the numerous systemic barriers to becoming a U.S. citizen—or even a permanent resident—keep many immigrant Latino/as from meaningful civic engagement in the communities where they live, work, pay taxes, worship, and raise their families.

The painful history of oppression and colonialism is felt long after the formal systems of social and political domination have fallen. Generations of people whose ancestors have been colonized may exhibit a deep-seated fear, anger, and distrust of political systems and leaders. It is fairly common among people who have been oppressed to encounter a mindset of powerlessness and fatalism that can lead to apathy or cynicism when it comes to political engagement. "Why bother? You can't change the system; you have to beat it." This mindset is contagious and is often reflected in the attitudes of Latino/a teens who cannot maneuver the complexities of U.S. educational, legal, health, and social welfare systems or access the resources they need to succeed educationally, economically, and socially.[6] A mindset of powerlessness is impossible to change without the actual experience of empowerment.

On the other hand, it is difficult to completely eliminate many of the attitudes and stereotypes that are formed in the culture of the colonizers, even generations after the formal colonial systems have been replaced by more egalitarian and democratic political structures. For example, the belief that everyone can make it in this country if they just "pull themselves up by the boot straps" is a prevalent mindset that blinds the majority from seeing how the systems and institutions that benefit them may actually serve to disenfranchise many others who cannot access the mythical American Dream.

Despite the numerous personal and systemic barriers facing Latino/as, they have a long history of political and social involvement in this country. In the 1920s and 40s, distinguished military service and the growth of the Latino middle class gave rise to numerous advocacy groups such as the League of United Latin Americans (LULAC), The Mexican American Legal Defense and Educational Fund (MALDEF), and the ASPIRA Association, dedicated to the educational and leadership development of Puerto Rican and Latino youth. These groups were primarily formed to protect the civil and human rights of Hispanics who were commonly discriminated against in schools and workplaces.

The dramatic social changes of the 1960s and 70s inspired many Latino/a youth and young adults to political action, social concern, volunteerism, and militancy. Groups such as the Brown Berets, FALM (for Puerto Rican Independence), and the United Farm Workers' Movement gave urgency to the long-neglected issues of Hispanics and paved the way for the political power of the 1980s when record numbers of Latinos were elected to national and local offices, including the mayors of Miami, San Antonio, and Denver. Other organizations were created to advocate for improved education for Latino/a children, such as the Association of Mexican-American Educators, the National Association for Bilingual Education, and the Intercultural Development Research Association that works with schools to create educational environments and programs that are effective for children of all cultures.

Also in the 1980s, many Latinos became socially and politically engaged through their church organizations. For example, IAF (Industrial Areas Foundation) community organizations rooted in urban Latino faith communities have mobilized significant numbers of economically poor Hispanics to find and use their collective power for the common good. These groups utilize the organizing principles of Sal Alinsky and the moral force of Christian social teaching to identify community concerns, train leaders, and pressure local governments to respond to their concerns. The IAF and its affiliates have won many local political battles, thereby improving the lives of countless disenfranchised people. In the process, they have formed thousands of Latino/a leaders whose activism is grounded in their Christian faith.

Still, it must be admitted that Christian churches have much more work to do in this area. For example, when the parents in the NSYR survey were asked about their church's level of political involvement, only 10% of the immigrant Hispanic parents and 14% of those born in the United States responded "very involved." In contrast, 36% of Black parents described their churches as "very involved" in the political process. This is troubling given the fact that, on the whole, both the Catholic and Protestant churches failed to provide an institutional base of support to the Latino civil rights movements of the 1960s and 70s, unlike the African American movements for civil rights that were birthed and fomented in their churches.

Is this history bound to be repeated in the present? The push for comprehensive immigration reform in 2006 and 2007 has galvanized a new generation of Latino/a political activists, and it provides an opportunity for churches to become involved in supporting the political activism of their young Latino/a members. At this writing, it is too early to know how the national political battle over illegal immigration will be resolved. However, the Catholic Church has already taken a stand in support of comprehensive immigration reform at the national level,[7] and individual bishops have been outspoken about the rights of immigrants—both documented and undocumented—in their dioceses. Nevertheless, it is not yet clear that the Church as a whole, especially at the grassroots level, has the will to be an effective advocate for immigration reform.

With or without church involvement, hundreds of thousands of Latino/a high school students who walked out of their classrooms on May 1, 2006 in solidarity with their undocumented parents, neighbors, and friends, came away from that experience with a new sense of empowerment and determination to make a difference in their world. Their experiences were not reflected in the NSYR survey and interview data described in the first section of this chapter, but parishes and congregations would do well to nurture their newfound political zeal and channel it in constructive efforts to address the issues they face—both in their local communities and at the state and national levels.

Politics and Christian discernment

While the NSYR findings may initially disappoint or disturb, they are actually a gift that can help us discern "the signs of the times" and the call to faithfully respond to the Gospel in this time and in this place, with a particular faith community. The following thoughts are the fruit of prayerful reflection on the gospels to see what Jesus' words and ministry have to say regarding political and social participation in our world today.

First of all, we must clarify what is meant by political, since this little word has such heavy baggage. For many people, it has the negative connotations of intrigue, corruption, manipulation, and/or the abuse of power. Actually, the roots of the word "political" are very positive—perhaps too much so. It comes from the Greek word for city (*polis*) and was used by Aristotle and Plato to describe the ideal society built cooperatively through the respectful and orderly relating of its citizens. While this image may be far from the reality of politics in the United States today, it is important to have a vision for what might be possible if we learn to live peacefully, cooperatively, and respectfully with one another.

As Christians, our vision for the world is not a utopian fantasy, but a firm belief in Jesus' proclamation that the Reign of God is coming and indeed is already in our midst. In other words, we must have eyes to see the signs of the Reign of God among us and discernment to participate in the continuation of Jesus' mission to bring it into its fullness. Discernment is at the heart of what it means to be a disciple of Jesus. It is a process of seeing the realities of life through eyes of faith in order to do what Jesus would do.

John's Gospel emphasizes that discipleship is about "seeing and believing." Just as the first disciples asked to know where Jesus lived, parents and youth workers today must help adolescents to ask this question, offering them the same invitation Jesus gave: "Come and see." (John 1:35-39) Come and see where and in what conditions Jesus lives today—in our neighborhood, our city, our world. How do we recognize him behind the many faces we see? How do we welcome him? How do we respond to his needs? How do we address the causes of his suffering as he carries the crosses imposed on him in our times?

Discernment is a way of seeing what is not obvious, what is hidden, what at times may be completely strange to us. It is the kind of sight described by the young woman in Dialog 7.1 at the beginning of this chapter, who responded to the question of why it is important to volunteer with the following: *"That one person you help could be an angel. It could be God, you know."* Discernment is the way to develop this kind of sight, and discernment is only fully Christian when it is practiced as a community. No one person can see the whole picture. When people from a variety of life situations come together in faith and trust to discern God's will, it becomes possible with the help of the Holy Spirit to bridge the gaps between rich and poor, English-speaking and Spanish-speaking, citizens and immigrants. It takes many pairs of eyes sharing their vantage points to truly come to see with the eyes of Jesus.

Jesus taught his disciples to see reality from God's point of view. He helped them to see the reality of the Reign of God, which according to Jesus *is* reality at its deepest level, where all people—especially the poor and oppressed—find the fullness of life and belonging. The Gospel of Luke describes a key moment of clarity for Jesus in the discernment of his own mission as a calling from God "to bring good news to the poor... to proclaim release to the captives and recovery of sight to the blind, to let the oppressed go free, to proclaim the year of the Lord's favor." (Luke 4:14-21) As members of the Body of Christ, Christians are called to continue this mission today and always, starting in their own homes, neighborhoods, and work or school environments.

The prophetic mission of Jesus

In effect, Jesus' mission was to be a prophet. As a messenger and spokesperson for God, Jesus announced the Good News of the new spiritual, social, *and* political order God wants to establish in this world. This is what Jesus called the "Reign of God." It became the core of his teaching and he used many parables to describe this reality as being present, yet not fully here. His mission therefore was to bring the fullness of God's Reign by proclaiming a vision of what God dreams for the world. At the same time, he reached out to heal and confront the sickness, suffering, violence, ignorance, and social injustice that prevent God's vision from being fully established in people's hearts and lives.

Jesus taught his disciples to see these menacing realties both in their symptoms and causes. A close review of the healing stories preserved by the gospel writers reveals that Jesus' miracles and physical healings always had a social and political dimension to them. He reached out to heal not only what was ailing the body, but also what was alienating the sick, sinful, or otherwise marginalized person from the community, helping them to find their place once again in society. He also confronted the religious and social laws that privileged certain groups to the detriment of many others. This dimension of his healing ministry is what got him into trouble with the powerful people of his time who were benefiting from the corrupt political and religious systems that kept so many people sick, unclean, illegal, and ostracized from the community.

As a true prophet, Jesus not only comforted the afflicted, but also *afflicted* the comfortable with the glaring light of truth. Light can be very discomforting for those who prefer to live in darkness, in the pretense of their self-sufficiency and privilege. Many of the gospel stories focus on the conflicts Jesus faced with the leaders of his day, how he dealt with them, and the heavy price he paid for his stance. He was usually very direct in his confrontations, even to the point of physically driving his opponents out of the temple; but there are also several stories in which Jesus cleverly engages them in their own Machiavellian logic in order to expose their true intentions of maintaining the status quo for their own benefit.

Luke 20:20-26 recounts such an encounter when Jesus' adversaries asked him if they were required to pay taxes to Rome. Jesus took a coin and asked them, "Whose head and whose title does it bear?" When they replied that it was Caesar's he said, "Then give to the emperor the things that are the emperor's, and to God the things that are God's." This provocative story has often been used to draw an imaginary line separating the secular world of politics and economics from the sacred world of religion and spirituality—but is it really possible to separate the two? Isn't the heart of Jesus' message that everything belongs to God, and that through God's graciousness we have been entrusted with stewardship of the goods of the earth? We have in our hands the power to decide what kind of stewards we will be. As disciples of Jesus in today's world, we are called to continue his prophetic and healing mission: to be simple but astute followers who can discern the signs of the times and boldly respond with love for our neighbor and with respect for all of God's creation.

Integral education and the Pastoral Circle

In this context, the question must be asked: how can we improve the way we educate Latino/a teenagers to be prophets and healers like Jesus in our parishes and congregations? In Spanish, the word for educating—*educar*—means much more than learning to read and write. It also means discovering a meaning and direction in life through mentoring, personal experience, and reflection; it entails learning *respeto,* respect. *Respeto* in Latino cultures is a social process of relating honorably to others, to God, and to one's self. Children learn *respeto* from their families, and the entire community has a role to play in making sure that children are *educados*—educated in how to properly treat and relate with others. Education in this sense is a holistic, formational process of integrating young people into the life, faith, and culture of the community.

Youth ministry in a Latino setting must build on the strengths of these foundations to call forth Latino/a teens to serve as leaders in their communities. Youth leaders need formation to acquire and strengthen skills for social and political action. A comprehensive program of formation for Hispanic adolescents must include multiple avenues for learning and practicing the following essential skills for leadership: self and cultural awareness, intercultural and intergenerational communication, conflict resolution, critical analysis, problem solving, discernment, planning, and above all collaborative action rooted in the gospel. Formation, therefore, is essentially a process of integral education whereby young people are guided and mentored into becoming active participants in the learning process and capable leaders in the community.

A process for integral education and discernment that has been historically very important for Latino faith communities is the same Pastoral Circle mentioned at the beginning of this chapter, commonly referred to in Spanish in its oldest and simplest form as *ver, juzgar, actuar* (see, judge, and act). This process begins with a close look *to see* both the social reality that is troubling the community and the pertinent assets or resources in the community that will facilitate a response to the challenge, taking into account all possible angles and different levels. Here, the young people engage in dialogue with those individuals and groups most affected by the reality. They study the symptoms of the reality by asking such questions as: When does it occur? How often? Where? Who is involved? Who is affected? Is it likely to be resolved on its own? What gifts exist in the community to help resolve the situation?

Understanding the symptoms of a problem is only the beginning. The teens must be empowered to probe deeper by asking the sometimes difficult questions about what is causing their troublesome reality. Questions such as the following are helpful in this phase: What is the history here? How is this reality related to other experiences? How is power being shared? Who is deciding? Who is benefiting? What systems or structures are involved in creating this reality? Who is resisting change? Who else might benefit from the creation of a more just social order? What are the potential consequences if action is taken to change the situation? Are we prepared to face the consequences of our action?

Once the teens have taken sufficient time to see the reality and try to understand its symptoms and causes, the next step is *to judge* the reality in the light of shared faith and values. The step of judging basically involves asking, "What do the Word of God and the teachings of our faith community have to say about this reality?" There are of course many ways to read the Bible. Sometimes we study how, when, and why it was written. Other times, we read it for inspiration and prayer, or to seek guidance in our lives. The process of judging social reality combines both of these approaches by prayerfully reflecting on the current challenges of the community in the light of the story of salvation and Jesus' proclamation of the Reign of God.

At this point it is important to remind the teens that *the Word of God is not meant to be applied literally to these realities.* The Scriptures were written in particular places, times, and for specific groups of people. Their situation was different from the circumstances we face today. However, the Word of God provides fundamental themes and images that apply to every place and time and culture. It is important for youth ministry leaders to identify these central themes in light of their particular denominational history and beliefs, and then to guide their adolescent members in making appropriate applications to the challenges they face in their lives.

The third step of the Pastoral Circle is *to act.* Action is the central piece of the cycle because it brings together prayer, study, reflection, and vision into a series of activities that will bring about a change in the community. A leader who seeks to be like Jesus is action-oriented. Leadership is not just talking about what is wrong with things, complaining, or wishing things could be different. True leaders put their faith into action. They make their values visible through loving service, educating others, resolving conflicts, confronting injustice, and creating new opportunities for peace and justice to flourish.

Christian leadership, however, is not about being a "Lone Ranger," someone who decides alone what action to take. Discipleship involves being part of a community of teachers and learners who together follow the one Master Teacher, Jesus. This insight is particularly important in youth ministry because adolescents are not in a position, either developmentally or socially, to tackle the enormous challenges that often plague low-income Hispanic communities, especially in urban settings. However, with appropriate guidance they can be empowered to name what is ailing their community and creatively work together for a healing that is within the sphere of their influence. Such action provides the teens with an experience of how Jesus lives among us, sending the Holy Spirit to inspire us as a community to continue his mission in our world today.

The call to participate in Jesus' active mission is essentially a call to work, to take action—but not just any work or action. As disciples, our action flows from critically "seeing" and "judging" in the light of our faith. If our work is to be a continuation of Jesus' mission, it must flow from what Jesus would have us do. When working with teens, it is important to remember not to impose responsibilities that they cannot bear, but neither should we create obstacles to their exercising leadership in the community according to their abilities. To find this balance, we must rely on the Holy Spirit guiding us through the shared wisdom of our sisters and brothers in the faith community and the tradition of our church. This is where youth leaders can help, because they often provide enthusiasm and creativity when strategizing for change. In our communities, we must equip these young leaders with the skills they need to help one another, sort through options, listen to each other, and decide with respect on a course of action.

Pastoral recommendations

This chapter began with the good news that most Latino/a youth are already very concerned about the wellbeing of the poor and the elderly, as well as racial equality. Lawrence Kohlberg identified these adolescent characteristics as the foundations of a post-conventional level of moral reasoning where fear of punishment or the desire for approval are no longer the primary motivators for ethical action (see pages 192-193). When adults nurture these foundations and model behaviors that build on them, teens begin to manifest what Carol Gilligan calls an "ethic of caring" that flows from a willingness to feel the pain of the other and respond to alleviate and prevent it.[8] As this ethic permeates their relationships, choices, and service to others, such adolescents learn to express compassion and empathy even to those who have no apparent way of reciprocating this kindness. These are skills and behaviors that will enable them to be strong, faithful, and moral leaders as adults. The following suggestions provide practical ways for parents and youth ministry leaders to help Hispanic teens develop their concern for others into a commitment to social justice and faithful citizenship.

> *Will the Lord be pleased with thousands of rams, with ten thousands of rivers of oil? Shall I give my firstborn for my transgression, the fruit of my body for the sin of my soul? He has told you, O mortal, what is good; and what does the Lord require of you but to do justice, and to love kindness, and to walk humbly with your God?*
>
> *– Micah 6:7-8*

1. **Mentor young people to take the lead in community service projects**

    For youth ministers, the most obvious systems to carefully examine are their churches and the influence of their structures, programs, and institutions on Latino/a teens and their families. Without question, the NSYR findings challenge youth ministers to examine their church's commitment to providing meaningful volunteer and community service opportunities for adolescents. For example, Table 7.2 on page 244 showed that 46% of the Protestant and 57% of the religiously "committed" Hispanic teens said that half or more of their service was organized by a religious group; yet only 9% of the Protestants and 23% of the "committed" respondents indicated that they "regularly" did volunteer work or community service. In other words, the service activities in most youth ministry programs tend to be occasional activities of direct service to people who are poor, sick, or elderly. Without diminishing the importance of such acts of charity and service, churches must go a step further especially when ministering with Hispanics.

    Given the history and personal realities of Latino/a adolescents, youth ministers should begin by educating the teens about the historical, ideological, cultural, and systemic causes of the suffering and injustice they have experienced or observed. The overall goal of this education is to foster in the young people a belief that our Christian faith can truly make a difference as we share power and work collaboratively to make our communities safer, more inclusive, and responsive to human needs. Engaging the teens in a reflection process based on the Pastoral Circle described in the last section has been a fruitful approach in many places. When the teens identify the issues for themselves and strategize together about how to address them, they become invested in carrying out an appropriate response and learn to see themselves as leaders and agents of change in their community.

2. Challenge pre-conceived notions about faith and politics

As important as it may be to ensure that government does not sanction and support a particular faith expression, being politically engaged and living out our Christian faith are not mutually exclusive endeavors. Rather, faith and social action are at the heart of the gospel and the teachings of many Christian denominational statements. Parents and youth ministers must draw on both Scripture and church teachings to educate young people about large social problems such as poverty and violence. For example, biblical themes such as the Reign of God, the gifts of the Spirit, and the prophetic and healing mission of Jesus could be explained and related to the events and circumstances of the teens' lives. In addition, the teens should be given the tools to tackle specific issues with their peers or with adults in the community, employing creative strategies appropriate to their age and level of development. In this way, the young people begin to see themselves as agents of change in the structures that directly impact their lives, such as their families, schools, and neighborhoods.

3. Empower Hispanic families to engage in political action

Youth ministers must find ways to invite Latino/a adolescents and their parents to participate in the political processes of this country. Because young Latinos often experience the tension of straddling two or more cultures with very distinct values, it is important to help them and their parents integrate their unique, Latino identity as truly "American" in the best sense of the term. As a nation of proud indigenous peoples and immigrants, our strength is founded on an unwavering commitment to a democracy that truly strives for unity in diversity and the protection of its weakest members. The strength of a democracy is only as great as the commitment of its citizens to be active participants in building the common good through inclusion and political participation.

A significant challenge lies in the fact that many (perhaps a majority) Latino families are completely excluded from the most basic form of political participation: voting. As non-citizens, the parents do not have the right to vote, and as underage citizens, neither do their children. Limited access to educational resources and analysis of local current events in Spanish, combined with a culture of religious determinism wherein one's circumstances and destiny in life are seen as being entirely in God's hands, lead many Hispanic adults to believe that they are powerless to change their situation or even participate in the political process. These are the attitudes and examples that they pass to their teenaged children despite the fact that many of the teens, as citizens and English-speakers, are in a better position to become politically active than their parents.

Churches need to work with both Hispanic adolescents and their parents in order to reverse these self-defeating attitudes and empower their political voice. As a first step, citizens who are not registered to vote should be encouraged to do so and provided with faith-based information in an appropriate language regarding the issues to be decided at the polls. Even non-citizens can be politically involved in a variety of ways, but they must be mentored on how to participate. Residents with legal immigration documents can openly support and participate in political action groups, but those without documents are in a more precarious position. The community would do well to obtain legal advice about how best to engage such parents in political processes without putting them in jeopardy. In any case, youth ministers should keep in mind that adolescents will become adults in a few years, and the children of immigrants may need extra guidance to become fully involved citizens as they reach the age of majority.

4. Address the needs of undocumented immigrants

As long as the political battle for comprehensive immigration reform continues, it will be important for Christian communities to work with their young Hispanic members to raise their voices and engage in the political process using a variety of strategies. The current debate has the potential to be a watershed moment in the political life of the Latino community in the United States. Every action the young people take will have an impact on the way they see themselves and their place in the society of the United States. If comprehensive reform can be achieved, the legalized immigration status of so many Latino parents will have a profound effect on their ability to advocate for themselves and their children in the political arena.

Whether comprehensive reform is achieved or not, immigrants will always be among the most vulnerable residents of any community. Out of solidarity with Latino/a immigrants both present and past, Hispanic young people should be encouraged to work for the protection of immigrants' human rights, irrespective of their immigration status. Just wages, educational opportunities, access to transportation and affordable housing, and discrimination will continue to be challenges for immigrants long after the debates over immigration reform have subsided. Youth ministers should be prepared to engage the Latino/a adolescents in their programs to develop responses to these challenges at the local level, according to their abilities.

5. Make sure that service activities are appropriate for the Latino/as

In middle and upper class suburban communities, youth ministers have become accustomed to building global awareness among their adolescent members by involving them in doing or supporting service projects in Latin America, Africa, or other parts of the developing world. Alternatively, they may bring a group of young people from their community to perform an act of service in a nearby low-income neighborhood. Such activities can be very useful in expanding the awareness of otherwise sheltered young people, especially if they are followed by a facilitated reflection process to help them recognize the structures that perpetuate the experiences of poverty and privilege in our world.

However, such activities make no sense in faith communities that serve low-income inner-city or rural populations. In these locations, it makes much more sense to engage the teens in service projects addressing needs found in their own neighborhoods. In this case, the experience is not about forming a young person's conscience to perform acts of charity for others who are "less fortunate," but rather of empowering them to bring about needed changes in their own lives and fostering in them a commitment to improve the lives of the people in their neighborhood as they grow into adulthood—even if they eventually move out of the barrio.

Finding an appropriate approach in an economically diverse urban community is especially challenging. In such communities, acts of charity developed and performed by the wealthier members often serve to emphasize their separation from the lower-income members, rather than helping them to see each other as co-responsible equals in the project. In addition, this approach leaves the lower-income members feeling objectified and disempowered. Even inviting young people from low-income families to participate with their wealthier peers in such projects can create feelings of alienation in them—both from the wealthier members of the larger community and from the people in their own family and neighborhood who are being served in the project.

This type of community is especially common in the Catholic Church. Since Catholic parishes tend to be much larger than the average Latino Protestant congregation, it is often the case that the parish is called to serve a culturally and economically diverse population. In addition, the Catholic Church in the United States is economically polarized on ethnic lines, with the Latino/a Catholics on average being poorer than Hispanic Protestants, while the white Catholics on average are wealthier than white Protestants (see Table 1.5 on page 31). In such communities, the youth ministry leaders should take special care to ensure that the voice of the low-income teens is not lost when doing an analysis of the needs of the community or strategizing about possible responses; inviting and developing youth leaders that reflect the diversity of the community is one way to promote full participation. In addition, all of the participants should be educated about the importance of working collaboratively to recognize and overcome unjust structures in the community. In this way, it is possible to build a spirit of mutual trust and unity in diversity among adolescent members of different backgrounds.

Another approach might be to structure youth ministry in the parish or congregation with multiple small groups, helping each teen to find a peer group that is socially, culturally, and linguistically appropriate for them. When the experiences of the teens in the small groups are similar, they usually feel more confident about sharing their experiences and proposing possible actions. In this case, each small group may be empowered to identify challenges and responses on its own, or the leaders might gather to strategize about how the various small groups might collaborate in addressing a more significant issue that is affecting the community. However the youth ministry programs might be structured, the objective should always be to ensure that the young Latino/as in the community are engaged as leaders and prophets, continuing the mission of Jesus in their families, neighborhoods, and in the faith community itself.

Questions for reflection

1. How is our faith community inviting young Hispanics into meaningful participation in the life and mission of the church through social action and volunteer opportunities? What more could be done?

2. What is our parish or congregation's record on political and social engagement in the community where it is located?

3. What are we doing to promote comprehensive immigration reform in our community? What services do we offer to assist immigrants and protect their human rights? What more could we do?

4. What types of service activities do we offer our adolescent members? Are they appropriately structured in view of their socioeconomic status? What impact do we hope to achieve in the lives of our Hispanic members by means of these activities?

5. What resources has our church invested in the formation of Latino/a youth leaders to help them discern the urgent social needs of our time and place, and to respond in faith with an action of their own design?

Chapter 8:
The Second Wave of the National Study of Youth and Religion

Ken Johnson-Mondragón, D.Min. cand.

Dialog 8.1 – 18 year-old Hispanic Catholic female from the West

I: *How would you describe yourself to me in terms of your religion?*

R: How would I describe myself? Um I do believe, I do believe in God, and I'm a Catholic, but like I said I'm leaning more towards my dad's perspective—where you can believe and everything but um, it doesn't mean that you have to go to church every Sunday. And um, that's where I'm leaning more towards now. I mean I still go to church but not as often.

I: *That makes sense... And how often do you go?*

R: Uh, like I said not as often as I used to, so maybe once or twice a month... If that sometimes.

I: *Are you involved in any youth group or other religious groups?*

R: Not at the moment. Um, well I mean I haven't really looked into any college group or anything like that. But like I said, I used to work with the youth, but that ended for the summer, so.

I: *How often do you pray?*

R: Every night. At least I try to [giggling].

I: *Do you read the Bible?*

R: No, not very often. I mean I used to when I was in youth, but now I don't.

I: *How much would you say religion is a part of your everyday life?*

R: Um, I would say a lot, because you know, during the day um... You know, if I pass a cross I do the sign of the cross. If I see something um, sometimes I'll say "God please this," or "God please that."

I: *Over the past couple of years, do you think you've become more religious, less religious, or stayed about the same?*

R: Um, I don't know if you'd call not going to church less religious or...

I: *Do you consider it less religious?*

R: No I don't... Yeah, I think I'm the same religious, but I just don't go to church. I think I've stayed as religious as I was, but I don't know. Like according to the church I would be less religious, but...

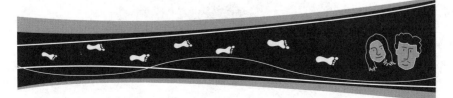

The Second Wave of the National Study of Youth and Religion

When work on this book started, it was envisioned as a pastoral reflection on the first wave of Hispanic data from the National Study of Youth and Religion. Since that time, data from the second wave of surveys and interviews has become available. Rather than mix the new data with the old, the themes developed in the previous chapters were based only on the first wave—the data collected while the respondents were all still teenagers. This chapter provides a statistical update and some reflections on the religious lives of these same Hispanic adolescents and young adults, now two to three years older than they were when first surveyed.

Before getting into the specific findings, it is important to recognize some of the limitations of the Wave 2 data. With respect to the surveys, the NSYR research team made every effort to contact all of the teens surveyed in the first wave, but many simply could not be found. Overall, about 79% of the teens surveyed in Wave 1 were reached again for the second wave, but the retention rate was only 63% among the Latino/a respondents. Of the 45 teens who answered the first survey in Spanish, only 42% were retained in the second wave, and none of the four teens interviewed in Spanish were among those interviewed the second time.

Not surprisingly, the teens from low-income and immigrant families were more likely than others to be missing in the second wave—the instability of their lives made them harder to find. Furthermore, since the Wave 2 survey was only conducted among Wave 1 respondents, it automatically excluded any immigrant Hispanic youth and young adults that arrived in the United States between 2002 and 2005. As a result, the Wave 2 data do not describe the full range of 16 to 20 year-old Latino/as in the U.S. since low-income and recent immigrant Hispanics are not proportionally represented.

Also, because there were only 294 weighted Latino/a respondents in Wave 2 compared to the 449 in the first wave,[1] there are often not enough responses to make statistically meaningful comparisons between subgroups of Hispanic teens, as was done in previous chapters. For example, many of the previous chapters compared the responses of religiously committed, engaged, sporadic, and disengaged teens on a variety of questions. In this chapter, those groupings were collapsed into just two categories so that there would be enough responses in each category to make a meaningful comparison.

The other significant difference between the two waves of surveys is that the second wave did not include a survey of the parents. This limitation especially impacts the way religious identity is categorized in Wave 2. In many cases, the adolescent respondents in both waves could not clearly identify their religious or denominational affiliation. In the first wave, if they stated that they attend church with their parents, then the parental religious affiliation was assigned to the child. For the purposes of this chapter, when the young person in the second wave survey responded that they were "just Christian," their Wave 1 religious tradition was utilized in order to distinguish between Catholics and Protestants.[2]

With respect to the personal interviews, the retention rate for Latino/a respondents between the first and second waves was even lower than for the surveys. Only 14 of the 38 Latino/a teens interviewed in Wave 1 received a second interview—six Catholics, five Protestants, and three without any religion. While these interviews are not a representative sample of the Latino/a teens and young adults in the U.S., they nevertheless provide excellent narrative examples of what is happening in the religious lives of young Hispanics as they mature from adolescence into young adulthood.

Religious switching

The analysis of religious affiliation and religious switching in Chapter 1 (see pages 20 to 23) found that Hispanic teens seldom switch religious affiliations on their own; they are much more likely to be religious followers of their parents if they should switch. As a follow-up to that analysis, it is very fitting to begin this chapter with a comparison between the religious tradition of teens in the Wave 1 survey and their expressed religious

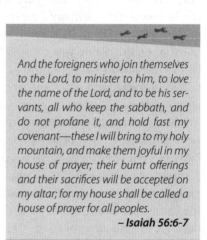

And the foreigners who join themselves to the Lord, to minister to him, to love the name of the Lord, and to be his servants, all who keep the sabbath, and do not profane it, and hold fast my covenant—these I will bring to my holy mountain, and make them joyful in my house of prayer; their burnt offerings and their sacrifices will be accepted on my altar; for my house shall be called a house of prayer for all peoples.
– Isaiah 56:6-7

affiliation in Wave 2. Table 8.1 provides a summary of that data, broken down for the Hispanic, white, and other racial/ethnic respondents.

In order to compensate for the effects of the sampling bias introduced in the second wave, the Wave 1 data reported in the table only include the responses from teens surveyed in Wave 2, so the numbers do not exactly match what was reported in Chapter 1 (cf. Chart 1.7 on page 21). In other words, the Wave 1 and Wave 2 numbers in the table represent the responses of the same young people to the same questions about their religious affiliation in 2002-2003 and in 2005. This approach highlights the religious changes that took place in the years between the two surveys.

A quick comparison reveals that the proportion of Protestant and Catholic respondents in all three ethnic/racial groups decreased slightly over the two years between surveys. The Catholic Hispanics had the largest drop of any group—three percentage points. Also, there was a notable increase in the number of teens reporting no religious affiliation in all three racial/ethnic

Table 8.1 – Religious tradition by race/ethnicity and NSYR Wave (percentages)			
	Race / Ethnicity		
	Hispanic	**White**	**Other**
Wave 1	N=294	N=1984	N=614
Protestant	20	53	70
Catholic	60	22	11
Other religion	5	11	7
No religion	10	12	9
Indeterminate	4	2	3
Wave 2			
Protestant	19	51	69
Catholic	57	20	10
Other religion	5	10	7
No religion	13	18	12
Indeterminate	5	2	4

groups. However, the overall proportions within each racial/ethnic group only tell part of the story. Further insight can be gained by considering how the religious identities of the Hispanic and white respondents in each religious tradition changed from Wave 1 to Wave 2, as shown in Table 8.2.

Religious changes by tradition

The phenomenon of Hispanics leaving the Catholic Church for evangelical and Pentecostal communities continues to be widely discussed and analyzed,[3] yet the NSYR surveys show that the *white* Catholics were twice as likely to become Protestant and nearly three times as likely to abandon their religious faith altogether. In fact, the Hispanic Catholics were the most stable group, with 87% retaining their religious identity from Wave 1 to Wave 2 and only 5% rejecting any religious identity—the lowest of all the groups. The loss of these Hispanic Catholics was more than offset by the non-religious and "other" Hispanic teens from Wave 1, 20% of whom had become Catholic by the time of the second wave survey.

Meanwhile, at 13% the Hispanic Protestants were as likely as the white Catholics to abandon their religious faith, and they were just as likely to become Catholic as the Latino/a Catholics were to become Protestant. Moreover, 7% of the Hispanic teens who were not categorized as Christians in Wave 1 identified themselves as Protestants in Wave 2. Thus, the slight decrease in Hispanic Protestants between Wave 1 and Wave 2 was primarily

Table 8.2 – Wave 2 religious tradition by race/ethnicity and Wave 1 religious tradition (percentages)

Wave 2 religious tradition	Wave 1 Catholics		Wave 1 Protestants		Wave 1 Others	
	Hispanic	White	Hispanic	White	Hispanic	White
	N=178	N=443	N=58	N=1061	N=59	N=480
Protestant	3	6	79	85	7	16
Catholic	87	79	3	3	20	3
Other religion	1	~	0	1	26	36
No religion	5	13	13	10	39	40
Indeterminate	5	2	4	1	9	5

due to the large number of Hispanic Protestant teens who no longer considered themselves religious by the time of the second wave survey, offset by a nearly equal number of Catholic and non-religious Hispanics who took on a Protestant identity.

Loss of Christian identity

In effect, the loss of young members to "no religion" should be of greater concern to both Catholics and Protestants than the much smaller proportion of their respective adherents switching between each other. This observation is supported by the fact that none of the Hispanics interviewed in the second wave had changed denominational affiliations, although one of the Catholics expressed serious doubts about the existence of God and two of the teens who had been Protestants in the first wave no longer identified themselves as Christian. The following example illustrates this point:

Dialog 8.2 – 16 year-old Hispanic ex-Christian female from the West

I: How would you describe yourself to me in terms of religion or spirituality?
R: Um, I'm confused, I don't really know...
I: Okay, what do you believe?
R: I believe in karma... That's all I can really say that I actually believe right now, is I believe in karma.
I: Okay, so you don't know right now whether you believe in God or not?
R: Uh-huh [doesn't know].
I: Or life after death? Heaven?
R: I really couldn't tell you. No, I'm totally confused on everything right now.
I: Okay, do you ever attend any religious services?
R: I used to, not anymore.
I: And you're not involved in any youth group or anything like that?
R: No.

I: *Do you pray ever?*

R: No.

I: *Do you ever read the Bible?*

R: No.

I: *So you wouldn't say that religion is a part of your everyday life at all?*

R: No.

I: *Was there anything that was behind that change, anything that happened in your life, or that you saw?*

R: No, nothing. Nothing really changed, just I just stopped.

I: *Okay. Was it a conscious decision, or did it just kind of...*

R: Just kind of did. I think it was both, conscious and it just kind of stopped. I don't really think too much about it.

It is helpful to take into account some of this girl's religious background based on her Wave 1 interview. Her biological parents were both Christians, but they never went to church when she was small. After they divorced and her dad remarried, her step-mother persuaded her to start going to a youth-friendly church recommended by a neighbor. She ended up going there by herself for about a year and a half, during which time she became very close to the youth pastor's wife and developed a strong friendship with a girl she met there. At the time, her dad and step-mother had been going to a different church, but everyone in the family stopped attending when the step-mother had surgery and could not go for a long time. After her step-mother's surgery, the daughter lost interest in church and became busy with other things in her life. By the time of the second interview two years later, she no longer identified herself as a Christian.

Religious beliefs and practices

Religious beliefs

One of the effects of young people like the girl in Dialog 8.2 abandoning their religious faith as they grow older is that there is a gradual "weeding out" of adolescents who only described themselves as Christians out of deference to their parents. As a result, those who retain their religious identity over time are more likely to be personally invested in the teachings of their faith tradition. Thus, it is not a surprise that on a number of measures the Catholic and Protestant teens in Wave 2 were more traditional or reported higher incidences of divine experiences than their Wave 1 counterparts, as shown in Table 8.3.

> Jesus heard that they had driven him out, and when he found him, he said, "Do you believe in the Son of Man?" He answered, "And who is he, sir? Tell me, so that I may believe in him." Jesus said to him, "You have seen him, and the one speaking with you is he." He said, "Lord, I believe." And he worshipped him.
> – *John 9:35-38*

Table 8.3 – Religious beliefs by race/ethnicity, religious tradition, and NSYR wave (percentages)

	Catholic		Protestant	
	Hispanic	White	Hispanic	White
Wave 1	N=276	N=556	N=94	N=1281
Believes in God as a personal being	78	80	90	86
Definitely believes in a judgment day	70	66	92	82
Definitely believes in life after death	42	47	53	58
Experienced a definite answer to prayer	41	40	73	61
Witnessed a miracle from God	38	37	63	54
Wave 2	N=169	N=394	N=55	N=1002
Believes in God as a personal being	80	76	95	86
Definitely believes in a judgment day	74	65	86	81
Definitely believes in life after death	36	44	61	63
Experienced a definite answer to prayer	51	39	83	64
Witnessed a miracle from God	39	28	75	49

There are two clear exceptions to the general trend of similar or higher levels of adherence to traditional teachings and experiences of God in the second wave. First, the Catholic respondents expressed lower confidence in a belief about life after death in the second survey. In contrast, the Protestant respondents expressed greater confidence in this belief the second time around. It is possible that some of the respondents were not clear about the meaning of the question, as in the following example:

Dialog 8.3 – 17 year-old Hispanic Christian male from the South

I: *Do you believe in life after death?*

R: No. Once you're dead, you're dead.

I: *Okay. No heaven, no hell?*

R: There's heaven. I mean, is that life after death? I mean I don't know. I've never been taught about that, I mean.

I: *Yeah, that's what I mean.*

R: Life after death to me is like reincarnation.

I: *Sorry. Heaven and hell. What happens when you die? Let's put it that way.*

R: To be honest I really have no idea.

I: *Do you think there's a heaven?*

R: I have no idea. I mean, I don't know.

I: *Okay, do you ever think about it?*

R: I think about it yeah, I mean.

I: *What do you think?*

R: I mean sometimes if I do something bad I'd be like, "Oh I'm going to hell for this," you know...

I: Well okay, like what would you go to hell for?
R: The stealing is the only thing I've really done bad...
I: And you thought to yourself, I'm going to hell for this?
R: Uh huh. [yes]

The second exception is that there was a clear drop in the number of white respondents who said that they had witnessed a miracle from God in the second survey. The drop was more pronounced among the white Catholics than for the white Protestants, but in both cases it is odd because one would think that if a person had witnessed a miracle from God at the time of the first survey, they would still remember that experience at the time of the second survey. One possible explanation is that as they get older, white adolescents tend to embrace a naturalistic/scientific worldview that seldom appeals to God as an explanation for life events, while Hispanic teens gravitate toward a more religious worldview in which the signs of God's activity are everywhere.

Religious practices

Instead of looking at individual religious practices in detail as was done in Chapters 2 and 3, Table 8.4 makes use of the religious types introduced in Chapter 2 (see pages 69-72) as a summary of all of those measures. Because

Table 8.4 – Religious type* by race/ethnicity, religious tradition, and NSYR wave (percentages)

	Catholic		Protestant	
	Hispanic	White	Hispanic	White
Wave 1	N=276	N=556	N=94	N=1281
Committed	4	8	28	19
Engaged	43	44	40	47
Sporadic	21	25	11	15
Disengaged	3	7	1	3
Mixed	28	16	20	16
Wave 2	N=169	N=394	N=55	N=1002
Committed	13	5	28	21
Engaged	28	36	48	37
Sporadic	23	32	8	20
Disengaged	3	1	1	2
Mixed	33	26	14	20

* See the Appendix on page 361 for definitions of the Wave 1 and Wave 2 religious types.

not all of the questions utilized as criteria for the religious types in Wave 1 were repeated in the Wave 2 survey, the religious types were not defined exactly the same way in both waves of the study, but every effort was made to make these variables as comparable as possible. The Appendix on page 361 provides a detailed explanation of the criteria that were used to determine religious type in each wave of the survey.

Despite the "weeding out" effect mentioned above, the overall change in religious commitment is quite mixed. Table 8.4 shows that the proportion of "committed" Christians increased from Wave 1 to Wave 2 among Latino/a Catholics and white Protestants, but only Hispanic Protestants increased in the "engaged" category. Also, the white respondents were more likely to be "sporadic" in the second wave, while their Hispanic counterparts were roughly unchanged in that category. Meanwhile, all but the Latino/a Protestants increased significantly in the "mixed" category.

Since Table 8.4 does not show how individual teens' religious type changed from the first wave to the second, it is difficult to determine from those statistics alone how the teens' religious dedication developed over the two years between the surveys—they only provide an overall average for each survey within each racial/ethnic and religious group.

Table 8.5 – Change in religious type* by race/ethnicity and religious tradition (percentages)

| | Wave 1 Type | | | |
| | Engaged / Committed | | Sporadic / Disengaged | |
	Hispanic	White	Hispanic	White
Wave 2 Catholics	N=87	N=235	N=39	N=100
Committed	13	8	8	0
Engaged	43	49	14	11
Sporadic	20	25	34	53
Disengaged	0	1	9	2
Mixed	24	16	35	34
Wave 2 Protestants	N=37	N=698	N=8**	N=155
Committed	34	27	N/A	5
Engaged	50	44	N/A	18
Sporadic	5	15	N/A	37
Disengaged	1	1	N/A	8
Mixed	10	14	N/A	32

* See the Appendix on page 361 for definitions of the Wave 1 and Wave 2 religious types.

** With only 8 responses, these results are not representative and do not merit reporting.

Table 8.5 provides additional clarity by following the committed/engaged and sporadic/disengaged teens from each religious tradition in Wave 1 to demonstrate how their religious dedication changed during the two years that followed.

Among the religiously committed and engaged teens from Wave 1, it was the Latino/a Protestants who were most likely to maintain their level of personal and communal religious involvement, followed in order by the white Protestants, the Hispanic Catholics, and lastly the white Catholics. Dialog 8.1 at the beginning of this chapter is an excellent example of how religious commitment after Confirmation often diminishes among young Latino/a Catholics—even those who have been very involved for a time. In contrast, the following conversation shows how one young Latino Protestant was able to maintain his religious commitment in college:

Dialog 8.4 – 20 year-old Hispanic Baptist male from the South

I: *How similar are your parents to you in religious belief and participation?*
R: We're pretty similar. They're probably a little more conservative than I am.
I: *What does that mean?*
R: I'm pretty conservative, but I'm probably like the new generation of conservative religious people. Not as hard core.
I: *What does that look like?*
R: Probably like, we're not going to home school our kids, and... The old school is like no dancing, you know. Definitely with the Baptist, it's a huge no-no.
I: *How would you describe yourself to me in terms of your religion?*
R: I would say I'm pretty religious, I think I have a pretty close relationship with God.
I: *You said you attended church?*
R: Yes.
I: *Are you involved in any college aged groups?*
R: Yes. Well like, religious groups? The BSM.
I: *The Baptist Student Mission?*
R: Yeah, that's about it.
I: *Do you pray?*
R: Yes.
I: *How often?*
R: Uh, pretty much every day. Some times I'll be working and I'll just pray while I'm working. I like to think I'm talking to somebody, so if I can't talk to somebody I might as well talk to God.
I: *How big of an impact would you say religion or spirituality has on your life?*
R: Um, I think it's a big impact. I mean... I grew up with it and went to religious schools all my life, so I definitely think it has an impact.
I: *Do you think your religion is the basis for how you live your life, or not?*
R: I think it should be, and I don't say that I always live my life, um how I probably should be doing it. That makes it sounds bad like I'm doing drugs or prostituting myself, which I'm not, but just like little things... Yeah, I think it should be the basis.
I: *Over the past couple of years, do you think you've become more religious, less religious, or stayed about the same?*

R: Pretty much about the same—maybe just a little bit less, maybe. Just because less church attendance, 'cause I haven't gone as much.

I: *You said you go once a week.*

R: I go once a week. At home, we go three times a week—Wednesday nights, Sunday night, and Sunday morning.

I: *How hard or easy has it been to maintain your religious faith, or being the kind of religious person you want to be, over the past couple of years?*

R: Um, it's not been hard, 'cause I mean, our school's so conducive to that... I often think about that, if I would be the exact same if I went to a different school. I don't know.

On the other hand, with respect to the sporadic and disengaged teens from Wave 1, it was the Hispanic Catholics who were most likely to move up to a higher level of involvement, followed by the white Protestants and lastly the white Catholics. There were not enough responses from sporadic or disengaged Hispanic Protestants in the second wave to be able to make a meaningful comparison. In any case, the following is a good example of how religious commitment increased among some of the Hispanic teens:

Dialog 8.5 – 16 year-old Hispanic Catholic male from the West

I: *How would you describe yourself to me in terms of your religion?*

R: I guess um, I'm pretty uh... faithful on it. I believe it's going to help me, so I go by it a lot. I do, like, I base most of my actions on it.

I: *And you attend church services? How often?*

R: Uh, every week. Every Sunday.

I: *Are you involved in any sort of class?*

R: Yeah... We all get together and... we'd have like a priest talk to us.

I: *So just for preparing for your First Communion, or is it like a catechism?*

R: Yeah, it's like, it's like a catechism, but it's like preparing for everything. 'Cause it's like one leads to another. So it's prepare for Communion, catechism... Like it's catechism preparing for our Communion, and uh, our Confirmation.

I: *And why do you do it?*

R: Oh, my Grandma put me into it... It was her choice. I was actually mad, 'cause my mom, my mom told me it wasn't her, so she was like, "Oh your Grandma put you in the catechism class." And I was like, "Huh?" I was like, "What do you mean catechism class?" And she was like, "Well if you don't like it you can quit." But I can't quit 'cause my Grandma's always there. So if I quit, if I quit she'll find out the same day, she'll be in the same house...

I: *And besides your Grandma and Grandpa and step-father, are there other important influences on your religious faith or spirituality in the past two years? Like events, experiences or other people?*

R: Actually yeah, there's a priest named Father Fernando, and he is explaining a lot to me. It's like whenever I have a question he'll always explain it.

I: *So you feel like you can go talk to him?*

R: Yeah, he's real friendly about things... When I was there, I guess he could tell that I didn't want to be in there, so he was being real friendly to me...

I: *How much would you say religion is a part of your everyday life?*

R: I base like all my wrong and right reactions on religion, most of the time.

I: *So would you say that your religion is the basis for how you live your life?*

R: Right now? Yeah, it's changed my life a lot. 'Cause before I'd never, I would have never thrown religion into what I would do. I'd just be like, "Oh, this seems okay." It was always, "Would this make my mom mad? Okay, I shouldn't do that." But now it's like, "Would that be okay for my religion?" And I'm like, "Oh, maybe I shouldn't do that."

I: *Over the past couple of years, do you think you've become more religious, less religious, or stayed about the same?*

R: More religious.

I: *More religious, in what ways?*

R: Understanding things more. Like if you hear enough of it, then you start... At first when you first hear it, it's real confusing. You're not sure what's going on. But after you hear it over and over and over and over, you start grasping the point. So I'm trying to grasp it.

I: *So just give me a couple of examples of things you thought initially were confusing, but now you're getting it?*

R: Like why it's important to believe or why it's important to have religion in your life. 'Cause before I thought like, "Why do you need religion if you believe in God?" And I'm starting to realize that it's not... Religion is not God. It's a way to get to him supposedly. So it's like uh, if you live your life according to religion, your whole entire life, you have no problems. But people don't always go by religion, so that's why there's problems. So it's almost like a walkway to a good life. So I'm starting to understand that now.

I: *And are there other religious groups that you could be involved in there?*

R: Uh, there is, but we haven't reached it—like you gotta be confirmed first. After that I think I'll be more involved... It's like my Grandma has done her part in it. The rest is up to me, and I'll keep up with it.

At the time of his first interview, this young man was a classic example of a moralistic therapeutic deist (see the description on page 72). However, through his grandmother's influence in getting him to church and the welcoming response of a priest, he has begun to see God as more central to his life and his faith as a motivator for his moral choices. He still seems to view religious observance primarily as a guarantor of a "good life," which he interprets as a life free from major problems. However, he also describes religion as a path to God, and he no longer relies on his grandmother to get him to church—he goes of his own will. In another part of the interview he mentions that he has persuaded his best friend to go with him as well.

Religious involvement at church

Although the religious development of the young man in Dialog 8.5 can certainly be taken as encouraging news for Catholic youth ministers

> So those who welcomed his message were baptized, and that day about three thousand persons were added. They devoted themselves to the apostles' teaching and fellowship, to the breaking of bread and the prayers.
> – Acts 2:41-42

and Confirmation catechists, it is important to note that at the time of the second interview he was still in the middle of his catechetical formation program. Three other Wave 2 Latino/a Catholic interviewees described how their religious commitment decreased after their Catholic school or Confirmation experience was finished. This decrease in religious commitment was most pronounced after high school—they did not have a peer community with which to connect, they began to attend Sunday liturgies less often, and they expressed doubts or outright rejected certain teachings of the Catholic Church, particularly regarding the obligation of Sunday Mass attendance and various aspects of sexual morality.

In contrast, of the four religiously active Wave 1 Hispanic Protestants who were interviewed again in Wave 2, three had become significantly more active at church, and the fourth (represented in Dialog 8.4 above) participated less but maintained his basic religious orientation in life and continued to attend worship services every Sunday. Of the three who had completed high school, two chose to go to colleges where they knew their faith would be supported strongly in the campus community, and the other joined a congregation with a large and dynamic college ministry group. All three fully accepted the teachings of their faith traditions, including the teachings on sexual morality, although one admitted she had recently changed her opinion to accept homosexual behavior between monogamous partners.

Church attendance

Since the number of interviews in the second wave of the NSYR was so small, and they were not conducted with a representative sample of Latino/a young people, it cannot be determined from the interviews alone whether these diverging patterns between young Catholic and Protestant Hispanics are typical in each faith tradition, or whether they are anomalies. However, the second wave survey data shown in Table 8.6 does provide some insights about what may be happening at a larger scale in U.S. faith communities. The comparable data from the first wave can be found in Tables 3.1 and 3.3 on pages 86 and 90.

Three patterns quickly emerge with respect to attendance at religious services. First, there is a significant drop in weekly attendance after high school (ages 18 and over) for all religious and racial/ethnic groups, the only exception being that of the Latino/a Protestants whose weekly attendance was unchanged. Second, Protestants in each age and ethnic group exceeded the weekly attendance of their respective Catholic peers by 11 to 19

Table 8.6 – Wave 2 church attendance and participation by age, religious tradition, and race/ethnicity (percentages)

	Catholic		Protestant	
	Ages 16 to 17	Ages 18 to 20	Ages 16 to 17	Ages 18 to 20
Hispanic	N=92	N=77	N=28*	N=27*
Attends worship services once a week or more	33	27	44	44
Attends 1 to 3 times a month, or many times a year	27	25	38	41
Attends a few times a year	21	33	18	11
Never attends	20	15	0	4
Has been confirmed or baptized (not infant baptism)	71	67	54	81
Currently participates in a youth group	13	18	48	51
Participates as a youth group leader	3	5	23	28
White	N=189	N=205	N=474	N=528
Attends worship services once a week or more	29	19	48	35
Attends 1 to 3 times a month, or many times a year	30	38	31	32
Attends a few times a year	22	29	14	21
Never attends	19	13	7	12
Has been confirmed or baptized (not infant baptism)	73	79	69	73
Currently participates in a youth group	20	12	55	34
Participates as a youth group leader	6	6	19	13

* With only 27 to 28 responses, these results have a sampling error of ±10%.

percentage points. Third, the Protestants were far less likely to report that they "never" attend worship services than their Catholic counterparts.

What these numbers reveal is that there is a strong trend toward lower church attendance as the teens move into young adulthood, even among those who have maintained their religious identity after the previously noted "weeding out" of many nominal Christians in the second wave of the study. They also suggest that when young Protestants stop going to church, they are much more likely than their Catholic counterparts to stop identifying themselves as Christian. This tendency was certainly evident in the interviews—the two least-involved Hispanic Protestant teens in the first interview identified themselves as having no religious affiliation in the second interview, while the least-involved Latina Catholic teen in the first interview continued to call herself Catholic in the second interview, despite the fact that religion clearly played no role in her life, as the following excerpt from her interview demonstrates:

Dialog 8.6 – 20 year-old Hispanic/Italian Catholic female from the Northeast

I: *How similar are your parents to you in terms of religious belief and participation?*

R: Um, my father is very religious. He's kind of like, um...

I: *Catholic, right?*

R: Catholic, right... But my mother, my mother is like, "What? What is God?" You know, like totally out of it. You know like, doesn't have any religious reference. But it's weird—her sister is like a religious freak. I mean, she's very involved in her religion, you know?

I: *And how similar are your parents to you in terms of religion?*

R: Oh, um, I guess I'm like my mom. Totally don't want to hear about it.

I: *Has that changed in the past couple years?*

R: No.

I: *How would you describe yourself to me in terms of your religion or spirituality?*

R: Non-existent.

I: *Do you identify as a Catholic? What does that mean to you?*

R: Nothing.

I: *Nothing, okay... Would you still say that [you are Catholic] if somebody asked you what religion you were?*

R: Yeah, I would.

I: *So why do you think that is?*

R: Because a lot of people want to hear it. They're like, "Oh, what religion are you?" "Oh, I'm a Catholic." "Oh, that's good..." like it just, it looks good.

I: *Okay. Do you have specific religious beliefs that you still have, even though you're not religious anymore?*

R: Um, let me see. Not really. No.

I: *Do you attend religious services?*

R: No.

I: *Are you involved in any youth group, or college-age group, or anything?*

R: Mm-mm (no).

I: *Do you pray?*

R: No.

I: *And you don't read the Bible?*

R: Actually it's weird, because... I used to work at the Cathedral and um, from there I had collected like a whole bunch of like children's Bibles, and I have a real Bible and like Bible stories, and like I have a little shelf in my room with all of them there and it's like... I mean, I know they're collecting dust, but like lately I've been looking over there like, "Wow, I could just pick that up and start to look at it," you know? But no, no, I won't. Like it's almost like no, I'm not gonna fall into that, so no.

I: *So not gonna fall into that... Is it like a dangerous thing? [giggles]*

R: Yeah. No, it's not like a dangerous thing. I just like, I just kind of feel like if I want to read something I should be reading my studies, you know? Not like reading these fairytales or these little Bible stories.

I: *Is that how you think of the Bible, as kind of a...*

R: Fairytale [giggles]... Yeah, I kind of do.

I: *Do you do have any other kind of religious or spiritual activities or practices?*

R: No.

I: *How big an impact would you say religion or spirituality have had your life?*

R: None.

Adolescent Confirmation and/or Baptism

Perhaps the loss of non-practicing members as they grow older provides a partial explanation for the large 27 percentage point difference in having been baptized between the older and younger Hispanic Protestants in Table 8.6, although the sampling error from such a small sample size also is a likely contributor. Furthermore, it is notable that the 13 percentage point Confirmation gap between Hispanic and white Catholic teens in Table 3.1 (see page 86) was reduced to just 2 percent among 16 and 17 year-old teens in the second wave survey, before going back up to 12 percentage points among the older respondents.

Some of this may be due to the Wave 2 sampling bias that excluded many low-income Hispanics who are less likely to be confirmed due to the instability of their lives, but it may also reflect the fact that the white Catholic teens abandoned their Catholic identity at a higher rate than their Latino/a peers. Since it is probable that a higher proportion of the "weeded out" Catholics were never confirmed, their elimination from the Catholic count raises the proportion of confirmed Catholics among the older white respondents more than it does among the older Hispanics.

Youth group participation

The final point of comparison in Table 8.6 has to do with participation in a youth group, either as a member or as a leader. Just as in the first wave survey (see Table 3.3 on page 90), the Protestant respondents were much more involved than their Catholic peers, both Hispanic and white. However, the pattern of participation from adolescence into young adulthood is distinctly different between the Hispanic and white respondents, whether they be Catholic or Protestant. In another article, I noted that the Wave 1 NSYR survey showed older Hispanic Catholic teens participating in a youth group more often than their younger peers—just the opposite of the pattern established among white Catholic teens.[4]

That pattern continues in the Wave 2 data, not only for the Hispanic Catholics, but now also for the Hispanic Protestants. In fact, youth group participation increased to 28% among the 20 year-old Latino/a Catholics surveyed, while holding steady at 13% for their white Catholic contemporaries (data not shown). There were not enough 20 year-old Hispanic Protestants surveyed to make a meaningful comparison with their white peers, but overall Hispanic Protestant youth group participation increased slightly after age 18 while there was a sharp drop among both the Catholic and Protestant white respondents.

A number of factors likely contribute to this divergent pattern of youth group involvement after high school, as well as to the higher rates of participation among Protestant teens and young adults when compared to their Catholic peers:

- As noted in Chapter 3, Catholic youth ministry as a whole has not been very effective at reaching low-income, immigrant, and second-generation Hispanic adolescents. It is most often prepared by and geared toward middle class people of the mainstream culture, leaving many immigrant and low-income Hispanics feeling excluded.

- Ministry for Catholic students on university and college campuses is also mostly geared toward middle class, mainstream students, but parishes have not been very effective at connecting graduating seniors with campus ministry programs, and few parishes offer any programs specifically for young adults. Those that do generally draw young adults who have completed college, leaving mainstream young adult Catholics who do not go to college with few options for a faith-based peer group.

- The Latin American model of *pastoral juvenil* (Hispanic youth and young adult ministry) serves older adolescents and single young adults together, and this approach has taken root to serve Spanish-speaking *jóvenes* (single youth and young adults) in many Catholic parishes across the country, as witnessed by the 2,000 delegates gathered for the First National Encuentro for Hispanic Youth and Young Adult Ministry in 2006.[5] Participation in such *grupos juveniles* (youth and young adult groups) or in popular apostolic movements such as the Charismatic Renewal could account for the fact that "youth group" participation increased by 5 percentage points after age 18 among Hispanic Catholics, yet the vast majority of the participants said that they were not serving as leaders in their group.

- Starting with much higher rates of participation than their Catholic peers, Protestant youth ministry programs have been much more effective at mentoring their older adolescent members into leadership positions in the group, as seen in the high percentage of white and Hispanic Protestants who served as youth group leaders in Table 8.6. For the young adults who do not leave their congregation after high school, as is common in many Hispanic families, opportunities usually exist to continue serving as leaders in ministry with younger adolescents.

- Without the heavy emphasis on the sacraments that is typical of Catholic parishes, Protestant congregations put much more energy into the ministry of the Word, fellowship, and pastoral care. Thus, they often strive to offer peer ministry groups for every stage in life, providing a clear path of advancement from one stage to the next as young people graduate from high school. Such continuity of opportunities for peer-group fellowship and religious formation is seldom found in Catholic parishes.

Pastoral recommendations

As young people make the transition from adolescence to young adulthood, one of their developmental tasks is to take responsibility for the important relationships in their lives. Their relationship with God is no exception. Some decide that God has no place in their lives, while others embrace God as the center of their life and seek out peer relationships that will help to nourish and sustain

Finally, beloved, whatever is true, whatever is honorable, whatever is just, whatever is pure, whatever is pleasing, whatever is commendable, if there is any excellence and if there is anything worthy of praise, think about these things. Keep on doing the things that you have learned and received and heard and seen in me, and the God of peace will be with you.
– Philippians 4:8-9

that primary relationship. Perhaps the majority of young people in the U.S. today opt for the path of moralistic therapeutic deism—acknowledging the existence of God, but spending very little time or energy thinking about their religious faith or developing their spiritual lives.

The question for parents and youth ministers in Christian faith communities is: what more can we do to nurture and sustain the faith and religious commitment of our young members in the transition from adolescence to young adulthood? Without a doubt, the first step is to build a solid foundation in adolescence on which to build. The rest of this book is filled with practical suggestions to enhance ministry with Latino/a teenagers during their high school years; that information will not be repeated here. Instead, the following five recommendations focus on strategies to carry that foundation forward in the transition to young adulthood.

1. Create diverse pastoral settings for young adult peer ministry

The increase in religious peer group participation after high school among Latino/a Catholics is a strong indication that *pastoral juvenil* and/or the apostolic movements are reaching a larger segment of that group than mainstream Catholic young adult and campus ministries. Nevertheless, with only one in five Hispanic Catholics participating, there is still much room to grow. Protestant congregations seem to be reaching a greater proportion of their young adults, but they are still missing nearly half of their Latino/a members and two-thirds of their white members after high school—and that does not count the large number that relinquish their Christian identity every year.

Christian communities would do well to reflect on the demographics of their area and ask themselves who they are reaching, and who they are not. If they have a ministry for college students, what are they doing for young adults who are not in college? If they have a ministry for Spanish-speaking *jóvenes,* what are they doing for English-speaking Hispanics, and vice-versa? If they have a ministry that mainly serves young adults of the cultural mainstream and/or the economic middle-to-upper class, what are they doing to reach out to people of other cultures or with limited economic resources? If they have a way to engage older teens as peer leaders, what are they doing for their spiritual and religious enrichment after high school graduation? If they have a ministry for young singles, what are they doing to support the faith development of young couples and parents? The answers to these questions will provide direction for new efforts to provide a more comprehensive outreach to young adults in the community, and the young people themselves—with the help of the Holy Spirit—will provide the hands to do the work.

2. Celebrate transitions and make connections

It is already fairly common in many faith communities to celebrate high school graduations, and the celebration of weddings and births is nearly universal—as it should be. Some other important moments that might merit celebration in the community are: college graduation, starting a new job, and moving into, or out of, the area. These are all events that are fairly common in the lives of young adults today, and recognizing their importance with a blessing of some kind would go a long way toward making young people feel accepted and welcome in the community.

Going one step further, youth and young adult ministers could help maintain continuity in the religious participation of older teens and young adults by working with them to find a new faith community when they move out of the area. For high school graduates going to college, this might mean speaking to the campus ministry team at the college they will be attending and making a personal introduction. When new jobs or family commitments call for a move to a new location, taking the time to find out what ministry opportunities are available there and providing personal contacts can facilitate their insertion into the new faith community.

3. Maintain contact and provide a home with a social commitment

When young adults depart their home town for college or work, they often leave family members and friends behind. For this reason, they often come back during the summer, or for occasional visits, especially at Thanksgiving, Christmas, or Easter. Organizing a welcome for young people returning at these times would help them to renew contacts with old friends and maintain their connection to the faith community.

One of the challenges in many low-income Hispanic communities is that when the young people go off to college, pastoral experience suggests that many do not come back except for occasional visits to family members they left behind. This deprives the community of some of its richest human resources and social capital. For inner-city communities, it is even more important to maintain relationships with young people who are becoming professionals and leaders in society. By inviting them to participate in community enrichment projects during their summer breaks, or calling on them to provide professional services at a discount, they become a resource and an inspiration for others in the community whose lives are still bound by limited opportunities and real suffering.

4. Call young adults to mission – and provide formation for ministry

The same principle that applies to the young adult professionals who have moved out of the area can also be relevant for the young adults who stay. As they move into their respective jobs and careers, many feel a loss of community and find it challenging to integrate into the life of the parish or congregation, especially in churches that are very family-oriented. These young adults are a wonderful asset for the community and should be called upon to participate in social enrichment projects and peer evangelization efforts. However, it will be important to mentor and support them in these efforts; providing formation and training opportunities will give them the confidence they need to fulfill their tasks, as well as creating fellowship and a deepening sense of connectedness to others in the community.

5. Provide resources and support for lifelong faith formation

At the heart of young adult ministry is the development of relationships—relationships with peers, across generations, and with the professional ministry staff in the faith community. However, not all young adults have the time or the desire to participate in a peer community on an ongoing basis. For these young people, communication is the vital link to the life of the parish or congregation. Providing information and announcing opportunities of interest to young adults in the weekly bulletin is one way to maintain contact. Another is to provide resources online—perhaps a section of the website that provides answers to common concerns or deals with issues faced by young adults—or by means of an email newsletter. By building on the relationships established while the young people were in youth ministry, the professional ministers in the community can provide suggestions for their spiritual reading, faith formation, or family life as they mature and move into other stages in their lives.

Conclusion

Based on the Wave 2 interviews with young Hispanics, one of the clearest differences between the young people whose religious commitment deepened after high school and those whose participation diminished was whether they had the opportunity to socialize, celebrate, and study their faith in a religious group of their peers. Among the Hispanic young adults interviewed who found such a group, it is notable that all of them intentionally sought it out for themselves. It also is interesting that most of the older Protestants interviewed chose to continue participating in a religious peer group after high school, while none of the Catholics did so. This is an unfortunate consequence of the small number of Hispanic interviews in the second wave, because it would have been very enlightening to learn more about the experiences of the 18% of older Hispanic Catholics surveyed who said that they were involved in a youth and/or young adult group.

In any case, the religious experiences associated with foregoing a faith-based peer group were pretty clear for most respondents: diminished attendance at church services, increased doubts about many teachings of their faith tradition, ambivalence or disinterest in learning about their religion, and a relationship with God that is largely detached from daily life. Of course, everyone has a right to make that choice in life if they so desire, but it is a tragedy for our faith communities when young people fall into this track simply because there was no other pathway open to them when they transitioned from high school into college or the working world.

Not all young Christians have the initiative or motivation to seek out a faith-based peer group after they graduate from high school. By employing some of the suggestions in this chapter, parents and youth ministers could make all the difference in the lives of the adolescents they care about. Pastoral experience suggests that young Hispanics as a whole—both Catholic and Protestant—are very receptive to gathering with their peers in a religious setting that is socially and culturally appropriate for them. The question is: will they be given that opportunity? If we want to endow Hispanic teens with pathways of hope and faith that do not end in adolescence but extend into young adulthood and beyond, then we must do all in our power to provide that opportunity.

Questions for reflection

1. How do the religious commitment and participation of the teens in our community change after they graduate from high school? Or after Baptism / Confirmation?

2. What pastoral settings are currently being provided for young adult peer groups in our community? What others might be needed based on the demographic characteristics of the young people in the area? Who might we invite to help meet those needs?

3. What more could we do to maintain relationships with young people after high school? How might they participate or contribute to the community whenever they come back to visit?

4. Is language an obstacle in our ministry? What are we doing to engage Spanish-speaking young adults in faith formation and community life?

5. How have we used email, the Internet, and other media to communicate with young adults in our community—both the locals and those who regularly come back to visit? What more could we do?

6. How often do we invite young adults to take a leadership role in a ministry or project of our faith community? How do we support them in those roles?

7. As a parent of an older teen or a young adult, how do I help or encourage my son or daughter to stay connected with the church?

Chapter 9:
The Religious Experience of Latino/a Protestant Youth

Edwin I. Hernández, Ph.D.

Dialog 9.1 – 16 year-old Hispanic Baptist female from the West

I: Can you tell me what God is like? Or who God is?

R: He's everything... He's a father... Even though you may not have a dad, He still is a father. He disciplines like a father... He's a provider, He cares.

I: Do you tend to think of God as more loving and forgiving, or demanding and judging?

R: Um... I know He's a balance of both. He, He is a merciful God, but He is also justice.

I: Okay, where do you think you learned this about God?

R: Um, because I grew up in a Christian home and my parents... they taught me this... They live it out every day to me in their lives, and so I see it through them. And then, then church, and Sunday School, and seeing other people there... listening to the pastor's message...

I: Okay. Can you tell me more about your own religious beliefs? I mean, what are some more important things you believe in?

R: Like I believe that Jesus is God's son and that he came and he died for me and for everyone else because we're all sinners. And that he didn't stay dead but he rose again, and he wants us to come live with him. And we just need to admit that we're sinners, and believe that he came and died on the cross and rose again, and just choose to follow him...

I: And who goes to heaven?

R: Those who trust in Jesus as their personal Lord and savior will go to heaven when they die, and those who don't will go to hell.

I: What do you think have been the most important influences on the development of your faith?

R: Um, watching how God has worked in other people's lives... reading his Word, being in it daily... stuff like that.

I: So you read the Bible every day?

R: Mm-hmm [yes].

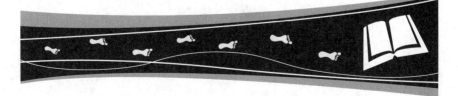

The Religious Experience
of Latino/a Protestant Youth

Perhaps one of the best barometers of a healthy congregation is how well its young people are integrated and committed to its life and faith. Congregations made up of young families and youth are more likely to be considered vibrant and growing.[1] This is certainly no less true in Latino faith communities than it is for congregations of the mainstream culture.

As the first chapter in this book shows, the Latino population will continue to grow exponentially in the coming decades in large part due to ongoing immigration and high birth rates. Furthermore, as a population, compared to both African Americans and Anglos, it is a very young population that will significantly impact our communities and the future character of our country. Is religion an asset for young people? Do religious belief and belonging in communities of faith result in positive life outcomes for them?

Understanding how religion is interwoven in the lives of adolescents to provide inspiration, community, moral conscience, protection, and the drive to pursue life's goals and dreams is foundational to any youth development effort, but particularly for those within religious institutions. The evidence provided by the unprecedented study of American youth and religion in the National Study of Youth and Religion[2] is that religion is a rich and powerful resource for young people predicting extraordinary life outcomes. It shows common themes and behavioral patterns that cut across the religious divide, but it also shows significant differences across ethnic and religious traditions. This has been the topic of this volume— to understand the religious experience of Latino/a young people in the United States.

Our colleagues in the preceding chapters have shared important findings coming out of the NSYR project and suggested valuable pastoral responses. The purpose of this chapter is to reflect and highlight the findings regarding the Latino/a Protestant youth gleaned from the previous chapters. A significant advantage of the NSYR data is that the Latino/a youth surveyed were drawn from the general population, but its major weakness is that its low sample size of Latino/a teens (N=451)—particularly among the non-Catholic Protestant youth (N=94)—prevents us from understanding important differences across the variety of non-Catholic religious communities such as mainline, evangelical, and Pentecostal traditions. Due to the low number of non-Catholic Hispanic Christians in the survey, they were collapsed together and given the generic label of Protestant youth. In order to have a better understanding of the Protestant youth experience it is beneficial to set this analysis within the larger religious landscape of Latinos in this country.

Latino religion in the United States

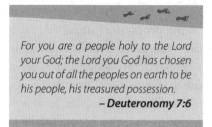

For you are a people holy to the Lord your God; the Lord you God has chosen you out of all the peoples on earth to be his people, his treasured possession.
– Deuteronomy 7:6

Recently, the Pew Forum on Religion and Public Life published the most extensive study ever conducted of Latino religion, entitled *Changing Faiths: Latinos and the Transformation of American Religion*.[3] The final report for the study presents the necessary population-wide trends among Latino/a adults in the United States to set our discussion in context.[4]

General beliefs and faith life of Hispanic Christians

The Pew Forum's portrait of Latino religious life in the U.S. shows a population that is 68% Catholic and 20% Protestant. Among the Protestants, 75% identify themselves as Evangelicals—with nearly half of these also identifying as Pentecostals—and the remaining 25% belong to mainline denominations. Latinos currently comprise about one-third (33%) of the Catholic population, and they make up about 6% of the evangelical Protestants in the United States.

In terms of religious beliefs and practices, Latino/as demonstrate high levels of religiosity. Among Hispanics, both the Catholics (68%) and the Protestants (80%) say that religion is very important to them. In terms of church attendance, 70% of the Evangelicals, 36% of the mainline Protestants, and 44% of the Catholics say they go at least once a week. Overall, 38% of Latino/a adults read their Bible at least weekly—though only 27% of the Catholics do so compared to 78% of the Evangelicals and 38% of the mainline Protestants.

Another key religious indicator is the extent to which people share their faith with others at least monthly; Evangelicals (79%) were more likely to do so than mainline Protestants (53%) and Catholics (32%). Participation at least monthly in prayer groups is also more likely to happen among Evangelicals (75%) than among mainline Protestants (47%) and Catholics (31%).

Most Hispanics believe that God is actively involved in the world today. For example, 75% of all Latino/as believe that "miracles still occur today as in ancient times." Half of all Latino/as (52%) believe that "Jesus will return to earth in my lifetime"—a belief that is most closely connected with Protestants, but interestingly Hispanic Catholics are more likely to hold this view (51%) than their mainline Protestant peers (36%).

When examining the degree to which churches are involved in providing social services, the Latino/a Evangelicals are significantly more likely to be involved in providing food or clothing, finding a job, financial assistance, housing, and child care than their Catholic counterparts. Also, when examining volunteering trends among Hispanics, 56% of Evangelicals, 34% of mainline Protestants, and 26% of Catholics say that in the past year they have volunteered for a church or religious group. Latino/as of all religious traditions were equally likely to volunteer for school or tutoring programs, while 36% of Evangelicals volunteered for neighborhood, business or youth group in contrast to 27% of mainline Protestants and 24% of Catholics.

The renewalist movement in Latino Christianity

One of the major findings of the Pew Forum study is the degree to which the renewalist movement has impacted Hispanic Christianity. *Renewalist* is an umbrella term to classify respondents who identified themselves as Pentecostal or charismatic. The report defined renewalist Christians as people who believe in "God's ongoing, day-to-day intervention in human affairs through the person of the Holy Spirit. Renewalists believe that the power of the Holy Spirit is manifested through such supernatural phenomena as speaking in tongues, miraculous healings and prophetic utterances and revelations." A majority of Latino/a Catholics (54%) are renewalists, meaning that they identified themselves as being either charismatic or Pentecostal.[5] Among Hispanic Protestants a total of 57% can be identified as renewalist, with 31% identifying as Pentecostals and 26% as charismatics.

There are important differences between the renewalist and non-renewalist Hispanic Catholics. The renewalists are more likely than non-charismatic Catholics to exhibit higher levels of religious commitment and to be involved in leadership positions in the parish. For example, the survey asked Catholics whether or not they were involved in the following five activities in their parish—lector (12%), Eucharistic minister (6%), choir member (4%), parish council member (8%) or leader of a small group or ministry (6%). A total of 22% of Latino/a Catholics were involved in at least one of the five roles. However, charismatic Latino/a Catholics are nearly twice as likely as their non-charismatic peers (28% vs. 15%) to participate in those roles.

Religious switching

One of the most important religious trends among Latino/a adults is that of conversion or religious switching. Though Latino/a Christians have historically found their home in the Catholic Church, for some their geographic relocation is paralleled by an equivalent denominational move. Although this trend toward religious conversion, or "switching" as sociologists call it, has received some attention over the past twenty years,[6] not until the current Pew Forum study has there been an exploration of the extent and causes of Latino/a conversion to Protestantism.

A significant majority of Latino/as (82%) has never experienced conversion or switching from one religious affiliation to another. However, almost one-in-five (18%) has changed and 70% of those are former Catholics. Among Hispanic Evangelicals, 43% were Catholics at one time in their lives, as were 26% of the mainline Protestants and 41% of the other Christians. The most common reason given for converting to evangelicalism was the "desire for a more direct, personal experience of God" (90%) followed by "the influence of a certain pastor" (42%). Furthermore, 61% of the former Catholics say that they view the Mass as unexciting and 36% said that they left because of this.

In sum, at the national level Latino/a adults living in the U.S. are a very religious people engaged with their religious communities. Important differences were found between the Catholic and Protestant Latinos, with the latter attending church, prayer groups, and sharing their faith more often. Among Hispanic Protestants, the Evangelicals are more engaged and hold to their beliefs in a more intense way. Finally, Hispanic Catholics and Protestants share very similar understandings with regard to the role of miracles in modern times and the belief that Christ will return again soon. Yet, important differences were found on volunteering behavior and provision of basic social services, with the Evangelicals indicating higher levels than the mainline Protestants and Catholics.

Finally, it appears that the renewalist form of religious belief and expression is prevalent among half or more of both Catholic and Protestant Latinos. Among Protestants, the differences exhibited between evangelical and mainline Protestants suggest that there are important differences within the umbrella category of Protestantism that require examining separately the subgroups. Unfortunately, due to the small size of the Latino Protestant sample in the NYSR surveys, we are unable to examine denominational or other subgroup differences. Despite this limitation, the trends summarized below provide an informative yet broad portrait of Latino/a Protestant teens.

Summary of key findings

The findings and narratives presented in the previous chapters provide an important understanding of how religion operates in the lives of

> As God's chosen ones, holy and beloved, clothe yourselves with compassion, kindness, humility, meekness, and patience.
>
> *– Colossians 3:12*

Latino/a young people. This section will summarize and highlight some of the most salient findings regarding Hispanic Protestant adolescents. First, we will explore the beliefs and participation levels of the Protestant youth, followed by family influences and educational behavior. Finally, we look at the moral behaviors of young Latino/a Protestants.

Religious beliefs and participation

As shown in Chapter 2, Latino/a youth—like their parents across denominations—have a high level of belief in God. However, interesting differences emerged in certain areas of belief. For example, Hispanic Protestant teens were more likely than their Catholic counterparts to express belief in a judgment day (92% vs. 70%), belief in miracles (82% vs. 60%), and in evil spirits (66% vs. 28%). In addition, Latino/a Protestants hold a more exclusive view of religious faith, with the majority (52%) saying that there is only one true religion, while only 19% of Hispanic Catholic teens believe that only one religion is true.

A critical element among Protestant youth is the degree to which their religious faith engulfs the totality of their lives. A large majority of them (73%) says that it is very important that religious faith shape their daily life, in contrast to 46% of their Catholic peers. In fact, 81% of the Latino/a Protestant youth say that they have "made a commitment to live life for God" versus 38% of the Catholic youth. This commitment translates into higher levels of religious practices such as church attendance, reading the Bible, reading religious books, attending music concerts, listening to religious music, praying, experiencing answer to prayer, and witnessing or experiencing miracles.

The Pew Forum survey identified a growing presence of the renewalist movement among Latino/a Protestants and Catholics. However, due to the small sample of Hispanic Protestant teens in the NYSR, we are unable to draw comparisons between Latino Protestant groups such as the mainline, evangelical, and Pentecostal traditions. However, based on what we know about "renewalists" they are represented among both Protestants and Catholics, and they are likely to live their faith more intensely than other Christians in their respective denominations.

There are a number of indicators that suggest the prevalence of "renewalist" characteristics among the Latino/a Protestant young people as described in Chapter 2: for example, their belief in a judgment day (92%), in divine miracles (82%), and in evil spirits (66%). Other important indicators of a "renewalist" experience of religion have to do with religious practices such as Bible reading, witnessing/evangelism, and listening to Christian music. For many Protestant youth, to be active in their faith means to engage in activities to bring others "to Christ," so it is not surprising that just over half (56%) of the Latino/a Protestant youth had shared faith with someone not of their faith. Interestingly, 7 out of 10 of them (71%) "listen to religious music or radio programs," suggesting how their faith influences and potentially transforms even their choice of music. Less than half of the Hispanic Protestant teens (48%) read religious books other than the Bible, and 50% read the Scriptures on their own once a week or more. Given that Bible reading is such a core value among Protestants, the fact that 50% of the youth are not reading the Bible frequently suggests an area for potential growth.

Latino/a Protestant youth also have a healthy desire to learn more about their faith, with 55% saying that they are "very interested" and 32% "somewhat interested." This apparent desire to deepen their faith and commitment presents a crucial opportunity for church leaders to respond. In this regard, participation in the life of congregations and youth groups are important activities that help to strengthen and deepen a young person's faith. Evidence related to participation from Chapter 3 shows that the Hispanic Protestant teens are considerably more involved in the life of their congregations than their Catholic counterparts. For example, 53% of Hispanic Protestant youth attend church one or more times a week, in contrast to 37% of Latino/a Catholic teens. And if it were left up to them to attend without their parents, the number of Latino/a Protestant youth attending weekly would actually increase (64%), while the level of attendance among their Catholic peers would remain roughly unchanged (36%). Furthermore, opportunities for Hispanic young people to be involved in "services, such as reading or praying aloud" are more likely to be experienced by Protestant than Catholic youth (76% vs. 48%).

Being engaged in a community of faith has far-reaching consequences. Regular participation in church life helps to strengthen social networks creates opportunities for learning the faith, and increases youth involvement in groups and in leadership opportunities. What does the evidence from the NYSR suggest? The responses from Hispanic teens reported in Chapter 3 provide a glimpse into what might be happening in the lives of their congregations. The high levels of church attendance among the young Protestants could be seen as a reflection of the fact that almost 6 out of every 10 (59%) said that they had "experienced very moving and powerful worship," while only about 3 out of 10 Latino/a Catholics had experienced the same. Clearly, worship experiences within Protestant churches seem to attract and connect their adolescent members. In short, the Latino/a Protestant teenagers are by far more likely to live their faith in intense and devout ways than their Catholic counterparts.

Furthermore, the Hispanic Protestant youth who regularly attend their church tend to experience their congregations in quite positive ways. They are more likely than their Catholic peers to say that their church makes them think about important things (71% vs. 52%), that their church is a warm and welcoming place (74% vs 66%), and that there is an adult in the congregation (not family) with whom they enjoy talking and who give them a lot of encouragement (78% vs. 59%). Their parents also share a positive view of their congregations, with 89% saying that ministry to teens is a very important priority in their congregations, compared to 62% of the attending Hispanic Catholic parents,

Close-knit relationship building opportunities, as in small groups, are powerful ways to enhance commitment to the faith, and they seem to be significantly more available among Latino/a Protestant teens. For example, the Protestant teens are twice as likely (44%) as the Catholic teens (20%) to say that they are currently involved in a youth group, and 40% have been involved in a youth group for two or more years, compared to only13% of the Latino Catholic cohort. About two-thirds (67%) attend Sunday school once a month or more, with 40% attending every week. Most Sunday school programming utilizes a curriculum that is age-specific, relevant, and engages adolescents in Bible study. Usually, Sunday school programs are directed by trusted and youth-friendly adults, thereby increasing the bonding between the teens and significant adults in their community, and providing the youth with adult mentors.

Table 3.5 on page 94 shows that Hispanic Protestant teens also report higher levels of participation than their Catholic peers in several other activities that can play a significant role in strengthening within-group social bonds as well as their faith commitment. In fact, a majority of the Latino/a Protestants (56%) had participated in one or more religious retreats, conferences, rallies, or congresses; in a religious summer camp (52%); and a sizable minority (40%) had been involved in religious mission teams or service projects.

In summary, the religious portrait of Latino/a Protestant youth coming from the NSYR findings shows a group of young people with high levels of commitment to God that encompasses all aspects of their lives. Because most of them believe that their faith is the only true one, and it appears to work for them—that is, they have experienced answers to their prayers and have witnessed divine miracles—they are excited and motivated to share it with others and to invite others to join their congregations.

Furthermore, the data show that the Latino Protestant congregations seem to make youth ministry a high priority, and significant majorities of their adolescent members perceive them as inviting and accepting. Large numbers of these teens have been involved in their youth group for two years or more, and of those who participate, nearly all (93%) say they like their youth group. In addition, they are involved in a variety of youth ministry activities such as Sunday school, retreats, summer camps, and mission projects that could potentially have powerful positive effects on their religious life.

Family influences and educational behavior

The evidence on the state of the family among Latino/a youth reported in Chapter 4 seems to indicate that they are strong and relatively healthy. On most family measures, Latino/a teens—both Protestant and Catholic—describe stable families and positive relationships with their parents, especially with their mothers. Most of the Protestants report feeling "very close" to their mothers (68%) and fathers (42%). They go on to say that their mothers (72%) and fathers (48%) praise and encourage them "fairly or very often." There is also a general sense that their parents understand them "some or a lot" (82%), and a vast majority (87%) says that their parents love and accept them "a lot." An area that appears challenging is how often these young people say that they share "personal subjects" with their parents. A total of 44% acknowledged that they talk with their mothers about personal subjects at least "fairly often," but only 16% did so with their fathers. In other words, the majority of Latino/a Protestant youth do not share personal matters with their parents, but among those who do, they are likely to share it only with their mothers.

When comparing the Latino/a Catholic and Protestant teens with respect to the quality of their family relationships, the major findings coming from the NSYR data are: 1) that there are no major differences between them with respect to the quality of their relationships with their parents; and 2) the degree to which fathers are perceived as less engaged than mothers on all of the family measures suggests that there is significant social distance between fathers and their adolescent children. Although the comparable data for white and African-American teens are not reported in Chapter 4, the NSYR data show that the pattern is equally prevalent among them, indicating that paternal disengagement is a larger social phenomenon that goes well beyond the boundaries of Hispanic families.

Findings from the NYSR have clearly shown that parents play a significant role in the religious lives of young people.[7] A critical element in this process is how parents live out their religious commitment in life. Table 4.6 on page 138 shows that the Latino Protestant families are significantly more likely (about 30% more) than their Catholic counterparts to do each of the following religious practices: give thanks before or after mealtime (69% vs. 40%); pray as a family other than at meal times (70% vs. 42%);

and talk about God, prayer, or the Scriptures at least weekly (76% vs. 43%). With such high levels of parental religious involvement and modeling, it is very likely that their children will follow in their footsteps.

No other issue facing Latino/a adolescents is as important for their future as their educational life. Recent findings suggest that religion plays a significant role in helping Hispanic youth stay on track educationally, improving their performance and strengthening parental responsibility for the educational life of their children.[8] As the evidence presented in Chapter 5 on educational issues shows, Latino/a teens still lag significantly behind their white counterparts in terms of educational aspirations and performance.

More specifically, is there evidence to show that religious commitment positively impacts educational outcomes? Table 5.2 on page 166 demonstrates that Hispanic youth that are religiously committed are more likely than their religiously disengaged peers to say that doing well in school is "extremely important" (66% vs. 44%). Also, Table 5.3 on page 169 shows that the Latino/a youth who have a high level of religious commitment tend to perform better in school than those with low religious commitment. In fact, more than half of the religiously "committed" and "engaged" Hispanic youth indicate that they get As and Bs or better in school, compared to about 42% of the youth with lower religious commitment. This suggests that their higher grades may be at least partly attributed to a higher degree of internal motivation to do well at school that is associated with religious participation and commitment.

On the other hand, the religiously committed Latino/a were actually slightly *less* likely to aspire to a bachelor's degree or higher than their peers with lower religious commitment. Furthermore, when asked how far they would "ideally" and "realistically" expect to go in school, the religiously disengaged Hispanics were actually twice as likely as the committed to say they hope or expect to get a master's degree or higher. Another critical finding is the disconnect between the high educational aspirations of young Latino/as as indicated in the survey responses and the fact that in their interviews, most of the Latino/as could not clearly articulate a connection between educational goals and future career plans. Thus, the connection between religious commitment and educational and career goals is at best somewhat ambiguous in the survey responses.

Nevertheles, the religiously committed Hispanics were more likely than their disengaged peers to see themselves as being a part of the popular group at school "a lot" (46% vs. 27%). Perhaps most importantly, the religiously committed were also significantly more likely than the disengaged to stay out of trouble and "stay on track" educationally. Cutting classes and being suspended are key factors that increase educational failure. The majority (56%) of the religiously committed Latino/as had never cut classes in the last year, compared to only about one-fourth (27%) of their disengaged counterparts. Similarly, 80% of the religiously committed had never been suspended in the last two years in comparison to only 57% of the disengaged.

Generational differences have always been a factor influencing educational outcomes. Third-generation Hispanic youth are significantly less likely to perform well in school than first- and second-generation youth. When asked what kind of grades they get, 55% of first-generation Latino/as indicated that they get "As and Bs or better," in contrast to 50% of second-generation, and 39% of third-generation adolescents. Since U.S.-born (second generation or higher) Hispanics are more prevalent among Protestant adolescents than among Catholics (see Chart 1.7 on page 21), it is noteworthy that the Latino/a Protestant teens were nevertheless able to match the grades of their Catholic peers.

Moral behavior

How are Latino/a youth faring in the area of moral behavior? Chapter 6 contains many interesting findings, the most important of which is the ambivalence between upholding moral standards and individual volition. Hispanic Protestant teens, when compared to their Catholic counterparts, are more likely to say that "people have lost a sense of right and wrong" (47% vs. 38%), and they are less likely to say that "morals are relative, there are no definite rights or wrongs" (40% vs. 52%). Yet the Latino/a Protestants are significantly less likely than the Catholics to say that there should be a "fix standard" for what is right and wrong (45% vs. 56%).

So while on the one had the Hispanic Protestants affirm that morals are not relative—that there are right and wrongs—they are ambivalent about whether there is a fixed standard to distinguish between the two. On the other hand, they are six times more likely than Catholics (31% vs. 5%) to say that they would "do what God or the Scriptures tell them is right" when they are unsure of what is right or wrong. Following God or the Scriptures is indeed a "fixed standard"—an apparent contradiction that is worth investigating in greater detail.

A closer look at the way Catholic and Protestant Latino/as make difficult moral decisions reveals that about one-third (32%) of the Protestant youth say that "they would follow the advice of a parent, teacher, or other adult," in contrast to almost half of the Catholics (49%). Protestant youth seem to exhibit a greater degree of individualism—a do-it-yourself style of moral decision-making. Even though the Hispanic Protestants are significantly more likely than their young Catholic peers to say that they would try to do what God and the Scriptures say is right, less than one-third of them overall affirm this position. As noted earlier, 50% of the Hispanic Protestant youth read the Bible once a week or more, yet only one out of every three is willing to consult God or the Scriptures to determine what is right when faced with uncertainty.

Perhaps this is a reflection of the fact that even though they read the Scriptures regularly, they are still young, and their moral character is still in the process of developing. When they make mistakes, the Latino/a Protestant teens say that religion is a significant resource to help relieve their guilty feelings, as shown in Table 6.2 on page 201. In fact, they are twice as likely as the Catholics (45% vs. 20%) to say that religion helped to relieve their guilty feelings "a lot."

Additionally, the guilty feelings just discussed may have to do with the young people engaging in at-risk behaviors such as drinking alcohol, use of illegal drugs, and premarital sexual behavior. As shown in Table 6.3 on page 203, about one-third (29%) of Latino/a Protestant youth drink alcohol a few times a year or more. Another 15% had been drunk once or more in the prior year, and 18% had used marijuana once or more in the same time frame. The rates for Hispanic Catholics were slightly higher on all three variables, but the Latino/a youth that had no religion were much more likely to use alcohol and illegal drugs than either their Catholic or Protestant peers.

Statistically, religion seems to fulfill a protective function among both Protestant and Catholic Latino/as, helping to keep the young people away from using substances harmful to them. Even so, since most Protestant denominations—particularly Evangelicals and Pentecostals—consider the consumption of tobacco, alcohol, and illegal drugs to be sinful practices, the use recorded here should be cause for concern. What additional factors contribute to increased use?

Parents can make a difference—not just in modeling good Christian behavior, but also keeping track of where their kids are. As Table 6.4 on page 204 shows, teens whose parents know what they are doing away from home are significantly less likely to engage in at-risk behaviors. Parental oversight even into the teen years can make a significant impact in the behavior of young people. Another factor that appears to make a difference with respect to substance abuse is the generation of the young people— whether they belong to the first, second, or third generation since their family's arrival in the United States. The more acculturated a young person is, the more dangerous their behavior is likely to be. For example, third-generation Hispanic youth are more likely to drink alcohol, get drunk, and use marijuana than their immigrant (first-generation) peers.

What is it about generational differences that significantly increases the chances that young people will engage in such behavior? To answer this question would go beyond the scope of this chapter. However, the findings here are consistent with other findings from a study within an evangelical denomination—the Seventh-day Adventist Church—that found the young Latino/as who experienced greater levels of acculturation were significantly more likely to participate in at-risk behaviors.[9] The implication is that maintaining a healthy appreciation of one's Latino cultural identity and language is an important resource related to a number of positive life outcomes. Thus, biculturalism should be promoted and made part of the church's ministry with adolescents and their families.

Another area of behavior with significant consequences for the moral and practical life of young people is sexuality. Are there any discernable and distinct issues facing Latino/a Protestant adolescents in the area of sexuality? Table 6.5 on page 206 highlights some interesting trends. A significant majority of them (73%) affirm that people should wait until marriage to have sex. However, 40% of them state that they "would consider living with a romantic partner before marriage." The practice of cohabitation before marriage is so common that many people do not have any moral conflicts with it. It dominates the public imagination of young people irrespective of their commitments to the sanctity and value of marriage. In fact, about a third of the Hispanic Protestant teens (32%) who said that people should wait until marriage to have sex, and four out of ten of their like-minded Catholic peers (40%), admitted that they would consider living with a romantic partner before marriage (data not in table).

Are sexual attitudes and behaviors interrelated? Several important findings related to the sexual activity of Hispanic teens are discussed in-depth in Chapter 6. Clearly, Latino/a youth are sexually active, and hardly any significant differences can be found between the Catholics and the Protestants. The argument and evidence presented shows that sexual activity among young people increases progressively from one stage to the next—from dating, to exposure to x-rated material, to physical intimacy, to oral sex, to sexual intercourse—not necessarily in this order of actual occurrence.

Notable findings related to the sexual activity of Latino/a Protestant youth are as follows: a third (31%) has watched x-rated movies in the last year; four out of ten (39%) have participated in physical intimacy "more than holding hands or light kissing;" 16% had oral sex; and 17% had sexual intercourse. Do the findings provide any direction about things that adolescents, their parents, or congregations can do to help prevent sexual activity before marriage? The answer is yes.

Table 6.7 on page 212 identifies some areas that are potentially controllable by individuals or family members. By controllable we mean that they have to do with attitudes, convictions, or beliefs, in contrast to characteristics that cannot be changed such as age, generation, or gender. For example, family members and congregations can help young people develop a healthy sexual ethic that includes abstaining from watching x-rated movies. Viewing x-rated material dramatically increases the likelihood of engaging in oral sex, sexual intercourse, and ultimately becoming or getting someone pregnant. Furthermore, guiding young people to develop an ethic of reserving sexual activity for marriage will help prevent early sexual activity. Additionally, young people who seek answers to what is right or wrong from God or the Scriptures are significantly less likely to engage in oral sex and sexual intercourse. Finally, when parents actively seek to know what their teenager is doing away from home, they significantly reduce the chances that their teenaged child will become sexually active in adolescence.

In summary, Protestant teens—like Catholics—who are religiously engaged are significantly less likely to participate in a broad range of at-risk behaviors such as smoking, drinking alcohol, drug abuse, and various forms of physical intimacy or sexual activity. Parents can have a positive impact on their children's moral development by modeling Christian behavior, being available to the teens, and keeping track of their whereabouts. The cultural pressures to explore and engage in sexual activity before adulthood and marriage are extraordinary. Contemporary youth culture celebrates sexual freedom, and cohabitation before marriage is seen as normal; in fact, it is often seen as an important trial period before "taking the plunge." Despite the pressures, teens who seek guidance from God and the Scriptures for what is right or wrong and who are connected to a network of adults who care about their wellbeing are less likely to make poor choices in adolescence that will negatively impact the rest of their lives.

The distinctiveness of the Latino Protestant experience

What factors help to explain the findings related to Latino/a Protestant youth that we have highlighted in this chapter? More particularly, what is it about the evangelical and Pentecostal forms of Christianity that has such a significant effect on their religious commitment as compared to their Catholic peers? Also, how

Everyone who believes that Jesus is the Christ has been born of God, and everyone who loves the parent loves the child. By this we know that we love the children of God, when we love God and obey his commandments. And his commandments are not burdensome, for whatever is born of God conquers the world. And this is the victory that conquers the world: our faith.
– Acts 2:41-42

does their religious commitment relate to the nationwide patterns of rapid church growth and high conversion rates among Latinos? The following six factors play a significant role in differentiating the Latino Protestant experience from the reality of most Catholic parishes, and they undoubtedly contribute to the continuing growth of Latino congregations, especially in evangelical and Pentecostal churches.

1. Congregational size

A key factor that differentiates Latino Protestant congregations from Catholic parishes is the size of their respective congregations. Catholic parishes are mostly large congregations that are established by the bishop to serve Catholics in a particular geographical area within the diocese. In contrast, Latino Protestant congregations are relatively small and located close to where Latinos live in order to serve their needs and attract them to the community of faith. Since most of the members of the congregation actually live close to one another, transportation is not an obstacle to building relationships and participating in church activities more than once a week.

Protestant growth strategies are entrepreneurial in nature, driven by a common core identity and a commitment to evangelization. Thus, there are many Protestant congregations that are truly *Latino* congregations, built from the ground up *by* Latinos, *for* Latinos. Building relationships among the diverse groups of adolescents in a geographically large, multicultural community can be fraught with challenges as shown in Chapters 3 and 4, but most Protestant Latino congregations do not have to deal with these challenges because of their size and homogeneity.

The size of Protestant churches also enables members to develop close-knit relationships across generations—providing the youth with opportunities to meet adults and develop mentoring relationships with them. Furthermore, smaller congregations create opportunities for young people to get involved in leadership roles and to participate as members of small groups. The small size also lends itself to creating relationships of mutual accountability and support, even among the adolescents. Such relationships help to strengthen a young person's commitment both to their faith and to the community in which it is expressed.

2. Evangelization and community outreach

Evangelism is the growth strategy used among Protestant denominations, particularly in evangelical and Pentecostal churches. Evangelization—actions taken by individuals or congregations to actively share the gospel and invite people to accept Christ and become members of the church—defines their core identity. In fact, pastors are judged to be successful or not based on whether their church experiences growth or produces good evangelists. Lay people are promoted in leadership within the group as a result of their success in bringing people to Christ. All members at all ages are encouraged and expected to share their faith—and the act of sharing and participating in evangelistic activities is seen as fundamental to Christian growth and discipleship.

When new members are brought into the church, their gifts and talents are put to use almost immediately. This is seen as a way to strengthen their faith and deepen their commitment. So whether it is cooking, singing, cleaning, or simply being part of the visitation team for "shut-ins"—elderly people who can't come to church—recent or older members are given some sort of active role or responsibility in the church. Likewise, giving adolescents an active role is seen as a retention and faith-strengthening strategy.

At the core, evangelization is understood as the best mechanism to effect broader social change, which always begins with a transformed heart. From this perspective, a life committed to Jesus is the first and primary step required to change society. Clearly, the cultural orientation in this approach to evangelization is highly individualistic—to claim a particular denominational label is not sufficient if it is not followed by observable actions, attitudes, and transformed relationships. In effect, behavioral change becomes the test of faithfulness. Thus, all that is required to change society is a converted individual; to change the individual is to begin a ripple effect that transforms the family, extended family, neighborhood, and society.

Sharing the Gospel by inviting people to come to church, conducting Bible studies in homes, providing a youth outreach ministry, and holding public evangelistic meetings are all part of the regular activities that are expected from a vibrant church. A key strategy for evangelization in Protestant churches is the use of small groups. Despite the fact that congregations are not usually very large in the first place, small group ministries are used as a growth strategy. Small groups function in the homes of members, and the objective is to invite friends and relatives that are not part of the church.

An added benefit of small churches or small group experiences is that they present opportunities to know the material and psychosocial needs of people and their families. Providing social services to individuals and their families or to the broader neighborhood is seen fundamentally as an extension of their evangelizing efforts. They reach out to touch individual lives because receiving assistance makes people more receptive to the Gospel message, to accepting Christ, and ultimately to becoming members of the church. For many immigrant families, the need for housing, food, clothing, money to pay a first month's rent, or assistance finding a job can provide an opening to share a treasure of more lasting value.

3. Religious education

Religious education and faith formation are taken seriously in most Protestant churches. Sunday school is a regular part of the weekly worship experience, and attendance is expected of all members. The textbook for Sunday school is the Bible, so both adult members and their children are encouraged to bring Bibles to church. Held every week before or after the main worship service, Sunday school is a time when the family is divided into classes by age groups—each with a Bible teacher, an age-appropriate curriculum, learning activities, and music.

Bible reading, study, and prayer are Christian habits strongly encouraged for all members to practice daily. Parents of young children are especially encouraged to do "family devotions"—a set time the family dedicates at home to study the Bible, pray, and share their faith together. Furthermore, realizing that they need to serve a growing number of second- and third-generation youth and young adults, many congregations are creating worship experiences in English to retain and attract them.

4. Entrepreneurial spirit

Protestant churches are driven by an entrepreneurial spirit, and their leadership usually arises from the Latino community itself. Most often, the people called to exercise pastoral leadership are energetic, charismatic, God-fearing, and devout individuals who experience a "call" to the ministry and respond by becoming pastors. Some pastors are recognized by their judicatories if they belong to an organized *concilio* or denomination. Others simply declare their newfound position and authority as pastors based solely on their individual "call" from God, authenticated by church members who recognize the calling as being legitimate due to the gifts of preaching, teaching, and counseling they exhibit. In most circumstances, these clergy do not have much theological education, if any at all.

The majority of Protestant clergy in Latino congregations are themselves Latino. The fact that they share the culture of the ethnic group most likely to be represented in their congregation or community facilitates relationship building. Most are also bi-vocational—meaning that in addition to pastoring, they hold another job to sustain their families financially. Governance in such congregations is usually decentralized—all decisions are made at the local congregational level. For example, if Latinos are moving to a new neighborhood due to gentrification, the congregation may decide to follow the population by moving the church. The decision to sell or buy a building to better meet the needs of the congregation is fairly simple, without requiring judicatory red tape or embroilment in denominational politics.

5. A clear message of salvation

The core message of salvation among Protestants is salvation through faith alone, which involves developing a personal relationship with Jesus Christ. In Latino congregations, this message is typically set within an apocalyptic time orientation which proclaims the belief in the imminent second coming of Christ. Emphasizing the second coming of Christ brings a sense of urgency to the preaching efforts of Protestant churches and their members. Characteristically, the message is a Bible-centered message; as such, it emphasizes reading the Bible and commitment to Jesus Christ as savior and Lord.

For Latino/a Protestants, the proclamation of salvation in Christ is set in the context of a faith orientation that is primarily charismatic or Pentecostal, emphasizing the miraculous power of God to effect a total transformation in individual lives. The Gospel is understood as providing a better way of life that calls for improved family relations, appropriate use of finances (not gambling), marriage, improved parenting practices, and total abstinence from tobacco, alcohol, and drugs. In fact, the use of these substances is understood to be sinful—behaviors that are fundamentally immoral in nature.

Thus, the scope of impact of Christian discipleship is the totality of life, impacting every waking hour of the day, every day of the week, and every dimension of human life—both personal and public. As such, the Christian way of life is seen as a "strict" code of behavior that is in high counter-cultural tension with the larger culture and society in which people live. All church members are expected to adhere to specific behavioral expectations and assent to certain biblical truths. This includes financially supporting the congregation through tithe and offerings to maintain and expand the ministries and mission of the church. The expectation also involves attending worship services not just once, but several times a week, spending anywhere between 5 and 8 hours a week in church-related activities.

In this context, it is no wonder that thick and deep relationships between members are developed, such that a young person's best friends frequently come from the congregation. Considering the small size of the congregation, the high behavioral expectations, the close family and friendship ties, and the time spent in worship, there is very little room for lax behavior, lukewarm commitment, or sporadic attendance.

In short, in the Latino evangelical Protestant context, there is no "free riding"—receiving benefits from the worshiping community without making significant time, financial, behavioral, and faith commitments. Since membership in the community is defined by total assent to strict norms of behavior and belief, it is easy to know who is falling short and who needs to be prayed for or otherwise supported. People who deviate are promptly counseled, cautioned, reprimanded, or provided a grace period. However, if the behavior persists, they risk church discipline which could result in expulsion from the community.

6. Vibrant and transforming worship

The worship experience in most Protestant congregations is best characterized as being expressive, emotive, and contemporary, with lively music usually led by a praise team of young people singing non-traditional hymns or *coritos* accompanied by a band using instruments such as an electric guitar or base, drums including congas, and rhythmic instruments. In short, the worship experiences are lively, interesting, and inspirational, especially to young people. Furthermore, the preaching is Bible-centered, teaching the use of the Bible as the rule for conduct and the authority on moral behavior. Adolescents are actively involved in worship as leaders, singers, or musicians—and because the worship is highly contemporary, it attracts them in greater numbers. The rituals and practices conducted in worship services function as a mechanism to strengthen commitment to the faith by showing that "faith works."

During most Latino Protestant worship services, it is very common to set aside time for *testimonios*—moments of sharing how God is working in the lives of individual members. To hear a *testimonio* is to listen to a first-hand witness to the powerful transformative power of Christianity in people's lives. During a *testimonio,* the congregation might hear:

- a man say how his conversion to Christ has liberated him from alcoholism and turned him into a loving father and husband
- a mother testify how her teenage son has returned home from his rebellious ways
- an unemployed person share how, after much prayer and supplication, God has opened doors to a job
- an elderly person talk about how God has healed her pain
- a lay chaplain describe how young men in jail are submitting their lives to Christ and turning into evangelists in prison
- a drug addict proclaim that he was transformed and cleaned through the power of the Holy Spirit.

In short, from the most mundane to the most extraordinary, *testimonios* provide the believer with irrefutable evidence that "Christianity works."[10] Because *testimonios* are shared in front of the congregation, they have a potentially powerful effect on the rest of the members: to the recent convert hearing such stories, they may affirm their decision to follow Christ;

to the young person struggling with personal issues, they may encourage and strengthen their resolve to persevere; and for the couple experiencing marital problems, listening to stories of reconciliation and forgiveness could save their marriage. Stories of deliverance, personal transformation, healing, miracles, and divine interventions in daily life have the potential to affirm people's faith, strengthen their social bonds and loyalty to the congregation, and legitimize—literally make true—the transformative claims of the gospel.

Areas for further research

Without a doubt, we are indebted to Dr. Christian Smith and his collaborators for the landmark work they are doing in compiling data for the National Study of Youth and Religion, for presenting the initial findings so compellingly in *Soul Searching*, and for his support and interest in advancing our understanding of Latino/a youth by giving us full access to study the same data. As with any good research, what is learned

> *The gifts he gave them were that some would be apostles, some prophets, some evangelists, some pastors and teachers, to equip the saints for the work of ministry, for building up the body of Christ, until all of us come to the unity of the faith and of the knowledge of the Son of God, to maturity, to the measure of the full stature of Christ.*
> *– Ephesians 4:11-13*

inevitably opens new areas for research as we probe ever deeper to understand the reality of our subject. With respect to Hispanic Protestant teens, four such areas stand out:

1. **Increase the Latino Protestant sample.** Future research efforts among Latino/a adolescents should seek to include a sufficiently large sample to adequately represent both Catholic and non-Catholic youth. This will probably require over-sampling for Latino/a non-Catholics. As noted earlier, the Pew Forum study found significant differences between the mainline, evangelical, and Pentecostal experiences of Christianity among Latino/as. With the NSYR data, there was no option but to collapse the various traditions into the general category we labeled Protestant. But the subgroup differences within the Protestant category can be very dramatic, so future research should ensure adequate representation. Future research should also address the following: a) provide comparability across religious groups; b) replicate a good number of the NYSR questions; and c) address issues particular to the Latino experience such as acculturation, language, socioeconomic status, and social environment.

2. **Explore the relationship between acculturation and religion.** A critical topic to research in more depth is that of acculturation. The process of adaptation and movement between two cultures has been shown to have a significant impact on the religious, educational, and other life outcomes of youth.[11] The previous chapters in this book also found significant differences on a number of issues between first-, second-, and third-generation Latino/a adolescents. Examining the process of acculturation in more depth is critical to understanding the role that religion will play in the lives of subsequent generations of Hispanics.

3. **Conduct congregational-level research.** Few studies have been conducted that examine Latino/a youth within the context of congregations. Understanding internal church dynamics can shed significant light on the culture of the church and the elements that are most successful at supporting positive outcomes among the young. There are a number of context variables and questions that should be explored in a congregational study. For example: What is the quality of the congregation's youth programming? How are teens involved in the community, and what is the impact of such involvement on their religious lives? How do the youth perceive the leadership of the church, including the pastor, and how important are church leaders in their lives? How does the issue of language affect the second- and third-generation Latino/as? How do the more acculturated youth relate to church services in Spanish?

4. **Youth ministry research.** Related to the previous recommendation is the need to understand the role of judicatory-level efforts to serve Latino/a adolescents. Latino churches that are affiliated with denominations often find themselves with limited financial resources and lacking overall institutional support. Studying how church organizational structures like dioceses, denominational offices, conferences, or *concilios* support Hispanic youth ministry is very important. Such a study should assess the leadership training needs of adult youth workers and help inform future capacity building efforts. Furthermore, such a study should focus on identifying effective youth ministry models within and across the religious spectrum. Can effective models be transferred across denominations? Can best practices be clearly described so they can be replicated? In short, studying the institutional structures can help identify youth ministry needs, align efforts within organizational structures, provide direction for leadership training, and multiply the awareness and utilization of programmatic best practices.

Pastoral recommendations

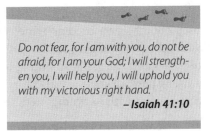

Do not fear, for I am with you, do not be afraid, for I am your God; I will strengthen you, I will help you, I will uphold you with my victorious right hand.
– Isaiah 41:10

In previous chapters, my colleagues have provided very useful and practical recommendations from a variety of points of view. Here I want to add and highlight some recommendations that I hope will speak relevantly to Hispanic youth ministry, both Protestant and Catholic.

1. Christ-centered Christianity

The teaching that Jesus is the way, the truth, and the life (John 14:6) is at the core of the Christian message. If it does nothing else, youth ministry must help young people understand and appreciate the centrality of Christ in their lives. Nothing could be more powerful, liberating, and ethnically affirming than for Hispanic teens to understand the richness of really knowing Jesus the Galilean.[12] To do so is to know that Jesus walks in the midst of—and affirms with the example of his life—those of us who live between two worlds, who experience marginality and cultural identity crisis. A Christ-centered message of hope, assurance, forgiveness, and affirmation will sustain, inspire, and transform the lives of our young.

2. Walking with God

It is important to help young people understand that the Christian life is a life-long process of daily communion with God. To belong to God is like belonging to our earthly parents. One is not a son or a daughter one day a week or once a month. Rather, every single minute of the day, one belongs to a particular family with a unique history and tradition. Similarly for those who have accepted Christ, nothing can separate us from the love of God in Christ (Romans 8:35-39). We have been adopted into the family of God—we belong to him. Seeking to learn and commune with God is a daily experience that must be nurtured in the lives of young people. Through the spiritual disciplines of prayer, Bible study, and sharing time with friends and family, faith grows and deepens.

3. Fun and recreation

Providing regular time and space for adolescents to socialize, have fun, and play in a wholesome environment is critical to enhancing positive life outcomes. Non-Christian parties usually present young people with very difficult choices and decisions. At most such parties, drinking alcohol as well as other compromising behaviors abound. When the church intentionally organizes social or recreational events for its teenagers, it is meeting an important need that can have a profoundly positive impact. It only takes one night of excessive drinking to ruin or destroy a life. Furthermore, such church-sponsored activities provide an alternative way to enjoy life without succumbing to the lure of our "live for the moment" partying culture. It is amazing what an outing to a museum or a camping trip can do for a young person's memory and appreciation of their church. A congregation that has fun with its young members will reap great results.

4. Friendship and leadership

Teenagers need adult friendships to guide and mentor them through the difficult decisions and phases they face at this critical time in their lives. Identifying, training, supporting, and equipping Latino/a leaders for youth ministry is a paramount need. Every church should develop a youth ministry leadership team composed of dedicated, fun-loving, religiously committed, positive individuals. Their task is to teach, love, care for, mentor, and lead the young people in the community.

Perhaps no other person in a local congregation is as important for the cause of youth ministry than the pastor of the congregation. The first task of a pastor should be to conduct a diagnostic evaluation of the youth ministry in the congregation. This would involve asking critical questions to understand the state of the youth in the church, and similarly to ascertain the depth of commitment and response of the larger congregation. The pastor, whose concern is for the drive and vision of the congregation, can set the tone of a youth-friendly church environment. Such an environment is characterized by:

- creating opportunities for youth involvement in church governance
- openness to providing bilingual church programming
- appointing and helping to train adult leaders
- spending time listening and talking to the youth
- maintaining a worship environment that is inspiring and relevant
- fostering a thinking environment where contemporary issues are addressed openly within a Christian perspective
- nurturing a church environment that is Christ-centered and grace-filled, where teens are loved, accepted, and supported.

5. Communal dimension of faith

The ideology of excessive individualism is increasingly influencing the understanding of the Gospel, distorting Christian living and witness. While it is true that the Gospel calls for a personal response to accept Jesus Christ as personal savior, it is also true that God's mission impacts communities, neighborhoods, cities, and nations. A communal understanding of the Gospel would counter the contemporary notion that one can live the Christian life apart from a community of faith. To be a Christian is to be nested within a community from which we connect to a rich historic legacy, deepen our faith, experience inspiration, calling, and spiritual nurture.[13]

A communal understanding of the Gospel also focuses the Christian walk on the broader issues of justice, mercy, and liberation. To give greater emphasis to personal salvation—while excluding concern for institutional injustice and active participation in alleviating the pain and suffering of the poor—is to distort and create an imbalance in our understanding of the Gospel.[14] The corporate and institutional understanding of both sin and salvation are areas that need greater clarity and attention within Protestant churches.

Furthermore, the social dimension of the Gospel is a concern of particular importance to the young. Adolescents care deeply for their communities and want to connect their spirituality to relevant issues of larger concern. Providing opportunities for teens to engage in community organizing, service projects, and broader community care activities can have a significant impact on their faith and commitment to their church.

6. Promoting positive lifestyles

At a time in their lives in which they are experimenting with different behaviors and identities while searching for greater independence, adolescents need positive reinforcement to develop healthy lifestyles. Religious institutions have a responsibility to communicate clearly the behavioral expectations that come as a response to God's saving grace. It is critically important to present in a positive way the message of total abstinence from life-threatening behaviors such as premarital sexual activity and the use of tobacco, alcohol, and drugs.

A first step is to make clear the connection between one's spirituality and the imperative of living a healthy lifestyle. Christ came into this world to give life abundantly, and the abundant life is not just a promise of eternal life but also a this-life ethic of wellness and health that enhances and prolongs life. In addition, helping young people select good friends and creating social environments that reinforce healthy life choices are an essential part of good youth ministry practice. Ultimately, how individuals experience mental, spiritual, and physical wellbeing depends on their understanding of God.[15] It is our hope that Latino congregations will become advocates and resources for health education and wellness practices to bring health to their adolescent and adult members, as well as their surrounding communities.

7. Family matters

As *Soul Searching* clearly demonstrates, parents play a significant role in the spiritual lives of teens. Parents can model the Christian life in many ways. Simply talking with their children about their faith and how much they value it is critical, and the evidence shows that the impact is even greater when both mother and father participate. When parents present consistent messages and a living example about the role of religion in their life, young people learn to appreciate its value, and parents avoid the criticism of hypocrisy. Dedicating time in the morning or evening for the family to share time together, pray, and read the Bible—even if it is a short period of time—helps to transmit spiritual practices to the next generation, highlights the importance of the spiritual life, and provides important teaching moments. Some call this time "family devotions" or *culto familiar*. Of particular importance is for the church to be a center for family life education; providing parenting training, marriage enrichment, and conflict resolution skills are some examples of what can be done in this area.

8. The life of the mind

One of the effects of involvement in a religious congregation is the development of skills and habits of the mind that are transferable to educational pursuits and civic life.[16] There is no other issue as important for the present and future of the Latino community, and the country at large, than the education of our youth. Our children and adolescents are paddling upstream against the currents of inadequate academic preparation, limited English proficiency, the lack of high expectations at school, and a peer oppositional culture that saps energy and suppresses academic ambition.

Congregations need to become more intentional about the powerful role they can play in the educational lives of Hispanic young people. Sunday school programming could be settings for evaluating literacy levels and offering referrals for enhancing literacy skills. Similarly, the bully pulpit could be used to advocate for communal norms of high expectations and academic achievement. However, the Latino community knows that rhetoric without action is empty noise, because too many promises for better education have been broken in the past.

While the political and educational establishments debate the merits of the "No Child Left Behind" legislation, churches could be providing tutoring, financial assistance, mentoring, resource materials, peer models, teacher-parent information, and much more. Furthermore, churches can adopt a public school and offer to provide educational support to the children in the school and neighborhood. Through mission storytelling and lifting up modern day heroes—many of whom are Christian men and women in their own congregations whose achievements are worthy of emulation—the vision of higher learning can be birthed and academic aspirations nurtured. The educational mission of the church should be to help young people to "Think Big"—to aspire through education to develop their God-given gifts and talents in order to build God's Reign.[17] In short, educating the mind is the best investment that parents and congregations can make—not just for their young members, but for their congregation and society at large—because a mind truly is a terrible thing to waste.

Conclusions

Nothing should be more important to parents and church leaders than to care for and nurture their children's faith and walk with God. The Judeo-Christian tradition calls parents to instruct their children, passing down rituals, values, and truths from one generation to the next (Deuteronomy 6:6-9), with the promise that if they do so, when the children grow older they will not stray from the right way (Proverbs 22:6). There is no greater responsibility of parenting than to nourish the moral development of our youth. Helping them to develop respect, love, and inspiration from sacred traditions, rituals, and texts solidifies and anchors their moral compass.

The portrait of Latino/a Protestant youth presented in these pages provides reasons to both celebrate and be concerned. Where spiritual growth is evident, careful attention should be given to fostering the spiritual maturity associated with higher levels of religious commitment. Spiritual practices such as small group involvement, prayer, Bible reading, faith sharing activities, and involvement in social service activities provide important opportunities to deepen faith and strengthen church loyalty.

In all of this, the role of adults in the spiritual formation of the young is fundamental. The most important are the parents whose modeling, sharing, and involvement in religious practices directly impacts the lives of their children. Close behind are the adults both young and old who seek to support, befriend, and open their hearts and homes to create encouraging environments where the Christian faith can be seen as an attractive and healthy way of life worthy of emulation and a lifelong commitment.

In a recent provocative article, Christian Smith argues that Christianity works because "the belief content of the Christian faith gives rise to certain practices and experiences—particularly emotional ones—that many people find highly engaging, compelling, persuasive, and convincing".[18] He presents an argument for why Christianity persists despite the challenges and attacks on its foundations. As a conclusion, we use Smith's argument to briefly answer the question, "How might Christianity work more powerfully for Latino/a young people?" Based on Smith's framework, we could say that Christianity works for Latino/a young people when:

1. They understand that they are not alone in this world, that there is a purpose for their lives, and that their daily life struggle's are noticed by a God who listens, acts, and desires the very best for them.

2. They recognize that they were created in God's image for a purpose and with infinite significance. Young people are priceless because their past and future is secure in the hands of their maker.

3. They accept the promise of unconditional love and acceptance from God. For young people who at times feel alienated and unloved, the knowledge of an all-loving God who pours out his love unconditionally and unmerited is fundamentally transforming.

4. They accept their state of sinfulness by confessing and seeking God's grace and forgiveness. By providing principles and norms for discerning between right and wrong, young people are guided to a life of meaning and positive outcomes.

5. They open their hearts to God's grace and forgiveness. When young people understand that their salvation was bought "at a cost beyond measure," it will inspire awe and move them to a life of devotion and faithfulness to the crucified Christ.

6. They collectively experience the grandeur and majesty of God through worship. Transformation of the self is enhanced when young people experience the divine on a weekly basis through the worship that includes music, songs, prayers, readings, sacraments, and *testimonios*— all pointing towards the majestic and awesome presence of God.

7. They are guided by the moral principles that enhance the quality of their lives. Young people who accept God's forgiveness and grace are now followers of Christ—and as such, embrace and obey the moral foundations for ethical behavior as found in Scripture.

8. They are nested within a community of faith. To belong to the triune God is also to belong to a community of believers. A grace-filled congregation creates an environment of acceptance and tolerance. It is in communities of faith that young people find meaning, identity, and inspirational resources to sustain them.

All of these factors when taken together, believed, and shared form a powerful web of meaning that attracts and sustains believers both young and old. It is our hope that Latino and Latina youth in all congregations can experience this rich knowledge in their minds and hearts, and that the experience will transform their lives and their communities.

Questions for reflection

1. What activities have helped you most in developing or maintaining a spiritual life? What may be preventing you from enjoying a more committed spiritual experience?

2. What memories do you cherish most about your family? In what ways did your family influence your spiritual life, positively or negatively?

3. Does your church provide opportunities for its young members to get together and socialize in wholesome ways? Would the youth of your church characterize your community of faith as a happy place where fun and recreation are valued? Why or why not?

4. What concrete ideas could your community implement to advance the educational lives of the children and teens in your congregation?

5. Do you agree with the idea that Christians should be people who live a healthy lifestyle that includes abstinence from using tobacco, alcohol, and drugs? Why or why not?

6. From your perspective, how could your congregation make a difference in the neighborhood where your church is located? Are feeding the hungry, helping people find a job, and defending workers' rights activities that belong to the mission of your church? Why or why not?

7. In your opinion, what could your congregation do to make the Christian life more inviting and attractive to young people?

8. What does it mean to be a youth-friendly congregation? What actions could your church take to become more youth-friendly? What could the teenagers do to contribute to a friendlier climate? What could the adults do? What could the pastor(s) do?

Chapter 10:
Passing the Faith to Latino/a Catholic Teens in the U.S.

Carmen M. Cervantes, Ed.D.
with
Ken Johnson-Mondragón, D.Min. cand.

Dialog 10.1 – 18 year-old Hispanic Catholic female from the West

I: *Can you tell me about how you were raised religiously? Do your parents believe in religion?*

R: Yeah, both my parents are Catholic and they raised us to be Catholic... I don't know, I guess like, we all used to go to church as a family when we were younger. I remember when I was like ten, we used to go to church like every Sunday morning, like 6:00 in the morning, every, you know, every Sunday. And we'd all wear little dresses and stuff like that. You know, everything was nice, but then like all of the sudden, it's like once I entered junior high, I remember, we just stopped going, like I don't know why.

I: *You don't remember why?*

R: I don't remember why. I just think like my dad, he never really went because he supposedly was claustrophobic. [laughs] He couldn't be around many people, you know. He hated it, you know. I don't like the standing up, but he forced us to go. "You better go. You guys better go."

I: *So you went with your mom?*

R: Yeah, I would go with my mom... The whole family would go, except for my dad. He would go and like relax at home, because you know he couldn't be there with like the crowds. So he'd just stay home and we would go, and um... I don't know, I guess we started getting older, like when I was like 13 or something like that, we just stopped going...

I: *So... does religion have any thing to do now in your family life?*

R: The only one that's really religious still is my mother. She's still like, she still lights her candles and things like that, you know. I mean I've never really learned why. I don't know what the Catholic religion is about and stuff like that. I don't really know... I mean I wish I did, but I don't, you know.

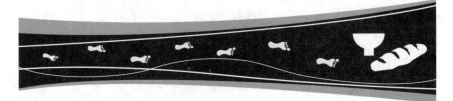

Passing the Faith to Latino/a Catholic Teens in the U.S.

All across the country I hear stories of Catholic parents, grandparents, godparents, priests, youth ministers, and catechists who are striving to pass their Christian faith and Catholic Tradition to the Latino/a teens in their lives and communities. In the face of the many challenges they encounter when trying to do so, they ask me, "Why is it so difficult? What can we do to have more success?"

Throughout this book, the Catholic Latino/a teens have come across as less savvy about Christian doctrine than their Protestant counterparts, and they participate less than Latino/a Protestant and white Catholic teens in the liturgy and other church-related activities. Although they say they pray more than their white Catholic peers at home, they are much less devoted than their Protestant brothers and sisters. Admittedly, the NSYR data show that Catholics and Protestants alike have a long way to go if they want to engage all of their young people as disciples of Christ, but why is it that our white Catholic and our Hispanic Protestant brothers and sisters are so much more successful at sharing Christ with their respective adolescent children, leading more of them to make a commitment to his church and his Gospel?

My experiences in the Catholic Church of the United States as an immigrant Latina trying to pass her faith to her own children, and as a lay ecclesial minister advocating for greater pastoral attention to young Hispanics, lead me to identify several variables that are hindering our efforts. Throughout this chapter, I will make use of my double lens as mother and lay ecclesial minister to analyze the NSYR data and some of the theories presented in this book, to offer some recommendations from the theological and pastoral perspectives, and to point to further research. It is my conviction that only by openly and assertively addressing each of these factors with an appropriate ecclesiological and pastoral approach, will the Catholic Church be able to make significant inroads in the evangelization and faith formation of its adolescent Latino/a members.

Key insights into the pastoral situation of Latino/a Catholic teens

Each of the authors in this book has provided a rich assortment of pastoral recommendations and insights, based on the NSYR research. Without diminishing the importance of what they have expressed, I would like to highlight the following realities:

> O God of my ancestors and Lord of mercy, who have made all things by your word, give me the wisdom that sits by your throne, and do not reject me from among your servants.
> *– Wisdom 9:1, 4*

- As a whole, Catholic teens are less articulate about their faith, are less engaged at church, and are more likely to subscribe to the tenets of moralistic therapeutic deism (MTD—see pages 72-74) than their Protestant peers.

- Latino/a teens will soon be more than half of all adolescent Catholics in the U.S., and as a group they are even more religiously inarticulate and disengaged than other Catholic teens, despite the fact that they participate in more personal and family-based spiritual practices, and their parents demonstrate greater commitment to their faith than do the white Catholic parents.

- A majority of the most religiously committed Hispanic Catholic parents has a difficult time getting their children to Sunday Mass and to participate in parish youth ministry programs, in sharp contrast to the experience of the most committed white Catholic parents and most Protestant parents, both white and Hispanic.

- The economic disparity between Latino and white Catholic families is tremendous, and the vast majority of Latino/a Catholic teens has at least one immigrant parent; these two facts alone present significant social barriers to the integration of all Hispanic and white Catholic teens in youth ministry settings.

- The diverse cultural, linguistic, educational, and economic circumstances among Latino/a Catholic teens and their families call for a differentiated approach to ministry with them in parishes and dioceses in order to effectively reach all segments of the population.

- The strengths and values of Hispanic families, together with the experience and apostolic zeal of Latino/a young adults, are assets that the Church must learn to leverage in order to provide for the evangelization and involvement of Hispanic Catholic teens in the life of the parish community.

Building on the findings of the NSYR, Instituto Fe y Vida (Fe y Vida) conducted a survey among the nearly 2,000 young adult delegates gathered at the First National Encounter for Hispanic Youth and Young Adult Ministry (*Encuentro*), held at the University of Notre Dame in June 2006. While the *Encuentro* process was designed to engage young Hispanic Catholics in both youth ministry and *pastoral juvenil* (ministry with single, Spanish-speaking youth and young adults), only 12 (1.5%) of the 804 Latino/a delegates surveyed were youth ministry leaders serving Hispanic teens in English, despite the fact that the NSYR survey found 68% of Hispanic Catholic teens to be English-dominant. Furthermore, only 42 (5%) of the delegates were youth ministry leaders serving Hispanic teens in Spanish or bilingually. Some other significant findings of the *Encuentro* survey are as follows:[1]

- 93% of the *grupos juveniles* (youth and young adult groups) represented by the *Encuentro* delegates included young adults over the age of 18
- 50% also included 16- and 17-year-old members
- 36% had 14- and 15-year-old members
- 12% even included 11- to 13-year-olds together with the young adults in the group
- Overall, 54% of the groups served minors together with young adults, 39% served only young adults, and only 7% served adolescents alone
- Of the delegates representing groups serving young adults alone or together with adolescents, 95% stated that their group was conducted in Spanish or bilingually

If the NSYR demonstrates that most youth ministry programs have failed to engage the full spectrum of Latino/a teens in our parishes, the *Encuentro* survey suggests that *pastoral juvenil* has been equally ineffective at reaching the majority of Latino/a Catholic teens that is English-dominant. Clearly there is a need for leaders in youth ministry and *pastoral juvenil* to work together to identify leaders and develop strategies to reach more of the young Hispanic Catholics that are currently being missed by both pastoral approaches.

Ten factors that need to be addressed in our Church

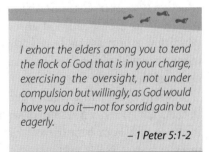

I exhort the elders among you to tend the flock of God that is in your charge, exercising the oversight, not under compulsion but willingly, as God would have you do it—not for sordid gain but eagerly.

– 1 Peter 5:1-2

The data from the NSYR has confirmed my experience and concern about the situation of the Latino/a teens in our Church. As adolescents, my own children eventually gave up trying to "fit in" in our parish's youth ministry program. The lack of alternative opportunities suitable for them, the frustration of trying to help Hispanic parents deal with their teenage children without church structures to support them, the lack of professional youth ministers capable of producing programs and resources for Latino/a teenagers… all are reflected in the statistical charts and excerpts from the interviews with Hispanic Catholic adolescents in the preceding chapters.

This does not mean that the situation for young Latino/a Catholics is equally bleak in all U.S. parishes. I personally know of parishes that are doing a great job, but parishes with excellent ministry for Latino/a teens must be the exception, or the data would have reflected otherwise. There is a need for further research to confirm or challenge perceptions in the field about appropriate pastoral care for Latino/a Catholic teens. Nevertheless, the impressive body of information gathered through the NSYR, together with my experience and attempts to improve and expand ministry with young Hispanics over the last twenty-five years, allows me to put forward with confidence the following ten factors that urgently need to be addressed by our Church if we do not want to lose a full generation of Latino/a Catholics due to *pastoral nearsightedness* (see page 106) and neglect.

1. History of racism and neglect

The poor pastoral attention being provided to Latino/a teens in our Church is not new. A complete overview of the history of Hispanic Catholics in the U.S. is beyond the scope of this book and this chapter. However, it is helpful to recall some facts that have shaped our history up to the present time.

The U.S. Catholic Church in the nineteenth century saw a tremendous increase of Catholics because of the influx of Irish, Italian, German, French, Polish, and other eastern European immigrants. The American bishops welcomed native European clergy and were successful in integrating the first and second generations through a system of national parishes. The Church also assisted immigrant families in their cultural transition with an effective system of Catholic schools, which was instrumental in fostering vocations to the priesthood and religious life, and provided an excellent education at a reasonable cost that allowed many Catholics to enter the labor force with a significant advantage. As these immigrants moved up the social ladder, so did the Church.[2]

On the other hand, when Puerto Rico was annexed to the United States in 1898, the American system of separation of church and state was imposed in the island. Four centuries of Catholicism entered into turmoil; Spanish priests and sisters left, and many schools and churches were confiscated. The largest influence from the U.S. Catholic church was in building schools; but, in comparison with the Protestants who soon started to prepare local clergy and opened their arms to Catholic ex-priests, Catholics were too focused on Americanization and on the very young. By taking an assimilationist approach, the Catholic Church failed to nurture native ministry vocations, leaving the space open to the ministry of many Protestant churches.[3]

A similar situation occurred with Catholic Spaniards and Mexicans in the Southwestern territory annexed to the United States in 1848.

Foreign priests and religious missionaries from Europe arrived in Texas, New Mexico, and California, and they soon outnumbered the few native Hispanic vocations that had developed there. With the tremendous influx of non-Hispanic Americans, particularly after Texas was granted statehood and gold was discovered in California, Hispanics found themselves more and more at the margins of society and also of the Catholic Church. By the end of the nineteenth century, Hispanics had very little leadership or voice in the institutional church. Nevertheless, the traditional faith and religious practices of the people continued to be nurtured at home and in devotional confraternities. In most cases this was done without much support from the hierarchy, with a few notable exceptions in areas that retained a high concentration of Hispanic residents.[4]

Immigration from Cuba was different: the first wave that left the island belonged to the professional and business class, and although they arrived penniless, their education and entrepreneurship allowed them to integrate into the middle class of the U.S. without loosing their culture. Later Cuban immigrations brought poor people from that country, but many have benefited from the social environment established by earlier Cuban arrivals, especially in areas like south Florida, New York, and Chicago. However, more recent immigrants from other Caribbean cultures, such as the Dominicans and Haitians, have followed the ranks of the poor in the U.S.

For centuries, the general attitude of superiority among Catholics of European background over those of Latin American origin with their lower educational and occupational status, led the Church to consider them primarily as objects of charity, instead of preparing them to become evangelizers and ministers. For example, a group of Puerto Rican women in New York City wrote to Cardinal Francis Spellman in 1951, reporting that "in New York, there are about 800 Puerto Rican Protestant ministers but not a single Catholic priest of Puerto Rican origin."[5] This was the common situation of Latino/a Catholics in the U.S. up to the middle of the twentieth century, when the Vatican II renewal called for the celebration of the Sacraments in the native language of the people. At that time, the small group of Hispanic priests and religious in the country decided to organize themselves and raise their prophetic voice in favor of their own people.

A series of three National Encounters for Hispanic Ministry—in 1972, 1977, and 1985, with their respective formation-in action leadership processes—and the proclamation of the U.S. Bishops' *National Pastoral Plan for Hispanic Ministry* in 1987 set the foundations for Hispanic ministry. These efforts, as well as the opening of diocesan offices for Hispanic ministry, the inclusion of Hispanic personnel in catechetical offices, the renewal of the permanent diaconate, and the creation of schools of ministry in

Spanish, came at the same time as a significant influx of immigrants from Mexico and every other part of Latin America. Just in the last 20 years of the past century, about 12 million Latin Americans immigrated to the United States, and they continued to come at the rate of about 650 thousand per year from 2000 to 2005.

The journey to develop adequate ministry programs and structures for Latino/a Catholics has not been easy, even with the help of thousands of mainstream U.S. priests and religious who have become bilingual in order to better serve them. Hispanic ministers usually have to play the roles of prophet and bridge-builder at the same time, denouncing the history of pastoral neglect while seeking allies and recruits to improve this poorly-funded and poorly-staffed ministry wherever they may be found. Although Hispanic liturgical ministry, pastoral ministry among adults, catechesis with children, and schools of ministry have all made great strides in the last twenty years, ministry with Latino/a teens has largely been left behind. The remaining nine factors described later in this section explain the main reasons why this has happened.

The pastoral situation of young Hispanic Catholics is complicated by the fact that the concept of youth in most Latin American cultures does not match the U.S. concept for this age group, so youth ministry and *pastoral juvenil* have traditionally taken very different approaches in ministry. Instituto Fe y Vida has published an article describing these differences in detail, so that information will not be repeated here, but it is vital for ministers working with young Latino/a Catholics to understand these cultural differences. The article is available as a free download from Fe y Vida's website.[6]

The founding of Instituto Fe y Vida in 1994 and the creation of the National Catholic Network de Pastoral Juvenil Hispana (La Red) in 1997 marked the beginning of serious efforts to advocate and train for appropriate ministry with young Latino/a Catholics (both adolescents and young adults). Developments in this ministry since 2000 include:

- Fe y Vida began to offer seminars for ministry with Hispanic adolescents
- La Red launched a ten-year initiative to develop leadership and resources for ministry with young Hispanics, and convoked the First National Encounter for Hispanic Youth and Young Adult Ministry, with a two-year process that began at the grassroots level in parishes and culminated at the national event in 2006
- The Mexican American Cultural Center (MACC) started to offer courses and a parish program for leadership development among Latino/a adolescents

- The Center for Ministry Development (CMD) integrated some additional training for ministry with Latino/a teens in its Certificate Program in Youth Ministry Studies

We are indeed in a new era for ministry with young Latino/as in the Catholic Church, and with God's grace, we are on our way to reverse the pastoral neglect that Latino young people and their parents have endured for centuries.

2. Cultural and religious gaps between Latino parents and their children

Education in the faith is easier when children are small; they do not ask difficult doctrinal and moral questions, and parents can usually involve them in religious traditions without being challenged about their meaning or being rebuked because they are "boring." The arrival of puberty, paired with the influence of the media, videogames, peers of other religions or no religion, and a secular consumer-oriented and individualistic culture, can make it very difficult for parents to set religious goals and ideals in the minds of their children as they guide their maturation in the faith.

Parents of U.S. Latino/a teenagers have several additional challenges. If they are immigrants (72% of Hispanic teens have at least one immigrant parent), they were most likely raised in a Catholic environment, where the extended family, neighbors, the general culture, and a myriad of daily faith-based rituals, sayings, and practices supported the efforts of their own parents to instill the faith in their children. In addition, as is typical of traditional cultures, children tended to respect the adults and authority figures. These conditions not only do not exist for most Hispanic parents in the U.S., but they find themselves at odds with the spirituality and catechetical style of Catholic ministers from the mainstream culture. In parishes that are mostly Hispanic or multicultural and poor, the absence of professional youth ministers with intercultural competence makes it nearly impossible to find advocates to help the parents articulate and remedy their frustrations with respect to the religious formation of their adolescent children.

Moving from a Catholic to a plurireligious environment is a challenge for many Latino Catholic families for two reasons. First, due to the lack of priests and the history of poor educational opportunities in many parts of Latin America, the Catholic identity has mainly been supported by practices of *popular Catholicism* (see page 140) incarnated in family and community-based cultural and religious celebrations. These foundations prove to be unstable when immigrant adults with only a basic understanding of Catholic Tradition are confronted by enthusiastic peers from other Christian traditions and a local Catholic parish that is not very responsive to their religious needs, or those of their adolescent children. Second, many evangelical and Pentecostal churches offer small and quite homogenous Latino communities, a Latino/a pastor, Bible-based instruction and spiritual guidance for people of all ages, lively and moving worship services, and an obvious spirit of mutual concern and support in the congregation. Most Catholic parishes cannot offer these benefits to their immigrant parishioners, and the pastoral staff is often not equipped to build on the religious foundations that were laid in Latin America.

The complexities of bilingualism and the acculturation process also hinder the ability of immigrant parents to nurture the faith of their teenage children (see pages 143-152). In most Hispanic Catholic families, parents either speak limited English or are functionally bilingual, but lack the religious and affective vocabulary necessary for prayer and meaningful conversations about faith and values in English. If they are religiously active, they tend to participate in Spanish-language Eucharists, prayer groups, and pious practices where they can live and express their faith. If their children feel comfortable in Spanish, they may join a *grupo juvenil* together with immigrant young adults, if there is one available. However, teens that feel more comfortable in English usually lack the vocabulary to maintain a religious conversation in Spanish, so *pastoral juvenil* is not an option for them and they are unlikely to find a peer group that supports their culture and spirituality in English.

In addition, the lack of adequate programs and resources for Latino parents to assist them in the transition to the catechetical style and content used in U.S. parishes, has made it difficult for them to support, or in some cases even understand, the religious formation of their children in mainstream youth ministry programs. Although it may seem logical to expect that the situation would be better for second- and third-generation Latino/a teens, the NSYR data and the survey conducted at the Encuentro suggest that it is even more difficult for many of them. The religious formation of these *culturally squeezed* teenagers (see page 152), who do not "fit in" with either the Spanish-speakers or the mainstream groups, represents a significant challenge for their parents and for the Church.

3. Inadequate church structures for ministry with Latino/a adolescents

From the parish level to the national scene, church structures have failed to serve young Latino/a Catholics. Mainstream youth ministers generally feel inadequately prepared for ministry with teens of other cultures,[7] and few take the initiative to serve them for a variety of reasons. Some of the most frequently cited reasons include:

- Pastoral nearsightedness that leads pastors and youth ministers to believe there are few or no Latino/a teens in their parish ("They all go to the parish down the road.")
- The difficulty of understanding and addressing the diverse needs of each pastoral segment (see pages 33-39)
- The youth minister's inability to speak Spanish and/or their lack of cultural competence
- Assuming that it is not their responsibility because others (i.e. the leaders in *pastoral juvenil*) have a ministry dedicated to them
- In some cases, there may be racism or classism on the part of the pastoral team

In addition, many times when Hispanic adults have attempted to minister to their teens, their pastoral action has been challenged by directors or coordinators of youth ministry, who see themselves as responsible for all of the teens in the parish or diocese, and who consider these other efforts to be divisive or even racist because they are not "inclusive" of everyone (see factor #5 below). In other cases Latino/a adults have their efforts blocked due to legitimate concerns over their adequate preparation for ministry with adolescents, yet they are seldom offered opportunities to prepare themselves through appropriate formation programs for them.

As the roots of the word "responsibility" imply, being responsible for something presupposes the "ability" to "respond" to that particular situation. History has shown that mainstream structures have not had the ability to respond to the complexities of youth ministry with Latino/a teens, and that Hispanic initiatives have been blocked or inadequately supported as described above, leaving no structures really "responsible" for youth ministry among Hispanics. The NSYR data, plus the general lack of ecclesial ministers and resources specialized in this ministry, demonstrate a *de facto* pastoral abandonment toward this significant portion of the church.

The celebration of the National *Encuentro* in 2005-2006 marked the beginning of a new era of collaboration between structures usually serving mainstream teens and Hispanic *jóvenes* (single Hispanic youth and young adults) separately. Although the conversations were sometimes strained due to historic and cultural misunderstandings, the dialogue that has occurred at the leadership levels and the good will that has been generated is surely a sign of hope for the future.

When speaking of teenagers, the future is now; a person is a teenager for only 7 years, the most difficult in the entire process of growth to maturity. According to socioreligious estimates, about 3.5 million young Latino/a Catholics in the U.S. are teenagers now, and at least 12 million will become teenagers in the next twenty years, not counting any immigrants that may arrive during that time. Thus, there is no time to waste in our efforts to improve the ecclesial structures for ministry with Latino/a adolescents.

4. Deficiencies in the ecclesiological approach to youth ministry

Some of the structural difficulties just mentioned are rooted in what appears to be a popular misconception among mainstream Catholic pastors and youth ministers: that creating multiple youth ministry programs within a single parish does harm to the Body of Christ—that it somehow is forming divisions in the church or creating a "parallel church." This misconception is grounded in a poor theological understanding of what a parish is, and how it relates to the diocese and the universal church. The following quotes shed light on the nature of the parish with respect to the topic at hand:

- "This Church of Christ is really present in all legitimately organized local groups of the faithful [parishes], which, in so far as they are united to their pastors, are also quite appropriately called Churches in the New Testament... In these communities, though they may often be small and poor, or existing in the diaspora, Christ is present through whose power and influence the One, Holy, Catholic and Apostolic Church is constituted. For the sharing in the body and blood of Christ has no other effect than to accomplish our transformation into that which we receive." – *Lumen Gentium*, §26

- The parish "gathers into a unity all the human diversities that are found there and inserts them into the universality of the Church." – *Apostolicam Actuositatem*, §10

- The parish "represents the visible Church constituted throughout the world... Efforts must be made to encourage a sense of community within the parish, above all in the common celebration of the Sunday Mass." – *Sacrosanctum Concilium*, §42

- "A parish is a definite community of the Christian faithful established on a stable basis within a particular church [a diocese]; the pastoral care of the parish is entrusted to a pastor as its own shepherd under the authority of the diocesan bishop." – Canon 515, §1

- "The parish initiates the Christian people into the ordinary expression of the liturgical life: it gathers them together in this celebration; it teaches Christ's saving doctrine; it practices the charity of the Lord in good works and brotherly love." – *Catechism of the Catholic Church*, §2179

The above quotes make it clear that the ecclesial nature of a parish is grounded in the communal celebration of the Eucharist, gathered around a pastor appointed by the bishop. To say that establishing two or more youth ministry programs or groups within a single parish is dividing the church or creating a "parallel church" is to deny the nature of the church as a communion of believers united by Baptism and a common creed, gathered around a duly appointed pastor ordained through apostolic succession, and constituted by an active participation in the celebration of the Eucharist.

When we all eat of the one Bread, we are formed into a single Body united by the living presence of the Holy Spirit, whether we participate in the Eucharist at 8:00 A.M., 5:30 P.M., in Spanish, in English, or in another language. Applying the "parallel church" principle throughout the parish would make it necessary to eliminate the St. Vincent de Paul Society, the Altar Society, the Knights of Columbus, the Charismatic Renewal, separate boy and girl scouts, children's religious education classes, and every other gathering apart from the liturgy, because such organizations are not directed to the entire parish community. Why is it that we can speak of being united with Catholics all over the world through our Baptism, creed, and the Eucharist, but we cannot see this unity in diversity when it relates to ministry with teenagers in two or more settings in our own parishes?

Herein lies the theological error in the "parallel church" assumption: it denies the power of the Holy Spirit to establish, build up, and renew the Body of Christ, the church, in and through the Sacraments, especially Baptism and the Eucharist. Whenever anyone participates in the sacrifice of the Mass—even if there are only two people present—the unity of the Body that is signified and sacramentally realized is a manifestation of the mystical unity of the church in Christ. Pope Benedict XVI recently expressed this reality in the following words:

> "It is significant that the Second Eucharistic Prayer, invoking the Paraclete, formulates its prayer for the unity of the church as follows: 'May all of us who share in the body and blood of Christ be brought together in unity by the Holy Spirit.' These words help us to see clearly how the *res* [Latin for "thing" or essence] of the sacrament of the Eucharist is the unity of the faithful within ecclesial communion. The Eucharist is thus found at the root of the church as a mystery of communion." – Apostolic Exhortation *Sacramentum Caritatis* (2007), §15

If youth ministry, *pastoral juvenil,* and every other ministry in the parish direct their participants to a fuller participation in the celebration of the Eucharist and foster the baptismal mission of their members, there can be no room for the suggestion that they are dividing the Body or creating a parallel church. On the other hand, a real division of the church occurs when Latino/a teens and their families are not offered pastoral care and religious formation in an appropriate sociocultural context for them, and they end up either being unchurched or seeking an ecclesial community elsewhere that is more responsive to their pastoral needs.

Establishing multiple youth groups or youth ministry programs may entail the creation of different *church substructures,* but that in itself does not make them "parallel." The word "parallel" implies that two or more groups *never* touch; at a minimum, the various groups are united in the person of the pastor who oversees them all, in the celebration of the Eucharist, and in fostering the baptismal call of their members. Ideally, they should also come together periodically for reflection and dialogue, celebration of their faith, pastoral action, and socialization as members of one parish community. If the leaders organize activities to bring the groups together, parallelism will not occur even at the substructural or programmatic levels.

Indeed, this approach to ministry is found throughout our Church. Every parish usually functions as a separate entity, but the leaders come together at the deanery, regional, and diocesan levels with certain periodicity, under the leadership of the local bishop. The same happens at the national and international levels with regard to bishops, other church leaders, and lay ecclesial ministers. Any parish with more than one ministerial department, religious education class, or Sunday liturgy has created different substructures, thereby helping individuals and families to gather to hear the Word of God, reflect together on its meaning for their lives, and forge relationships of accountability and support in their journey with Christ.

An advantage that our Protestant brothers and sisters have is their ability to establish small ecclesial communities where Latino/a pastors can attend to the particular pastoral needs of their people and form networks of support among families with similar situations and challenges. The beauty of our Catholic Church is its universality—the opportunity to live the faith united in the Spirit and in the Eucharist, while being enriched by the diversity of its members. As noted above, there is no theological reason to prevent the Catholic Church from offering both treasures to its teenage members; it is a matter of shifting the paradigm away from youth ministry in a single group, which has resulted in the structural exclusion of millions of Catholic teens from their parish youth ministry programs.

5. Erroneous identification of "pastoral segmentation" with "segregation"

Apart from the misconception about parish unity outlined above, many youth ministers feel compelled to maintain a single youth ministry group or program based on their sensitivity to the injustice implied in any kind of "segregation." This is the cultural context from which many U.S. Catholics operate: it does harm to our sensibilities when we begin to separate people on racial or ethnic lines; we feel like we are leading our people back to the kind of racial separation and discrimination that preceded the civil rights movement of the 1960s.

It is true that any ministry program that requires teens to form groups along racial or ethnic lines would be a form of segregation. However, that is not what is being proposed here. In order to adequately serve the adolescents in parishes with Hispanics at different levels of acculturation or cultural integration (see pages 143-152), the youth ministry team must develop and coordinate culturally appropriate programs, events, and leadership development activities for the various sociocultural segments of the community. However, one should never presume that because teens are Hispanic, they belong with a particular community or group; rather, they should be allowed to find their own comfort zone in the group of their choice, just as adult Catholics do.

When the Reign of God is ushered into its fulfillment at the end of time, the unity of the Body of Christ will be perfectly manifested for ever. In the meantime, many kinds of differences can make harmonious human relationships difficult—language, educational levels, experiences of prejudice and discrimination, social class, culture, and even spirituality itself, to name a few. In a utopia, people of every race, class, culture, and language would come together in love to grow in faith, hope, and charity. For a diverse group of particularly mature adults, such an experience may even be possible, assuming they share a common language. However, for adolescents who are trying to understand themselves and find out where they fit in a world marked by clear religious, social, and cultural boundaries, asking them to do this as a prerequisite to participation in the parish youth ministry is asking more than many can give.

Youth ministers often make the mistaken assumption that becuase teens are in school together, it should not be a problem to ask them to come together in a youth group as well. In reality, there are hundreds of thousands of home-schooled, alternative-schooled, detained, recent immigrant, and high school drop-out Catholic teenagers who are *not* in school with the other students in their parish's youth ministry program. Even if they do go to the same school or work in similar part-time jobs, groups of friends spontaneously form along the lines of social and cultural similarities and comfort with each other. It is extremely rare for impoverished teens to socialize with the economic elite of their school, or for mainstream students to seek their friends in English as a Second Language (ESL) classes. Youth ministers should not underestimate the importance of the NSYR's finding that there are stark differences in socioeconomic status and educational attainment between most Hispanic and white Catholic families, which accentuate their cultural, racial, and linguistic differences.

At a younger age, socioeconomic and educational factors weigh less than during adolescence. The reason is simple: among children the differences in clothing, entertainment, and conversations tend to be less

336 PATHWAYS OF HOPE AND FAITH AMONG HISPANIC TEENS

abrasive. In adolescence, these differences reflect social contexts that provide radically different opportunities and social horizons to each group. For example, the cost of one teen's weekend activities may be equivalent to the entire entertainment budget for a family of six for a month. As a result, conversations are quite different with respect to lived experiences, cultural references (television, music, history, etc.), and expectations for the future. Adding the social influence of classism and racism, many teens from middle- to upper-class families and Euro-American ancestry tend to look down on their low-income peers of color, who in turn are inclined to develop lower self-esteem and lower self-confidence. Some even acquire a deep-seated anger and attitude of resistance toward people of the dominant culture/class as a result of the various forms of prejudice and discrimination they and their loved ones have suffered.

Because attending youth ministry and church activities is voluntary, those teens who feel that they do not "fit in" usually opt not to participate. I still remember the words of a teenage boy from California to his pastor when the Latino and mainstream youth groups were merged and the Latino/a teens did not return: "I have to suffer in this brown skin all day at school, and you want me to feel the same way at church?" In contrast, Hispanic teens that feel fine in mainstream groups usually have no problem participating in them, but the NSYR data show that they are a very small group—mostly those in the middle to upper income levels, who belong to families accustomed to moving in the mainstream.

When teens on the cultural and social margins opt out, youth ministry ends up serving a homogenized group of mainstream adolescents who feel pretty good about being together. That is a powerful and wonderful thing—it creates a sense of Catholic identity that will carry them into their adulthood. But for those who do not fit, the parish has created a sense of alienation, unwelcome, and perhaps even isolation or rejection that diminish their ability to integrate their faith in a constructive way into their developing personal identity. Unless their parents are able to transmit their faith and religious identity rooted in something other than participation in the life of the community, such adolescents will likely develop a very weak sense of Catholic identity, or perhaps none at all.

When the social prerequisites to participation in youth ministry are too high, or when they create excessive anxiety related to cultural or social dissonance, teens will opt not to participate. The NSYR data show that culturally squeezed Hispanic teens are especially prone to make this choice. If creating a program, a group, an event, or a service especially for them would foster their participation in a faith community where they can comfortably celebrate and express their Catholic identity, should we not encourage youth ministers to do so?

This is not a form of segregation, but rather an intentional pastoral segmentation according to the diverse needs of the adolescents in the parish. If we do not develop appropriate pastoral responses for marginalized teens, we are in effect doing the opposite of what Jesus the Good Shepherd would do—we are giving up on the sheep in the wilderness in order to protect and care for only those already in the sheepfold.

History tells us that over time and generations, the children, grandchildren, and great-grandchildren of immigrants will find their place in the dominant culture in the United States, making choices about elements of their cultural heritage that they would like to retain. Anglo and Hispanic Catholics already experience common ground in the Eucharist and their shared Catholic identity. In due time, that common identity will be strengthened by social and cultural ties, as well as the experience of partnership in the mission of the church—and both segments of our Catholic community will be changed by this spiritual and cultural encounter. Even so, it is unfair to expect of today's Latino/a adolescents what will be ingrained in their grandchildren.

A larger question confronting the Catholic Church is: will its young Hispanics remain Catholic in adulthood? The most recent research from the Pew Hispanic Center shows that 74% of Hispanic immigrant adults are Catholic, compared to 58% of Hispanic adults born in the United States.[8] It will take a concerted effort to reverse the effects of generations of pastoral neglect among Hispanic families, but the consequence of not making that effort is that another generation may become secularized, alienated, and excluded from the life and mission of the Catholic Church—if they do not find a more welcoming ecclesial community somewhere else.

6. Inadequate attention to the multicultural dimension of youth ministry

Some of the limitations and misunderstandings that were described in the earlier sections of this chapter were addressed by the U.S. Bishops in their 1997 pastoral letter on youth ministry, yet the field has been slow to implement the bishops' recommendations for developing a multicultural youth ministry. This dimension is identified as one of the seven overarching themes that inform the practice of youth ministry in all of its components, and it involves two complementary considerations:

> "Ministry with adolescents is multicultural when it focuses on a specialized ministry to youth of particular racial and ethnic cultures and promotes multicultural awareness among all youth." – *Renewing the Vision: A Framework for Catholic Youth Ministry* (USCCB, 1997), 22-23.

The first consideration is that parishes *may* need to provide particular cultural groups with specialized ministry programs, apart from the mainstream youth group(s). The document goes on to describe how such programs should: a) build on the cultural identity and respond to the social and cultural needs of the participants; b) develop adolescent leaders and consult with parents that reflect the diversity of the participants; c) provide training to staff members to increase their cultural competence; and d) balance cultural awareness with the concept of unity in diversity that characterizes the universal church.

The second consideration is that *all* adolescents need to be provided with training in multicultural awareness as an integral element of youth ministry programming. Diversity awareness activities may include: cross-cultural experiences, programs in racism and oppression awareness, development of intercultural communication skills, reflection on the social barriers to achievement and how to overcome them, and modeling of fairness and nondiscrimination by the leaders—both teens and adults.

The NSYR data has made it clear that there is a great need for our Catholic Church to provide more specialized ministry programs for Latino/a teens. Nevertheless, youth ministry teams should consult with parents and carefully assess the needs of the teens in their own parish before making a decision about how to structure their programs. In parishes where most of the young Hispanics are already participating in youth ministry, it may be enough to provide the diversity awareness activities described above in a program that gathers all of the parish teens in a single group. However, if there are significant numbers of marginalized or recently arrived Latino/a teens, it will be necessary to organize missionary activities to reach out to them with programs directed to their particular needs.

Attempting to do diversity awareness activities in a multicultural youth group with teens at different levels of acculturation can be counterproductive. Consider for example the experience of ethnic minority teens being asked to share some aspect of their cultural heritage on a youth group multicultural night. This process gives teens of the dominant culture a sense that their experience is the "objective norm" by which all other cultural expressions are to be judged. It may also make the minority teens feel uncomfortable, forcing them to make a spectacle of the "differentness" of their lifestyle from the perspective of the dominant culture. When such activities focus on traditional folkloric elements that are not part of daily life, they do little to help teens of either culture understand the deeper differences that shape the way they see and experience the world, or to help ethnic minority teens appreciate the values of their heritage and integrate them in the broader social context of the U.S. mainstream.

On the other hand, when teens of a particular culture are given the space and time to delve deeply into their own religious and cultural heritage in a group of peers with the same background, they will feel empowered and accepted when asked to prepare an artistic expression of their identity to share with other groups—knowing that *all* of the other groups will be doing the same. In this scenario, no one cultural group is perceived as the norm, but all are invited to share their own traditions and cultural traits, and to appreciate those of the others.

Two challenges stand out in this process: ensuring that the mainstream teens do not feel unappreciated or excluded because they think they "have no cultural heritage," which is a common misperception; and securing the guidance of culturally competent leaders to help the teens in each group to understand their own culture and how it differs from other cultures, without judging or creating stereotypes about each other. The teens also need to have a certain level of spiritual and psychosocial maturity so that they can experience these activities as enriching and not as a cause of alienation for young people of a particular culture.

7. Limited integration of evangelization in youth ministry

Teens of every culture are engaged in a process of identity construction with many dimensions, including the religious. Youth ministry is charged with evangelizing and catechizing young people to help them appropriate their Catholic identity. Youth ministers and missionaries have a great deal in common: in a sense they are both trying to incarnate the Gospel in the lives of people of a different culture—in this case youth culture(s). If youth ministers in multicultural parishes were to integrate a missionary identity into their programs, they would see their task as one of building up the teens to be evangelizers of their peers and families in their particular social and cultural environments.

Pope Paul VI's Apostolic Exhortation *Evangelii Nuntiandi* does not reflect specifically on the role of adolescents in the work of evangelization, but his statement that "evangelizing is in fact the grace and vocation proper to the Church, her *deepest identity*. [Emphasis added.] She exists in order to evangelize..." (§14) must be applied as much to them as it is to the adults in the church. The document goes on to say that evangelization does not reach is completion until the evangelized becomes the evangelizer. (§24) The implication is clear: unless adolescents take up the call to evangelize their peers, their families, their neighbours, and even the world, they have not fully experienced what it means to be a Catholic Christian.

Despite this fact, many youth ministers and Confirmation catechists continue to treat adolescents as if they were catechumens at the stage of inquiry, trying to decide whether being Catholic is for them. They are not—they are baptized members of the Body of Christ who have been called to carry out Christ's mission in the world, according to their still-developing ability to do so. Even children are called to fulfill this mission according to their ability, but that is a story for another book.

How can we honestly expect them to assume their baptismal identity if they are deprived of the one experience that is the "deepest identity" of the church—bringing the light of the Good News to people still living in darkness and working to transform the injustices that still remain in our world? They should be mentored into the practice of evangelization and assisted in reflecting on how they will give expression to their religious faith in their lives (their vocation).

A comparison of church involvement between Catholics and Protestants with respect to the children of sporadic/disengaged parents (see Tables 3.7 and 3.8 on pages 98 and 99) suggests that Catholic youth ministers depend heavily on the initiative of parents to sign up their adolescent children and bring them to youth ministry events and activities. If evangelization of, with, and by adolescents were implemented well in parish youth ministry programs, the Catholic Church would be reaching far more of its teenaged members of all socioeconomic classes and cultural backgrounds, because the teens themselves would be reaching out to their peers to get them involved. This approach would even raise the possibility of reaching the Catholic teens whose families do not regularly come to church, even for the Eucharist.

8. Lack of follow through on the Hispanic ministry documents

Many of the key NSYR findings listed at the beginning of this chapter have come as an unwelcome surprise to a lot of pastors and youth ministry workers in the Catholic Church. In part, this is understandable—they regularly encounter the small minority of Catholic teens that are deeply committed to their faith and involved in the life of the parish, so they see no basis in their experience for the description of Catholic teens as incredibly "inarticulate and disengaged."

The NSYR data suggest that religiously committed teens only make up about 7% of all Catholic teens (see Table 2.6 on page 71), but with about 6 million 13- to 17-year-old Catholics in our 19,000 Catholic parishes, that averages out to about 22 committed high school-aged kids per parish. Undoubtedly, some parishes have a much larger share of these kids than the average—especially the parishes with a professional youth minister on staff. That is enough to convince a lot of priests and youth ministers that they are meeting the religious needs of the Catholic teens in their parish.

For the first time, the NSYR data has made it possible to assess the religious development of Catholic teens that are *not* participating in the parish youth group, so it should not be surprising that its results are out of step with prior research. For example, *Renewing the Vision* based its assessment of Catholic youth ministry's success on a social scientific portrait of the Catholic teens who were youth ministry participants:

> "The 1996 study of parish youth ministry program participants, *New Directions in Youth Ministry*, offers the first data on a national level specifically on Catholic youth ministry. The study is good news for the Church because it shows that adolescents who participate in parish youth ministry programs identify faith and moral formation as a significant contribution to their life, have a profound sense of commitment to the Catholic Church, attend Sunday Mass regularly, and show continued growth while they remain involved in youth programs." – *Renewing the Vision*, 5.

This optimistic picture of the practice of Catholic youth ministry stands in stark contrast to the assessment of youth ministry in the U.S. Hispanic ministry documents. Based on a communitarian analysis of the pastoral reality instead of sociological research, these documents have consistently decried the state of pastoral care for Hispanic adolescents, starting with the *Proceedings of the Second National Encuentro for Hispanic Ministry* in 1978, and continuing unabated in all the main Hispanic documents up to the publication of *Encuentro and Mission* in 2002. The following are two typical descriptions found in these documents:

- The situation of Hispanic youth—both male and female—is as follows: "A large number is alienated from the Church. Generally lack adequate attention and pastoral care. [Are] victims of materialism and consumerism. Experience difficulty in finding their own identity as they exist between different languages and cultures. Feel strong... pressures toward drugs, crime, gangs and dropping out of school." – *National Pastoral Plan for Hispanic Ministry* (USCCB, 1987), §§51 and 55

- "The traditional model of parish youth ministry does not, for the most part, reach Hispanic young people because of economic, linguistic, cultural, age, and educational differences. At the same time, there is resistance to accepting, affirming, and supporting emerging models that attempt to fill the void by reaching out to Hispanic young people, particularly new immigrants. Generally speaking, the majority of parish youth ministry programs serve a population that is mostly European white, mainstream, middle class, and English-speaking." – *Encuentro and Mission* (USCCB, 2002), 22.

It should be noted here that when *Encuentro and Mission* speaks of the "traditional model" of parish youth ministry, it is contrasting the current practice of Catholic youth ministry in most parishes with *pastoral juvenil hispana* and other "emerging models." It is not making any comment about what many youth ministers may think of as the "traditional model," namely youth ministry as it was practiced in parish youth groups prior to the emphasis on comprehensive youth ministry in *Renewing the Vision*.

In any case, pastoral nearsightedness prevents a lot of youth ministers from seeing the needs of the young people who do not participate in their programs. On the other hand, Hispanic ministers have been more keenly aware of this problem because they are in constant contact with the religiously committed parents whose children resist participating in the parish youth ministry programs, as confirmed by the NSYR data. A truly adequate pastoral assessment that looks at the broader situation and needs of the Catholic teens within the geographic boundaries of the parish would go a long way toward remedying this challenge.

Although the assessment of Hispanic youth ministry presented in the *National Pastoral Plan for Hispanic Ministry* is correct, and ministry with the young was identified as one of the four missionary "preferential options" in Hispanic ministry, the Plan has rarely received the financial and human resources to succeed at the parish, diocesan, regional, and national levels, especially with respect to ministry with young Hispanics. In addition, dioceses generally lack coordination between youth ministry, catechesis, evangelization, Catholic education, and Hispanic ministry offices/personnel. As a result, most mainstream youth ministers have never read the Hispanic ministry documents and are not aware that they have a key role to play in their implementation. The general lack of coordination between mainstream youth ministry and *pastoral juvenil* has meant that almost no one has taken responsibility to address the needs of the culturally squeezed Latino/a teens who do not "fit in" in either sociocultural context.

9. The challenge of maintaining safe environments

In 2002, the USCCB published the *Charter for the Protection of Children and Young People,* and since then most dioceses have complied by requiring all adults in the church who work with minors to undergo a background check and receive training on establishing and maintaining safe environments. The problem for *pastoral juvenil hispana* arises in view of the fact that the U.S. and Latin American concepts of "youth," "young adult," and *"joven"* do not match. *Pastoral juvenil* has traditionally served Latino/a immigrants across the boundary between adolescence and young adulthood, because in Latin America *jóvenes* are usually considered to be single young people over the age of 15.

Latin American parents have always been aware of the risks in *grupos juveniles* because of the presence of older young adults in the same group with their teenage children, especially their daughters. They usually take it upon themselves to send their daughters with trusted chaperons (older brothers, cousins, etc.) to make sure the older participants do not take advantage of them. This practice has continued among Latino/a immigrants in the U.S., and although the risks remain, parents are also aware of certain benefits for their older adolescent children:

- The *grupo juvenil* provides religious formation in a language and cultural context that is appropriate for their children, and in a religious style or spirituality that embraces the practices of Latin American popular Catholicism, so that parents can easily understand and support what is happening in the group

- As a peer-led ministry, older adolescents are mentored in leadership and in their faith by people their own age or slightly older, which often helps to reduce adolescent rebellion against the religious instruction of their parents

- The optimism, religious enthusiasm, and apostolic zeal of the immigrant *jóvenes* create an atmosphere that the teens experience as more religiously serious than what they typically see in mainstream parish youth ministries

Many parents feel that these benefits outweigh the potential risks of bringing young adults and older adolescents together in the same group. Nevertheless, it is still important for these groups to follow the safe environment guidelines of their bishops and pastors. A significant challenge lies in the fact that many of the older *jóvenes* are undocumented, so going through a background check is not an option for them. Consequently, some parishes and dioceses have begun to separate the minors and older *jóvenes* into two distinct Spanish-language ministries.

As mentioned earlier in this chapter (see page 325), the survey conducted at the National *Encuentro* in 2006 found that about 54% of the *grupos juveniles* in the U.S. are simultaneously serving both young adults and adolescents, while 39% are attending only young adults and 7% only adolescents—all mostly in Spanish. Separating the age groups typically has little impact on the religious and cultural atmosphere of the older groups, but it can dramatically change the experience for the teens. In many places, parishes struggle to find adequately prepared, bilingual, bicultural, documented adults to lead the adolescent group. With poorly trained adult leaders, the teens often lose the opportunity to grow as leaders themselves, it is difficult to maintain the same religious seriousness and contagious optimism that is found in the combined groups, and the adolescent group may end up dying, especially if it is expected to serve a mixture of immigrant and U.S.-born teens. In such circumstances, only the *grupo juvenil* survives, now as a group that serves only young adults.

These difficulties are not insurmountable, especially if bicultural adults can be recruited and trained as leaders for the Latino/a youth ministry. The effort can be worthwhile since adolescent-only groups offer certain advantages over combined groups, such as:

- Having the ability to tailor the content of the program to the developmental needs of Hispanic adolescents

- Offering the teens opportunities to participate in large-group events or activities with their peers in the English-speaking youth group(s) in the parish, or in neighboring parishes
- Providing the teens *greater* opportunities to exercise their leadership skills than they had in the combined group, if the adult leaders are well-prepared to implement a comprehensive youth ministry program
- Affording Latino/a adults the opportunity to exercise their vocation and apply their gifts in service to the adolescents in their community, which may lead some of them to consider a career in ministry, where Hispanics are severely underrepresented (see factor #10 below)

Despite these potential benefits, the challenge of maintaining adolescent-only ministries in Spanish or bilingually is reflected in the small number of Hispanic adolescent groups that were represented by the delegates at the *Encuentro*. In talking to leaders across the country, I have often heard that they tried to separate the age groups, but they gave up trying to do so because it was too divisive for the community, or because they simply could not find suitable adult leaders to work with the Latino/a adolescents.

As a result, some parishes have structured their *grupo juvenil* as an intergenerational ministry, modeled on the whole community approach to catechesis, in which certain adults are certified and responsible for the formation and protection of the adolescent participants. Ultimately, it is the responsibility of the bishop and his pastors to establish criteria for what approaches are acceptable, striving to maintain a healthy balance between the requirements of the Charter and responding adequately to the social, religious, and cultural needs of both the younger and older *jóvenes*.

10. Limitations in leadership training and ministry formation

Formation for ministry specialized in Latino/a teens has just started in the past eight years, and few programs are currently available. Because of this, the nation lacks mentors, youth ministry leaders, and youth ministry coordinators for this ministry, both from the mainstream and the Hispanic cultures. Both mainstream ministers and Hispanics—particularly those that are immigrants—usually need to acquire intercultural competence in order to minister effectively to Latino/a teens: the former with respect to the Hispanic cultures and religiosity, and the latter regarding the cultural diversity and acculturation processes among Latino/a teens in this country.

Beyond youth ministry, the adequate formation of Hispanic leaders for ministry continues to be a challenge in general. In addition, few parishes in the inner city and rural areas where most Hispanics live have the financial resources to provide stable leadership over a period of years. Consequently, they depend on volunteers who seldom have appropriate knowledge and skills to serve teenagers. Lack of an adequate effort to address these issues at the diocesan and national levels has led to a crisis in Hispanic leadership for ministry with young people in our Church.

The low educational attainment of adult Hispanic Catholics nation-wide is a significant obstacle to their ability to serve as professional lay ecclesial ministers, and it means that the leadership crisis we currently face will not go away anytime soon. *Encuentro and Mission* identified advocacy and mentoring for Latino/a education as one of its top priorities in ministry with young Hispanic Catholics,[9] yet the vast network of Catholic schools and universities has only had a small impact in addressing the educational crisis among Latino/a Catholic teens and young adults. As an example, only one of the 16 Latino/a Catholic teens interviewed for the NSYR was attending a Catholic school, and only 6% of the Hispanic Catholic teens surveyed overall were in Catholic schools.

The thousands of parish youth ministry leaders and Catholic school personnel in the U.S. are in an excellent position to lay the foundation for overcoming the Hispanic leadership crisis in the Catholic Church over the next twenty years. The urgent need for more Hispanic leaders to serve the church in the 21st century calls Catholic educators and ministers to envision, advocate for, and provide better educational and pastoral opportunities for low-income, at-risk, immigrant, and second-generation Latino/a teens, as well as those from other impoverished groups. The Cristo Rey, San Miguel, and Nativity schools provide an important example of what can be done to address these needs at the local level when dedicated Catholic educators, local businesses, and parents work together to find solutions for the academic and religious formation of low-income teens.

Envisioning the Church as a community of communities

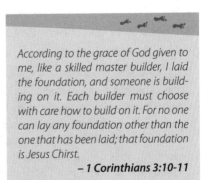

According to the grace of God given to me, like a skilled master builder, I laid the foundation, and someone is building on it. Each builder must choose with care how to build on it. For no one can lay any foundation other than the one that has been laid; that foundation is Jesus Chirst.
– *1 Corinthians 3:10-11*

When thinking about how to structure an appropriate youth ministry for a multicultural parish that seeks to be united in spirit and mission, enriched by its diversity, and able to inculturate the Gospel in the various ethnic and cultural milieus of the faithful, the model of the church as a "community of communities" stands out. This model is grounded in the experience of the first ecclesial communities as described in the New Testament, in an ecclesiology of the

Eucharist, and in the recommendations of Pope John Paul II in his Apostolic Exhortation *Ecclesia in America.*

Biblical and ecclesiological foundations

The New Testament gives ample witness to the fact that the Gospel was preached and incarnated in different ways according to the needs of each faith community. Communities of Jewish Christians were quite different from those made up of gentiles; the language spoken was different, and preaching took place in the language and according to the socioreligious and cultural traits of each community. At the same time, all of the communities were united through the same Spirit, Baptism, creed, Eucharist, and pastoral leadership. St. Paul's collection for the needs of the church in Jerusalem (see Romans 15:25 and 1 Corinthians 16:1-4) shows that the unity of the various communities even extended to financial support.

In biblical times as well as throughout the history of the Catholic Church, the strength of all these elements has united Christians into the one Body of Christ. Structures such as the diocese and the parish were created to help the Church fulfill its evangelizing mission. When the pastoral structures created to organize ministry in the Church begin to exclude large segments of the faithful they are intended to serve, as has clearly happened in the case of many parish youth ministries that revolve around a single youth group, it is time to reflect on alternative approaches that will allow parishes and dioceses to fulfill their mission.

The following quotes from Pope John Paul II and the recent gathering of Latin American bishops at Aparecida, Brazil, build on the concept of the parish as a Eucharistic communion of believers gathered from a variety of small communities, as outlined earlier in this chapter on pages 332-334, and point to the soundness of envisioning the church as a community of communities:

- "One way of renewing parishes, especially urgent for parishes in large cities, might be to consider the parish as a community of communities and movements. It seems timely therefore to form ecclesial communities and groups of a size that allows for true human relationships. This will make it possible to live communion more intensely, ensuring that it is fostered not only 'ad intra,' but also with the parish communities to which such groups belong, and with the entire diocesan and universal church. In such a human context, it will be easier to gather to hear the word of God, to reflect on the range of human problems in the light of this word, and gradually to make responsible decisions inspired by the all-embracing love of Christ." – Pope John Paul II, Apostolic Exhortation *Ecclesia in America* (1999), §41

• The renewal of the parish at the beginning of the third millennium calls for a reformulation of its structures, so that it may be a network of communities and groups, capable of linking together to make their members really become disciples and missionaries of Jesus Christ in communion...

All of these ecclesial communities and groups will bear fruit according to the measure by which the Eucharist is the center of their life and the Word of God is a light for their path and their activity in the one Church of Christ. – *Documento de Aparecida*, V Conferencia General del Episcopado Latinoamericano y del Caribe, §§172 and 180.

Value of the "community of communities" approach in ministry with young Catholics

A strong cultural trait of Hispanics is that we are a very family and community-oriented people. The fact that so few Latino/a Catholics are involved in parish youth ministry programs strongly challenges current pastoral practice, because it indicates that the barriers to participation are so high that they even overcome their cultural inclination to gather as a community.

The development of a "community of communities" model of parish ministry allows for the active participation of many more people, irrespective of their linguistic abilities or intercultural competence. In this approach, the faith of the people is allowed to flourish within the comfort zone of familiar linguistic and cultural conventions, and the small community members are continually called to recognize and serve the needs of the larger community. The cultural warmth and hospitality of the Latino people lends itself to evangelization by inviting friends, relatives, and acquaintances into participation in the small community.

Because every small community requires leadership in order to function, the creation of small communities gives many more people the opportunity to grow as leaders through a process of formation-in-action. In other words, they learn leadership skills by serving as leaders, with appropriate pastoral accompaniment from an adviser—perhaps a member of the parish pastoral staff. The use of small ecclesial communities in youth ministry can be an effective way to teach young Catholics how to practice peer ministry in a community, to nurture the Christian vocation to service, and to foster vocations to the priesthood, religious life, and lay ministry. For all of these reasons, the *National Pastoral Plan for Hispanic Ministry* privileges ministry in small communities as an effective way to promote unity in the church while incarnating the Gospel in the diverse sociocultural contexts of a multicultural parish (§§37 and 44-47).

When young Catholics gather together to pray, to study the faith, and to discern their personal and communal response to Christ's invitation to become disciples, they have a greater opportunity to support, encourage, and even hold one another accountable to the demands of the Gospel. The small community can overcome the isolation and alienation felt by many Latino/a teens in ways that a large parish youth group for everyone simply cannot. This support and encouragement is especially important in the Hispanic community, since it faces serious challenges in overcoming substance abuse, violence, discrimination, and poverty. The mutual encouragement and accountability found in small communities can be the first step toward empowerment for the evangelization of culture and the transformation of the social environment to which each baptized person is called.

Need for a paradigm shift

Implementing youth ministry within the framework of a parish that sees itself as a community of communities can be an effective way to promote ecclesial unity while serving teens of various languages, cultures, and situations, according to their particular needs. However, this approach entails more than merely creating separate groups; it is necessary to undertake a paradigm shift in the way the youth ministry team thinks about its work, and even the nature of the parish as a whole. This paradigm shift can be achieved in three steps as follows:

1. Recognize the existence of the small communities already present in the parish, and lead them to embrace the vision of their work as members of a community of communities. All parishes are composed of a variety of small and not-so-small faith communities that operate relatively independently of one another, even though most of the participants speak the same language. The Saturday Mass community, the ten o'clock Sunday Mass community, the community of catechists, the choir(s), the women's group, the pastoral council, the charismatic prayer group, and many others—these can all be seen as small communities in their own right. Individual communities have a great deal of freedom to set their own agenda, develop their own spirituality, and do the ministry they feel called to do.

A parish that sees itself as a community of communities develops structures of accountability to coordinate, accompany, and create a spirit of communion among its various ministry groups and small communities. These structures ensure that each small community understands its role in accomplishing the mission of the parish and create a sense of partnership among them. This is what the Hispanic ministry documents mean when they speak of *pastoral de conjunto,* or "communion in mission."

At first it may seem that creating mostly homogeneous small communities is counterproductive for building the unity of multicultural parishes. However, the process of fostering unity among the various communities provides many fruits: the leaders engage in joint pastoral action; a spirit of mutual support animates the parish; intercultural reflections and cross-cultural prayers are more meaningful; members of the small communities participate in whole parish activities; and special multicultural liturgies are valued and fully lived. The parish then becomes a more inclusive and welcoming place for people of every race, culture, language, and social class.

Perhaps the greatest challenge lies in convincing the existing small communities and movements that accountability to the parish pastoral plan and communion with other communities are vital. Essentially, we are asking them to recognize that they form church with one another. In this vision of parish, each community has a responsibility to support the wellbeing and mission of the others. For example, the St. Vincent de Paul society will work with the youth group in a service project; the catechists will work together with liturgical ministers to engage young people in the liturgy; and all communities will work together with a spirit of mutual service for the parish festival, caring for the poor, and special celebrations such as the Easter vigil.

Given the fact that most parishes have already established a multitude of small groups or communities in order to fulfill their pastoral mission, it should not be too much of a stretch to envision structuring youth ministry with a variety of groups, programs, and activities designed to meet the spiritual, cultural, social, emotional, and intellectual needs of the various segments of the parish's adolescent population. The key in this approach is to ensure that each small community sees itself as an integral part of the larger parish and its mission. This is effectively communicated when the small communities are brought together for large-group events and activities, in which each small community is responsible to prepare some element of the event as a service to the others.

2. Acknowledge the right of each young Catholic to find a group of peers in their parish with whom they can grow in faith and exercise their evangelizing mission. Participation in church cannot be forced upon a person, and teens quickly decide whether they will participate depending on how welcome, comfortable, and valued they feel. The same can be said about adults. For example, the cultural and societal tensions experienced by most first- and many second-generation Latino/a immigrants often lead them to seek spiritual and social support in a faith community. How do they decide what parish to attend?

Although mobility and time constraints are often deciding factors for immigrant families, if given a choice they will seek: a community in which they can express themselves in the language of their personal prayer life; a parish that is responsive to their worldview, their values system, and their ways of praying and of experiencing God; a priest that understands what they experience at home and offers helpful suggestions for handling their suffering, conflicts, and problems. All of these elements are vital when living the faith in community, so there is a tendency for adults to join a parish that offers an affinity to their personal way of being.

In a similar way, the formation of multiple small communities for youth ministry in multicultural parishes allows first- and second-generation immigrant teens to find the environment in which they can relate to God, learn about their faith, pray, and support each other. If this is important for the adults, it is even more relevant for adolescents.

Another important factor to consider is the geographical situation and the relatively limited mobility of many Latino/a teenagers and their parents. Because of this, large inner city and rural parishes may need to adjust the organization of the small communities away from the parish campus, keeping in mind that the parish includes all of its territory, not only the terrain where the buildings are located.

When teens can gather in small Christian communities in homes, schools, and other sites throughout the parish, many obstacles to participation are removed, and it becomes easier for them to be leaven for the Reign of God in the world. I believe this is what was envisioned by the *General Directory for Catechesis* (1997) when it stated that the parish "must continue to be the prime mover and pre-eminent place for catechesis, while recognizing that in certain occasions, it cannot be the center of gravity for all of the ecclesial functions of catechesis and must integrate itself into other institutions." (§257)

3. Focus on leadership formation, pastoral accompaniment, and coordination. The pastor of a parish organized as a community of communities seldom suffers from pastoral nearsightedness because the small community leaders are in constant communication with him, making him aware of the needs of the people in every sector of the parish. In a similar way, youth ministry coordinators can multiply their impact in the life of parish teens by offering pastoral accompaniment, direction, and sharing opportunities to the adult leaders coordinating each small group. Working closely with the small community leaders, the parish youth minister and the pastor can effectively assure that the needs of the different subgroups of young people will be addressed.

The youth minister in a multicultural parish organized as a community of communities has three main tasks with respect to serving the Latino young people:

- Identify and recruit Hispanic leaders, preferably but not exclusively bilingual and bicultural, and secure appropriate leadership training for them in their ministry with Latino/a adolescents in small communities
- Support the small community leaders with the help of a core group of Latino/a youth, young adults, and parents who function as a planning and advisory committee

- Work with the small community leaders to ensure that they are responding to the needs of their teens in a way that reflects the pastoral vision of the parish and the goals of youth ministry, and to plan and coordinate large group activities, using simultaneous translation if needed

Youth ministers should be aware of two challenges that may arise when small community leaders do not have adequate formation for their roles. First of all, some novice leaders have a tendency to form dictatorships, taking control of the small community, imposing their own agenda, and refusing to identify and promote other leaders. This style of leadership can be a death knell for the community, so the youth minister should supervise the leaders and ensure that they receive training on how to create and maintain structures for shared leadership and responsibility in the community.

Secondly, as the experience of solidarity and mutual support in the community grows, some adolescents may share intimate details of their personal lives that require pastoral counseling beyond the leader's ability to handle in the group. Alternatively, there may be theological questions or behavioral issues that go beyond the leader's competence to address. Novice leaders often try to handle these situations on their own in inappropriate ways, so it is the responsibility of the youth minister to communicate with them about issues that arise in the course of their community meetings and provide mentoring on how to handle difficult situations or questions. In particularly challenging moments, the youth minister or parish pastor should step in to facilitate a group process or address an issue one-on-one with a teen.

So what would youth ministry in a multicultural parish united by the "community of communities" approach look like? It would definitely be an "integrated" youth ministry because teens of every background would find a comfortable place to grow in faith and service to one another and the larger community, and they would all be reflected in the leadership structures. Some other notable characteristics would be:

- Respect for the dignity, leadership, and gifts of each community or group
- A call to mutual accountability and participation in the life of the community of communities (*pastoral de conjunto*)
- Solidarity with the weak, the poor, and the marginal communities, and mutual service among all communities
- A commitment to reconciliation and conflict resolution to overcome divisions that may arise within and between small communities
- An evangelizing praxis of invitation to, and multiplication of, small communities with a preferential option for outreach to the poor, the marginalized, and the alienated Catholic teens in the parish

- Unity of vision and direction, amid a diversity of expressions—and a humble respect for the unfamiliar ways of other groups
- Most importantly, becoming a Eucharistic community of communities, such that the parish celebration of the Eucharist truly becomes the greatest longing, the sign of unity, the source and summit of the Christian life for all the small communities that make up the parish youth ministry

The bottom line is that the "community of communities" approach, if done well, creates spaces for diverse groups to participate in the life of the parish by overcoming the cultural and socioeconomic differences that usually lead to alienation and separation. From the perspective of Hispanic ministry, this is the pastoral framework for ministry in multicultural parishes that offers the greatest promise to empower Latino/a Catholic teens in the U.S. to develop and offer their gifts for the service of the Catholic Church in the coming century and beyond.

Areas for further research

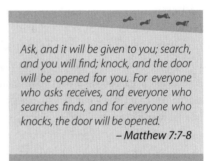

The NSYR has provided the Catholic Church with a wealth of information regarding the faith development, religious formation, and pastoral care of young Latino/a Catholics. However, as any good research does, it has also raised a lot of questions that merit investigation. What stands out is that

Ask, and it will be given to you; search, and you will find; knock, and the door will be opened for you. For everyone who asks receives, and everyone who searches finds, and for everyone who knocks, the door will be opened.
– Matthew 7:7-8

the current successes and challenges of ministry with Hispanic teens in youth ministry and *pastoral juvenil* settings are still not sufficiently understood. For example:

- Currently there is not enough information available to estimate the number of groups operating in Spanish with Catholic adolescents and young adults, either together or separately. Nor has a really good assessment of how many adolescents are being reached in these groups been done. As a result, it is difficult to gauge their success or advocate for the development of resources to serve them.

- Both waves of the NSYR showed that as young Hispanic Catholics get older, they become slightly more involved in church groups. However, the participation rate remains low, and there was not enough data to indicate what type of groups they were participating in: high school youth ministry, religious education and/or sacramental preparation, *pastoral juvenil,* campus ministry, or young adult ministry.

- Among the Hispanic Catholic teens selected for personal interviews in the NSYR, only two were involved in youth ministry programs—and both were preparing for Confirmation, which is usually considered religious education, not a "youth group" or "*grupo juvenil.*" As a result, the interviews offered no insight into the experience of Hispanic teens in the more typical youth ministry and *pastoral juvenil* settings.

- Stories continue to circulate about parishes that are doing exemplary work with their adolescent Hispanic members, but there is very little documentation of what they are doing and why it is working in their particular setting, nor has there been an objective assessment of how effective they have been in addressing the full spectrum of pastoral needs among the Hispanic teens in their communities.

- Diocesan leaders of *pastoral juvenil* are aware that a variety of apostolic movements are actively engaged in the evangelization and catechesis of Latino/a teens and young adults, but these organizations tend to work in isolation from one another and from the diocesan offices. This makes it difficult to determine how many teens they are reaching, what methods they are using, or what additional resources they need to improve their ministry.

- Recent studies have made a case that as many as half of Latino/a Catholic adults in the U.S. are charismatic,[10] yet only 16% of the Hispanic Catholic parents surveyed in the NSYR identified themselves as charismatic or Pentecostal (see Table 3.6 on page 96). Furthermore, there were no clear indications of a charismatic identity in any of the Hispanic Catholics interviewed in either wave. It seems likely that the presence or absence of a charismatic spirituality in youth ministry and *pastoral juvenil* settings plays a role in attracting or alienating Latino/a Catholic teens, but it is not known to what extent this is a factor.

Given these gaps in our understanding of the landscape for ministry with Latino/a Catholic teens and young adults in the U.S., the following research strategies would go a long way toward providing youth ministry professionals at every level with the information and tools they need to be more effective in their ministries, and for publishers to create better resources to help them in their efforts:

1. Conduct a survey among diocesan directors of Hispanic Ministry and of Youth and Young Adult Ministry, as well as national leaders of apostolic movements that serve Hispanic youth and young adults, to identify the number and proportion of parishes with significant Hispanic populations that are actively serving Hispanic youth, and the settings in which they do so. For example: (a) together with immigrant young adults in Spanish; (b) integrated in mainstream youth ministry;

(c) in multicultural ministry settings; (d) in groups of mostly or only Hispanic teens, whether in English, Spanish, or bilingually; (e) in occasional retreats or workshops, in English, Spanish, or bilingually.

2. Identify the pastoral models that are successful in ministry with Hispanic youth and young adults in different settings (i.e. urban multicultural, suburban, rural, generational mix, proportion of Hispanics in the parish, etc.).

3. Conduct focus groups around the country with Latino parents of preadolescent and adolescent children, and with youth ministers and young adult leaders ministering with Latino/a teens, in order to identify specific challenges for a successful ministry and brainstorm appropriate responses.

4. Conduct interviews of a broad cross-section of Hispanic Catholic teens in the focus group cities to learn more about their experiences of cultural and religious differences with their Catholic peers, with a particular focus on the influence of the charismatic renewal, prayer groups, and Spirit-centered spirituality in their lives.

5. Identify the pastoral resources published with a focus on ministry with Latino/a teens or for multicultural adolescent ministry; conduct a critical analysis of their purpose and quality, and publish an annotated bibliography.

6. Conduct in-depth community studies of parishes with a variety of demographic characteristics: (a) communities that have a long history and tradition of serving Hispanics; (b) communities in transition from being mostly mainstream to bicultural; (c) communities whose population has recently transitioned to being mostly immigrant Latino/as; and (d) long-established Hispanic communities that are dealing with a wave of new Latino/a immigrants.

Although these strategies are described from the point of view of a national research project, local faith communities can and should take up some of these actions as a way to develop more responsive pastoral programs and activities for their adolescent members. Such community studies should provide a demographic portrait of the community, an analysis of the pastoral needs of the teens and the concerns of their parents, and a description of the models, successes, challenges, and limitations of current pastoral efforts. Research methods might include analysis of census data, other public records, and summaries of parish membership lists, as well as focus group meetings with the pastoral staff, participating adolescents, non-participating Catholic adolescents, parents of teens that are involved, parents of teens that are not involved, and conversations with school officials, local law enforcement officers, public health officials, and social workers regarding the well-being of the Hispanic teens in the area.

Summary

Looking back on my experience as an immigrant Latina raising three children in the United States, I thank God for the small community of Hispanics from various countries who helped me transmit my faith to them. That community reinforced our Hispanic communitarian values and fostered in them a sincere respect for

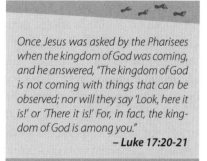

Once Jesus was asked by the Pharisees when the kingdom of God was coming, and he answered, "The kingdom of God is not coming with things that can be observed; nor will they say 'Look, here it is!' or 'There it is!' For, in fact, the kingdom of God is among you."
– Luke 17:20-21

their elders, particularly in their teenage years when they were challenged by the different lifestyle of most of their peers. From the time they were little, they learned to pray in community and participated in theological reflections with their adopted "grandma" and "uncles." These were the people who took the place of my husband as mentors in the faith, because illness prevented him from assuming responsibility for their education.

Forming an extended family with people of the same culture and faith is invaluable for immigrants. The values my community helped to instill in my children are the same ones that other Latino parents seek for their adolescent children when they allow them to be part of a group with Latino/a *jóvenes*—if *pastoral juvenil* is available in their parish. In many cases it is their only realistic option, even if it may not be their ideal, because so many parishes do not provide an appropriate youth ministry for the majority of their Latino/a teens.

Small ecclesial communities are already quite common among the Hispanic people above and beyond the *grupos juveniles* already mentioned. Some are charismatic prayer groups or apostolic movements; others center on sharing faith amid the joys and challenges of daily life; still others are dedicated to social action or service in the parish, such as the communities of catechists and liturgical ministers. However, as the NSYR data show, many of the teenage children of the religiously committed parents in these communities have not found a place for themselves in our Church.

In my many years as a lay ecclesial minister and national speaker, if I had to identify the single cause for the greatest pain, frustration, discouragement, and even anger and bitterness among Latino parents, it is seeing their teenage children going astray in their human development and spiritual formation. This experience shatters the hopes and dreams they or their own parents had when they came to this country seeking a better life for their family. Although serious and ample inroads have been made in catechesis for Hispanic children since 1979 when I first arrived in the United States, the NSYR only confirms the painful experience of pastoral abandonment that awaits most Hispanic teens in our Church.

In the parish *grupos juveniles* that serve youth and young adults together, many Latino/a adolescents have been able to mature in their faith, and today may be found among the young adult leaders in this peer-led ministry. Nevertheless, it can be challenging to develop a comprehensive ministry for adolescents in this pastoral model, and it is clearly not a solution for the majority of young Latino/a Catholics born in the U.S.

At the same time, mainstream youth ministry programs have also encountered serious challenges in their efforts to reach Latino/a teens. Low-income multiracial parishes in the inner city are seldom able to hire an experienced youth minister, so their programs flourish or fail according to the gifts and available time of the volunteer leaders. Some wealthy parishes and rural communities have developed ministries to meet the sacramental needs of immigrants working in domestic and janitorial services, fast-food, restaurants, or the lower strata in blue-collar occupations, but the children of immigrant workers tend to be abandoned once they reach adolescence. In theory they are welcome to join the mainstream teens in the parish's youth ministry program, but the socioeconomic distance between the two groups is usually too great for them to overcome. Ethnically diverse middle class parishes should have the easiest task, but cultural and religious differences by generation, and the widespread lack of Latino/a role models in youth ministry settings, may call for a missionary approach to reach those who do not readily fit in with their peers of other ethnic backgrounds.

In all of these cases, leadership formation is of the utmost importance. One of the key efforts that our Church needs to undertake is identifying vocations to youth ministry among Hispanic adults and young adults, and offering them training in the language that they prefer. Mainstream youth ministers, both paid and volunteer, also need appropriate training for ministry with teens of a culture different from their own. Finally, pastors need to become aware of the diverse needs of young Latino/a Catholics, their history of pastoral neglect in our Church, and the opportunity to reach many more teens by structuring youth ministry as a community of communities.

The NSYR challenges our Church once again to develop appropriate responses to the pastoral needs of *all* the young Hispanics in our parishes. The prophetic voices of the Latino/a young adults gathered at the *Encuentro* clamored for more services and resources directed to them and their adolescent peers. They also clearly stated their profound commitment to build unity with other cultures, to carry out meaningful evangelization and missionary outreach efforts in their communities, and to foster Latino leadership... In one way or another, they identified all ten of the factors mentioned above, either in their analysis of the pastoral reality or in their suggested responses for ministry with Latino/a adolescents.

The participation of national and diocesan leaders from mainstream youth and young adult ministry in the *Encuentro,* and the creation of a partnership between La Red and several other national organizations to implement the conclusions of the *Encuentro,* are also signs of hope for the future. I am confident that when Hispanic ministers, young adult leaders, and parents join forces with pastors, parish staffs, and mainstream youth ministry leaders, our Church can significantly improve the pastoral care and accompaniment of Latino/a teens in just ten years. To do this, it is vital to address the ten factors mentioned in this chapter intentionally and assertively at the national, diocesan, and parish levels.

Making the paradigm shift to see the parish and youth ministry as a community of communities may be at the core of the solution. While this vision has two main challenges—identifying and training leaders for the small communities, and developing the skills to coordinate the parish and/ or youth ministry as a community of communities—the potential rewards for the vitality of the Catholic Church and the wellbeing of the Hispanic people in the United States are worth of the effort.

Whatever steps are taken, our Catholic Church needs to assume "responsibility" for its young Latino population. It is urgent that we acquire the vision and the "ability to respond" as soon as possible. We must not squander the hope and trust of the Latino/a young adult leaders gathered at the national *Encuentro,* who together composed a Creed that included the following statements:[11]

- We believe that we can build the Reign of God, without cultural boundaries, bearing witness that God lives among Hispanic young people, nurturing and forming us in our faith, and overcoming the obstacles that we encounter in life.

- We believe in leading a life of communion and solidarity, in exercising a prophetic leadership grounded in prayer and the sacraments, and in taking risks and maintaining a serious commitment to the evangelization of young people by young people.

- We believe in a profound commitment to the community of the young, and that we can foster life in community and love for people of other races and communities, in solidarity with the most disadvantaged and the recently arrived immigrants, so that they may fully develop themselves through academic and spiritual formation.

- We believe that, with the power of prayer, the sacraments, and a missionary spirit, we can develop a new generation of prophetic and active leaders, so that we may highlight the true gospel values through our culture, comprehensive formation, and openness to other cultures.

- We believe that Hispanic young people are capable of developing a comprehensive, bilingual, and united *pastoral juvenil,* of creating new forms of evangelization, and of finding new ways to face the challenges of life in general.
- We believe that our Hispanic culture is a gift to our Church, that we are capable of breaking down language barriers to relate with other cultural groups without forgetting our roots, and that we can be recognized as equals in the Church and as a source of hope for the entire nation.

Of the young adult delegates at the national *Encuentro,* nearly half (49%) said that they began participating in *pastoral juvenil* as teenagers, and almost half of those (44%) had been active for five years or more. The simple fact that 2,000 volunteer Latino/a young adult leaders could be convened at the national level to discuss their ministry—and that they could articulate their faith in God, their commitment to the Church, their passion for the Gospel, and their hope for the future with such maturity—is a testament to what is possible when the Catholic Church provides consistent pastoral care and accompaniment to its young Hispanic members over time. Our task today is to empower these young leaders to multiply their ministry and extend it to reach the adolescent Latino/a Catholics who have not yet found a suitable space in which to develop and exercise their baptismal call in our Church and in the world.

Questions for reflection

1. How well are we meeting the spiritual, intellectual, moral, and social needs of *all* of the Catholic teens and their families in our [parish, diocese, city, region, etc.]?
2. What needs stand out as being urgent or pressing issues for the life of the community and the wellbeing of its adolescent members?
3. What more could we do with the resources available to us to effectively address the urgent pastoral needs of Latino/a Catholic adolescents in our [parish, diocese, city, region, etc.]?
4. How intentional are we about identifying Latino/a leaders with abilities to minister to adolescents, and offering them appropriate training in their preferred language?
5. How effectively are we fostering small faith communities of young people in order to provide more options for the diverse segments of young Catholics in the parish?
6. How well integrated is youth leadership development and youth evangelization into all youth programs and activities in our [parish, diocese, city, region, etc.]?

7. To what degree are Latino parents considered in needs assessments and planning for youth ministry in our [parish, diocese, city, region, etc.]?

8. To what degree is our [parish, diocese, city, region, etc.] youth ministry comprehensive and attentive to Latino families?

9. How frequent and how deep is the formation for intercultural communication and cultural competence that we offer youth ministry leaders in our area?

Appendix:

Compound Variable Definitions

Throughout this book, the NSYR survey data has been analyzed by making comparisons between Catholic and Protestant teens, Hispanic and white teens, and a wide variety of other variables or combinations of variables. The purpose of making these comparisons is to highlight the correlations between differences in background and differences in religious beliefs and practices, church involvement, family life, educational goals, moral behaviors, and social or political activities.

In most cases, the independent variables utilized in the tables correspond directly to one of the questions asked in the NSYR survey or one of the variables defined by the NSYR researchers at the University of North Carolina at Chapel Hill. However, several variables were created to simplify the work of this book by combining information from several of the questions in the survey. The *Stata*™ syntax for the variable definitions is included at the end of each section so that these variables may be used by other NSYR researchers to make their own analyses comparable to what is reported in this book.

One of the challenges in creating these variables was the fact that in order to have meaningful comparisons, there should be at least 30 survey respondents in each category for each of the groups being compared. Since there were only 94 weighted Hispanic Protestant respondents in the survey, this means that ideally none of the variables created for this research should have more than three possible responses. An exception was made for the religious type variables in order to follow the pattern established by Christian Smith and Melinda Lundquist Denton in *Soul Searching*.

Economic status

A family's economic status has a direct effect on the opportunities available to its adolescent members in school, at church, in their neighborhoods, and at home. While household income is a common measure of economic status, it is only part of the picture. The intention in creating this variable was to use some of the other family economic indicators in the NSYR survey to obtain a broader perspective on the living situation of the teens.

A significant challenge in creating these categories was the fact that the largest numbers of the Hispanic and white families were at opposite ends of the economic spectrum from one another. This meant that the three economic status categories had to be skewed toward the lower end of the economic spectrum in the United States in order to have sufficient numbers of Hispanic teens in the higher categories to make meaningful comparisons between the Hispanic and white teens within the Catholic and Protestant religious traditions.

As a result, many of the families in the "middle" economic status category would probably be considered lower middle class by most people in the United States, and some families in the "high" category would be considered middle class by most standards. With that in mind, the economic status categories were defined as follows:

- **Low:** (Annual household income is $20K or less) OR (household income is $20K to $30K AND family does not own their home AND family does not have any savings) OR (household income was not reported AND (family has a lot of debt OR (family is just breaking even AND family does not own their home))).

- **Middle:** (Annual household income is $30K to $50K) OR (household income is $20K to $30K AND (family owns their home OR family has some savings)) OR (household income is $50K to $60K AND family does not own their home AND family does not have any savings) OR (household income was not reported AND family has some savings).

- **High:** (Annual household income is more than $60K) OR (household income is $50K to $60K AND (family owns their home OR family has some savings)) OR (family has a lot of savings and assets, irrespective of annual income).

- **Unknown:** All others.

```
generate econstat=555
replace  econstat=1 if  pincome<3  |  (pincome==3 & pown>1 &
    pdebt<3) | (pincome>12 & (pdebt==1 | (pdebt==2 & (pown==2
    | pown==3))))
replace econstat=2 if pincome==4 | pincome==5 | (pincome==3 &
    (pown==1 | pdebt==3)) | (pincome==6 & (pown==2 | pown==3)
    & pdebt<3) | (pincome>12 & pdebt==3)
replace econstat=3 if (pincome>6 & pincome<12) | (pincome==6 &
    (pown==1 | pdebt==3)) | pdebt==4
label def econstat 1 Low 2 Middle 3 High 555 Unknown
label variable econstat "Family economic status"
```

Teen's religious type

As mentioned in Chapter 2, the definitions of the teen religious types used in this book are slightly different from those used by Christian Smith and Melinda Lundquist Denton in *Soul Searching*. The purpose of this change was to develop definitions that did not emphasize so heavily the types of personal religious practices that have historically been associated with Protestant forms of religious devotion by adding some indicators of Catholic religious devotion. It should also be noted that "committed" and "engaged" were combined into the "high religious commitment" category in Table 5.4, and "sporadic" and "disengaged" were combined into the "low religious commitment" category. The categories were defined as follows:

- **Committed:** (Attends church services at least once a week) AND (faith is extremely or very important in their daily life) AND (feels extremely or very close to God) AND ((prays alone at least a few times a week) OR (in the last year has: prayed with parents other than at meals or church AND ((gone to Confession or a Reconciliation liturgy) OR (prayed the rosary, a novena, or to a special saint) OR (participated in a pilgrimage, procession, or way of the cross) OR (celebrates the Virgin of Guadalupe or another national devotion to Mary))) OR (reads the Scriptures alone at least once a week)) AND (family talks about religious or spiritual things at least once a week) AND (considers him/herself to be part of a particular religion, denomination, or church)

- **Engaged:** (Attends church at least 2 to 3 times a month) AND (faith is at least "somewhat" or "not very" important in shaping daily life) AND (teen does not qualify as "committed" above)

- **Sporadic:** ((Attends church "many times a year" or less, but at least "a few times a year") OR (does not know or refused to answer how often goes to church)) AND (faith is less than "very important" in daily life) AND (teen does not qualify as "disengaged" below)

- **Disengaged:** ((Never attends church) AND (faith is not "very important" or "extremely important" in daily life) AND ((feels "somewhat close" or less to God) OR (doesn't know or refused to answer how close they feel to God)) AND (not in a religious youth group, or doesn't know/refused to answer if in a youth group) AND (prays alone twice a month or less, or doesn't know/refused to answer how often prays alone) AND (reads the Scriptures twice a month or less, or doesn't know/refused to answer how often reads the Scriptures) AND (family talks about religious or spiritual things "a few times a month" or less)) OR ((doesn't consider him/herself to be part of a particular religion, denomination, or church) AND (attends church less than once a month) AND (faith is "somewhat important" or less in daily life) AND (reads the Scriptures twice a month or less) AND (is not in a religious youth group) AND (prays alone twice a month or less) AND (feels "somewhat close" or less to God))

- **Mixed:** All others.

```
generate reltype=555
replace reltype=2 if (attend==4 | attend==5 | attend==6) & (faith1==1
   | faith1==2 | faith1==3 | faith1==4)
replace reltype=1 if (attend>=5 & attend<=6) & (faith1==1 | faith1==2)
   & (godclose==5 | godclose==6) & ((prayalon>=5 & praya-
   lon<=7) | (praypar==1 & (confess==1 | rosary==1 | pilgrim==1
   | celvirg==1)) | (readbibl>=4 & readbibl<=7)) & (talkrel>=1 &
   talkrel<=3) & atheist==999
replace reltype=3 if (attend==1 | attend==2 | attend==3 | at-
   tend==777 | attend==888) & faith1>2
replace reltype=4 if (attend==0 & faith1>2 & (godclose<5 | god-
   close==777 | godclose==888 | godclose==999) & (ythgrp2==0 |
   ythgrp2==777 | ythgrp2==888) & (prayalon<4 | prayalon==777 |
   prayalon==888) & (readbibl<4 | readbibl==777 | readbibl==888)
   & talkrel>=4) | (atheist<999 & attend<3 & faith1>2 & readbibl<4
   & ythgrp2!=1 & prayalon<4 & godclose<5)
label def reltype 1 Committed 2 Engaged 3 Sporadic 4 Disengaged 555
   Mixed
label variable reltype "Teen's religious type"
```

Responding parent's religious type

Since the parents were not asked the same questions as their children, it was not possible to use exactly the same religious type definitions as were used for the teens. Thus, the parent religious types were defined as follows:

- **Committed:** (Attends church services at least once a week) AND (faith is extremely or very important in their daily life) AND ((in the last year has prayed with teen other than at meals) OR (family regularly prays together at meal times)) AND (family talks about religious or spiritual things at least once a week) AND (has encouraged teen to participate in a religious youth group "a lot") AND (prays for teen every day)

- **Engaged:** (Attends church at least 2 to 3 times a month) AND (faith is at least "somewhat" or "not very" important in shaping daily life) AND (has encouraged teen to participate in a religious youth group at least "a little") AND ((in the last year has prayed with teen other than at meal times) OR (family regularly prays together at meal times) OR (prays for teen at least a few times a week)) AND (parent does not qualify as "committed" above)

- **Sporadic:** ((Attends church "many times a year" or less, but at least "a few times a year") OR (does not know or refused to answer how often goes to church)) AND (faith is less than "very important" in daily life) AND (parent does not qualify as "disengaged" below)

- **Disengaged:** (Attends church "a few times a year" or less) AND (faith is not "very important" or "extremely important" in daily life) AND (has never encouraged teen to participate in a religious youth group, or doesn't know/refused to answer how often encourages teen to participate) AND (family talks about religious or spiritual things less than once a week, or doesn't know/refused to answer how often family talks about religious or spiritual things)

- **Mixed:** All others.

```
generate preltype=555
replace preltype=2 if (pattend==1 | pattend==2 | pattend==3) & (pim-
   prel>=1 & pimprel<=4) & (prlygask>=1 & prlygask<=3) & (pray-
   par==1 | grace==1 | prlpray==1 | prlpray==2)
replace preltype=1 if (pattend>=1 & pattend<=2) & (pimprel==1 | pim-
   prel==2) & (praypar==1 | grace==1) & (talkrel>=1 & talkrel<=3)
   & prlygask==1 & prlpray==1
replace preltype=3 if (pattend==6 | pattend==5 | pattend==4 | pat-
   tend==777 | pattend==888) & pimprel>2
replace preltype=4 if (pattend==7 | pattend==6) & pimprel>2 &
   prlygask>3 & talkrel>=4
label def preltype 1 Committed 2 Engaged 3 Sporadic 4 Disengaged 555
   Mixed
label variable preltype "Responding parent's religious type"
```

Teen's religious type in Wave 2

Because so few of the older respondents in Wave 2 were members of a religious youth group, and some of the Catholic questions from Wave 1 were not repeated in Wave 2, it was necessary to make some minor changes in the religious type definitions for the second wave. As a result, the Wave 2 religious types were defined as follows:

- **Committed:** (Attends church services at least once a week) AND (faith is extremely or very important in their daily life) AND (feels extremely or very close to God) AND ((prays alone at least a few times a week) OR (in the last year has prayed with parents other than at meals or church) OR (reads the Scriptures alone at least once a week)) AND ((family talks about religious or spiritual things at least once a week) OR (talks with close friends about religious beliefs or experiences)) AND (considers him/herself to be part of a particular religion, denomination, or church)

- **Engaged:** (Attends church at least 2 to 3 times a month) AND (faith is at least "somewhat" or "not very" important in shaping daily life) AND (does not qualify as "committed" above)

- **Sporadic:** ((Attends church "many times a year" or less, but at least "a few times a year") OR (does not know or refused to answer how often goes to church)) AND (faith is less than "very important" in daily life) AND (does not qualify as "disengaged" below)

- **Disengaged:** ((Never attends church) AND (faith is not "very important" or "extremely important" in daily life) AND ((feels "somewhat close" or less to God) OR (doesn't know, refused to answer, or was not asked how close they feel to God)) AND (not in a religious youth group, or doesn't know/refused to answer if in a youth group) AND (prays alone twice a month or less, or doesn't know/refused to answer how often prays alone) AND (reads the Scriptures twice a month or less, or doesn't know/refused to answer how often reads the Scriptures) AND (family talks about religious or spiritual things "a few times a month" or less)) OR ((doesn't consider him/herself to be part of a particular religion, denomination, or church) AND (attends church less than once a month) AND (faith is "somewhat important" or less in daily life) AND (reads the Scriptures twice a month or less) AND (is not in a religious youth group) AND (prays alone twice a month or less) AND (feels "somewhat close" or less to God))

- **Mixed:** All others.

```
generate reltype_w2=555
replace reltype_w2=2 if (attend_w2==4 | attend_w2==5 | attend_
   w2==6) & (faith1_w2==1 | faith1_w2==2 | faith1_w2==3 |
   faith1_w2==4)
replace reltype_w2=1 if (attend_w2>=5 & attend_w2<=6) & (faith1_
   w2==1 | faith1_w2==2) & (godclose_w2==5 | godclose_w2==6)
   & ((prayalon_w2>=5 & prayalon_w2<=7) | praypar_w2==1
   | (readbibl_w2>=4 & readbibl_w2<=7)) & ((talkrel_w2>=1 &
   talkrel_w2<=3) | frndtlkrel_w2>0 | sfrndtlkrel_w2>0) & atheist_
   w2==999
replace reltype_w2=3 if (attend_w2==1 | attend_w2==2 | attend_
   w2==3 | attend_w2==777 | attend_w2==888) & faith1_w2>2
replace reltype_w2=4 if (attend_w2==0 & faith1_w2>2 & (god-
   close_w2<5 | godclose_w2==777 | godclose_w2==888 | god-
   close_w2==999) & (ythgrp2_w2==0 | ythgrp2_w2==777 |
   ythgrp2_w2==888) & (prayalon_w2<4 | prayalon_w2==777 |
   prayalon_w2==888) & (readbibl_w2<4 | readbibl_w2==777 |
   readbibl_w2==888) & talkrel_w2>=4) | (atheist_w2<999 & at-
   tend_w2<3 & faith1_w2>2 & readbibl_w2<4 & ythgrp2_w2!=1 &
   prayalon_w2<4 & godclose_w2<5)
```

```
label def reltype_w2 1 Committed 2 Engaged 3 Sporadic 4 Disengaged
    555 Mixed
label variable reltype_w2 "Teen's religious type - Wave 2"
```

Teen's generation since family's arrival in the United States

Sociologists recognize that there are important differences from one generation to the next from the time of a family's arrival in the United States. For Hispanic families, it is important to consider these generational differences, so a variable was created to make these comparisons, based on responses from the teen and parent surveys in Wave 1. The generations were defined as follows:

- **First generation:** (Teen was not born in the United States)
- **Second generation:** (Teen was born in the United States) AND ((responding parent was not born in the United States) OR (responding parent's spouse was not born in the United States))
- **Third generation or greater:** (Teen was born in the United States) AND (responding parent was born in the United States) AND ((responding parent's spouse was born in the United States) OR (responding parent has no spouse))
- **Unknown:** All others.

```
generate generation=555
replace generation=1 if native==0
replace generation=2 if native==1 & (pnative==0 | pspnativ==0)
replace generation=3 if native==1 & pnative==1 & pspnativ>0
label def generation 1 First 2 Second 3 Third 555 Unknown
label variable generation "Teen's generation since family's arrival in the
    U.S."
```

Teen's dominant language

Dominant language is often used by sociologists and psychologists as a marker of cultural assimilation for Hispanics in the United States. The NSYR teen survey provided a rich set of four questions relating to the teen's use of the Spanish and English languages. This information was combined into a single variable for comparisons between English-dominant and Spanish-dominant Hispanic teens, as follows:

- **Spanish-dominant:** (Teen responded to the survey in Spanish) OR ((teen was not born in the United States) AND (reads and speaks Spanish and English equally)) OR (speaks mostly or only Spanish at home) OR (speaks mostly or only Spanish with friends) OR (thinks mostly or only in Spanish)
- **English-dominant:** All others.

```
generate domlang=1
replace domlang=2 if rlpy==2 | (native==0 & lang1==5) | lang2==3 |
    lang2==4 | lang3==3 | lang3==4 | lang4==3 | lang4==4
label def domlang 1 English 2 Spanish
label variable domlang "Teen's dominant language"
```

Responding parent's dominant language

There were not as many questions regarding the responding parent's use of the Spanish and English languages in the survey, so the parent's dominant language was defined as follows:

- **Spanish-dominant:** (Parent responded to the survey in Spanish) OR (((parent is Hispanic) OR (teen is Hispanic)) AND (English is not the primary language spoken at home))

- **Other dominant language:** (Parent responded to the survey in English) AND (English is not the primary language spoken at home) AND (parent is not Spanish-dominant as defined above)

- **English-dominant:** All others.

```
generate pdomlang=1
replace pdomlang=3 if rlp==1 & plang==0
replace pdomlang=2 if rlp==2 | ((prace==3 | teenrace==3) &
    plang==0)
label def pdomlang 1 English 2 Spanish 3 Other
label variable pdomlang "Responding parent's dominant language"
```

Notes and Resources

Introduction

Notes

[1] For descriptive purposes, the NSYR researchers weighted the survey results to adjust for the number of teenagers in the household and the number of household telephone numbers. Weighting is a statistical process that is used to compensate for the fact that households with a lot of telephone numbers are more likely to appear in the survey, and teens with a lot of siblings are less likely to appear since only one child was interviewed in each household. These weighted results are generally acknowledged to provide a more reliable and representative portrait of the target population, so they are used throughout this book for all NSYR survey results, unless otherwise indicated.

One of the consequences of using weighted responses is that the number of responses listed in the tables (the Ns) is somewhat inflated. For example, the weighted number of Hispanic survey respondents in Wave 1 is 451, and it is 297 in Wave 2. Although these may seem like large increases compared to the 385 and 242 actual Hispanic respondents, the weighted number of respondents of other ethnic groups also increased. As a result, the overall weighted number of respondents in Waves 1 and 2 were 3,671 and 2,901 respectively, so the proportional change is not as dramatic.

It should be noted that the NSYR researchers also developed weights to adjust for census region of residence and household income. For the purposes of this book it was decided not to use these additional adjustments for several reasons:

- When adjusting for these factors, the number of Hispanic respondents actually *decreased* slightly relative to the overall population, despite the fact that Hispanic teens were underrepresented in the sample.
- Since the weight does not adjust for ethnicity, and ethnic comparisons within religions traditions (i.e. comparisons between white and Hispanic Catholics) form an important part of this book, it was felt that the regional and income-based adjustments may affect these comparisons in ways that are not representative of the target populations.

- Two other significant research reports have already utilized the weighted NSYR data without adjustments for census region and income: *The National Study of Youth and Religion: Analysis of the Population of Catholic Teenagers and Their Parents,* by Charlotte McCorquodale, Victoria Shepp, and Leigh Sterten (Washington, DC: National Federation for Catholic Youth Ministry, 2004) and "Youth Ministry and the Socioreligious Lives of Hispanic and White Catholic Teens in the U.S.," by Ken Johnson-Mondragón (Stockton, CA: Instituto Fe y Vida, 2005). Maintaining the use of the same weights allows for coherence and comparability with these reports.

- The census region and income weights were readjusted for Wave 2 of the NSYR to compensate for the fact that not all of the adolescent participants in Wave 1 were included in the second wave survey. However, Wave 2 cannot be taken as a representative sample of young Hispanics in the U.S. for two reasons:

  ○ Hispanics were overrepresented among the teens who were not found, and therefore not included, in the second wave of the survey.

  ○ From 2003 to 2005, many young people arrived in the United States as immigrants from Latin American countries: according to the U.S. Census Bureau's Current Population Survey, the proportion of immigrants rose from 26% of 13 to 17 year-old Hispanic U.S. residents in March, 2003 to 32% of the same age cohort in March, 2006. These additional young immigrants are not represented in Wave 2 of the NSYR survey. Using the census-adjusted weights adds an air of representation to the Wave 2 numbers that in fact cannot be sustained, especially with regard to the Hispanic population.

[2] Probability theory provides a formula for estimating how closely the sample statistics are clustered around the value one would obtain by surveying every member of the target population. This estimate is known as the *sampling error,* and the formula contains three factors: the parameter P, the sample size N, and the standard error s. P is equal to the number of respondents giving a particular response divided by the total number of respondents in the sample. The formula is written as follows:

$$s=\sqrt{\frac{P-P^2}{N}}$$

As an example, 60% of the 278 weighted Hispanic Catholic respondents in Table 2.1 stated that they definitely believe in angels. In this case, $P=0.6$ (for 60%) and $N=278$, so applying the formula gives $s=0.029$. In probability theory, this means that if we repeatedly took random samples of 278 Hispanic Catholic teens in the United States, asking them the same question each time, about 68% of the time their tabulated responses would be within ±2.9% of the 60% found in the original sample. By doubling the standard error, their tabulated responses would be within ±5.8% of the 60% found in the original sample about 95% of the time. The margin of error in social-scientific surveys is usually reported at the 95% confidence level—in this case about ±5.8%—so tabulated results that differ by less than twice the standard error are not considered to be statistically significant.

Chapter 1:
Socioreligious Demographics
of Hispanic Teenagers

Notes

[1] Barry A. Kosmin and Seymour P. Lachman, *One Nation Under God: Religion in Contemporary American Society* (New York: Harmony Books, 1993), 114-154.

[2] Rodolfo O. de la Garza, et al., *Latino Voices: Mexican, Puerto Rican, and Cuban Perspectives on American Politics* (Boulder, CO: Westview Press, 1993).

[3] Barry A. Kosmin and Ariela Keysar, *Religion in a Free Market: Religious and Non-Religious Americans* (Ithaca, NY: Paramount Market Publishing, 2006), 235-259.

[4] Roberto Suro, et al., *2002 National Survey of Latinos: Summary of Findings* (Washington, DC: Pew Hispanic Center, 2002), 52-55.

[5] President's Advisory Commission on Educational Excellence for Hispanic Americans, *From Risk to Opportunity: Fulfilling the Educational Needs of Hispanic Americans in the 21st Century* (Washington, DC: White House Initiative on Educational Excellence for Hispanic Americans, 2003), 2.

[6] Richard Fry, *Hispanic Youth Dropping Out of U.S. Schools: Measuring the Challenge* (Washington, DC: Pew Hispanic Center, 2003), 5-8.

[7] Ana María Díaz-Stevens and Anthony Stevens-Arroyo, *Recognizing the Latino Resurgence in U.S. Religion: The Emmaus Paradigm* (Boulder, CO: Westview Press, 1998), 224.

[8] U.S. Dept. of Commerce, Bureau of the Census, *American Community Survey (ACS): Public Use Microdata Sample, 2005* [Computer file] (Washington, DC: U.S. Dept. of Commerce, Bureau of the Census, 2006).

[9] National Youth Gang Center, *National Youth Gang Survey Analysis (2006)*, retrieved on March 7, 2007 from http://www.iir.com/nygc/nygsa .

[10] Melissa Sickmund, "Juveniles in Corrections," in *Juvenile Offenders and Victims National Report Series Bulletin for June 2004* (Washington, DC: U.S. Department of Justice, Office of Justice Programs, Office of Juvenile Justice and Delinquency Prevention (OJJDP), 2004).

Additional resources

Books and articles

Boran, George. "Hispanic Catholic Youth in the United States." In *Bridging Boundaries: The Pastoral Care of U.S. Hispanics,* ed. Kenneth G. Davis and Yolanda Tarango, 95-105. Scranton, PA: University of Scranton Press, 2000.

_____. *The Pastoral Challenges of a New Age.* Dublin, Ireland: Veritas, 1999.

Cervantes, Carmen M., ed. *Hispanic Young People and the Church's Pastoral Response / La Juventud Hispana y la Respuesta Pastoral de la Iglesia.* Winona, MN: Saint Mary's Press, 1994.

_____. *Evangelization of Hispanic Young People / Evangelización de la Juventud Hispana.* Winona, MN: Saint Mary's Press, 1995.

Jackson, Lonnie. *Gangbusters: Strategies for Prevention and Intervention.* Lanham, MD: American Correctional Association, 1998.

Johnson-Mondragón, Ken. *The Status of Hispanic Youth and Young Adult Ministry in the United States: A Preliminary Study.* Stockton, CA: Instituto Fe y Vida, 2002.

Larson, Scott, and Karen Free, eds. *City Lights: Ministry Essentials for Reaching Urban Youth.* Loveland, CO: Group Publishing, 2003.

Suro, Roberto, et al. *Changing Faiths: Latinos and the Transformation of American Religion.* Washington, DC: Pew Hispanic Center, 2007.

Valdés, M. I. *Marketing to American Latinos: A Guide to the In-Culture Approach, Part 2.* Ithaca, NY: Paramount Market Publishing, Inc, 2002.

Websites

www.census.gov/pubinfo/www/NEWhispML1.html

www.feyvida.org

www.idra.org

www.iir.com/nygc

latinostudies.nd.edu/cslr

mumford1.dyndns.org/cen2000/HispanicPop/HspPopData.htm

www.pewhispanic.org

depthome.brooklyn.cuny.edu/risc

www.urban.org

Chapter 2:
Personal Religious Beliefs and Experiences

Notes

¹ *The American Heritage Dictionary of the English Language, Fourth Edition* (Boston: Houghton Mifflin Company, 2000).

² Trent C. Butler, ed., *Holman Bible Dictionary* (Nashville, TN: Broadman & Holman Publishers, 1991).

³ *The American Heritage Dictionary.*

⁴ Ken Johnson-Mondragón, "Youth Ministry and the Socioreligious Lives of Hispanic and White Catholic Teens in the U.S." (Stockton, CA: Instituto Fe y Vida, 2005), 20.

⁵ Christian Smith and Melinda Lundquist Denton, *Soul Searching: The Religious and Spiritual Lives of American Teenagers* (New York: Oxford University Press, 2005), 162-163.

Additional resources

Books and articles

Bass, Dorothy C. and Don C. Richter, D.C. *Way to Live: Christian Practices for Teens.* Nashville, TN: Upper Room Books, 2002.

Blackaby, Henry T. *Experiencing God: Knowing and Doing the Will of God.* Nashville, TN: LifeWay Press, 1993.

Davis, Kenneth G. *Misa, Mesa, y Musa: Liturgy in the U.S. Hispanic Church, Second Edition.* Schiller Park, IL: World Library Publications, 2004.

Dean, Kenda Creasy. *Youth and the Church of 'Benign Whatever-ism': Reflections on the Church, American Teenagers, and Where We Go from Here.* New York: Oxford University Press, 2007.

De Luna, Anita. *Faith Formation and Popular Religion: Lessons from the Tejano Experience.* Lanham, MD: Rowman & Littlefield Publishers, 2002.

Díaz-Stevens, Ana María and Anthony M. Stevens-Arroyo. *Recognizing the Latino Resurgence in U.S. Religion: The Emmaus Paradigm.* Boulder, CO: Westview Press, 1998.

Elizondo, Virgilio P. and Timothy M. Matovina. *Mestizo Worship: A Pastoral Approach to Liturgical Ministry.* Collegeville, MN: The Liturgical Press, 1998.

Francis, Mark R. and Arturo J. Pérez-Rodríguez. *Primero Dios: Hispanic Liturgical Resource.* Chicago, IL: Liturgy Training Publications, 1997.

Jones, Stephen D. *Faith Shaping: Youth and the Experience of Faith, Revised Edition.* Valley Forge, PA: Judson Press, 1987.

Maldonado, David, ed. *Protestantes / Protestants: Hispanic Christianity Within Mainline Traditions.* Nashville, TN: Abingdon Press, 1999.

Matovina, Timothy, ed. *Beyond Borders: Writings of Virgilio Elizondo and Friends.* Maryknoll, NY: Orbis Books, 2000.

Matovina, Timothy and Gary Riebe-Estrella, eds. *Horizons of the Sacred: Mexican Traditions in U.S. Catholicism.* Ithaca, NY: Cornell University Press, 2002.

Pocock, Michael and Joseph Henriques. *Cultural Change and Your Church: Helping Your Church Thrive in a Diverse Society.* Grand Rapids, MI: Baker Books, 2002.

Wilkerson, Barbara, ed. *Multicultural Religious Education.* Birmingham, AL: Religious Education Press, 1997.

Websites

www.biblegateway.com

www.buenasnuevas.com

www.catholic.net

www.christiansunite.com

www.exemplarym.com

www.iglesia.net

www.pulpithelps.com

www.thesource4ym.com

www.youthministry.com

www.youthworks.com

Chapter 3:
Participation in Church and Youth Ministry

Notes

[1] Robert Wuthnow, "Youth and Culture in American Society: The Social Context of Ministry to Teenagers," *The Princeton Lectures on Youth, Church, and Culture,* 1996, 67-75. Retrieved August 3, 2004 from http://www.ptsem.edu/iym/research/lectures/lectures96.htm

[2] United States Conference of Catholic Bishops, *Renewing the Vision: A Framework for Catholic Youth Ministry* (Washington, DC: USCCB Publishing, 1997), 9-18.

³ Ken Johnson-Mondragón, "Youth Ministry and the Socioreligious Lives of Hispanic and White Catholic Teens in the U.S.," *Perspectives on Hispanic Youth and Young Adult Ministry 2* (Stockton, CA: Instituto Fe y Vida, 2005), 12.

⁴ Ibid., 15-16.

⁵ Christian Smith with Melinda Lundquist Denton, *Soul Searching: The Religious and Spiritual Lives of American Teenagers* (New York: Oxford University Press, 2005), 261.

⁶ Justo González, *Santa Biblia: The Bible Through Hispanic Eyes* (Nashville, TN: Abingdon Press, 1996), 44-45.

⁷ Pope Paul VI, *Evangelii Nuntiandi,* §14. Retrieved December 5, 2005 from http://www.vatican.va/holy_father/paul_vi/apost_exhortations/documents/hf_p-vi_exh_19751208_evangelii-nuntiandi_en.html

⁸ George Boran, "Hispanic Youth in the United States," in Kenneth G. Davis and Yolanda Tarango, eds., *Bridging boundaries: The pastoral care of U.S. Hispanics* (Scranton, PA: University of Scranton Press, 2000), 105.

Additional resources

Books and articles

Acosta, Larry. "The Morphing of Urban Ministries." *Network Magazine* (Winter 2003).

Aguilera-Titus, Alejandro. "Youth Ministry in a Culturally Diverse Church." *Origins* 36 (October 12, 2006), 277-283.

Boran, George. *The Pastoral Challenges of a New Age.* Dublin: Veritas, 1999.

Cervantes, Carmen M., ed. *Hispanic Young People and the Church's Pastoral Response / La Juventud Hispana y la Respuesta Pastoral de la Iglesia.* Winona, MN: Saint Mary's Press, 1994.

_____. *Evangelization of Hispanic Young People / Evangelización de la Juventud Hispana.* Winona, MN: Saint Mary's Press, 1995.

Copeland Jr., Nelson E., Rev. *The Heroic Revolution: A New Agenda for Urban Youthwork.* Nashville, TN: James C. Winston Publishing Company, Inc., 1995.

Dahm, Charles W. *Parish Ministry in a Hispanic Community.* Mahwah, NJ: Paulist Press, 2004.

Davis, Kenneth G. "Architects of Success." *America* 186 (April 29, 2002).

Dean, Kenda Creasy, Chap Clark, and Dave Rahm, eds. *Starting Right: Thinking Theologically about Youth Ministry.* Grand Rapids, MI: Zondervan Publishing Houses, 2001.

Dean, Kenda Creasy and Ron Foster. *The Godbearing Life: The Art of Soul Tending for Youth Ministry.* Nashville, TN: The Upper Room, 1998.

Foster, Charles R. and Grant S. Shockley, eds. *Working with Black Youth: Opportunities for Christian Ministry.* Nashville, TN: Abingdon Press, 1989.

González, Justo. *Santa Biblia: The Bible Through Hispanic Eyes.* Nashville, TN: Abingdon Press, 1996.

Johnson-Mondragón, Ken. *The Status of Hispanic Youth and Young Adult Ministry in the United States: A Preliminary Study.* Stockton, CA: Instituto Fe y Vida, 2002.

Larson, Scott and Karen Free, eds. *City Lights: Ministry Essentials for Reaching Urban Youth.* Loveland, CO: Group Publishing, 2003.

Lytch, Carol E. *Choosing Church: What Makes a Difference for Teens.* Louisville, KY: Westminster John Knox Press, 2004.

McNerney, Eileen. *A Story of Suffering and Hope: Lessons from Latino Youth.* Mahwah, NJ: Paulist Press, 2005.

Singer-Towns, Brian, ed. *Vibrant Worship with Youth: Keys for Implementing From Age to Age: The Challenge of Worship with Adolescents.* Winona, MN: Saint Mary's Press, 2000.

Strommen, M. P. & Hardel, R. A. *Passing on the Faith: A Radical New Model for Youth and Family Ministry.* Winona, MN: Saint Mary's Press, 2000.

Ward, Pete. *God at the Mall: Youth Ministry that Meets Kids Where They're At.* Peabody, MA: Hendrickson Publishers, 1999.

West, B. and West, G. *Dynamic Preteen Ministry.* Loveland, CO: Group Publishing, 2000.

Websites

www.amen-amen.net

www.buenasnuevas.com

www.cmdnet.org

www.cultivationministries.com

www.disciplesnow.com

www.feyvida.org

www.group.com

www.lideresjuveniles.com

www.lifeteen.org

www.ministryandmedia.com

www.nfcym.org

www.paralideres.org

www.ptsem.edu/iym/

www.smp.org

www.usccb.org

www.youthministry.com

www.youthspecialties.com

www.youthworks.com

Chapter 4:
Faith and Culture in Hispanic Families

Notes

[1] *Lumen Gentium,* §§27, 28, 32, and 51.

[2] Ibid., §11.

[3] Joan D. Koss-Chioino and Luis A. Vargas, *Working with Latino Youth* (San Francisco, CA: Editorial Jossey-Bass, 1999).

[4] Survey on Vocations and Ministry among Leaders in Pastoral Juvenil Hispana, conducted at the First National Encounter for Hispanic Youth and Young Adult Ministry (Stockton, CA: Instituto Fe y Vida, 2006), unpublished.

[5] *Gaudium et Spes,* §52.

[6] Johnny Ramírez-Johnson and Edwin Hernández, *Avance: A Vision for a New Mañana* (Loma Linda, CA: Loma Linda University Press, 2003), 84.

[7] Allan G. Johnson, *The Blackwell Dictionary of Sociology, Second Edition* (Malden, MA: Blackwell Publishers, Inc., 2000), 73.

[8] Carmen M. Cervantes, ed., *Hispanic Young People and the Church's Pastoral Response,* Vol. 1 of the Prophets of Hope Series (Winona, MN: Saint Mary's Press, 1994), 81.

[9] Ibid.

[10] Based on Bryan Kim and José Abreu, "Acculturation Measurement: Theory, Current Instruments, and Future Directions" in Joseph G. Ponterotto, J. Manuel Casas, Lisa Suzuki, and Charlene Alexander, *Handbook of Multicultural Counseling: Second Edition* (Thousand Oaks, CA: Sage Publications, 2001), 398. Where Kim and Abreu used the term "integration," this book opts to use "biculturalism" in order to avoid confusion with the concept of racial integration in society, which is unrelated to the dynamics of acculturation.

[11] Adapted from Alejandro Portes, Patricia Fernandez-Kelly, and William Haller, "Segmented Assimilation on the Ground : The New Second Generation in Early Adulthood," *Ethnic and Racial Studies* 28 (2005): 1000-1040.

Additional resources

Books and articles

Avalos, Hector, ed. *Introduction to the U.S. Latina and Latino Religious Experience.* Boston, MA: Brill Academic Publishers, 2004.

Badillo, David A. *Latinos and the New Immigrant Church.* Baltimore, MD: Johns Hopkins University Press, 2006.

Brankin, Patrick. *Bilingual Ritual of Hispanic Popular Catholicism.* New Hope, KY: New Hope Publications, 2002.

Brendtro, Larry and Mary Shahbazian. *Troubled Children and Youth: Turning Problems into Opportunities.* Champaign, IL: Research Press, 2004.

Burns, Jim in collaboration with Larry Acosta, Jeffrey De León, and Russ Cline. *El Ministerio Juvenil Dinámico.* Miami, FL: Editorial Unilit, 1997.

Cervantes, Carmen M., ed. *Evangelization of Hispanic Young People / Evangelización de la Juventud Hispana.* Winona, MN: Saint Mary's Press, 1995.

_____. *Latino Catholic Youth and Young Adults in the United States: Their Faith and their Culture.* Stockton, CA: Instituto Fe y Vida, 2002.

Covey, Stephen R. *The Seven Habits of Highly Effective Families.* New York: Golden Books, 1997.

De Luna, Anita. *Faith Formation and Popular Religion: Lessons from the Tejano Experience.* Lanham, MD: Rowman & Littlefield Publishers, 2002.

Elizondo, Virgilio P. and Timothy M. Matovina. *Mestizo Worship: A Pastoral Approach to Liturgical Ministry.* Collegeville, MN: The Liturgical Press, 1998.

Johnson-Mondragón, Ken. "Welcoming Hispanic Youth/Jóvenes in Catholic Parishes and Dioceses." Stockton, CA: Instituto Fe y Vida, 2003.

Matovina, Timothy and Gary Riebe-Estrella, eds. *Horizons of the Sacred: Mexican Traditions in U.S. Catholicism.* Ithaca, NY: Cornell University Press, 2002.

Romero, C. Gilbert. *Hispanic Devotional Piety: Tracing the Biblical Roots.* Maryknoll, NY: Orbis Books, 1991.

Santiago-Rivera, Azara L., Patricia Arredondo, and Maritza Gallardo-Cooper. *Counseling Latinos and La Famlia: A Practical Guide.* Thousand Oaks, CA: Sage Publications, 2002.

Sue, Derald Wing, and David Sue. *Counseling the Culturally Diverse: Theory and Practice, 4th Edition.* New York: John Wiley & Sons, 2003.

Websites

www.ChristianityToday.com/home/communities.html

www.family.org

www.familyministries.org

www.foryourmarriage.org

www.gospelcom.net/ministries

www.hcfm.org

family.nadadventist.org

www.usccb.org/laity/marriage

Chapter 5:
The Moral Imperative of Latino/a
Educational Investment

Notes

¹ Thomas D. Snyder, Alexandra G. Tan, and Charlene M. Hoffman, *Digest of Education Statistics 2005* (Washington, DC: National Center for Education Statistics, 2006), 181-185.

² Richard Fry, "Hispanic Youth Dropping Out of U.S. Schools: Measuring the Challenge," (Washington, DC: Pew Hispanic Center, 2003), 5-7.

³ Carola Suárez-Orozco and Irina L.G. Todorova, eds., *Understanding the Social Worlds of Immigrant Youth* (San Francisco: Jossey-Bass, 2003), 20-21.

⁴ Ken R. Crane, *Latino Churches: Faith, Family, and Ethnicity in the Second Generation* (New York: LFB Scholarly Publishing, 2003), 166.

⁵ Sonia Nieto, *Affirming Diversity: The Sociopolitical Context of Multicultural Education, 4th ed.* (Boston: Pearson Education, 2004), 268-269.

⁶ Desirée Baolian Qin-Hilliard, "Gendered expectations and gendered experiences: Immigrant students' adaptation in schools," in *Understanding the Social World of Immigrant Youth,* ed. Carola Suárez-Orozco and Irina L.G. Todorova (Hoboken, NJ: John Wiley & Sons, Inc., 2003), 104-105.

⁷ H. Richard Niebuhr, *Christ and Culture* (New York: Haper & Row, 1951).

⁸ Pope Paul VI, *Evangelii Nuntiandi,* 1975, §20.

⁹ Orlando Crespo, *Being Latino in Christ: Finding Wholeness in Your Ethnic Identity* (Downers Grove, IL: InterVarsity Press, 2003).

¹⁰ See for example the American Bible Society ESL curriculum.

Additional resources

Books and articles

Bredekamp, S. and C. Copple. *Developmentally Appropriate Practice in Early Childhood Programs.* Washington, DC: National Association for the Education of Young Children, 1997.

Carle, Robert D. and Louis A. DeCaro, Jr. *Signs of Hope in the City: Ministries of Community Renewal.* Valley Forge, PA: Judson Press, 1999.

Conn, Harvey M. *The Urban Face of Mission: Ministering the Gospel in a Diverse and Changing World.* Philipsburg, NJ: P&R Publishing, 2002.

Davey, Andrew. *Urban Christianity and Global Order: Theological Resources for an Urban Future.* Peabody, MA: Hendrickson Publishers, 2002.

Elizondo, Virgilio. *Galilean Journey: The Mexican-American Promise.* New York: Orbis Books, 1991.

Federal Interagency Forum on Child and Family Statistics. *America's Children: Key National Indicators of Well-Being.* Washington, DC: U.S. Government Printing Office, 2002.

Hunter III, George G. *Radical Outreach: The Recovery of Apostolic Ministry & Evangelism.* Nashville, TN: Abdingdon Press, 2003.

Ivory, Luther D. *Toward a Theology of Radical Involvement: The Theological Legacy of Martin Luther King, Jr.* Nashville, TN: Abingdon Press, 1997.

Linthicum, Robert C. *City of God, City of Satan: A Biblical Theology of the Urban Church.* Grand Rapids, MI: Zondervan Publishing House, 1991.

Myers, Bryant L. *Walking With the Poor: Principles and Practices of Transformational Development.* Maryknoll, NY: Orbis Books, 2002

Simpson, Gary M. *Critical Social Theory: Prophetic Reason, Civil Society and Christian Imagination.* Minneapolois, MN: Fortress Press, 2002.

Sterns, C. and S. Watanbe. *Hispanic Serving Institutions: Statistical Trends from 1990—1999* (NCES 2002-051). U.S. Department of Education, NCES. Washington, DC: U.S. Government Printing Office, 2002.

Villafane, Eldin. *Seek the Peace of the City: Reflections on Urban Ministry.* Grand Rapids, MI: Eerdmans Publishing Co., 1995.

Warburton, E.C., R. Bugarin, A. Nunez, and C. D. Carroll. *Bridging the Gap: Academic Preparation and Postsecondary Success of First-Generation Students* (NCES 2001-153). U.S. Department of Education, National Center for Education Statistics. Washington, DC: U.S. Government Printing Office, 2001.

Wehlage, G., R. Rutter, G. Smith, N. Lesko, and R. Fernandez. *Reducing the Risk: Schools as Communities of Support.* London: The Falmer Press, 1989.

Websites

www.CristoReyNetwork.org

www.hsf.net

www.idra.org

www.LaRaza.org

latinostudies.nd.edu/cslr

www.nativitymiguelschools.org

www.pewhispanic.org

Chapter 6:
Insights into the Moral Life of Hispanic Youth

Notes

¹ Melanie Killen and Judith Smetana, eds., *Handbook of Moral Development* (Mahwah, NJ: Lawrence Erlbaum Associates, 2006), xi.

² John W. Santrock, *Adolescence, Eleventh Edition* (New York: McGraw-Hill, 2007), 239.

³ Lawrence Kohlberg, "Stages of Moral Development as a Basis for Moral Education," in *Moral Development, Moral Education, and Kohlberg: Basic Issues in Philosophy, Psychology, Religion, and Education,* ed. Brenda Munsey (Birmingham, AL: Religious Education Press, 1980), 91-98.

⁴ Augusto Blasi, "Moral Functioning: Moral Understanding and Personality," in *Moral Development, Self, and Identity,* ed. Daniel K. Lapsley and Darcia Narvaez (Mahwah, NJ: Lawrence Erlbaum Associates, 2004), 335-347.

⁵ Peter L. Berger, *The Sacred Canopy: Elements of a Sociological Theory of Religion* (New York: Doubleday, 1967), 45-48.

⁶ Felipe Korzenny and Betty Ann Korzenny, *Hispanic Marketing: A Cultural Perspective* (Burlington, MA: Elsevier, 2005), 246-247.

⁷ Mark D. Regnerus, *Forbidden Fruit: Sex & Religion in the Lives of American Teenagers* (New York: Oxford University Press, 2007), 107-112.

⁸ Ibid., 163-171.

⁹ Ibid., 130-134.

¹⁰ Ibid., 98-100 and 137.

¹¹ Francisco A. Villaruel, Daniel F. Perkins, Lynne M. Borden, and Joanne G. Keith, eds., *Community Youth Development: Programs, Policies, and Practices* (Thousand Oaks: Sage Publications, 2003).

¹² Johnny Ramírez-Johnson and Edwin I. Hernández, *Avance: A Vision for a New Mañana* (Loma Linda, CA: Loma Linda University Press, 2003), 28.

¹³ Ibid., 52.

¹⁴ Leslie Reese, "Morality and Identity in Mexican Immigrant Parents' Vision of the Future," *Journal of Ethnic and Migration Studies* 27 (13), 455-484.

¹⁵ Merton P. Strommen and Richard A. Hardel, *Passing On the Faith: A Radical New Model for Youth and Family Ministry* (Winona, MN: Saint Mary's Press Christian Brothers Publications, 2000).

¹⁶ Santrock, 151-159.

¹⁷ Carola Suárez-Orozco and Marcelo M. Suárez-Orozco, *Children of Immigration* (Cambridge, MA: Harvard University Press, 2001), 107-112.

[18] David White, *Practicing Discernment with Youth: A Transformative Youth Ministry Approach* (Cleveland, OH: The Pilgrim Press, 2005), 88-199. Arturo Chavez develops a similar style of reflection in Chapter 7, where he employs three tasks: see, judge and act. There are many variations on these.

[19] Jennifer G. Roffman, Carola Suárez-Orozco, and Jean E. Rhodes, "Facilitating Positive Development in Immigrant Youth: The Role of Mentors and Community Organizations," in *Community Youth Development: Programs, Policies and Practices,* ed. Francisco A. Villaruel et al. (Thousand Oaks, CA: Sage Publications, 2003), 90-117.

[20] Ramirez-Johnson and Hernández, 83.

[21] Ibid., 93.

[22] Ibid., 94.

[23] Ibid., 91.

[24] Strommen and Hardel, 158-185.

[25] Shepherd Zeldin, Annette K. McDaniel, Dimitri Topitzes, and Matt Calvert, *Youth in Decision Making: A Study on the Impact of Youth and Adults on Organizations* (Chevy Chase, MD: Innovation Center for Youth and Community Development and University of Wisconsin Extension, 2000), 23-30.

Additional resources

Books and articles

Ahearn, David O. and Peter R. Gathje, eds. *Doing Right and Being Good: Catholic and Protestant Readings in Christian Ethics.* Collegeville, MN: Liturgical Press, 2005.

Bass, Dorothy C. and Don C. Richter, D.C. *Way to Live: Christian Practices for Teens.* Nashville, TN: Upper Room Books, 2002.

Boran, George. "Hispanic Catholic Youth in the United States." In *Bridging Boundaries: The Pastoral Care of U.S. Hispanics,* ed. Kenneth G. Davis and Yolanda Tarango, 95-105. Scranton, PA: University of Scranton Press, 2000.

Calva, Cecilia, Marilú Covani, Petra Alexander, et al. *Mis 15 Años / My 15th Birthday: Teaching Material for Quinceañera Formation, Bilingual Edition.* Boston, MA: Pauline Books & Media, 2003.

Erevia, Angela. *Quince Años: Celebrando una Tradición / Celebrating a Tradition.* San Antonio, TX: Missionary Catechists of the Divine Providence, St. Andrew's Convent, 1985.

Garcia, Ismael. *Dignidad: Ethics Through Hispanic Eyes.* Nashville, TN: Abingdon Press, 1997.

Gustafson, James M. *Protestant and Roman Catholic Ethics: Prospects for Rapprochement.* Chicago, IL: The University of Chicago Press, 1978.

Lovin, Robin W. *Christian Ethics: An Essential Guide.* Nashville, TN: Abingdon Press, 2000.

Mahdi, Louise C., Nancy G. Christopher, and Michael Meade. *Crossroads: The Quest for Contemporary Rites of Passage.* Chicago, IL: Open Court Publishing, 1996.

Maldonado, Jorge E. and Elizabeth Conde-Frazier. *Criando a Nuestros Hijos en Dos Culturas.* Bell Gardens, CA: Centro Hispano de Estudios Teológicos, 2001.

Rhodes, Jean E. *Stand by Me: The Risks and Rewards of Mentoring Today's Youth.* Cambridge, MA: Harvard University Press, 2004.

United States Conference of Catholic Bishops. *United States Catholic Catechism for Adults.* Washington, DC: USCCB Publishing, 2006, 319-337.

Chapter 7:
The Social and Political Involvement of Latino/a Youth

Notes

[1] For a more complete description of the Catholic understanding of the relationship between good works and justification, see the *Joint Declaration on the Doctrine of Justification by the Lutheran World Federation and the Catholic Church,* §§37-38. It can be found on the Vatican website at: http://www.vatican.va/roman_curia/pontifical_councils/chrstuni/documents/rc_pc_chrstuni_doc_31101999_cath-luth-joint-declaration_en.html

[2] *The Augsburg Confession* (1530), Article IV. Retrieved on June 24, 2007 from http://www.ctsfw.edu/etext/boc/ac/augustana04.asc

[3] *The Westminster Confession of Faith* (1647), Chapter XVI, §§2-3. Retrieved on June 24, 2007 from http://www.pcanet.org/general/cof_chapxvi-xx.htm

[4] For an exemplary study and some bibliographic references, see Robert A. Rhoads, "In the Service of Citizenship: A Study of Student Involvement in Community Service," *The Journal of Higher Education,* 1 May 1998. Retrieved on June 20, 2007 from http://www.highbeam.com/DocPrint.aspx?DocId=1G1:20757353

[5] Martin L. Hoffman, "Implications for Socialization and Moral Education," in *Empathy and Moral Development: Implications for Caring and Justice* (New York: Cambridge University Press, 2000), 287-298.

[6] Carola and Marcelo Suárez-Orozco, *Transformations: Migration, Family Life, and Achievement Motivation Among Latino Adolescents* (Stanford, CA: Stanford University Press, 1995), 55-57.

⁷ On May 10, 2005, the United States Conference of Catholic Bishops announced the launch of *Justice for Immigrants: A Journey of Hope. The Catholic Campaign for Immigration Reform* together with 19 other Catholic national organizations. In addition, the U.S. and Mexican bishops issued a joint pastoral letter regarding the pastoral care of migrants in 2003 entitled *Strangers No Longer: Together on the Journey of Hope.* Information about both is available at http://www.usccb.org

⁸ Carol Gilligan, *In a Different Voice: Psychological Theory and Women's Development* (Cambridge, MA: Harvard University Press, 1982).

Additional resources

Books and articles

Baez-Chávez, Mary and Arturo Chávez. *RESPETO: Latino Youth Leadership Formation.* San Antonio, TX: The Mexican American Cultural Center, 2002.

Bright, Thomas J., Mike Poulin, Sean T. Lansing, and Joan Weber. *Ministry Resources for Justice and Service.* Winona, MN: Saint Mary's Press, 2004.

Burke, John F. *Mestizo Democracy: The Politics of Border Crossing.* College Station, TX: Texas A&M University Press, 2002.

Carrasquillo, Angela L. *Hispanic Children and Youth in the United States: A Resource Guide.* New York: Garland Publishing, Inc., 1991.

Conn, Harvie M. and Manuel Ortiz. *Urban Ministry: The Kingdom, the City, and the People of God.* Downers Grove, IL: InterVarsity Press, 2001.

Davis, Kenneth G. and Leopoldo Pérez, eds. *Preaching the Teaching: Hispanics, Homiletics, and Catholic Social Justice Doctrine.* Scranton, PA: University of Scranton Press, 2005.

Espinosa, Gastón, Virgilio Elizondo, and Jesse Miranda, eds. *Latino Religions and Civic Activism in the United States.* New York: Oxford University Press, 2005.

Fernandez-Kelly, Patricia. "From Estrangement to Affinity: Dilemmas of Identity Among Hispanic Children." In *Borderless Borders: U.S. Latinos, Latin Americans, and the Paradox of Interdependence,* ed. Frank Bonilla, Edwin Melendez, Rebecca Morales, and Maria de los Angeles Torres. Philadelphia: Temple University Press, 1998.

Fitzgerald, Hiram E., Barry M. Lester, and Barry S. Zuckerman, eds. *Children of Color: Research, Health, and Policy Issues.* New York: Garland Publishing, Inc., 1999.

Grant, Joseph. *Justice and Service Ideas for Ministry with Young Teens.* Winona, MN: Saint Mary's Press, 2000.

Law, Eric H.F. *The Wolf Shall Dwell with the Lamb.* St. Louis, MO: Chalice Press, 1993.

Lupton, Robert D. *Compassion, Justice and the Christian Life: Rethinking Ministry to the Poor.* Ventura, CA: Regal Books, 2007.

National Federation for Catholic Youth Ministry. *Living Justice, Proclaiming Peace: 2004 Youth Ministry Resource Manual.* Washington, DC: National Federation for Catholic Youth Ministry, 2004.

Perkins, John M. *Restoring At-Risk Communities: Doing It Together and Doing It Right.* Grand Rapids, MI: Baker Books, 1996.

Romo, Harriet D. and Toni Falbo. *Latino High School Graduation: Defying the Odds.* Austin, TX: University of Texas Press, 1996.

Roberto, John, ed. *Justice: Access Guides to Youth Ministry.* New Rochelle, NY: Don Bosco Multimedia, 1990.

Search Institute. *Step by Step: A Young Person's Guide to Positive Community Change.* Minneapolis, MN: The Search Institute, 2001.

United States Conference of Catholic Bishops. *Renewing the Vision: A Framework for Catholic Youth Ministry.* Washington, D.C.: United States Catholic Conference, 1997.

_____. *Strangers No Longer: Together on the Journey of Hope.* Washington, D.C.: United States Conference of Catholic Bishops, 2003.

Wood, Richard L. *Faith in Action: Religion, Race, and Democratic Organizing in America.* Chicago, IL: The University of Chicago Press, 2002.

Websites

www.amae.org

www.elca.org/youth/links.html

www.industrialareasfoundation.org

www.lulac.org

www.nabe.org

www.nclr.org

www.search-institute.org

www.usccb.org/faithfulcitizenship

Chapter 8:
The Second Wave of the National Study of Youth and Religion

Notes

[1] In most of this book, the number of Hispanic respondents to the Wave 1 survey is based on 451 weighted responses. However, at the time of the second

wave, it was discovered that some of the ages of the teens in the first survey were entered improperly, such that a few teens were inadvertently surveyed who were not between the ages of 13 and 17. For the sake of comparison with the Wave 2 surveys, their responses were invalidated and not counted. For an explanation of the weighting process, see note 1 from the Introduction on page 369.

[2] In the Wave 2 survey, 316 respondents identified themselves as "just Christian" or "just Protestant" and could not identify a specific denominational congregation where they attend religious services. Of these, 33 were classified as Catholics in Wave 1, four of whom were Hispanic. Admittedly, imputing Wave 1 religious affiliations to respondents in Wave 2 is not a perfect solution, since it is possible that some of these young people who were classified as Catholics in Wave 1 may have actually left the Catholic Church and joined a non-denominational Christian congregation, or simply adopted a Christian identity without any particular congregational affiliation. Nevertheless, the alternative was to omit the responses of hundreds of teens who identified themselves as Christian, which would have impoverished the Wave 2 data and made comparisons with Wave 1 more difficult. For reference, the following Stata™ syntax was used to create the simplified Wave 2 religious tradition variable from the survey responses:

```
generate int simplerel_w2 = relaff_w2
replace simplerel_w2 = 1 if relaff_w2<3 | relaff_w2==9 |
    relaff_w2==10
replace simplerel_w2 = 2 if relaff_w2==3
replace simplerel_w2 = 3 if relaff_w2==5
replace simplerel_w2 = 4 if relaff_w2==4 | relaff_w2==6 |
    relaff_w2==7
replace simplerel_w2 = 5 if relaff_w2==8
replace simplerel_w2 = 1 if relaff_w2==8 & relig0_w2==2
replace simplerel_w2 = 2 if relaff_w2==8 & (relig0_w2==1 |
    (relig0_w2==2 & reltrad==4))
replace simplerel_w2 = 5 if relaff_w2==8 & relig0_w2==2 &
    reltrad==9
label def simplerel_w2 1 Protestant 2 Catholic 3 "Not Religious"
    4 Other 5 Indeterminate
label val simplerel_w2 simplerel_w2
label variable simplerel_w2 "Simple teen religious type in Wave 2"
```

[3] For a recent analysis of this phenomenon, see Roberto Suro et al., *Changing Faiths: Latinos and the Transformation of American Religion* (Washington, DC: Pew Hispanic Center, 2007), 41-48.

[4] Ken Johnson-Mondragón, "Youth Ministry and the Socioreligious Lives of Hispanic and White Catholic Teens in the U.S.," *Perspectives on Hispanic Youth and Young Adult Ministry* 2 (Stockton, CA: Instituto Fe y Vida, 2005), 9, 14-16.

⁵ For a discussion of current issues in the practice of Catholic youth ministry, young adult ministry, and pastoral juvenil, see Carmen M. Cervantes and Ken Johnson-Mondragón, "Pastoral Juvenil Hispana, Youth Ministry, and Young Adult Ministry: An Updated Perspective on Three Different Pastoral Realities," *Perspectives on Hispanic Youth and Young Adult Ministry* 3 (Stockton, CA: Instituto Fe y Vida, 2007).

Additional resources

Books and articles

Consejo Episcopal Latinoamerican (CELAM). *Civilización del Amor: Tarea y Esperanza.* Santafé de Bogotá, Colómbia: CELAM, 1996.

Hayes, Mike. *Googling God: The Religious Landscape of People in their 20s and 30s.* Mahwah, NJ: Paulist Press, 2007.

Parks, Sharon Daloz. *Big Questions, Worthy Dreams: Mentoring Young Adults in their Search for Meaning, Purpose, and Faith.* San Francisco: Jossey-Bass, 2000.

Shenk, Sara Wenger. *Thank You for Asking: Conversations with Young Adults about the Future of the Church.* Scottsdale, PA: Herald Press, 2005.

Sweet, Leonard. *Postmodern Pilgrims—First Century Passion for the 21ˢᵗ Century World.* Nashville: Broadman & Holman, 2000.

United States Conference of Catholic Bishops (USCCB). *Sons and Daughters of the Light: A Pastoral Plan for Ministry with Young Adults.* Washington, DC: USCCB Publishing, 1996.

Weber, Joan. "The Faith Formation of Young Adults: Opportunities and Challenges," in *Lifelong Faith: The Theory and Practice of Lifelong Faith Formation* Vol 1.1 (Spring 2007), 29-38. Naugatuck, CT: LifelongFaith Associates LLC.

Websites

www.bibliaparajovenes.org

www.bustedhalo.com

www.intervarsity.org

www.larepjh.org

www.lideresjuveniles.com

www.lifelongfaith.com

www.ncyama.org

Chapter 9:
The Religious Experience
of Latino/a Protestant Youth

Notes

[1] Robert Wuthnow, *After the Baby Boomers: How Twenty- and Thirty-Some-things Are Shaping the Future of American Religion* (Princeton, NJ: Princeton University Press, 2007).

[2] Christian Smith and Melinda L. Denton, *Soul Searching: The Religious and Spiritual Lives of American Teenagers* (New York: Oxford University Press, 2005).

[3] Roberto Suro, et al., *Changing Faiths: Latinos and the Transformation of American Religion* (Washington, DC: Pew Hispanic Center, 2007). The data in this report is based on a nationally representative sample of 4,016 Latino/a respondents age 18 and older. Of the total, 2,025 were Catholics and 905 were Protestants. This is the largest representative sample to date of Latino religious trends. For more information on the survey go to: http://pewforum.org/surveys/hispanic/

[4] The information in this section comes from this report.

[5] This finding was so surprising to the researchers that they it prompted a follow-up survey of Latino/a Catholics to explore this issue further. The call-back survey confirmed that indeed the renewalist movement is a significant part of the contemporary Catholic experience in the US. They further found that renewalist Catholics retain a strong identity as Catholics, and in fact are more likely than non-charismatic Catholics to pray the rosary and serve in their parishes.

[6] Important studies over the last 20 years include: Andrew Greeley, "Defection among Hispanics," *America* 159 (July 30, 1988): 61-62; Andrew Greeley, "Defection among Hispanics" *America* 177 (September 27, 1997): 12-14; Larry L. Hunt, "The Spirit of Hispanic Protestantism in the United States: National Survey Comparisons of Catholics and Non-Catholics" *Social Science Quarterly* 79 (1998): 828-45; and Edwin I. Hernández, "Moving from the Cathedral to Storefront Churches: Understanding Religious Growth and Decline Among Latino/a Protestants," in *Protestantes/Protestants: Hispanic Christianity within Mainline Traditions*, ed. David Maldonado, Jr. (Nashville, TN: Abingdon Press, 1999).

[7] Smith and Denton, 261.

[8] David Sikkink and Edwin I. Hernández, "Religion Matters: Predicting Schooling Success Among Latino Youth" *Interim Reports* 2003.1 (Notre Dame, IN: Institute for Latino Studies, University of Notre Dame, 2003).

[9] Johnny Ramírez and Edwin I. Hernández, *AVANCE: A Vision for a New Mañana* (Loma Linda, CA: Loma Linda University Press, 2003).

[10] Christian Smith, "Why Christianity Works: An Emotions-Focused Phenomenological Account" *Sociology of Religion* 68 (2007): 165-178.

[11] Ramírez and Hernández, 2003.

[12] Virgilio Elizondo introduced the rich theological meaning of mestizaje and related it to the experience of Hispanics living in the United States in two classic works: *The Future Is Mestizo: Life Where Cultures Meet* (Boulder, CO: University of Colorado Press, 2000) and *The Galilean Journey* (Maryknoll, NY: Orbis Books, 2000).

[13] Tod E. Bolsinger, *It Takes a Church to Raise a Christian* (Grand Rapids, MI: Brazos Press, 2004).

[14] Ronald J. Sider, *One-Sided Christianity? Uniting the Church to Heal a Lost and Broken World* (Grand Rapids, MI: Zondervan, 1993) and *Rich Christians in an Age of Hunger: Moving from Affluence to Generosity* (New York: Thomas Nelson, 2005).

[15] Harold J. Ellens, *Radical Grace: How Belief in a Benevolent God Benefits our Health* (Westport, CT: Praeger Publishers, 2007).

[16] Sikkink and Hernández, 2003. See also Sidney Verba, Kay Lehman Schlozman, and Henry E. Brady, *Voice and Equality: Civic Voluntarism in American Politics* (Cambridge, MA: Harvard University Press, 1995).

[17] Ben Carson and Cecil Murphey, *Think Big: Unleashing Your Potential for Excellence* (Grand Rapids, MI: Zondervan, 2006).

[18] Smith, "Why Christianity Works," 167.

Additional resources

Books and articles

Bass, Dorothy C. and Don C. Richter, D.C. *Way to Live: Christian Practices for Teens.* Nashville, TN: Upper Room Books, 2002.

Clark, Chap and Kara E. Powell. *Deep Ministry in a Shallow World.* Grand Rapids, MI: Zondervan, 2006.

Conn, Harvie M. and Manuel Ortiz. *Urban Ministry: The Kingdom, the City, and the People of God.* Downers Grove, IL: InterVarsity Press, 2001.

Dean, Kenda Creasy. *Youth and the Church of 'Benign Whatever-ism': Reflections on the Church, American Teenagers, and Where We Go from Here.* New York: Oxford University Press, 2007.

Elizondo, Virgilio. *A God of Incredible Surprises: Jesus of Galilee.* New York: Rowman & Littlefield Publishers, 2003.

Espinosa, Gastón, Virgilio Elizondo, and Jesse Miranda, eds. *Latino Religions and Civic Activism in the United States.* New York: Oxford University Press, 2005.

Lupton, Robert D. *Compassion, Justice and the Christian Life: Rethinking Ministry to the Poor.* Ventura, CA: Regal Books, 2007.

Lytch, Carol E. *Choosing Church: What Makes a Difference for Teens.* Louisville, KY: Westminster John Knox Press, 2004.

Ortiz, Manuel. *The Hispanic Challenge: Opportunities Confronting the Church.* Downers Grove, IL: InterVarsity Press, 1993.

Regnerus, Mark D. *Forbiden Fruit: Sex & Religion in the Lives of American Teen-agers.* New York: Oxford University Press, 2007.

Romo, Harriet D. and Toni Falbo. *Latino High School Graduation: Defying the Odds.* Austin, TX: University of Texas Press, 1996.

Ward, Pete. *God at the Mall: Youth Ministry that Meets Kids Where They're At.* Peabody, MA: Hendrickson Publishers, 1999.

White, David. *Practicing Discernment with Youth: A Transformative Youth Ministry Approach.* Cleveland, OH: The Pilgrim Press, 2005.

Websites

www.cyfm.net

www.group.com

www.healthymarriageinfo.org

latinostudies.nd.edu/cslr

www.pewhispanic.org

www.thesource4ym.com

www.youthministry.com

www.youthworks.com

www.uywi.org

Chapter 10:
Passing the Faith to Latino/a Catholic Teens in the U.S.

Notes

[1] Carmen M. Cervantes and Ken Johnson-Mondragón, "*Pastoral Juvenil Hispana,* Youth Ministry, and Young Adult Ministry: An Updated Perspective on Three Different Pastoral Realities," *Perspectives on Hispanic Youth and Young Adult Ministry* #3 (Stockton, CA: Instituto Fe y Vida, 2007), 4.

[2] Thomas Bohenkotter, *Concise History of the Catholic Church* (New York: Doubleday, 1979), 378-396.

[3] Anthony Stevens-Arroyo, "Puerto Rican Migration," in *Frontiers of Hispanic Theology,* ed. Allan F. Deck (Maryknoll, NY: Orbis Books, 1992), 269-270.

[4] Moisés Sandoval, *On the Move: A History of the Hispanic Church in the United Sates Since 1513* (Maryknoll, NY, Orbis Books, 1990). Rodolfo Acuña, *Occupied America: A History of Chicanos* (New York: Harper-Collins, 1988). Also Timothy

Matovina and Gerald E. Poyo, eds., *¡Presente! U.S. Latino Catholics from Colonial Origins to the Present* (Maryknoll, NY: Orbis Books, 2000), 45-58.

⁵ Matovina and Poyo, 113.

⁶ See Cervantes and Johnson, "Pastoral Juvenil Hispana, Youth Ministry, and Young Adult Ministry," available at http://www.feyvida.org/research/researchpubs.html

⁷ Charlotte McCorquodale, "The Emergence of Lay Ecclesial Youth Ministry as a Profession Within the Roman Catholic Church" (Ph.D. diss., Louisiana State University, 2001), 76.

⁸ Roberto Suro, et al., *Changing Faiths: Latinos and the Transformation of American Religion* (Washington, DC: Pew Hispanic Center, 2007), 7.

⁹ United States Conference of Catholic Bishops, *Encuentro and Mission: A Renewed Pastoral Framework for Hispanic Ministry* (Washington, DC: USCCB Publishing, 2002), 14.

¹⁰ Roberto Suro, et al., *Changing Faiths*, 29-41.

¹¹ National Catholic Network de Pastoral Juvenil Hispana, *First National Encounter for Hispanic Youth and Young Adult Ministry (PENPJH): Conclusions* (Washington, DC: National Catholic Network de Pastoral Juvenil Hispana, 2007).

Additional resources

Books and articles

Aguilera-Titus, Alejandro. "Youth Ministry in a Culturally Diverse Church." *Origins* 36 (October 12, 2006), 277-283.

Badillo, David A. *Latinos and the New Immigrant Church*. Baltimore, MD: The Johns Hopkins University Press, 2006.

Brennan, Patrick J. *The Mission Driven Parish*. Maryknoll, NY: Orbis Books, 2007.

Canales, Arthur D. "A Reality Check: Addressing Catholic Hispanic Youth Ministry in the United States of America (Part 1)." *Apuntes* 25 (Spring 2005): 4-23.

_____. "Reaping What We Sow: Addressing Catholic Hispanic Youth Ministry in the United States of America (Part 2)." *Apuntes* 25 (Summer 2005): 44-74.

Cervantes, Carmen M., ed. *Hispanic Young People and the Church's Pastoral Response / La Juventud Hispana y la Respuesta Pastoral de la Iglesia*. Winona, MN: Saint Mary's Press, 1994.

_____. *Evangelization of Hispanic Young People / Evangelización de la Juventud Hispana*. Winona, MN: Saint Mary's Press, 1995.

Cervantes, Carmen M. and Ken Johnson-Mondragón. "Pastoral Juvenil Hispana, Youth Ministry, and Young Adult Ministry: An Updated Perspective on Three Different Pastoral Realities." *Perspectives on Hispanic Youth and Young Adult Ministry* 3. Stockton, CA: Instituto Fe y Vida, 2007.

Crane, Ken R. *Latino Churches: Faith, Family, and Ethnicity in the Second Generation.* New York: LFB Scholarly Publishing, 2003.

Dahm, Charles W. *Parish Ministry in a Hispanic Community.* Mahwah, NJ: Paulist Press, 2004.

Deck, Allan F., Yolanda Tarango, and Timothy M. Matovina, eds. *Perspectivas: Hispanic Ministry.* Kansas City, MO: Sheed & Ward, 1995.

Johnson-Mondragón, Ken. "Youth Ministry and the Socioreligious Lives of Hispanic and White Catholic Teens in the U.S." *Perspectives on Hispanic Youth and Young Adult Ministry* 2. Stockton, CA: Instituto Fe y Vida, 2005.

McCorquodale, Charlotte, Victoria Shepp, and Leigh Sterten. *The National Study of Youth and Religion: Analysis of the Population of Catholic Teenagers and Their Parents.* Washington, DC: National Federation for Catholic Youth Ministry, 2004.

Phan, Peter C. and Diana Hayes. Many Faces, One Church: Cultural Diversity and the American Catholic Experience. Chicopee, MA: Sheed & Ward, 2005.

Sheffield, Dan. *The Multicultural Leader: Developing a Catholic Personality.* Toronto: Clements Publishing, 2005.

Yancey, George. *One Body One Spirit: Principles of Successful Multiracial Churches.* Downers Grove, IL: InterVarsity Press, 2003.

Websites

www.bibliaparajovenes.org

www.catholic.net

www.cmdnet.org

www.cultivationministries.org

www.disciplesnow.com

www.feyvida.org/publications

www.group.com

www.laredpjh.org

www.nfcym.org

www.smp.org